Course	Annual Editions: The Developing World, 24e
Course Number	**by Robert J. Griffiths**

http://create.mheducation.com

ISBN-10: 1308008813   ISBN-13: 9781308008813

Contents

Credits

Preface

The developing world continues to play an increasingly important role in world affairs. It is home to the vast majority of the world's population, and it has an increasingly significant impact on the international economy. From the standpoint of international security, developing countries are not only sites of conflicts and humanitarian crises, but also a source of continuing concern about state weakness or failure and their connection to international terrorism. Developing countries also play a critical role in the efforts to protect the global environment.

The developing world demonstrates considerable ethnic, cultural, political, and economic diversity, thus making generalizations about such a diverse group of countries difficult. Increasing differentiation among developing countries further complicates our comprehension of the challenges of modernization, development, and globalization that they face. A combination of internal and external factors shape the current circumstances throughout the developing world. Issues of peace and security, international trade and finance, poverty, the environment, human rights, and gender illustrate the complexity of these challenges and highlight the effects of globalization and growing interdependence. The implications of these issues demonstrate the importance of a greater understanding of the challenges that face the developing world as well as the most effective ways to address those challenges.

The twenty-fourth edition of *Annual Editions: Developing World* seeks to help students understand the diversity and complexity of the developing world and acquaint them with the challenges that these nations face. I remain convinced of the need for greater awareness of the problems that face the developing world. The international community must make a commitment to address these issues more effectively, particularly because of the increasingly important role developing countries are playing in international affairs. I hope that this volume contributes to students' knowledge and understanding of current trends in the developing world and their implications.

I hope the articles are both interesting and informative and that they can serve as a basis for further student research and class discussion. The units deal with what I regard as the major issues facing the developing world. In addition, I have attempted to suggest the similarities and differences between developing countries, the nature of their relationships with the industrialized nations, and the different perspectives that exist regarding the causes of and approaches to the issues.

Several learning features are included to aid students and expand critical thinking about each article topic. *Learning Outcomes accompany each article* and outline the key concepts that students should focus on as they are reading the material. *Critical Thinking* questions, located at the end of each article, allow students to test their understanding of the key points of the article. A *Topic Guide* assists students in finding other articles on a given subject within this edition, while a list of recommended *Internet References at the end of each article* guides them to sources of additional information. Each article is now also correlated with chapters in *Global Politics* by Mark A. Boyer, Natalie F. Hudson, and Michael J. Butler.

I would again like to thank McGraw-Hill for the opportunity to put together a reader on a subject that is the focus of my teaching and research. I would also like to thank those who have offered comments and suggestions. I have tried to take these into account in preparing the current volume. No book on a topic as broad as the developing world can be completely comprehensive. There certainly are additional and alternative readings that might be included. Any suggestions for improvement are welcome.

Editor

Robert J. Griffiths is Associate Professor of Political Science at the University of North Carolina at Greensboro. His teaching and research interests are in the field of comparative and international politics with a focus on Africa. He teaches courses on the politics of the non-Western world, African politics, international law and organization, international security, and international political economy. His recent publications include "Democratizing South African Civil-Military Relations: A Blueprint for Post-Conflict Reform?" in *War and Peace in Africa: History, Nationalism, and the State,* edited by Toyin Falola and Raphael C. Njoku (2009) and "Parliamentary Oversight of Defense in South Africa" in *Legislative Oversight and Budgeting: A World Perspective,* Rick Stapenhurst, Riccardo Pelizzo, David Olson, and Lisa von Trapp, edited by World Bank Institute Development Studies (2008).

Academic Advisory Board

Members of the Academic Advisory Board are instrumental in the final selection of articles for the *Annual Editions* series. Their review of the articles for content, level, and appropriateness provides critical direction to the editor(s) and staff. We think that you will find their careful consideration reflected in this book.

Correlation Guide

The *Annual Editions* series provides students with convenient, inexpensive access to current, carefully selected articles from the public press. **Annual Editions: Developing World 14/15** is an easy-to-use reader that presents articles on important topics such as *democracy, emerging markets, human rights,* and many more. For more information on other McGraw-Hill Create™ titles and collections, visit www.mcgrawhillcreate.com.

This convenient guide matches the articles in **Annual Editions: Developing World 14/15** with Global Politics by Boyer/Hudson/Butler.

Annual Editions: Developing World 14/15	Global Politics by Boyer/Hudson/Butler
How the ANC Lost Its Way	**Chapter 3:** Nations, States, and Identity
Between Democracy and Militancy: Islam in Africa Islamism After the Arab Spring	**Chapter 4:** Globalization: Politics from Above and Below
Not Ready for Prime Time: Why Including Emerging Powers at the Helm Would Hurt Global Governance Own the Goals: What the Millennium Development Goals Have Accomplished	**Chapter 5:** International Organizations: Global and Regional Governance
Girls in War: Sex Slave, Mother, Domestic Aide, Combatant A New Kind of Korea Uprisings Jolt the Saudi-Iranian Rivalry World Peace Could Be Closer Than You Think	**Chapter 6:** Pursuing Security
Central America's Security Predicament Humanitarian Intervention Comes of Age A New Kind of Korea The True Costs of Humanitarian Intervention Uprisings Jolt the Saudi-Iranian Rivalry World Peace Could Be Closer Than You Think	**Chapter 7:** Conflict and Conflict Management
Increasing Women's Access to Justice in Post-Conflict Societies	**Chapter 8:** International Law and Transitional Justice
The Democratic Malaise Haiti Doesn't Need Your Old T-Shirt The Post-Washington Consensus: Development after the Crisis Role Reversal	**Chapter 9:** Global Political Economy—Protecting Wealth in the Dominant System
Best. Decade. Ever. Broken BRICs A Few Dollars at a Time: How to Tap Consumers for Development Haiti Doesn't Need Your Old T-Shirt How Development Leads to Democracy: What We Know about Modernization Is Indonesia Bound for the BRICS?It's Economics, Stupid: Mobile Technology in Low-Income Countries Lions, Tigers, and Emerging Markets: Africa's Development Dilemmas The Mixed News on Poverty The New Mercantilism: China's Emerging Role in the Americas Own the Goals: What the Millennium Development Goals Have Accomplished Please, Don't Send Food Role Reversal	**Chapter 10:** Global Political Economy—A Searching for Equity in the Dependent System
The Awakening Divergent Paths: The Future of One-Party Rule in Singapore Gender and the Revolution in Egypt Girls in War: Sex Slave, Mother, Domestic Aide, Combatant The Global Glass Ceiling: Why Empowering Women Is Good for Business Good Soldier, Bad Cop Human Rights Last Justice and Development: Challenges to the Legal Empowerment of the Poor Not Ready for Prime Time: Why Including Emerging Powers at the Helm Would Hurt Global Governance One Step Forward, Two Steps Back Why Do They Hate Us? The Women's Crusade	**Chapter 11:** Human Rights: A Tool for Preserving and Enhancing Human Dignity
Bangladesh's Climate Displacement Nightmare Climate Change and Food Security The End of Easy Everything A Light in the Forest: Brazil's Fight to Save the Amazon and Climate Change Diplomacy The New Geopolitics of Food The New Population Bomb: The Four Megatrends That Will Change the World Women in the Shadow of Climate Change The World's Water Challenge	**Chapter 12:** Global Political Ecology

Topic Guide

This topic guide suggests how the selections in this book relate to the subjects covered in your course.

All the articles that relate to each topic are listed below the bold-faced term.

Unit 1

UNIT

Prepared by: Robert J. Griffiths, *University of North Carolina at Greensboro*

Understanding the Developing World

The diversity of the countries that make up the developing world has always made it difficult to categorize these countries and specify their role in international affairs. The task has become even more difficult as economic growth rates have varied, and many developing countries have implemented political reforms producing even further differentiation among developing countries. "Developing world" has always been a catchall term that lacks precision and explanatory power. It has been used to describe both societies that are desperately poor as well as those rich in resources. The term also refers to societies ranging from traditional to modernizing and from authoritarian to democratic. To complicate things even further, there is also debate over what actually constitutes development. For some, it is economic growth or progress toward democracy, while for others it involves cultural changes associated with modernization. Some also emphasize greater empowerment and dignity. There are also differing views on why progress toward development has been uneven. The West tends to see the problems of development as stemming from poor governance, institutional weakness, and failure to embrace free-market principles. Critics from the developing world cite the legacy of colonialism and the nature of the international political and economic structures as the reasons for the lack of development. Not only are there differing views on the causes of lagging development, but there is also considerable debate on how best to tackle these issues. The Millennium Development Goals (MDGs) seek to eradicate extreme poverty and hunger and address issues of education, health, gender, and the environment. There has been significant but uneven progress in this effort so far. This has contributed to the debate on the best way to achieve development. Critics maintain that the top-down ideology of development epitomized in the MDGs focuses attention at the macro level of development and ignores the importance of fostering local, grassroots solutions, while supporters say that recent progress demonstrates the benefits of focusing global attention and engaging in a concerted effort to address critical global problems. The emphasis of development has broadened as well; it now extends beyond the traditional focus on poverty reduction to include issues like civil and political rights, human security, and environmental sustainability. Reflecting this broader emphasis is a growing list of actors that includes nongovernmental organizations and philanthropic organizations involved in development efforts. In any case, lumping together the 120-plus nations that make up the developing world obscures the disparities in size, population, resources, forms of government, level of industrialization, distribution of wealth, ethnicity, and a host of other indicators making it difficult generalize about the developing world.

Despite their diversity, many nations in the developing world share some characteristics. Many developing countries have large populations, with annual growth rates that often exceed 2 percent. Although there has been some progress in eradicating poverty, it continues to be widespread in both rural and urban areas, with rural areas often containing the poorest of the poor. Moreover, while many have risen out of poverty, evidence suggests that many also have slipped back into poverty. While the majority of the developing world's inhabitants continue to live in the countryside, there is a massive rural-to-urban migration under way, cities are growing rapidly, and some developing countries are approaching urbanization rates similar to those of industrialized countries. Wealth is unevenly distributed, making education, employment opportunities, and access to healthcare luxuries that only a relative few enjoy. A lack of legal protection further disadvantages the poor. Corruption, mismanagement, and ineffective government are also common features. With very few exceptions, these nations share a colonial past that has affected them both politically and economically. The neocolonial perspective charges that the structure of the international economy and the West's political, military, and cultural links with the developing world contribute to undue influence.

The roots of the diverging views between the rich and the poor nations on development emerged shortly after the beginning of the independence era. The neocolonial viewpoint encouraged efforts to alter the international economic order during the 1970s. While the New International Economic Order (NIEO) succumbed to neo-liberalism in the 1980s, developing countries still frequently seek solidarity in their interactions with the West although the increasing diversity makes coordinated efforts more complicated. Nevertheless, developing countries still view Western prescriptions for development skeptically and have chafed under the Washington Consensus, which dictates the terms for the access to funds from international financial institutions and foreign aid. Furthermore, some critics suggest that Western development models result in inequitable development and give rise to cultural imperialism. In contrast to the developing world's criticism of the West, industrial countries continue to maintain the importance of institution-building and following the Western model that emphasizes a market-oriented approach to development. As the developing world comes to play a more prominent role in economic, security, and environmental issues and problems continue in the industrialized countries, the West's ability to dictate the terms on which development occurs will diminish. Moreover, the West is facing global demographic changes that, when combined with the effects of the global economic crisis, are producing shifts in power that will have a major impact on the industrialized countries' ability to meet future challenges.

There is a clear difference of opinion between the industrialized countries and the developed world on a wide range of development issues. Ultimately the development process will be shaped primarily by the countries experiencing it. The industrialized countries can, however, continue to contribute to this process although their influence will be affected by substantial demographic, economic, and political changes.

Article

How Development Leads to Democracy

What We Know about Modernization

Ronald Inglehart and Christian Welzel

In the last several years, a democratic boom has given way to a democratic recession. Between 1985 and 1995, scores of countries made the transition to democracy, bringing widespread euphoria about democracy's future. But more recently, democracy has retreated in Bangladesh, Nigeria, the Philippines, Russia, Thailand, and Venezuela, and the Bush administration's attempts to establish democracy in Afghanistan and Iraq seem to have left both countries in chaos. These developments, along with the growing power of China and Russia, have led many observers to argue that democracy has reached its high-water mark and is no longer on the rise.

That conclusion is mistaken. The underlying conditions of societies around the world point to a more complicated reality. The bad news is that it is unrealistic to assume that democratic institutions can be set up easily, almost anywhere, at any time. Although the outlook is never hopeless, democracy is most likely to emerge and survive when certain social and cultural conditions are in place. The Bush administration ignored this reality when it attempted to implant democracy in Iraq without first establishing internal security and overlooked cultural conditions that endangered the effort.

The good news, however, is that the conditions conducive to democracy can and do emerge—and the process of "modernization," according to abundant empirical evidence, advances them. Modernization is a syndrome of social changes linked to industrialization. Once set in motion, it tends to penetrate all aspects of life, bringing occupational specialization, urbanization, rising educational levels, rising life expectancy, and rapid economic growth. These create a self-reinforcing process that transforms social life and political institutions, bringing rising mass participation in politics and—in the long run—making the establishment of democratic political institutions increasingly likely. Today, we have a clearer idea than ever before of why and how this process of democratization happens.

The long-term trend toward democracy has always come in surges and declines. At the start of the twentieth century, only a handful of democracies existed, and even they fell short of being full democracies by today's standards. There was a major increase in the number of democracies following World War I, another surge following World War II, and a third surge at the end of the Cold War. Each of these surges was followed by a decline, although the number of democracies never fell back to the original base line. By the start of the twenty-first century, about 90 states could be considered democratic.

Although many of these democracies are flawed, the overall trend is striking: in the long run, modernization brings democracy. This means that the economic resurgence of China and Russia has a positive aspect: underlying changes are occurring that make the emergence of increasingly liberal and democratic political systems likely in the coming years. It also means that there is no reason to panic about the fact that democracy currently appears to be on the defensive. The dynamics of modernization and democratization are becoming increasingly clear, and it is likely that they will continue to function.

The Great Debate

The concept of modernization has a long history. During the nineteenth and twentieth centuries, a Marxist theory of modernization proclaimed that the abolition of private property would put an end to exploitation, inequality, and conflict. A competing capitalist version held that economic development would lead to rising living standards and democracy. These two visions of modernization competed fiercely throughout much of the Cold War. By the 1970s, however, communism began to stagnate, and neither economic development nor democratization was apparent in many poor countries. Neither version of utopia seemed to be unfolding, and critics pronounced modernization theory dead.

Since the end of the Cold War, however, the concept of modernization has taken on new life, and a new version of modernization theory has emerged, with clear implications for our understanding of where global economic development is likely to lead. Stripped of the oversimplifications of its early versions, the new concept of modernization sheds light on ongoing cultural changes, such as the rise of gender equality the recent wave of democratization, and the democratic peace theory.

For most of human history, technological progress was extremely slow and new developments in food production were offset by population increases—trapping agrarian economies in a steady-state equilibrium with no growth in living standards. History was seen as either cyclic or in long-term decline from a past golden age. The situation began to change with the Industrial Revolution and the advent of sustained economic growth—which led to both the capitalist and the communist visions of modernization. Although the ideologies competed fiercely, they were both committed to economic growth and social progress and brought mass participation in politics. And each side believed that the developing nations of the Third World would follow its path to modernization.

At the height of the Cold War, a version of modernization theory emerged in the United States that portrayed underdevelopment as a direct consequence of a country's psychological and cultural traits. Underdevelopment was said to reflect irrational traditional religious and communal values that discouraged achievement. The rich Western democracies, the theory went, could instill modern values and bring progress to "backward" nations through economic, cultural, and military assistance. By the 1970s, however, it had become clear that assistance had not brought much progress toward prosperity or democracy—eroding confidence in this version of modernization theory, which was increasingly criticized as ethnocentric and patronizing. It came under heavy criticism from "dependency theorists," who argued that trade with rich countries exploits poor ones, locking them into positions of structural dependence. The elites in developing countries welcomed such thinking, since it implied that poverty had nothing to do with internal problems or the corruption of local leaders; it was the fault of global capitalism. By the 1980s, dependency theory was in vogue. Third World nations, the thinking went, could escape from global exploitation only by withdrawing from global markets and adopting import-substitution policies.

More recently, it has become apparent that import-substitution strategies have failed: the countries least involved in global trade, such as Cuba, Myanmar (also called Burma), and North Korea, have not been the most successful—they have actually grown the least. Export-oriented strategies have been far more effective in promoting sustained economic growth and, eventually, democratization. The pendulum, accordingly, has swung back, and a new version of modernization theory has gained credibility. The rapid economic development of East Asia, and the subsequent democratization of South Korea and Taiwan, seem to confirm its basic claims: producing for the world market enables economic growth; investing the returns in human capital and upgrading the work force to produce high-tech goods brings higher returns and enlarges the educated middle class; once the middle class becomes large and articulate enough, it presses for liberal democracy—the most effective political system for advanced industrial societies. Nevertheless, even today, if one mentions modernization at a conference on economic development, one is likely to hear a reiteration of dependency theory's critique of the "backward nations" version of modernization theory, as if that were all there is to modernization theory—and as if no new evidence had emerged since the 1970s.

The New Modernization

In retrospect, it is obvious that the early versions of modernization theory were wrong on several points. Today, virtually nobody expects a revolution of the proletariat that will abolish private property, ushering in a new era free from exploitation and conflict. Nor does anyone expect that industrialization will automatically lead to democratic institutions; communism and fascism also emerged from industrialization. Nonetheless, a massive body of evidence suggests that modernization theory's central premise was correct: economic development does tend to bring about important, roughly predictable changes in society, culture, and politics. But the earlier versions of modernization theory need to be corrected in several respects.

First, modernization is not linear. It does not move indefinitely in the same direction; instead, the process reaches inflection points. Empirical evidence indicates that each phase of modernization is associated with distinctive changes in people's worldviews. Industrialization leads to one major process of change, resulting in bureaucratization, hierarchy, centralization of authority, secularization, and a shift from traditional to secular-rational values. The rise of postindustrial society brings another set of cultural changes that move in a different direction: instead of bureaucratization and centralization, the new trend is toward an increasing emphasis on individual autonomy and self-expression values, which lead to a growing emancipation from authority.

Thus, other things being equal, high levels of economic development tend to make people more tolerant and trusting, bringing more emphasis on self-expression and more participation in decision-making. This process is not deterministic, and any forecasts can only be probabilistic, since economic factors are not the only influence; a given country's leaders and nation-specific events also shape what happens. Moreover, modernization is not irreversible. Severe economic collapse can reverse it, as happened during the Great Depression in Germany, Italy, Japan, and Spain and during the 1990s in most of the Soviet successor states. Similarly, if the current economic crisis becomes a twenty-first-century Great Depression, the world could face a new struggle against renewed xenophobia and authoritarianism.

Second, social and cultural change is path dependent: history matters. Although economic development tends to bring predictable changes in people's worldviews, a society's heritage—whether shaped by Protestantism, Catholicism, Islam, Confucianism, or communism—leaves a lasting imprint on its worldview. A society's value system reflects an interaction between the driving forces of modernization and the persisting influence of tradition. Although the classic modernization theorists in both the East and the West thought that religion and ethnic traditions would die out, they have proved to be highly resilient. Although the publics of industrializing societies are becoming richer and more educated, that is hardly creating a uniform global culture. Cultural heritages are remarkably enduring.

Third, modernization is not westernization, contrary to the earlier, ethnocentric version of the theory. The process of industrialization began in the West, but during the past few decades, East Asia has had the world's highest economic growth rates, and Japan leads the world in life expectancy and some other aspects of modernization. The United States is not the model for global cultural change, and industrializing societies in general are not becoming like the United States, as a popular version of modernization theory assumes. In fact, American society retains more traditional values than do most other high-income societies.

Fourth, modernization does not automatically lead to democracy. Rather, it, in the long run, brings social and cultural changes that make democratization increasingly probable. Simply attaining a high level of per capita GDP does not produce democracy: if it did, Kuwait and the United Arab Emirates would have become model democracies. (These countries have not gone through the modernization process described above.) But the emergence of postindustrial society brings certain social and cultural changes that are specifically conducive to democratization. Knowledge societies cannot function effectively without highly educated publics that have become increasingly accustomed to thinking for themselves. Furthermore, rising levels of economic security bring a growing emphasis on a syndrome of self-expression values—one that gives high priority to free choice and motivates political action. Beyond a certain point, accordingly, it becomes difficult to avoid democratization, because repressing mass demands for more open societies becomes increasingly costly and detrimental to economic effectiveness. Thus, in its advanced stages, modernization brings social and cultural changes that make the emergence and flourishing of democratic institutions increasingly likely.

The core idea of modernization theory is that economic and technological development bring a coherent set of social, cultural, and political changes. A large body of empirical evidence supports this idea. Economic development is, indeed, strongly linked to pervasive shifts in people's beliefs and motivations, and these shifts in turn change the role of religion, job motivations, human fertility rates, gender roles, and sexual norms. And they also bring growing mass demands for democratic institutions and for more responsive behavior on the part of elites. These changes together make democracy increasingly likely to emerge, while also making war less acceptable to publics.

Evaluating Values

New sources of empirical evidence provide valuable insights into how modernization changes worldviews and motivations. One important source is global surveys of mass values and attitudes. Between 1981 and 2007, the World Values Survey and the European Values Study carried out five waves of representative national surveys in scores of countries, covering almost 90 percent of the world's population. (For the data from the surveys, visit www.worldvaluessurvey.org.) The results show large cross-national differences in what people believe and value. In some countries, 95 percent of the people surveyed said that God was very important in their lives; in others, only 3 percent did. In some societies, 90 percent of the people surveyed said they believed that men have more of a right to a job than women do; in others, only 8 percent said they thought so. These cross-national differences are robust and enduring, and they are closely correlated with a society's level of economic development: people in low-income societies are much likelier to emphasize religion and traditional gender roles than are people in rich countries.

These values surveys demonstrate that the worldviews of people living in rich societies differ systematically from those of people living in low-income societies across a wide range of political, social, and religious norms. The differences run along two basic dimensions: traditional versus secular-rational values and survival versus self-expression values. (Each dimension reflects responses to scores of questions asked as part of the values surveys.)

The shift from traditional to secular-rational values is linked to the shift from agrarian to industrial societies. Traditional societies emphasize religion, respect for and obedience to authority, and national pride. These characteristics change as societies become more secular and rational. The shift from survival to self-expression values is linked to the rise of postindustrial societies. It reflects a cultural shift that occurs when younger generations emerge that have grown up taking survival for granted. Survival values give top priority to economic and physical security and conformist social norms. Self-expression values give high priority to freedom of expression, participation in decision-making, political activism, environmental protection, gender equality, and tolerance of ethnic minorities, foreigners, and gays and lesbians. A growing emphasis on these latter values engenders a culture of trust and tolerance in which people cherish individual freedom and self-expression and have activist political orientations. These attributes are crucial to democracy—and thus explain how economic growth, which takes societies from agrarian to industrial and then from industrial to postindustrial, leads to democratization. The unprecedented economic growth of the past 50 years has meant that an increasing share of the world's population has grown up taking survival for granted. Time-series data from the values surveys indicate that mass priorities have shifted from an overwhelming emphasis on economic and physical security to an emphasis on subjective well-being, self-expression, participation in decision-making, and a relatively trusting and tolerant outlook.

Both dimensions are closely linked to economic development: the value systems of high-income countries differ dramatically from those of low-income countries. Every nation that the World Bank defines as having a high income ranks relatively high on both dimensions—with a strong emphasis on both secular-rational and self-expression values. All the low-income and lower-middle-income countries rank relatively low on both dimensions. The upper-middle-income countries fall somewhere in between. To a remarkable degree, the values and beliefs of a given society reflect its level of economic developments—just as modernization theory predicts.

This strong connection between a society's value system and its per capita GDP suggests that economic development tends to produce roughly predictable changes in a society's beliefs and values, and time-series evidence supports this hypothesis. When one compares the positions of given countries in successive waves of the values surveys, one finds that almost all the countries that experienced rising per capita GDPs also experienced predictable shifts in their values.

The values survey evidence also shows, however, that cultural change is path dependent; a society's cultural heritage also shapes where it falls on the global cultural map. This map shows distinctive clusters of countries: Protestant Europe, Catholic Europe, ex-communist Europe, the English-speaking countries, Latin America, South Asia, the Islamic world, and Africa. The values emphasized by different societies fall into a remarkably coherent pattern that reflects both those societies' economic development and their religious and colonial heritage. Still, even if a society's cultural heritage continues to shape its prevailing values, economic development brings changes that have important consequences. Over time, it reshapes beliefs and values of all kinds—and it brings a growing mass demand for democratic institutions and for more responsive elite behavior. And over the quarter century covered by the values surveys, the people of most countries placed increasing emphasis on self-expression values. This cultural shift makes democracy increasingly likely to emerge where it does not yet exist and increasingly likely to become more effective and more direct where it does.

Development and Democracy

Fifty years ago, the sociologist Seymour Martin Lipset pointed out that rich countries are much more likely than poor countries to be democracies. Although this claim was contested for many years, it has held up against repeated tests. The causal direction of the relationship has also been questioned: Are rich countries more likely to be democratic because democracy makes countries rich, or is development conducive to democracy? Today, it seems clear that the causality runs mainly from economic development to democratization. During early industrialization, authoritarian states are just as likely to attain high rates of growth as are democracies. But beyond a certain level of economic development, democracy becomes increasingly likely to emerge and survive. Thus, among the scores of countries that democratized around 1990, most were middle-income countries: almost all the high-income countries already were democracies, and few low-income countries made the transition. Moreover, among the countries that democratized between 1970 and 1990, democracy has survived in every country that made the transition when it was at the economic level of Argentina today or higher; among the countries that made the transition when they were below this level, democracy had an average life expectancy of only eight years.

The strong correlation between development and democracy reflects the fact that economic development is conducive to democracy. The question of why, exactly, development leads to democracy has been debated intensely, but the answer is beginning to emerge. It does not result from some disembodied force that causes democratic institutions to emerge automatically when a country attains a certain level of GDP. Rather, economic development brings social and political changes only when it changes people's behavior. Consequently, economic development is conducive to democracy to the extent that it, first, creates a large, educated, and articulate middle class of people who are accustomed to thinking for themselves and, second, transforms people's values and motivations.

Today, it is more possible than ever before to measure what the key changes are and how far they have progressed in given countries. Multivariate analysis of the data from the values surveys makes it possible to sort out the relative impact of economic, social, and cultural changes, and the results point to the conclusion that economic development is conducive to democracy insofar as it brings specific structural changes (particularly the rise of a knowledge sector) and certain cultural changes (particularly the rise of self-expression values). Wars, depressions, institutional changes, elite decisions, and specific leaders also influence what happens, but structural and cultural change are major factors in the emergence and survival of democracy.

Modernization brings rising educational levels, moving the work force into occupations that require independent thinking and making people more articulate and better equipped to intervene in politics. As knowledge societies emerge, people become accustomed to using their own initiative and judgment on the job and are also increasingly likely to question rigid and hierarchical authority.

Modernization also makes people economically more secure, and self-expression values become increasingly widespread when a large share of the population grows up taking survival for granted. The desire for freedom and autonomy are universal aspirations. They may be subordinated to the need for subsistence and order when survival is precarious, but they take increasingly high priority as survival becomes more secure. The basic motivation for democracy—the human desire for free choice—starts to play an increasingly important role. People begin to place a growing emphasis on free choice in politics and begin to demand civil and political liberties and democratic institutions.

Effective Democracy

During the explosion of democracy that took place between 1985 and 1995, electoral democracy spread rapidly throughout the world. Strategic elite agreements played an important role in this process, facilitated by an international environment in which the end of the Cold War opened the way for democratization. Initially, there was a tendency to view any regime that held free and fair elections as a democracy. But many of the new democracies suffered from massive corruption and failed to apply the rule of law, which is what makes democracy effective. A growing number of observers today thus emphasize the inadequacy of "electoral demomcy," "hybrid democracy," "authoritarian democracy," and other forms of sham democracy in which mass preferences are something that political elites can largely ignore and in which they do not decisively influence government decisions. It is important, accordingly, to distinguish between effective and ineffective democracies.

The essence of democracy is that it empowers ordinary citizens. Whether a democracy is effective or not is based on not only the extent to which civil and political rights exist on paper but also the degree to which officials actually respect these rights. The first of these two components—the existence of rights on paper—is measured by Freedom House's annual rankings: if a country holds free elections, Freedom House tends to rate it as "free," giving it a score at or near the top of its scale. Thus, the new democracies of eastern Europe receive scores as high as those of the established democracies of western Europe, although in-depth analyses show that widespread corruption makes these new democracies far less effective in responding to their citizens' choices. Fortunately, the World Bank's governance scores measure the extent to which a country's democratic institutions are actually effective. Consequently, a rough index of effective democracy can be obtained by multiplying these two scores: formal democracy, as measured by Freedom House, and elite and institutional integrity, as measured by the World Bank.

Effective democracy is a considerably more demanding standard than electoral democracy. One can establish electoral democracy almost anywhere, but it will probably not last long if it does not transfer power from the elites to the people. Effective democracy is most likely to exist alongside a relatively developed infrastructure that includes not only economic resources but also widespread participatory habits and an emphasis on autonomy. Accordingly, it is closely linked to the degree to which a given public emphasizes self-expression values. Indeed, the correlation between a society's values and the nature of the country's political institutions is remarkably strong.

Virtually all the stable democracies show strong self-expression values. Most Latin American countries are underachievers, showing lower levels of effective democracy than their publics' values would predict. This suggests that these societies could support higher levels of democracy if the rule of law were strengthened there. Iran is also an underachiever—a theocratic regime that allows a much lower level of democracy than that to which its people aspire. Surprising as it may seem to those who focus only on elite-level politics, the Iranian public shows relatively strong support for democracy. Conversely, Cyprus, Estonia, Hungary, Poland, Latvia, and Lithuania are overachievers, showing higher levels of democracy than their publics' values would predicts—perhaps reflecting the incentives to democratize provided by membership in the European Union.

But do self-expression values lead to democracy, or does democracy cause self-expression values to emerge? The evidence indicates that these values lead to democracy. (For the full evidence for this claim, see our book *Modernization, Cultural Change, and Democracy.*) Democratic institutions do not need to be in place for self-expression values to emerge. Time-series evidence from the values surveys indicates that in the years preceding the wave of democratization in the late 1980s and early 1990s, self-expression values had already emerged through a process of an intergenerational change in values—not only in the Western democracies but also within many authoritarian societies. By 1990, the publics of East Germany and Czechoslovakia—which had been living under two of the most authoritarian regimes in the world—had developed high levels of self-expression values. The crucial factor was not the political system but the fact that these countries were among the most economically advanced countries in the communist world, with high levels of education and advanced social welfare systems. Thus, when the Soviet leader Mikhail Gorbachev renounced the Brezhnev Doctrine, removing the threat of Soviet military intervention, they moved swiftly toward democracy.

In recent decades, self-expression values have been spreading and getting stronger, making people more likely to directly intervene in politics. (Indeed, unprecedented numbers of people took part in the demonstrations that helped bring about the most recent wave of democratization.) Does this mean that authoritarian systems will inevitably crumble? No. A rising emphasis on self-expression values tends to erode the legitimacy of authoritarian systems, but as long as determined authoritarian elites control the army and the secret police, they can repress pro-democratic forces. Still, even repressive regimes find it costly to check these tendencies, for doing so tends to block the emergence of effective knowledge sectors.

Modern Strategy

This new understanding of modernization has broad implications for international relations. For one thing, it helps explain why advanced democracies do not fight one another. Recent research provides strong empirical support for the claim that they do not, which goes back to Adam Smith and Immanuel Kant. Since they emerged in the early nineteenth century, liberal democracies have fought a number of wars, but almost never against one another. This new version of modernization theory indicates that the democratic peace phenomenon is due more to cultural changes linked to modernization than to democracy per se.

In earlier periods of history, democracies fought one another frequently. But the prevailing norms among them have evolved over time, as is illustrated by the abolition of slavery, the gradual expansion of the franchise, and the movement toward gender equality in virtually all modern societies. Another cultural change that has occurred in modern societies—which tend to be democracies—is that war has become progressively less acceptable and people have become more likely to express this preference and try to affect policy accordingly. Evidence from the World Values Survey indicates that the publics of high-income countries have much lower levels of xenophobia than do the publics of low-income countries, and they are much less willing to fight for their country than are the publics of low-income countries. Moreover, economically developed democracies behave far more peacefully toward one another than do poor democracies, and economically developed democracies are far less prone to civil war than are poor democracies.

Modernization theory has both cautionary and encouraging implications for U.S. foreign policy. Iraq, of course, provides a cautionary lesson. Contrary to the appealing view that democracy can be readily established almost anywhere, modernization theory holds that democracy is much more likely to flourish under certain conditions than others. A number of factors made it unrealistic to expect that democracy would be easy to establish in Iraq, including deep ethnic cleavages that had been exacerbated by Saddam Hussein's regime. And after Saddam's defeat, allowing physical security to deteriorate was a particularly serious mistake. Interpersonal trust and tolerance flourish when people feel secure. Democracy is unlikely to survive in a society torn by distrust and intolerance, and Iraq currently manifests the highest level of xenophobia of any society for which data are available. A good indicator of xenophobia is the extent to which people say they would not want to have foreigners as neighbors. Across 80 countries, the median percentage of those surveyed who said this was 15 percent. Among Iraqi Kurds, 51 percent of those polled said they would prefer not to have foreigners as neighbors. Among Iraqi Arabs, 90 percent of those polled said they would not want foreigners as neighbors. In keeping with these conditions, Iraq (along with Pakistan and Zimbabwe) shows very low levels of both self-expression values and effective democracy.

Modernization theory also has positive implications for U.S. foreign policy. Supported by a large body of evidence, it points to the conclusion that economic development is a basic driver of democratic change—meaning that Washington should do what it can to encourage development. If it wants to bring democratic change to Cuba, for example, isolating it is counterproductive. The United States should lift the embargo, promote economic development, and foster social engagement with, and other connections to, the world. Nothing is certain, but empirical evidence suggests that a growing sense of security and a growing emphasis on self-expression values there would undermine the authoritarian regime.

Similarly, although many observers have been alarmed by the economic resurgence of China, this growth has positive implications for the long term. Beneath China's seemingly monolithic political structure, the social infrastructure of democratization is emerging, and it has progressed further than most observers realize. China is now approaching the level of mass emphasis on self-expression values at which Chile, Poland, South Korea, and Taiwan made their transitions to democracy. And, surprising as it may seem to observers who focus only on elite-level politics, Iran is also near this threshold. As long as the Chinese Communist Party and Iran's theocratic leaders control their countries' military and security forces, democratic institutions will not emerge at the national level. But growing mass pressures for liberalization are beginning to appear, and repressing them will bring growing costs in terms of economic inefficiency and low public morale. On the whole, increasing prosperity for China and Iran is in the United States' national interest.

More broadly, modernization theory implies that the United States should welcome and encourage economic development around the world. Although economic development requires difficult adjustments, its long-term effects encourage the emergence of more tolerant, less xenophobic, and ultimately more democratic societies.

Critical Thinking

1. What is modernization? How does this process make democratization more likely?
2. How has modernization theory evolved over time?
3. What changes in emphasis need to be made to ensure modernization's continued relevance?
4. What values are important to democracy?
5. What is the connection between economic development and democracy?

Ronald Inglehart is Professor of Political Science at the University of Michigan and Director of the World Values Survey. **Christian Welzel** is Professor of Political Science at Jacobs University Bremen, in Germany. They are the co-authors of *Modernization, Cultural Change, and Democracy*.

Article

The New Population Bomb: The Four Megatrends That Will Change the World

JACK A. GOLDSTONE

Forty-two years ago, the biologist Paul Ehrlich warned in The Population Bomb that mass starvation would strike in the 1970s and 1980s, with the world's population growth outpacing the production of food and other critical resources. Thanks to innovations and efforts such as the "green revolution" in farming and the widespread adoption of family planning, Ehrlich's worst fears did not come to pass. In fact, since the 1970s, global economic output has increased and fertility has fallen dramatically, especially in developing countries.

The United Nations Population Division now projects that global population growth will nearly halt by 2050. By that date, the world's population will have stabilized at 9.15 billion people, according to the "medium growth" variant of the UN's authoritative population database World Population Prospects: The 2008 Revision. (Today's global population is 6.83 billion.) Barring a cataclysmic climate crisis or a complete failure to recover from the current economic malaise, global economic output is expected to increase by two to three percent per year, meaning that global income will increase far more than population over the next four decades.

But twenty-first-century international security will depend less on how many people inhabit the world than on how the global population is composed and distributed: where populations are declining and where they are growing, which countries are relatively older and which are more youthful, and how demographics will influence population movements across regions.

These elements are not well recognized or widely understood. A recent article in *The Economist,* for example, cheered the decline in global fertility without noting other vital demographic developments. Indeed, the same UN data cited by *The Economist* reveal four historic shifts that will fundamentally alter the world's population over the next four decades: the relative demographic weight of the world's developed countries will drop by nearly 25 percent, shifting economic power to the developing nations; the developed countries' labor forces will substantially age and decline, constraining economic growth in the developed world and raising the demand for immigrant workers; most of the world's expected population growth will increasingly be concentrated in today's poorest, youngest, and most heavily Muslim countries, which have a dangerous lack of quality education, capital, and employment opportunities; and, for the first time in history, most of the world's population will become urbanized, with the largest urban centers being in the world's poorest countries, where policing, sanitation, and health care are often scarce. Taken together, these trends will pose challenges every bit as alarming as those noted by Ehrlich. Coping with them will require nothing less than a major reconsideration of the world's basic global governance structures.

Europe's Reversal of Fortunes

At the beginning of the eighteenth century, approximately 20 percent of the world's inhabitants lived in Europe (including Russia). Then, with the Industrial Revolution, Europe's population boomed, and streams of European emigrants set off for the Americas. By the eve of World War I, Europe's population had more than quadrupled. In 1913, Europe had more people than China, and the proportion of the world's population living in Europe and the former European colonies of North America had risen to over 33 percent. But this trend reversed after World War I, as basic health care and sanitation began to spread to poorer countries. In Asia, Africa, and Latin America, people began to live longer, and birthrates remained high or fell only slowly. By 2003, the combined populations of Europe, the United States, and Canada accounted for just 17 percent of the global population. In 2050, this figure is expected to be just 12 percent—far less than it was in 1700. (These projections, moreover, might even understate the reality because they reflect the "medium growth" projection of the UN forecasts, which assumes that the fertility rates of developing countries will decline while those of developed countries will increase. In fact, many developed countries show no evidence of increasing fertility rates.) The West's relative decline is even more dramatic if one also considers changes in income. The Industrial Revolution made Europeans not only more numerous than they had been but also considerably richer per capita than others worldwide. According to the economic historian Angus Maddison, Europe, the United States, and Canada together produced about 32 percent of the world's GDP at the beginning of the nineteenth century. By 1950, that proportion had increased to a remarkable 68 percent of the world's total output (adjusted to reflect purchasing power parity).

This trend, too, is headed for a sharp reversal. The proportion of global GDP produced by Europe, the United States, and Canada fell from 68 percent in 1950 to 47 percent in 2003 and will decline even more steeply in the future. If the growth rate of per capita income (again, adjusted for purchasing power parity) between 2003 and 2050 remains as it was between 1973 and 2003—averaging 1.68 percent annually in Europe, the United States, and Canada and 2.47 percent annually in the rest of the world—then the combined GDP of Europe, the United States, and Canada will roughly double by 2050, whereas the GDP of the rest of the world will grow by a factor of five. The portion of global GDP produced by Europe, the United States, and Canada in 2050 will then be less than 30 percent—smaller than it was in 1820.

These figures also imply that an overwhelming proportion of the world's GDP growth between 2003 and 2050—nearly 80 percent—will occur outside of Europe, the United States, and Canada. By the middle of this century, the global middle class—those capable of purchasing durable consumer products, such as cars, appliances, and electronics—will increasingly be found in what is now considered the developing world. The World Bank has predicted that by 2030 the number of middle-class people in the developing world will be 1.2 billion—a rise of 200 percent since 2005. This means that the developing world's middle class alone will be larger than the total populations of Europe, Japan, and the United States combined. From now on, therefore, the main driver of global economic expansion will be the economic growth of newly industrialized countries, such as Brazil, China, India, Indonesia, Mexico, and Turkey.

Aging Pains

Part of the reason developed countries will be less economically dynamic in the coming decades is that their populations will become substantially older. The European countries, Canada, the United States, Japan, South Korea, and even China are aging at unprecedented rates. Today, the proportion of people aged 60 or older in China and South Korea is 12–15 percent. It is 15–22 percent in the European Union, Canada, and the United States and 30 percent in Japan. With baby boomers aging and life expectancy increasing, these numbers will increase dramatically. In 2050, approximately 30 percent of Americans, Canadians, Chinese, and Europeans will be over 60, as will more than 40 percent of Japanese and South Koreans.

Over the next decades, therefore, these countries will have increasingly large proportions of retirees and increasingly small proportions of workers. As workers born during the baby boom of 1945–65 are retiring, they are not being replaced by a new cohort of citizens of prime working age (15–59 years old).

Industrialized countries are experiencing a drop in their working-age populations that is even more severe than the overall slowdown in their population growth. South Korea represents the most extreme example. Even as its total population is projected to decline by almost 9 percent by 2050 (from 48.3 million to 44.1 million), the population of working-age South Koreans is expected to drop by 36 percent (from 32.9 million to 21.1 million), and the number of South Koreans aged 60 and older will increase by almost 150 percent (from 7.3 million to 18 million). By 2050, in other words, the entire working-age population will barely exceed the 60-and-older population. Although South Korea's case is extreme, it represents an increasingly common fate for developed countries. Europe is expected to lose 24 percent of its prime working-age population (about 120 million workers) by 2050, and its 60-and-older population is expected to increase by 47 percent. In the United States, where higher fertility and more immigration are expected than in Europe, the working-age population will grow by 15 percent over the next four decades—a steep decline from its growth of 62 percent between 1950 and 2010. And by 2050, the United States' 60-and-older population is expected to double.

All this will have a dramatic impact on economic growth, health care, and military strength in the developed world. The forces that fueled economic growth in industrialized countries during the second half of the twentieth century—increased productivity due to better education, the movement of women into the labor force, and innovations in technology—will all likely weaken in the coming decades. College enrollment boomed after World War II, a trend that is not likely to recur in the twenty-first century; the extensive movement of women into the labor force also was a one-time social change; and the technological change of the time resulted from innovators who created new products and leading-edge consumers who were willing to try them out—two groups that are thinning out as the industrialized world's population ages.

Overall economic growth will also be hampered by a decline in the number of new consumers and new households. When developed countries' labor forces were growing by 0.5–1.0 percent per year, as they did until 2005, even annual increases in real output per worker of just 1.7 percent meant that annual economic growth totaled 2.2–2.7 percent per year. But with the labor forces of many developed countries (such as Germany, Hungary, Japan, Russia, and the Baltic states) now shrinking by 0.2 percent per year and those of other countries (including Austria, the Czech Republic, Denmark, Greece, and Italy) growing by less than 0.2 percent per year, the same 1.7 percent increase in real output per worker yields only 1.5–1.9 percent annual overall growth. Moreover, developed countries will be lucky to keep productivity growth at even that level; in many developed countries, productivity is more likely to decline as the population ages.

A further strain on industrialized economies will be rising medical costs: as populations age, they will demand more health care for longer periods of time. Public pension schemes for aging populations are already being reformed in various industrialized countries—often prompting heated debate. In theory, at least, pensions might be kept solvent by increasing the retirement age, raising taxes modestly, and phasing out benefits for the wealthy. Regardless, the number of 80- and 90-year-olds—who are unlikely to work and highly likely to require nursing-home and other expensive care—will rise dramatically. And even if 60- and 70-year-olds remain active and employed, they will require procedures and medications—hip replacements, kidney transplants, blood-pressure treatments—to sustain their health in old age.

All this means that just as aging developed countries will have proportionally fewer workers, innovators, and consumerist young households, a large portion of those countries' remaining economic growth will have to be diverted to pay for the medical bills and pensions of their growing elderly populations. Basic services, meanwhile, will be increasingly costly because fewer young workers will be available for strenuous and labor-intensive jobs. Unfortunately, policymakers seldom reckon with these potentially disruptive effects of otherwise welcome developments, such as higher life expectancy.

Youth and Islam in the Developing World

Even as the industrialized countries of Europe, North America, and Northeast Asia will experience unprecedented aging this century, fast-growing countries in Africa, Latin America, the Middle East, and Southeast Asia will have exceptionally youthful populations. Today, roughly nine out of ten children under the age of 15 live in developing countries. And these are the countries that will continue to have the world's highest birthrates. Indeed, over 70 percent of the world's population growth between now and 2050 will occur in 24 countries, all of which are classified by the World Bank as low income or lower-middle income, with an average per capita income of under $3,855 in 2008.

Many developing countries have few ways of providing employment to their young, fast-growing populations. Would-be laborers, therefore, will be increasingly attracted to the labor markets of the aging developed countries of Europe, North America, and Northeast Asia. Youthful immigrants from nearby regions with high unemployment—Central America, North Africa, and Southeast Asia, for example—will be drawn to those vital entry-level and manual-labor jobs that sustain advanced economies: janitors, nursing-home aides, bus drivers, plumbers, security guards, farm workers, and the like. Current levels of immigration from developing to developed countries are paltry compared to those that the forces of supply and demand might soon create across the world.

These forces will act strongly on the Muslim world, where many economically weak countries will continue to experience dramatic population growth in the decades ahead. In 1950, Bangladesh, Egypt, Indonesia, Nigeria, Pakistan, and Turkey had a combined population of 242 million. By 2009, those six countries were the world's most populous Muslim-majority countries and had a combined population of 886 million. Their populations are continuing to grow and indeed are expected to increase by 475 million between now and 2050—during which time, by comparison, the six most populous developed countries are projected to gain only 44 million inhabitants. Worldwide, of the 48 fastest-growing countries today—those with annual population growth of two percent or more—28 are majority Muslim or have Muslim minorities of 33 percent or more.

It is therefore imperative to improve relations between Muslim and Western societies. This will be difficult given that many Muslims live in poor communities vulnerable to radical appeals and many see the West as antagonistic and militaristic. In the 2009 Pew Global Attitudes Project survey, for example, whereas 69 percent of those Indonesians and Nigerians surveyed reported viewing the United States favorably, just 18 percent of those polled in Egypt, Jordan, Pakistan, and Turkey (all U.S. allies) did. And in 2006, when the Pew survey last asked detailed questions about Muslim-Western relations, more than half of the respondents in Muslim countries characterized those relations as bad and blamed the West for this state of affairs.

But improving relations is all the more important because of the growing demographic weight of poor Muslim countries and the attendant increase in Muslim immigration, especially to Europe from North Africa and the Middle East. (To be sure, forecasts that Muslims will soon dominate Europe are outlandish: Muslims compose just three to ten percent of the population in the major European countries today, and this proportion will at most double by midcentury.) Strategists worldwide must consider that the world's young are becoming concentrated in those countries least prepared to educate and employ them, including some Muslim states. Any resulting poverty, social tension, or ideological radicalization could have disruptive effects in many corners of the world. But this need not be the case; the healthy immigration of workers to the developed world and the movement of capital to the developing world, among other things, could lead to better results.

Urban Sprawl

Exacerbating twenty-first-century risks will be the fact that the world is urbanizing to an unprecedented degree. The year 2010 will likely be the first time in history that a majority of the world's people live in cities rather than in the countryside. Whereas less than 30 percent of the world's population was urban in 1950, according to UN projections, more than 70 percent will be by 2050.

Lower-income countries in Asia and Africa are urbanizing especially rapidly, as agriculture becomes less labor intensive and as employment opportunities shift to the industrial and service sectors. Already, most of the world's urban agglomerations—Mumbai (population 20.1 million), Mexico City (19.5 million), New Delhi (17 million), Shanghai (15.8 million), Calcutta (15.6 million), Karachi (13.1 million), Cairo (12.5 million), Manila (11.7 million), Lagos (10.6 million), Jakarta (9.7 million)—are found in low-income countries. Many of these countries have multiple cities with over one million residents each: Pakistan has eight, Mexico 12, and China more than 100. The UN projects that the urbanized proportion of sub-Saharan Africa will nearly double between 2005 and 2050, from 35 percent (300 million people) to over 67 percent (1 billion). China, which is roughly 40 percent urbanized today, is expected to be 73 percent urbanized by 2050; India, which is less than 30 percent urbanized today, is expected to be 55 percent urbanized by 2050. Overall, the world's urban population is expected to grow by 3 billion people by 2050.

This urbanization may prove destabilizing. Developing countries that urbanize in the twenty-first century will have far lower per capita incomes than did many industrial countries when they first urbanized. The United States, for example, did not reach 65 percent urbanization until 1950, when per capita income was nearly $13,000 (in 2005 dollars). By contrast, Nigeria, Pakistan, and the Philippines, which are approaching similar levels of urbanization, currently have per capita incomes of just $1,800–$4,000 (in 2005 dollars).

According to the research of Richard Cincotta and other political demographers, countries with younger populations are especially prone to civil unrest and are less able to create or sustain democratic institutions. And the more heavily urbanized, the more such countries are likely to experience Dickensian poverty and anarchic violence. In good times, a thriving economy might keep urban residents employed and governments flush with sufficient resources to meet their needs. More often, however, sprawling and impoverished cities are vulnerable to crime lords, gangs, and petty rebellions. Thus, the rapid urbanization of the developing world in the decades ahead might bring, in exaggerated form, problems similar to those that urbanization brought to nineteenth-century Europe. Back then, cyclical employment, inadequate policing, and limited sanitation and education often spawned widespread labor strife, periodic violence, and sometimes—as in the 1820s, the 1830s, and 1848—even revolutions.

International terrorism might also originate in fast-urbanizing developing countries (even more than it already does). With their neighborhood networks, access to the Internet and digital communications technology, and concentration of valuable targets, sprawling cities offer excellent opportunities for recruiting, maintaining, and hiding terrorist networks.

Defusing the Bomb

Averting this century's potential dangers will require sweeping measures. Three major global efforts defused the population bomb of Ehrlich's day: a commitment by governments and nongovernmental organizations to control reproduction rates; agricultural advances, such as the green revolution and the spread of new technology; and a vast increase in international trade, which globalized markets and thus allowed developing countries to export foodstuffs in exchange for seeds, fertilizers, and machinery, which in turn helped them boost production. But today's population bomb is the product less of absolute growth in the world's population than of changes in its age and distribution. Policymakers must therefore adapt today's global governance institutions to the new realities of the aging of the industrialized world, the concentration of the world's economic and population growth in developing countries, and the increase in international immigration.

During the Cold War, Western strategists divided the world into a "First World," of democratic industrialized countries; a "Second World," of communist industrialized countries; and a "Third World," of developing countries. These strategists focused chiefly on deterring or managing conflict between the First and the Second Worlds and on launching proxy wars and diplomatic initiatives to attract Third World countries into the First World's camp. Since the end of the Cold War, strategists have largely abandoned this three-group division and have tended to believe either that the United States, as the sole superpower, would maintain a Pax Americana or that the world would become multipolar, with the United States, Europe, and China playing major roles.

Unfortunately, because they ignore current global demographic trends, these views will be obsolete within a few decades. A better approach would be to consider a different three-world order, with a new First World of the aging industrialized nations of North America, Europe, and Asia's Pacific Rim (including Japan, Singapore, South Korea, and Taiwan, as well as China after 2030, by which point the one-child policy will have produced significant aging); a Second World comprising fast-growing and economically dynamic countries with a healthy mix of young and old inhabitants (such as Brazil, Iran, Mexico, Thailand, Turkey, and Vietnam, as well as China until 2030); and a Third World of fast-growing, very young, and increasingly urbanized countries with poorer economies and often weak governments. To cope with the instability that will likely arise from the new Third World's urbanization, economic strife, lawlessness, and potential terrorist activity, the aging industrialized nations of the new First World must build effective alliances with the growing powers of the new Second World and together reach out to Third World nations. Second World powers will be pivotal in the twenty-first century not just because they will drive economic growth and consume technologies and other products engineered in the First World; they will also be central to international security and cooperation. The realities of religion, culture, and geographic proximity mean that any peaceful and productive engagement by the First World of Third World countries will have to include the open cooperation of Second World countries.

Strategists, therefore, must fundamentally reconsider the structure of various current global institutions. The G-8, for example, will likely become obsolete as a body for making global economic policy. The G-20 is already becoming increasingly important, and this is less a short-term consequence of the ongoing global financial crisis than the beginning of the necessary recognition that Brazil, China, India, Indonesia, Mexico, Turkey, and others are becoming global economic powers. International institutions will not retain their legitimacy if they exclude the world's fastest-growing and most economically dynamic countries. It is essential, therefore, despite European concerns about the potential effects on immigration, to take steps such as admitting Turkey into the European Union. This would add youth and economic dynamism to the EU—and would prove that Muslims are welcome to join Europeans as equals in shaping a free and prosperous future. On the other hand, excluding Turkey from the EU could lead to hostility not only on the part of Turkish citizens, who are expected to number 100 million by 2050, but also on the part of Muslim populations worldwide.

NATO must also adapt. The alliance today is composed almost entirely of countries with aging, shrinking populations and relatively slow-growing economies. It is oriented toward the Northern Hemisphere and holds on to a Cold War structure that cannot adequately respond to contemporary threats. The young and increasingly populous countries of Africa, the Middle East, Central Asia, and South Asia could mobilize insurgents much more easily than NATO could mobilize the troops it would need if it were called on to stabilize those countries. Long-standing NATO members should, therefore—although it would require atypical creativity and flexibility—consider the logistical and demographic advantages of inviting into the alliance countries such as Brazil and Morocco, rather than countries such as Albania. That this seems far-fetched does not minimize the imperative that First World countries begin including large and strategic Second and Third World powers in formal international alliances.

The case of Afghanistan—a country whose population is growing fast and where NATO is currently engaged—illustrates the importance of building effective global institutions. Today, there are 28 million Afghans; by 2025, there will be 45 million; and by 2050, there will be close to 75 million. As nearly 20 million additional Afghans are born over the next 15 years, NATO will have an opportunity to help Afghanistan become reasonably stable, self-governing, and prosperous. If NATO's efforts fail and the Afghans judge that NATO intervention harmed their interests, tens of millions of young Afghans will become more hostile to the West. But if they come to think that NATO's involvement benefited their society, the West will have tens of millions of new friends. The example might then motivate the approximately one billion other young Muslims growing up in low-income countries over the next four decades to look more kindly on relations between their countries and the countries of the industrialized West.

Creative Reforms at Home

The aging industrialized countries can also take various steps at home to promote stability in light of the coming demographic trends. First, they should encourage families to have more children. France and Sweden have had success providing child care, generous leave time, and financial allowances to families with young children. Yet there is no consensus among policymakers—and certainly not among demographers—about what policies best encourage fertility.

More important than unproven tactics for increasing family size is immigration. Correctly managed, population movement can benefit developed and developing countries alike. Given the dangers of young, underemployed, and unstable populations in developing countries, immigration to developed countries can provide economic opportunities for the ambitious and serve as a safety valve for all. Countries that embrace immigrants, such as the United States, gain economically by having willing laborers and greater entrepreneurial spirit. And countries with high levels of emigration (but not so much that they experience so-called brain drains) also benefit because emigrants often send remittances home or return to their native countries with valuable education and work experience.

One somewhat daring approach to immigration would be to encourage a reverse flow of older immigrants from developed to developing countries. If older residents of developed countries took their retirements along the southern coast of the Mediterranean or in Latin America or Africa, it would greatly reduce the strain on their home countries' public entitlement systems. The developing countries involved, meanwhile, would benefit because caring for the elderly and providing retirement and leisure services is highly labor intensive. Relocating a portion of these activities to developing countries would provide employment and valuable training to the young, growing populations of the Second and Third Worlds.

This would require developing residential and medical facilities of First World quality in Second and Third World countries. Yet even this difficult task would be preferable to the status quo, by which low wages and poor facilities lead to a steady drain of medical and nursing talent from developing to developed countries. Many residents of developed countries who desire cheaper medical procedures already practice medical tourism today, with India, Singapore, and Thailand being the most common destinations. (For example, the international consulting firm Deloitte estimated that 750,000 Americans traveled abroad for care in 2008.)

Never since 1800 has a majority of the world's economic growth occurred outside of Europe, the United States, and Canada. Never have so many people in those regions been over 60 years old. And never have low-income countries' populations been so young and so urbanized. But such will be the world's demography in the twenty-first century. The strategic and economic policies of the twentieth century are obsolete, and it is time to find new ones.

Reference

Goldstone, Jack A. "The new population bomb: the four megatrends that will change the world." *Foreign Affairs* 89.1 (2010): 31. *General OneFile.* Web. 23 Jan. 2010. http://0-find.galegroup .com.www.consuls.org/gps/start.do?proId=IPS& userGroupName=a30wc.

Critical Thinking

1. What will be the second order impacts of future population growth?
2. In the developed countries, population will age and decline relative to developing countries. How will these changes strain world governance structures and generate instability and violence?

Article

Best. Decade. Ever.

The first 10 years of the 21st century were humanity's finest—even for the world's bottom billion.

CHARLES KENNY

The past 10 years have gotten a bad rap as the "Naughty Aughties"—and deservedly so, it seems, for a decade that began with 9/11 and the Enron scandal and closed with the global financial crisis and the Haiti earthquake. In between, we witnessed the Asian tsunami and Hurricane Katrina, SARS and swine flu, not to mention vicious fighting in Sudan and Congo, Afghanistan and, oh yes, Iraq. Given that our brains seem hard-wired to remember singular tragedy over incremental success, it's a hard sell to convince anyone that the past 10 years are worthy of praise.

But these horrific events, though mortal and economic catastrophes for many millions, don't sum up the decade as experienced by most of the planet's 6-billion-plus people. For all its problems, the first 10 years of the 21st century were in fact humanity's finest, a time when more people lived better, longer, more peaceful, and more prosperous lives than ever before.

Consider that in 1990, roughly half the global population lived on less than $1 a day; by 2007, the proportion had shrunk to 28 percent—and it will be lower still by the close of 2010. That's because, though the financial crisis briefly stalled progress on income growth, it was just a hiccup in the decade's relentless GDP climb. Indeed, average worldwide incomes are at their highest levels ever, at roughly $10,600 a year—and have risen by as much as a quarter since 2000. Some 1.3 billion people now live on more than $10 a day, suggesting the continued expansion of the global middle class. Even better news is that growth has been faster in poor places like sub-Saharan Africa than across the world as a whole.

There are still 1 billion people who go to bed each night desperately hungry, but cereal prices are now a fraction of what they were in the 1960s and 1970s. That, alongside continued income growth, is why the proportion of the developing world's population classified as "undernourished" fell from 34 percent in 1970 to 17 percent in 2008, even at the height of a global spike in food prices. Agricultural productivity, too, continues to climb: From 2000 to 2008, cereal yields increased at nearly twice the rate of population growth in the developing world. And though famine continues to threaten places such as Zimbabwe, hundreds of millions of people are eating more—and better—each day.

We're also winning the global battle against infectious disease. The 2009 swine flu has killed more than 18,000 people so far, according to the World Health Organization. But its impact has been far less severe than the apocalyptic forecasts of a few years ago, fueled by nightmare scenarios of drug-resistant, Airbus-hopping viruses overwhelming a hot, flat, and crowded world. The truth is that pandemics are on the wane. Between 1999 and 2005, thanks to the spread of vaccinations, the number of children who died annually from measles dropped 60 percent. The proportion of the world's infants vaccinated against diphtheria, whooping cough, and tetanus has climbed from less than half to 82 percent between 1985 and 2008.

There are dark spots still, not least the continuing tragedy of the HIV/AIDS epidemic. But though the 15 countries with the highest HIV prevalence still see life expectancies more than three years lower than their 1990 peak, at least the trend has started ticking back up in the last decade. The overwhelming global picture is of better health: From 2000 to 2008, child mortality dropped more than 17 percent, and the average person added another two years to his or her life expectancy, now just one shy of the biblical standard of three score and 10.

We can thank improved literacy, which has played a role in spreading vital knowledge in low-income societies, for some of these health gains. More than four-fifths of the world's population can now read and write—including more than two-thirds of Africans. The proportion of the world's young people who go on to university climbed from below one-fifth to above a quarter from 2000 to 2007 alone. And progress in education has been particularly rapid for women, one sign of growing gender equity. Although no one would argue the struggle is complete, the gains are striking—the worldwide proportion of women parliamentarians, for instance, increased from 11 percent in 1997 to 19 percent in 2009.

If you had to choose a decade in history in which to be alive, the first of the 21st century would undoubtedly be it.

Even the wars of the last 10 years, tragic as they have been, are minor compared with the violence and destruction of decades and centuries past. The number of armed conflicts—and their death toll—has continued to fall since the end of the Cold War. Worldwide, combat casualties fell 40 percent from 2000 to 2008. In sub-Saharan Africa, some 46,000 people died in battle in 2000. By 2008, that number had dropped to 6,000. Military expenditures as a percentage of global GDP are about half of their 1990 level. In Europe, so recently divided into two armed camps, annual military budgets fell from $744 billion in 1988 to $424 billion in 2009. The statistical record doesn't go back far enough for us to know with absolute certainty whether this was the most peaceful decade ever in terms of violent deaths per capita, but it certainly ranks as the lowest in the last 50 years.

On the other hand, humanity's malignant effect on the environment has accelerated the rate of extinction for plants and animals, which now reaches perhaps 50,000 species a year. But even here there was some good news. We reversed our first man-made global atmospheric crisis by banning chlorofluorocarbons—by 2015, the Antarctic ozone hole will have shrunk by nearly 400,000 square miles. Stopping climate change has been a slower process. Nonetheless, in 2008, the G-8 did commit to halving carbon emissions by 2050. And a range of technological advances—from hydrogen fuel cells to compact fluorescent bulbs—suggests that a low-carbon future need not require surrendering a high quality of life.

Technology has done more than improve energy efficiency. Today, there are more than 4 billion mobile-phone subscribers, compared with only 750 million at the decade's start. Cell phones are being used to provide financial services in the Philippines, monitor real-time commodity futures prices in Vietnam, and teach literacy in Niger. And streaming video means that fans can watch cricket even in benighted countries that don't broadcast it—or upload citizen reports from security crackdowns in Tehran.

Perhaps technology also helps account for the striking disconnect between the reality of worldwide progress and the perception of global decline. We're more able than ever to witness the tragedy of millions of our fellow humans on television or online. And, rightly so, we're more outraged than ever that suffering continues in a world of such technological wonder and economic plenty.

Nonetheless, if you had to choose a **decade** in history in which to be alive, the first of the 21st century would undoubtedly be it. More people lived lives of greater freedom, security, longevity, and wealth than ever before. And now, billions of them can tweet the good news. Bring on the 'Teenies.

Critical Thinking

1. Why does Kenny think the first decade of the 21st century is the best?
2. In what ways have conditions in the developing world improved?
3. What challenges remain?
4. Why do the reality and perceptions of global decline continue to be at odds?

Charles Kenny, a contributing editor to *Foreign Policy* is author of the forthcoming book *Getting Better: Why Global Development Is Succeding and How We Can Improve the World Even More.*

Article

Prepared by: Robert J. Griffiths, *University of North Carolina at Greensboro*

The Mixed News on Poverty

"To make progress toward moving a majority of the worlds population into better circumstances, we must adopt a more nuanced view of what constitutes poverty."

ANIRUDH KRISHNA

Learning Outcomes

After reading this article, you will be able to:

- Explain the reasons for the mixed news on poverty reduction.
- Identify the factors that cause people to fall into poverty.

Progress in poverty reduction has been spectacular, unprecedented, and widespread over the past quarter-century. Here's the evidence: In 1981, more than 50 percent of the world's population lived below the international poverty line (currently, $1.25 per day, adjusted for cost-of-living differences). This share was cut nearly in half, falling to 25.7 percent by 2005. The number of people's in poverty fell from 1.9 billion to 1.4 billion. The number living below a lower poverty line of $1 per day fell even more sharply, from 1.5 billion in 1981 to 0.8 billion in 2005. These improvements are far better than anything achieved over comparable periods in the past.

Clearly, there is much to celebrate. But look closer at the evidence and you may not feel quite so triumphant. Those who escaped poverty have not moved very far above the poverty line; many are in danger of backsliding. And despite the recent successes, large numbers remain mired in poverty. Fifty-one percent of the population in sub-Saharan Africa, 40 percent in South Asia (including India), and 17 percent in East Asia (including China) continue to live below the $1.25 poverty line. These numbers need to be halved and then halved again.

Business as usual will not succeed in reducing world poverty to single-digit percentages. Policies that have helped reduce poverty in the past have lost some of their edge, and are unlikely to be equally effective in the future. Newer and better-focused policies are required to address three areas of continuing concern that have received relatively little attention in the past. Only with attention to these concerns can we hope to achieve a world in which the majority of people live in dignity and reach their potential.

Persistent Problems

The first of these concerns relates to the resurgence of poverty. Moving people out of poverty is not the entire solution, because people fall into poverty in large numbers. Investigations that I conducted together with colleagues in different countries show that more than one-third of all poor people were not born into poverty. Rather, they fell into poverty, and in the majority of cases have remained persistently poor. Assistance of different kinds is being provided to these individuals and families. It seems odd and grimly ironic that support is extended only after people have become impoverished. Much more can be done to prevent these occurrences, saving a great deal of human misery and substantial taxpayer funds. Yet policies aimed at poverty prevention have not been put in place in most countries. As a result, what is gained on one hand is lost on the other; new people fill spaces vacated by the formerly poor.

A second concern relates to the special problems of chronic and intergenerational poverty, on which current policies have had very little effect. Stubborn pockets of poverty remain, in particular locations and among members of groups that are discriminated against or marginalized by geography or politics. Whole families remain poor for generations: Poverty is passed on from parents to children and grandchildren. Such chronically poor people are estimated to number between 320 million and 400 million across the world, a sizeable group requiring special attention.

A third area concerns the nature and quality of escapes from poverty. Sure, it is a happy occasion when some individual crosses over the poverty line. But how much more do formerly poor individuals typically end up achieving? Are the destinations at which they arrive commensurate with their personal capabilities and hard work? Or do even the most capable and hardworking tend to get trapped beneath low glass ceilings?

Not a great deal of knowledge is available on this score, but for what they are worth the aggregate statistics are far from encouraging. Between 1981 and 2005, the number of people living in acute poverty (below $1.25 per day) fell by 500 million across the world. What we did not see, and what is less often discussed, is that simultaneously the number of those in near-poverty (between $1.25 and $2) went up by an even larger number: 600 million. The entire reduction in the numbers of the acutely poor thus seems to have been absorbed within the ranks of the near-poor, with those escaping poverty climbing above but still remaining close to the poverty line—a realization that takes the luster off the reported achievements.

More people need support to rise, not just above the poverty line, but as high as each one is individually capable. Unfortunately, current policies do not help achieve this goal. Talented individuals are born in large numbers even within very poor households. Our investigations revealed that hardly anyone among them was able to achieve a high-paying position.

Many have moved out of poverty, but only a tiny number have risen very far.

Economic growth, which has helped raise millions out of poverty in the past, will not be equally successful as an anti-poverty measure in the future. Already, calculations show that the poverty-reducing impacts of growth have shrunk, especially within countries where growth has helped most in the past. One reason for this is that economic growth is not a sufficient antidote for any of these three remaining concerns, which will require new policies assisted by disaggregated data collection and innovative analytical tools.

Hidden Flows

Continuing inattention to the concerns discussed above can be blamed in part on gaps in poverty data. An intense, worldwide focus on stimulating economic growth as the primary antipoverty measure has resulted in the collection only of national-aggregate poverty statistics. Surveys carried out by national governments and international agencies estimate the total number of people who are poor in a country at particular moments in time. We can deduce the net change in the stock of poverty between successive measurements, but there is nothing in these data that reveals precisely how many people escaped poverty, much less about the quality of individual escapes; nor do the data show how many fell into poverty, or anything about the numbers and conditions of the chronically poor.

For the sake of illustration, consider the following hypothetical example. The level of poverty in Country X, which was 32 percent in 2000, fell to 24 percent by 2010. Should we be optimistic or disheartened? More important, what can we deduce from these statistics, the only ones usually available, about what needs to be done in terms of future policy design?

The answers to these questions, it turns out, depend largely on the nature of the underlying poverty flows. We need to know: How did this 8 percentage point reduction actually come about? Did (a) 8 percent of the population escape poverty, and no one fell into poverty over the same period (which, if it were true, would be very encouraging); or (b) did 16 percent escape poverty, while 8 percent concurrently became poor; or (c) causing most distress, did 24 percent escape poverty and 16 percent fall into poverty? None of these possibilities can be discounted. The available data are compatible with any of these (and innumerable other) flow possibilities, all resulting in an 8 percent net reduction of the national poverty level.

If statistics tell us nothing about different flow possibilities, we are powerless to design effective policies. Critically, escapes from poverty and descents into poverty are not responsive to the same remedies. People escape poverty on account of one set of reasons; they fall into poverty on account of a different set of reasons. Because separate factors are associated with each poverty flow, separate and parallel policies are required.

One set of policies—let's call them promotional policies—is required to promote more poverty escapes. Concurrently, another set—preventive policies—is required for holding poverty descents in check. The faster the pace of descents in some country or region, the more urgent is the need for preventive policies. But where descents are fewer in number, resources can be concentrated, instead, on promotional strategies. Different combinations of promotional and preventive policies are required, therefore, depending on the particular circumstances of a nation or region.

In order to give shape to the appropriate policy mix, it is critical to have disaggregated data that help differentiate escapes from descents. Such data have not been available in the past. Policy makers; unable to view the magnitude, far less the sources, of this problem, have been blind to poverty descents. As a result, preventive policies have been enacted in only a handful of countries, developing or rich—and these are the countries that have the lowest poverty rates, not those with the highest growth rates or the largest per capita incomes.

The same nexus—non-availability of data leading to policy inattention—applies to the second and third areas of concern: chronic poverty, and a dearth of opportunities resulting in a low glass ceiling for poor individuals. Recent studies give some indication of the magnitude of these problems and ideas about what needs to be done. In particular, improving health care is critical for preventing future poverty. Simultaneously, investments must be made in education, infrastrucmre, and information provision.

Ups and Downs

Planners are fixated on promotional strategies, but the only way in which inattention to poverty descents can be justified is by assuming that all poor people must have been born poor. A swath of evidence from different parts of the world shows that nothing could be further from the truth. Recent research employing a variety of methods has tracked flows into and out of poverty. The results are broadly similar: Everywhere, poverty simultaneously falls and rises.

In a series of investigations undertaken between 2001 and 2010, I traced which households have come out of poverty and which others fell into poverty (and why) in a varied sample of nearly 400 communities in India, Kenya, Peru, Uganda, and the US state of North Carolina. In association with colleagues in these countries I studied more than 35,000 households.

In each case, we found, encouragingly, that large numbers of people have moved out of poverty. In 36 Ugandan communities that I analyzed, 370 households (almost 15 percent of the total) emerged from poverty between 1994 and 2004. In Gujarat, India, 10 percent of a sample of several thousand households emerged from poverty between 1980 and 2003. In Kenya, 18 percent of a sample of households came out of poverty between 1990 and 2004.

Unfortunately, people moving out of poverty are only half the story. The other, gloomier half is about the thousands of people who fall below the poverty line each year. In Kenya, for example, more households, 19 percent, fell into poverty than emerged from it. In Gujarat, 7 percent of all households fell into poverty, even as 10 percent were moving out. In Egypt, Peru, South Africa, Bangladesh, and every other country where such studies have been carried out, concurrent escapes and descents have been similarly exposed.

In remote rural areas as well as throbbing metropolises, the numbers are large both for those who have escaped poverty and for others who have become poor. In many places, the newly impoverished constitute the majority of the poor. Worse, many of those who fall into poverty take a long time to move out, with some becoming persistently poor. Nearly 60 percent of all those who slipped into poverty 15 or more years ago were still poor at the time of our investigations.

The Health Care Trap

Preventive policies are urgently required. There is nothing inevitable about falling into poverty. In fact, there are many opportunities to prevent it. People usually fall into poverty over a period of time, bit by bit, and not all of a sudden. A number of factors contribute to poverty descents, and they differ in importance within and across countries. A chain of everyday events, rather than any single catastrophe, is most often involved.

However, the leading culprit is poor health care. Tracking thousands of households in the five countries we studied, my colleagues and I found that poor health and high health care expenses are the leading cause for people's reversals of fortune. The story of a man from Cachachi, a district in Peru, is illustrative. "I was much better off than my neighbors when my wife of 25 years became ill," he said. It was diagnosed as uterine cancer. "I was obliged to sell my animals, cows, oxen, and donkeys, and I also went into debt in order to care for her, and later, to bury her. Today, old and sick, I have to find work as a day laborer."

Among households that fell into poverty in 20 villages of western Kenya, 74 percent cited ill health and high health care costs as the most important cause of their economic decline. Eighty-eight percent of people who fell into poverty in 36 villages in India's Gujarat state placed the blame principally on health care costs. In Peru, 67 percent of the recently impoverished in two provinces cited ill health, hard-to-reach medical facilities, and high health care costs. In comparison, drunkenness, drug abuse, and laziness together accounted for no more than 3 percent of all poverty descents.

People are not poor because they wish to be poor or because of some character defect. Most have become poor due to influences beyond their personal control, including, particularly, health care.

Once families are hit by a health crisis, it is often hard to recover. One major illness typically reduces family income by up to one-fifth. Successive illnesses ensure an even faster spiral into persistent poverty. Public health researchers have detected a "medical poverty trap" in many countries. A combination of ill health and indebtedness has forced large numbers of households in Asia and Africa into poverty, including many who were once quite well off: The phenomenon exists in wealthy nations as well. More than half of all personal bankruptcies in the United States occur due to high medical expenses.

Millions of people are living one illness away from poverty. And existing poverty alleviation measures are ill suited to respond to the challenge. Economic growth does not by itself remove the medical poverty trap. Health care is not automatically better or cheaper where economic growth rates have been high. In Gujarat, which has regularly achieved 8 percent growth rates for many years, the dearth of affordable health care remains a severe problem, and thousands have fallen into poverty for health-related reasons. Health care in fast-growing Gujarat is no better than in other, often poorer, states of India. Indeed, Gujarat ranked fourth from the bottom among twenty-five states in terms of proportion of state income spent on health care.

Perversely, rapid economic growth often weakens existing social safety nets and raises the danger of falling into poverty. In places as diverse as rural India, Kenya, Uganda, and North Carolina, I observed how community and family support is crumbling as market-based transactions overtake community networks.

Making affordable and high-quality health care accessible to all is the most important preventive policy of the future. Poverty is lowest in those countries and communities where residents can get a loved one's illness treated without having to lose their shirts. The poverty rate in Japan is 2 percent, among the lowest in the world. By the same measure, 14 percent of the United States' population is poor, even though the country boasts one of the highest annual per capita incomes in the world—nearly $50,000.

Higher incomes and economic growth undoubtedly helped in Japan, but so, too, did an entirely different set of policies. Quite early in the country's postwar recovery, Japanese officials recognized the critical relationship among illness, health care services, and poverty creation, and they responded by implementing universal health care as early as the 1950s. Sweden, Denmark, and all other countries with single-digit poverty rates have also invested in high-quality, universally accessible health care.

Improving health care will reduce future poverty by stemming the inflow of newly impoverished people. It will also improve the prospects of the existing poor. People who know that they are protected against downslides will more readily take risks and invest in their futures.

Future poverty cannot be controlled without introducing better health care.

Chronic Adversity

Both promotional and preventive policies are also required to deal with the problems of chronic poverty. People remain chronically poor not for lack of trying or because nothing happens to change their lifestyles. More often, for them, one step forward is followed by two steps back. Over time, families face different combinations of adverse and positive events. Adverse events—a loved one's illness, the death of a spouse—tend to pitch families into a downward spiral. But positive events also occur: Someone acquires education and lands a job; someone else obtains a profitable supply contract. The buoyancy produced by positive events is offset, however, when families experience negative events.

The balance of events—positive and adverse—determines whether a family will climb up, go down, or stay in place. The object of policy should be to change this balance, inducing more positive and fewer adverse events. Improving health care will help enhance the balance of events, including for the chronic poor.

Three other factors require special mention. First, there is a spatial dimension to chronic poverty, which is more often found in rural than in urban areas. It is especially acute in remote rural regions. The prospects of rising out of poverty are lower (while the odds of falling into poverty are higher) among habitations located far from towns and cities. In many countries, urban areas and villages located close to major cities provide the lion's share of physical and social infrastructures. In remote areas, a lack of transportation, schools, and clinics combine to keep people trapped in chronic poverty, which is multidimensional in nature—the chronically poor are more often sick, they are less often educated, and they find it hard to connect with market opportunities. A hard core of chronic poverty is frequendy found among forest dwellers and mountain folk.

These handicaps are made worse by social exclusion and political discrimination directed against members of particular ethnic groups. In India, for instance, scheduled castes (former untouchables) and scheduled tribes (indigenous people) have been historically discriminated against and still carry a higher burden of poverty. Gender discrimination is another concern in many countries. Female headed households are among the poorest of the poor, being (or becoming) chronically poor in a vast number of cases.

A third chronic poverty trap has to do with civil wars and limited citizenship. Prolonged civil strife with refugees moving across borders has given rise to persistent poverty, especially in sub-Saharan Africa, where the chronic poor constitute 15 to 20 percent of the population.

Having little or no education, lacking roads and communication, isolated, and often refugees or victims of social discrimination to boot, the chronically poor have few means to avail themselves of the benefits of economic growth. They need targeted policies that can equip them better for participating in the growth process. Improving health and especially education is critical; there are many illiterate people and their wages are very low. Building better connections to outlying areas is another priority. Rapidly spreading cell phones have in some places and to some extent helped, but other forms of physical and social infrastructure are also necessary.

Marginal Escape

To make progress toward moving a majority of the world's population into better circumstances, we must adopt a more nuanced view of what constitutes poverty. A binary view considering only two possible states—above and below the poverty line—has unfortunately informed poverty policies of the past. Because reducing the aggregate numbers in poverty was the overriding concern, the quality of individual escapes was not separately monitored. A marginal escape above the $1.25 poverty line—from, say, $1.23 to $1.27 per day—was counted as a success. A more substantial escape, 79 cents to $2.50, was counted in much the same way. This manner of compiling poverty statistics has provided relatively little knowledge about individual poverty escapes.

Recent data from grassroots investigations help fill these gaps, in poverty knowledge. The picture they show is similar to what we have seen in global statistics. Many have moved out of poverty, but only a tiny number have risen very far. Most of those who escaped poverty in the countries I studied have found positions working as maids, gardeners, chauffeurs, pushcart vendors, security guards, rickshaw pullers, mason's assistants, and the like. Hardly anyone has become a software engineer, university professor, business magnate, or airline pilot. Further investigations have shown that even the sons and daughters of these maids and pushcart vendors are rarely able to achieve higher-paying positions.

Everywhere, poverty simultaneously falls and rises.

What is holding back these individuals? It is certainly not lack of effort or ambition. Again and again, in interviews with poor mothers and fathers, I was brought back to one essential fact: One's own poverty is easier to bear with fortitude if future opportunities for one's children are bright. People of all socioeconomic levels are deeply concerned about their children's future. Data from around the developing world show an explosive rise in school attendance. Many are investing more than they can afford in sending their children to schools.

Few among these investments have delivered rich rewards. People from poorer communities, even the more educated and hardworking ones, tend to get stuck with low-paying positions. I inquired in a diverse group of communities about what the residents have achieved in the past and what current residents, especially younger ones, aspire to achieve in the future. Separately, I examined the social and educational backgrounds of young people who have been recruited recently as engineers or managers or who found other high-paying positions. There are many happy parts to the stories I heard, but the sad part is that none among these new recruits was brought up poor.

Two factors have militated against greater achievement. First, the quality of education in poor communities is poor. The schools that poorer children attend are poorly resourced. Teachers are scantily supervised and poorly motivated; teacher absenteeism is rife. There is hardly any after-school activity. Despite going to school for the same number of years, children in poorer communities learn less than their peers in better schools.

Intensifying the limitations imposed by lower-quality education is an acute shortage of career information. Employment exchanges, career counseling services, college guides, vocational centers, and other institutions that provide information and career guidance do not exist in poor communities. And the only role models available in such communities are those who achieved low-paying positions in the past. The absence of high-achieving role models and mentors along with a lack of reliable information about pathways and opportunities keeps thousands of bright-eyed young people trapped within low-productivity, low-compensation situations. Even those who have innate ability and the will to excel are unable to do so because they cannot get plugged into better opportunities.

Faster economic growth will open new opportunities, but who will benefit from them? There are concerns that income inequality is rising worldwide, hampering the poverty-reducing impact of economic growth. Investing in education and information is, therefore, an urgent need. Individuals will benefit and countries will grow faster when a greater share of their talent pool can connect with higher-productivity opportunities.

Promote and Prevent

Progress in poverty reduction has been laudable in the past few decades, but we cannot afford to be complacent, hoping that what has worked in the past will continue to deliver in the future. Promoting faster economic growth is critical, particularly in countries, including many in sub-Saharan Africa, where growth rates have been historically low. In addition, different and targeted policies are required.

And this means preventive as well as promotional policies. It does litte good that large numbers of new recruits enter the pool of poverty while strenuous efforts are made to move people out of this pool. People who escaped poverty in the past have not gone very far, and many others are in danger of impoverishment. Cutting off the flow of people into poverty is a critical priority for the future. Diverse factors are responsible for this constant flow, and bad health is primary among them. Future poverty cannot be controlled without introducing better health care.

Reducing chronic poverty is another priority. The chronic poor constitute a special group that is not automatically assisted by economic growth. Better physical and social infrastructures are required to deal with their problems, in addition to legislation and grassroots actions against discrimination.

Moving beyond a narrow concern with dollar-a-day poverty, improving social mobility among the poor is another priority for the future. Imagine if someone like Albert Einstein had been born poor. Would it have been enough to have moved him just above one dollar a day? The antipoverty achievements of the past are brought into question because many who escaped poverty have joined the ranks of the near-poor. Doing better in the future will require investing in more effective promotional policies. Nurturing talent, no matter where it emerges, requires higher-quality education for all. Simultaneously, there is a need for institutions that provide poor people with information about diverse career opportunities, helping individuals put their capabilities to better use.

Small-scale examples, sparks of light from across the world, pioneered variously by nongovernmental organizations, government agencies, businesses, and volunteer groups, show how these efforts can be successful. Achieving a world without poverty is not beyond our reach, but it will require expanding current thinking, doing new things, and adopting different ways.

Critical Thinking

1. Who are the persistently poor?
2. How does the current data on poverty reduction disguise what is happening among the poor?
3. How does the cost of health care push people into poverty?
4. What are the two types of policy required to boost people out of poverty and prevent them from falling back into it?
5. What other factors affect poverty levels?

Create Central

www.mhhe.com/createcentral

Internet References

Africa Index on Africa
www.afrika.no/index

African Studies WWW (U. Penn)
www.sas.upenn.edu/African_Studies/AS.html

United Nations Development Program
http://undp.org

Anirudh Krishna is a professor of public policy and political science at Duke University's Sanford School of Public Polity and associate dean of its international academic programs. His recent publications include One Illness Away: Why People Become Poor and How They Escape Poverty (Oxford University Press, 2010) and Poverty, Participation, and Democracy: A Global Perspective (Cambridge University Press, 2008).

Article

Prepared by: Robert J. Griffiths, *University of North Carolina at Greensboro*

Own the Goals: What the Millennium Development Goals Have Accomplished

JOHN W. MCARTHUR

Learning Outcomes

After reading this article, you will be able to:

- List the Millennium Development Goals.
- Discuss the reasons for progress on several of the goals and how that progress can be sustained.

For more than a decade, the Millennium Development Goals—a set of time-bound targets agreed on by heads of state in 2000—have unified, galvanized, and expanded efforts to help the world's poorest people. The overarching vision of cutting the amount of extreme poverty worldwide in half by 2015, anchored in a series of specific goals, has drawn attention and resources to otherwise forgotten issues. The MDGS have mobilized government and business leaders to donate tens of billions of dollars to life-saving tools, such as antiretroviral drugs and modern mosquito nets. The goals have promoted cooperation among public, private, and nongovernmental organizations (NGOS), providing a common language and bringing together disparate actors. In his 2008 address to the UN General Assembly, the philanthropist Bill Gates called the goals "the best idea for focusing the world on fighting global poverty that I have ever seen."

The goals will expire on December 31, 2015, and the debate over what should come next is now in full swing. This year, a high-level UN panel, co-chaired by British Prime Minister David Cameron, Liberian President Ellen Johnson Sirleaf, and Indonesian President Susilo Bambang Yudhoyono, will put forward its recommendations for a new agenda. The United States and other members of the UN General Assembly will then consider these recommendations, with growing powers, such as Brazil, China, India, and Nigeria, undoubtedly playing a major role in forging any new agreement. But prior to deciding on a new framework, the world community must evaluate exactly what the mdg effort has achieved so far.

Working on a Dream

The MDGS are not a monolithic policy following a single trajectory. Ultimately, they are nothing more than goals, established by world leaders and subsequently reaffirmed on multiple occasions. The MDGS were not born with a plan, a budget, or a specific mapping out of responsibilities. Many think of the MDGS as the UN's goals, since the agreements were established at UN summits and UN officials have generally led the follow-up efforts for coordination and reporting. But the reality is much more complicated. No single individual or organization is responsible for achieving the MDGS. Instead, countless public, private, and nonprofit actors-working together and independently, in developed and developing countries- have furthered the goals. Amid this complexity, the achievements toward reaching the MDGS are all the more impressive. The goals have brought the diffuse international development community closer together.

Before the MDGS were crafted, there was no common framework for promoting global development. After the Cold War ended, many rich countries cut their foreign aid budgets and turned their focus inward, on domestic priorities. In the United States, for example, the foreign aid budget hit an all-time low in 1997, at 0.09 percent of gross national income. Meanwhile, throughout the 1990s, institutions such as the World Bank and the International Monetary Fund (IMF) encouraged developed and developing countries to scale back spending on public programs—in the name of government efficiency—as a condition for receiving support.

The results were troubling. Africa suffered a generation of stagnation, with rising poverty and child deaths and drops in life expectancy. Economic crises and the threat of growing inequality plagued Asia and Latin America. The anti-globalization movement gained such force that in November and December 1999, at what has come to be called "the Battle in Seattle," street protesters forced the World Trade Organization to cancel major meetings midstream.

The suspicions on the part of civil society carried over into policy debates. In the late 1990s, the Organization for Economic

Cooperation and Development proposed "international development goal" benchmarks for donor efforts. The OECD'S proposal was later co-signed by leaders of the imf, the World Bank, and the UN. In response, Konrad Raiser, then head of the World Council of Churches, hardly a fire breathing radical, wrote UN Secretary-General KofiAnnan to convey astonishment and disappointment that Annan had endorsed a "propaganda exercise for international finance institutions whose policies are widely held to be at the root of many of the most grave social problems facing the poor all over the world."

That proposal never got off the ground, but the international community made other progress in the lead-up to 2000 that helped set the groundwork for the MDGS. Most notably, G-8 leaders took a major step forward when they crafted a debt-cancellation policy at their 1999 summit in Cologne, Germany. Under this new policy, countries could receive debt relief on the condition that they allocated savings to education or health. This helped reorient governments toward spending in social sectors after many years of cutbacks.

At the 2000 UN Millennium Summit, which was the largest gathering of world leaders to date, heads of state accepted that they needed to work together to assist the world's poorest people. Looking at the challenges of the new century, all the UN member states agreed on a set of measurable, time-bound targets in the Millennium Declaration. In 2001, these targets were organized into eight MDGS: eradicate extreme poverty and hunger; achieve universal primary education; promote gender equality and empower women; reduce child mortality; improve maternal health; combat hiv/aids, malaria, and other diseases; ensure environmental sustainability; and forge global partnerships among different countries and actors to achieve development goals. Each goal was further broken down into more specific targets. For example, the first goal involves cutting in half "between 1990 and 2015, the proportion of people whose income is less than $1 a day."

In practical terms, the MDGS were actually launched in March 2002, at the UN International Conference on Financing for Development, in Monterrey, Mexico. The attendees, including heads of state, finance ministers, and foreign ministers, agreed that developed countries should step in with support mechanisms and adequate financial aid to help poor countries committed to good governance meet the mdg targets. Crucially, leaders set a benchmark for burden sharing when they urged "developed countries that have not done so to make concrete efforts towards the target of 0.7 percent of gross national income (GNI) as official development assistance to developing countries." At the time of the conference, the 22 official OECD donor countries allocated an average of 0.22 percent of gni to aid. Thus, working toward a 0.7 target implied more than tripling total global support. The Monterrey conference established the MDGS as the first global framework anchored in an explicit, mutually agreed-on partnership between developed and developing countries.

The Global Conversation

These historic intergovernmental agreements have inspired much debate. Some NGO leaders, including participants in the annual World Social Forum, distrusted any agreement that involved international financial institutions and was negotiated behind closed doors. Human rights activists were dismayed that the MDGS excluded targets for good governance, which they considered a contributor to development and a key outcome unto itself. Some environmental activists were bothered by the narrow formulation of the targets, which ignored major issues, such as climate change, land degradation, ocean management, and air pollution.

To be sure, the mdg framework is imperfect. Several issues, such as gender equality and environmental sustainability, are defined too narrowly. The education goal is limited to the completion of primary school, overlooking concerns about the quality of learning and secondary school enrollment levels. In addition, some academics, such as the economist William Easterly, argue that the remarkable ambition of the goals is unfair to the poorest countries, which have the furthest to go to meet the targets, and minimizes what progress those countries do achieve. Sure enough, if the child survival goal were to cut mortality by half, instead of by two-thirds, 72 developing countries would already have met the target by 2011. Instead, the two-thirds goal has been achieved by only 20 developing countries so far. In addition, the MDGS' emphasis on human development issues, such as education and health, sometimes downplays the importance of investments in energy and infrastructure that support economic growth and job creation.

Nonetheless, the framework has provided a global rallying point. In 2002, with a mandate from Annan and Mark Malloch Brown, then the administrator of the UN Development Program, the economist Jeffrey Sachs launched the UN Millennium Project, which brought together hundreds of experts from around the world from academia, business, government, and civil-society organizations to construct policy plans for achieving the goals. Sachs also tirelessly lobbied government leaders in both developed and developing countries to expand key programs, especially in health and agriculture, in order to meet the mdg targets.

In the lead-up to the 2005 G-8 summit, in Gleneagles, Scotland, advocacy organizations worldwide championed the MDGS. In developing countries, NGO leaders, such as Amina Mohammed, Kumi Naidoo, and Salil Shetty, encouraged civil-society leaders to hold their governments accountable for meeting the goals. In developed countries, organizations such as one, co-founded by the activist Jamie Drummond, the rock star Bono, and others, petitioned politicians and conducted public awareness campaigns to demand that world leaders step up their efforts to meet the targets. At the summit, British Prime Minister Tony Blair and Gordon Brown, then British chancellor of the exchequer, put the MDGS and foreign aid commitments at the top of the agenda. Leaders at Gleneagles committed to increasing global aid by $50 billion by 2010 and set the groundwork for larger commitments to be made by 2015. However, one powerful player on the world stage, the United States, remained hesitant to embrace the mdg agenda.

Players on the Bench

U.S. President George W. Bush launched the Millennium Challenge initiative in 2002, promising a 50 percent increase in U.S. foreign aid within three years, with money going to countries committed to good governance. The initiative drew inspiration from the MDGS, as the name suggests, but confusingly, it did not directly link to the targets. Ten months later, in his 2003 State of the Union address, Bush launched the President's Emergency Plan for AIDS Relief, which has dramatically improved access to aids treatment in the developing world. This program was in many ways in line with the mdg effort but did not explicitly link to the goals. Bush even endorsed the UN Millennium Declaration and the Monterrey agreements, but he refused to support the MDGS, largely because his administration viewed them as un-dictated aid quotas.

Holding a similar view, State Department officials regularly claimed that they supported the targets of the Millennium Declaration but not the MDGS, despite the fact that the mdg targets were drawn directly from the Millennium Declaration. U.S.-UN tensions over the Iraq war were a critical backdrop, with the Bush administration reticent to support a major UN initiative. Washington's aversion was so strong that many U.S. advocacy groups avoided using the term "Millennium Development Goals" for fear of losing influence. When John Bolton became the U.S. ambassador to the UN in August 2005, one of his first actions was to suggest deleting all references to the MDGS in the drafted agreement of the upcoming UN World Summit. The subsequent uproar from other countries and U.S. media outlets forced Washington to modify its position. In his summit speech, Bush finally endorsed the MDGS, using the phrase "Millennium Development Goals" publicly for the first time.

By refusing to directly engage with the MDGS in their early years, the United States missed an opportunity to highlight its contributions to development efforts and foster international goodwill. In the early years of this century, the United States helped revolutionize global health, a central pillar of the MDGS, first through Bush's aids initiative and later through efforts on malaria and other deadly diseases. Furthermore, by resisting a project on which most of the world was actively collaborating, Washington missed easy opportunities to build political capital for solving much thornier and divisive international issues.

Diplomatic tensions have subsided under the Obama administration, which has given much stronger rhetorical support to the MDGS and has continued the previous administration's basic development policies, in addition to launching a major initiative to reduce poverty by supporting small farms around the world. Nevertheless, many officials in Washington remain either skeptical or disengaged when it comes to the MDGS, most likely because of a long-standing aversion to fixed foreign aid spending, especially when defined by an international agreement. This fear, however, is baseless. The MDGS do not dictate any aid commitments, and the only related figure, the 0.7 aid target, which countries agreed to work toward in Monterrey in 2002, was endorsed by Bush. It was only later that some countries, such as the United Kingdom, made timetables to meet this aid target.

The World Bank has similarly missed out. Although the bank has championed the framework at senior political levels, it has not adequately facilitated mdg efforts on the ground. Early resistance was in part due to bureaucratic resentment of the UN for its having been given such a prominent role on development issues. In addition, as an institution dominated by economists, the bank is prone to prioritize economic reforms over investment in social sectors. Even more, there is widespread distrust among the bank's staff that donor countries will provide adequate financing for the MDGS. Such concerns are not without merit, as the G-8 ended up falling more than $10 billion short on its Africa pledges for 2010 alone.

Nevertheless, the bank, as a main interlocutor with the developing world, should have helped poor countries assess how they could achieve the MDGS and sounded the alarm about donor financing gaps. Furthermore, the bank has a self-serving reason to get onboard: the MDGS spurred a major budgetary expansion for the International Development Association, the branch of the bank devoted to supporting the poorest countries. Fortunately, the United States and the World Bank are coming around on the MDGS, attracted by the proven success of the framework.

It's a Small World after All

As of late 2010, five years before the deadline, the world had already met the overarching mdg of cutting extreme poverty by half. The estimated share of the developing-world population living on less than $1.25 per day (the technical mdg measurement of extreme poverty) had dropped from 43 percent in 1990 to roughly 21 percent in 2010. This statistic is somewhat skewed by progress that was under way in China and other Asian countries long before the MDGS were adopted. The framework is not solely responsible for all of the advancements of the past 12 years. Many other forces, such as the expansion of global markets and the creation of groundbreaking health and communications technologies, have helped the developing world. Moreover, the goals relating to hunger, sanitation, and the environment have not been met. Poverty reduction, however, has progressed in every region since 2000. Even excluding China from the global calculation, the world's share of impoverish people fell from 37 percent in 1990 to 25 percent in 2008, and forthcoming data should show an even greater drop.

Most important, the MDGS have kick-started progress where it was lacking, especially in Africa, where unprecedented economic growth and poverty reduction are now taking place. From 1981 to 1999, extreme poverty in sub-Saharan Africa rose from 52 percent of the population to 58 percent. But since the launch of the MDGS, it has declined sharply, to 48 percent in 2008. Much of this was likely driven by mdg-backed investments in healthier and better-educated work forces in the region. The global mdg campaign has also prompted support for small subsistence and cash-crop farms, which has boosted growth in many low-income countries, such as Malawi.

Primary education rates have increased around the world, too, with South Asia and sub-Saharan Africa experiencing particularly big jumps in enrollment. Much of this has been the result of funding from mdg-linked initiatives, such as the Global Partnership for Education, launched in 2002 by the World Bank and other development organizations to help poor countries "address the large gaps they face in meeting education mdg 2 and 3, in areas of policy, capacity, data, finance." These same efforts have helped nearly every world region achieve gender parity in classrooms.

The greatest mdg successes undoubtedly concern health. The MDGS have invigorated multilateral institutions, such as the gavi Alliance (formerly called the Global Alliance for Vaccines and Immunization), which seeks to achieve MDGS "by focusing on performance, outcomes and results." The goals have also inspired a huge increase in private sector aid. Ray Chambers, a respected philanthropist and co-founder of a New York private equity firm, first learned of the goals in 2005. Since then, working with Sachs and others, Chambers has coordinated a worldwide coalition of policy, business, and NGO leaders in an effort to help the developing world meet the goal for malarial treatment and prevention. Thanks in part to this global effort, malaria-related mortality has dropped by approximately 25 percent since 2000, with most of those gains probably occurring since 2005. Many pharmaceutical companies have also put forth major efforts to make their medicines more widely available in poor countries, and new initiatives are continuing to take shape. The mdg Health Alliance, founded in 2011, is comprised of business and NGO leaders around the world working toward the mdg health targets, including the elimination of mother-to-child HIV transmission.

The combined results of these campaigns are remarkable. For example, in Senegal, child mortality has plummeted by half since 2000. In Cambodia, it has dropped by 60 percent. Rwanda has recorded a ten percent average annual reduction since 2000, one of the fastest declines in history. Even China has seen a significant decrease in child deaths, possibly because the expanded global emphasis on health has encouraged the country's policymakers to pay more attention to relevant issues. Overall, despite rapid global population growth, there has been a decrease in children dying worldwide before their fifth birthdays, from 11.7 million in 1990 to 9.4 million in 2000 and 6.8 million in 2011.

No issue has been more closely interconnected with the MDGS than the HIV/AIDS treatment campaign. In 2000, nearly 30 million people were infected, the vast majority in Africa, where only approximately 10,000 people were in treatment and over one million people were dying every year from the disease. The next year, the head of the U.S. Agency for International Development publicly deemed large-scale aids treatment in Africa impossible. Undeterred, Annan launched the Global Fund to Fight AIDS, Tuberculosis and Malaria, which aims to achieve "long-term outcome and impact results related to the Millennium Development Goals."

Spurred by the launch of the MDGS, Jim Yong Kim, then head of the World Health Organization's HIV/AIDS department, introduced the "3 by 5" initiative in 2003, which aimed to have three million people living with AIDS in the developing world receiving treatment by 2005. By the end of 2005, only 1.3 million people were receiving treatment-fewer than half of the target. But thanks to the interwoven aids-mdg campaign, the notion of service delivery targets has sunk in globally, helping expand AIDS treatment by orders of magnitude: also in 2005, the G-8 and the UN General Assembly endorsed a target of universal access to treatment by 2010, backed by major financial commitments. The mdg movement has expanded the world's ambitions in tackling health crises and made extraordinary progress. In 2011, more than eight million people worldwide were receiving AIDS treatment.

Next-Generation Goals

The MDGS have proved that with concentration and effort, even the most persistent global problems can be tackled. The post-2015 goals should remain focused on eliminating the multiple dimensions of extreme poverty, but they also need to address emerging global realities. These new challenges include the worsening environmental pressures affecting the livelihoods of hundreds of millions of people, the growing number of middle-income countries with tremendous internal poverty challenges, and rapidly spreading non-communicable diseases.

The new goals also need to be matched with resources. Without the Monterrey agreements of 2002 and the financial commitments made at the Gleneagles summit in 2005, the MDGS might well have faded from the international agenda. It is crucial that the post-2015 negotiations not be left solely to foreign and development ministries. Finance ministries will need an equal say on many of the most central issues and therefore need to be included from the beginning. Other relevant ministries, such as those that deal with health and environmental issues, should be consulted regularly. Additionally, in preparation for 2015, multilateral organizations, such as the World Bank and UN agencies, should conduct independent external reviews of their contributions to the MDGS and identify benchmarks for post-2015 success based on the results. And the United States needs to join the international community in making a solid commitment to long-term, goal-oriented foreign aid.

The MDGS have helped mobilize and guide development efforts by emphasizing outcomes. They have encouraged world leaders to tackle multiple dimensions of poverty at the same time and have provided a standard that advocates on the ground can hold their governments to. Even in countries where politicians might not directly credit the MDGS, the global effort has informed local perspectives and priorities. The goals have improved the lives of hundreds of millions of people. They have shown how much can be achieved when ambitious and specific targets are matched with rigorous thinking, serious resources, and a collaborative global spirit.

Looking forward, the next generation of goals should maintain the accessible simplicity that has allowed the MDGS to succeed and also facilitate the creation of better accountability mechanisms both within and across governments. In addition, the new goals need to give low and middle-income countries a greater voice in shaping the agenda. Most important, momentum matters. Just as progress in individual mdg areas has inspired other campaigns, so work done now, in the final stretch, will affect what happens in the future. The results achieved by

2015 will mark an endpoint, but even more, they will provide a springboard for the next generation of goals. There is no time to lose.

Critical Thinking

1. What have the MDGs accomplished?
2. What are the shortcomings of the MDGs?
3. How can their replacement be more effective?

Create Central

www.mhhe.com/createcentral

Internet References

Africa Index on Africa

www.afrika.no/index

African Studies WWW (U. Penn)

www.sas.upenn.edu/African_Studies/AS.html

United Nations Development Program

http://undp.org

John W. McArthur is a Senior Fellow at the Fung Global Institute and the UN Foundation and a Nonresident Senior Fellow at the Brookings Institution. From 2002 to 2006, he was Manager and Deputy Director of the UN Millennium Project. Follow him on Twitter @ mcarthur.

Article

Prepared by: Robert J. Griffiths, *University of North Carolina at Greensboro*

Justice and Development

Challenges to the Legal Empowerment of the Poor

Magdy Martínez-Solimán

Learning Outcomes

After reading this article, you will be able to:

- Identify the connections between development and legal empowerment.
- Discuss the ways in which a lack of legal empowerment adversely affects the poor.

We have made great strides in reducing poverty and enabling human development. Ever since poverty trends began to be monitored, the number of people living in extreme poverty and poverty rates declined in every developing region, including in sub-Saharan Africa. The global poverty rate at $1.25 a day declined in 2010 by less than half the 1990 rate. The first target of the Millennium Development Goals (MDGs)—halving the extreme poverty rate to its 1990 level—will have been achieved at the global level well before 2015.[1]

Yet, while overall poverty has been reduced, we face considerable challenges in human development today, largely shaped by growing inequalities within countries.[2] Bad governance, poor health, low quality in education, the impact of climate change and environmental degradation continue to be the catalysts for universal poverty. As United Nations Secretary-General Ban Ki-moon has stated: "Poverty is not simply the lack of material goods and opportunities such as employment, ownership of productive assets and savings. It is also the lack of intangible assets and social goods, such as legal identity, good health, physical integrity, freedom from fear and violence, organizational capacity, the ability to exert political influence, and the ability to claim rights and live in respect and dignity."[3]

With its emphasis on social justice and equity, the legal empowerment of the poor addresses structural causes of poverty and exclusion, and could thus be central in tackling these interlinked challenges. As the process to formulate the post-MDG development agenda is now in full swing, it is a good time to reflect on the challenges to the legal empowerment of the poor as critical to the rule of law in development. Indeed, in the recent Declaration of the High-level Meeting of the General Assembly on the Rule of Law at the National and International Levels, Member States recognized "that the rule of law and development are strongly interrelated and mutually reinforcing" and "that this interrelationship should be considered in the post-2015 international development agenda".[4]

Current Development Trends

Despite gains related to the MDGs, the poor and the marginalized continue to be plagued by severe obstacles to their empowerment and human development. For example, vulnerable employment has decreased only marginally over 20 years, hunger remains a global challenge, and the number of people living in slums continues to grow.[5] For the many urban poor and marginalized, their lives and livelihoods are guided by informal systems of economy, employment, housing and often violent social control that do not allow them to utilize existing legal frameworks to protect their assets, homes, businesses or personal security, or to access the basic services and social protection to which they are entitled.

The rural poor and marginalized whose livelihoods and welfare are most closely linked to natural resources and management will, therefore, bear the greatest social costs of unsustainable environmental practices. They are also more vulnerable to natural disasters and to the impact of climate change, and bear the immediate burden when ecological resources and services deteriorate. In Mexico, the women in Mayan coastal communities in Yucatan and the Tarahumaras in the Chihuahua deserts are among the most vulnerable people in the country—vulnerable to climate, to crises and to shocks. This vulnerability is comparable to that of the tribes that live in the Chittagong Hill Tracts in Bangladesh thousands of miles away, and suffer from the same historical poverty, human underdevelopment and climate vulnerability. In Chihuahua and in Chittagong, they suffer from inequality before the law: lack of knowledge, lack of access, lack of empowerment and, as a result, have little trust in the State.

These trends are as prevalent today as in 2008 when the Report of the Commission on the Legal Empowerment of the

Poor (CLEP) and its co-chairs, Madeleine Albright and Hernando de Soto, placed the concept of legal empowerment of the poor squarely on the development map. CLEP argued that 4 billion people worldwide were excluded from the rule of law, and were thus unable to properly protect and utilize their resources. Vulnerability based on gender, minority or other marginalized status further contributed to the deprivation of rights and the denial to participate on equal terms.[6]

Legal disempowerment leads to vulnerability and corruption. The United Nations Development Programme (UNDP) has partnered with UN Women and the Huairou Commission to build the knowledge based on the impact of corruption on women, the strategies adopted by them to combat corruption and to increase the accountability and transparency of governments. The study, "Seeing Beyond the State: Grassroots Women's Perspectives on Corruption," found that women experience corruption in basic services such as health and education from a very young age. They especially suffer abuse when accessing or applying for public documentation, such as identity cards, certificates, property documents and licences, and when dealing with law enforcement agencies. The police are generally not friendly towards poor women as well. As development practitioners, it is important to analyse the lack of legal empowerment in people's daily lives. This is why we ask for particular attention to the collateral misery that attacks women while accessing public services: sexual exploitation, harassment and physical abuse.

What Is Legal Empowerment?

CLEP's report describes legal empowerment as "a process of systemic change through which the poor and excluded become able to use the law, the legal system, and legal services to protect and advance their rights and interests as citizens".[7] The foundation is the rule of law and access to justice, understood broadly as a basic public service and better justice outcomes. At its core, legal empowerment seeks to protect the basic rights that enable poor people and marginalized groups, such as women, to fully realize their social and economic potential and improve their livelihoods, recognizing the importance and potential of the informal sector.

The focus is ensuring legal identity and literacy or awareness as a gateway to access and participation; identifying and removing legal and institutional bottlenecks constraining the poor and marginalized from accessing and exercising legal rights to improve their lives and livelihoods; and the effective implementation of decent laws. Legal implementation is crucial for translating law reform into poverty alleviation and to prevent the abuse of legal rights by stronger parties to the detriment of the poor and marginalized.

Legal empowerment is a multifaceted field, which assists in addressing a range of development outcomes related to basic services such as health, education, livelihoods, and acquisition of a remedy or entitlement, social inclusion and legal status, peaceful dispute or conflict resolution and environmental sustainability. There is an increasing body of evidence on the impact of legal empowerment. Nonetheless, it is often difficult to envision legal empowerment. A range of examples of impact:[8]

A grass-roots organization working with traditional justice systems helps women protect their inheritance, land and other property rights against those in the community who otherwise would capitalize on their ignorance or powerlessness.

- Parents learn how to register the births of their children, ensuring their access to education and other services later in life. Civil registration systems are improved.
- The urban poor and their allies lobby for reform of housing laws that provide them with greater security of tenure, enabling them to seek or retain nearby jobs, upgrade the physical infrastructure of their communities and otherwise improve their lives.
- Paralegals (laypersons, often drawn from the groups they serve, who receive specialized legal training and who provide various forms of legal education, advice and assistance) help their fellow farmers employ tenurial laws and regulations to gain greater control of their land. This helps to increase their incomes and provides them with sustained economic security.
- A grass-roots organization working with traditional justice systems helps women protect their inheritance, land and other property rights against those in the community who otherwise would capitalize on their ignorance or powerlessness.
- A government public health programme enables impoverished beneficiaries to understand and act on their legal rights to basic medical services, thereby reducing infant mortality.
- Market vendors negotiate the right to operate legally and free of police harassment in order to protect their livelihoods. Police conduct is improved.

The Post-2015 Agenda

The MDGs have been successful on many levels, as they could be understood by all and be implemented universally. They have become the development horizon for 140 governments in the South and the coherent cooperation agenda for another 50 governments in the North. Clear, quantifiable and time-bound goals and targets were at the core of this success. Progress can be measured and compared.

However, some developmental challenges were not included at the time, and new challenges have arisen. From a UNDP perspective, we have certainly learned from the MDGs that in order for development to be effective, inclusive and effective governance values, systems and institutions are needed.

In the process of coming up with an actionable agenda, it will thus be important to establish which facets of the rule of law are most critical to the poor and marginalized to make progress for human development and which can be adequately measured. In this regard, using a legal empowerment lens can be helpful.

George Soros and Sir Fazle Abed argue that legal identity and birth registration are universal rights which should be included in the next development agenda, as they are key to the enjoyment of many development goals including education, health and access to employment.[9] Such a target has global resonance: indigenous peoples in developing countries and the Roma people in developed nations share the lowest proportion of financial inclusion and legal empowerment in their respective societies. Concrete suggestions like the one championed by Soros and Abed can help to clearly put forward the legal dimensions of development in the post-2015 process.

Notes

1. United Nations, *Millennium Development Goals Report 2012,* Overview, p. 4.
2. See "Sustainability and Equity: A Better Future for All", *Human Development Report 2011.*
3. Report of the Secretary-General, "Legal empowerment of the poor and the eradication of poverty" (A/64/133), 13 July 2009, para. 7.
4. "Declaration of the High-level Meeting of the sixty-seventh session of the General Assembly on the Rule of Law at the National and International Levels" (A/67/L.1), para. 7.
5. *Millennium Development Goals Report 2012,* Overview, p. 5.
6. Commission on Legal Empowerment of the Poor, Making the Law Work for Everyone (Vol. 1), Report of the Commission on Legal Empowerment of the Poor (New Jersey, United States: Toppan Printing Company America Inc., 2008), p. 2.
7. Ibid., p. 3.
8. See "Legal Empowerment: Substantive Report and Guidance Tool Prepared for the United Nations Development Programme", Stephen Golub (2010).
9. *Financial Times,* "Opinion: Rule of law can rid the world of poverty", George Soros and Fazle Hasan Abed, 26 September 2012.

Create Central

www.mhhe.com/createcentral

Critical Thinking

1. What is legal empowerment?
2. How is legal empowerment connected to development?
3. How can insuring legal empowerment have a positive impact on the lives of the poor?

Internet References

Africa Index on Africa
www.afrika.no/index

African Studies WWW (U. Penn)
www.sas.upenn.edu/African_Studies/AS.html

United Nations Development Program
http://undp.org

MAGDY MARTÍNEZ-SOLIMÁN is Deputy Assistant Administrator and Deputy Director, Bureau for Development Policy, United Nations Development Programme.

Article

The Democratic Malaise

Globalization and the Threat to the West

CHARLES A. KUPCHAN

A crisis of governability has engulfed the world's most advanced democracies. It is no accident that the United States, Europe, and Japan are simultaneously experiencing political breakdown; globalization is producing a widening gap between what electorates are asking of their governments and what those governments are able to deliver. The mismatch between the growing demand for good governance and its shrinking supply is one of the gravest challenges facing the Western world today.

Voters in industrialized democracies are looking to their governments to respond to the decline in living standards and the growing inequality resulting from unprecedented global flows of goods, services, and capital. They also expect their representatives to deal with surging immigration, global warming, and other knock-on effects of a globalized world. But Western governments are not up to the task. Globalization is making less effective the policy levers at their disposal while also diminishing the West's traditional sway over world affairs by fueling the "rise of the rest." The inability of democratic governments to address the needs of their broader publics has, in turn, only increased popular disaffection, further undermining the legitimacy and efficacy of representative institutions.

This crisis of governability within the Western world comes at a particularly inopportune moment. The international system is in the midst of tectonic change due to the diffusion of wealth and power to new quarters. Globalization was supposed to have played to the advantage of liberal societies, which were presumably best suited to capitalize on the fast and fluid nature of the global marketplace. But instead, mass publics in the advanced democracies of North America, Europe, and East Asia have been particularly hard hit—precisely because their countries' economies are both mature and open to the world.

In contrast, Brazil, India, Turkey, and other rising democracies are benefiting from the shift of economic vitality from the developed to the developing world. And China is proving particularly adept at reaping globalization's benefits while limiting its liabilities—in no small part because it has retained control over policy instruments abandoned by its liberal competitors. State capitalism has its distinct advantages, at least for now. As a consequence, it is not just the West's material primacy that is at stake today but also the allure of its version of modernity. Unless liberal democracies can restore their political and economic solvency, the politics, as well as the geopolitics, of the twenty-first century may well be up for grabs.

Deer in the Headlights

Globalization has expanded aggregate wealth and enabled developing countries to achieve unprecedented prosperity. The proliferation of investment, trade, and communication networks has deepened interdependence and its potentially pacifying effects and has helped pry open nondemocratic states and foster popular uprisings. But at the same time, globalization and the digital economy on which it depends are the main source of the West's current crisis of governability. Deindustrialization and outsourcing, global trade and fiscal imbalances, excess capital and credit and asset bubbles—these consequences of globalization are imposing hardships and insecurity not experienced for generations. The distress stemming from the economic crisis that began in 2008 is particularly acute, but the underlying problems began much earlier. For the better part of two decades, middle-class wages in the world's leading democracies have been stagnant, and economic inequality has been rising sharply as globalization has handsomely rewarded its winners but left its many losers behind.

These trends are not temporary byproducts of the business cycle, nor are they due primarily to insufficient regulation of the financial sector, tax cuts amid expensive wars, or other errant policies. Stagnant wages and rising inequality are, as the economic analysts Daniel Alpert, Robert Hockett, and Nouriel Roubini recently argued in their study "The Way Forward," a consequence of the integration of billions of low-wage workers into the global economy and increases in productivity stemming from the application of information technology to the manufacturing sector. These developments have pushed global capacity far higher than demand, exacting a heavy toll on workers in the high-wage economies of the industrialized West. The resulting dislocation and disaffection among Western electorates have been magnified by globalization's intensification of transnational threats, such as international crime, terrorism, unwanted immigration, and environmental degradation. Adding to this nasty mix is the information revolution; the Internet and the profusion of mass media appear to be fueling ideological polarization more than they are cultivating deliberative debate.

Voters confronted with economic duress, social dislocation, and political division look to their elected representatives for help. But just as globalization is stimulating this pressing demand for responsive governance, it is also ensuring that its provision is in desperately short supply. For three main reasons, governments in the industrialized West have entered a period of pronounced ineffectiveness.

First, globalization has made many of the traditional policy tools used by liberal democracies much blunter instruments. Washington has regularly turned to fiscal and monetary policy to modulate economic performance. But in the midst of global competition and unprecedented debt, the U.S. economy seems all but immune to injections of stimulus spending or the Federal Reserve's latest moves on interest rates. The scope and speed of commercial and financial flows mean that decisions and developments elsewhere—Beijing's intransigence on the value of the yuan, Europe's sluggish response to its financial crisis, the actions of investors and ratings agencies, an increase in the quality of Hyundai's latest models—outweigh decisions taken in Washington. Europe's democracies long relied on monetary policy to adjust to fluctuations in national economic performance. But they gave up that option when they joined the eurozone. Japan over the last two decades has tried one stimulus strategy after another, but to no avail. In a globalized world, democracies simply have less control over outcomes than they used to.

Second, many of the problems that Western electorates are asking their governments to solve require a level of international cooperation that is unattainable. The diffusion of power from the West to the rest means that there are today many new cooks in the kitchen; effective action no longer rests primarily on collaboration among like-minded democracies. Instead, it depends on cooperation among a much larger and more diverse circle of states. The United States now looks to the G-20 to rebalance the international economy. But consensus is elusive among nations that are at different stages of development and embrace divergent approaches to economic governance. Challenges such as curbing global warming or effectively isolating Iran similarly depend on a collective effort that is well beyond reach.

Third, democracies can be nimble and responsive when their electorates are content and enjoy a consensus born of rising expectations, but they are clumsy and sluggish when their citizens are downcast and divided. Polities in which governance depends on popular participation, institutional checks and balances, and competition among interest groups appear to be better at distributing benefits than at apportioning sacrifice. But sacrifice is exactly what is necessary to restore economic solvency, which confronts Western governments with the unappetizing prospect of pursuing policies that threaten to weaken their electoral appeal.

One Problem, Three Flavors

In the United States, partisan confrontation is paralyzing the political system. The underlying cause is the poor state of the U.S. economy. Since 2008, many Americans have lost their houses, jobs, and retirement savings. And these setbacks come on the heels of back-to-back decades of stagnation in middle-class wages. Over the past ten years, the average household income in the United States has fallen by over ten percent. In the meantime, income inequality has been steadily rising, making the United States the most unequal country in the industrialized world. The primary source of the declining fortunes of the American worker is global competition; jobs have been heading overseas. In addition, many of the most competitive companies in the digital economy do not have long coattails. Facebook's estimated value is around $70 billion, and it employs roughly 2,000 workers; compare this with General Motors, which is valued at $35 billion and has 77,000 employees in the United States and 208,000 worldwide. The wealth of the United States' cutting-edge companies is not trickling down to the middle class.

These harsh economic realities are helping revive ideological and partisan cleavages long muted by the nation's rising economic fortunes. During the decades after World War II, a broadly shared prosperity pulled Democrats and Republicans toward the political center. But today, Capitol Hill is largely devoid of both centrists and bipartisanship; Democrats campaign for more stimulus, relief for the unemployed, and taxes on the rich, whereas Republicans clamor for radical cuts in the size and cost of government. Expediting the hollowing out of the center are partisan redistricting, a media environment that provokes more than it informs, and a broken campaign finance system that has been captured by special interests.

The resulting polarization is tying the country in knots. President Barack Obama realized as much, which is why he entered office promising to be a "post-partisan" president. But the failure of Obama's best efforts to revive the economy and restore bipartisan cooperation has exposed the systemic nature of the nation's economic and political dysfunction. His $787 billion stimulus package, passed without the support of a single House Republican, was unable to resuscitate an economy plagued by debt, a deficit of middle-class jobs, and the global slowdown. Since the Republicans gained control of the House in 2010, partisan confrontation has stood in the way of progress on nearly every issue. Bills to promote economic growth either fail to pass or are so watered down that they have little impact. Immigration reform and legislation to curb global warming are not even on the table.

Ineffective governance, combined with daily doses of partisan bile, has pushed public approval of Congress to historic lows. Spreading frustration has spawned the Occupy Wall Street movement—the first sustained bout of public protests since the Vietnam War. The electorate's discontent only deepens the challenges of governance, as vulnerable politicians cater to the narrow interests of the party base and the nation's political system loses what little wind it has in its sails.

Europe's crisis of governability, meanwhile, is taking the form of a renationalization of its politics. Publics are revolting against the double dislocations of European integration and globalization. As a consequence, the EU's member states are busily clawing back the prerogatives of sovereignty, threatening the project of European political and economic integration set in motion after World War II. As in the United States, economic conditions are the root of the problem. Over the past two decades, middle-class incomes in most major European economies have been falling and inequality has been rising. Unemployment in Spain stands at over 20 percent, and even Germany, the EU's premier economy, saw its middle class contract by 13 percent between 2000 and 2008. Those who slip through the cracks find a fraying safety net beneath them; Europe's comfortable welfare systems, which have become unsustainable in the face of global competition, are being dramatically scaled back. The austerity stemming from the ongoing debt crisis in the eurozone has only made matters worse. Greeks are as angry about the EU-enforced belt-tightening as Germans are about having to bail out Europe's economic laggards.

Europe's aging population has made immigration an economic necessity. But the lack of progress in integrating Muslim immigrants into the social mainstream has intensified discomfort over the EU's willingness to accept more outsiders into its midst. Far-right parties have been the beneficiaries of this anxiety, and their hard-edged nationalism targets not only immigrants but also the EU. Generational change is taking its own toll on popular enthusiasm for European integration. Europeans with memories of World War II see the EU as Europe's escape route from its bloody past. But younger Europeans have no past from which to flee. Whereas their elders viewed the European project as an article of faith, current leaders and electorates tend to assess the EU through a cold—and often negative—valuation of costs and benefits.

The collective governance that the EU desperately needs in order to thrive in a globalized world rests uneasily with a political street that is becoming decidedly hostile to the European project. Europe's institutions could descend to the level of its politics, which would effectively reduce the EU to little more than a trade bloc. Alternatively, national politics could again be infused with a European calling, which would breathe new legitimacy into an increasingly hollow union. The latter outcome is much preferable, but it will require leadership and resolve that, at least for now, are nowhere to be found.

Japan, for its part, has been politically adrift since Junichiro Koizumi stepped down as prime minister in 2006. Thereafter, the Liberal Democratic Party (LDP), which had dominated Japanese politics throughout most of the postwar era, stumbled badly, losing power to the Democratic Party of Japan (DPJ) in 2009. The consolidation of a two-party system had the potential to improve governance but instead produced only gridlock and declining public confidence. Japan has cycled through six prime ministers in the last five years. This past summer, public approval of the DPJ stood at 18 percent. The DPJ and the LDP are as internally divided as they are at loggerheads. Policymaking has ground to a halt even on urgent issues; it took over 100 days for the Diet to pass legislation providing relief to the victims of last year's earthquake, tsunami, and nuclear disaster.

The trouble began with the bursting of Japan's asset bubble in 1991, a setback that exposed deeper problems in the country's economy and led to a "lost decade" of recession. Japanese manufacturers suffered as jobs and investment headed to China and the "Asian tigers." The country's traditional social compact, by which corporations provided lifetime employment and comfortable pensions, was no longer sustainable. The past two decades have brought a long slide in middle-class incomes, rising inequality, and a spike in the poverty rate from roughly seven percent in the 1980s to 16 percent in 2009. In 1989, Japan ranked fourth in the world in terms of per capita GDP; by 2010, its rank had plummeted to 24th.

It was to address such problems that Koizumi embarked on ambitious efforts to liberalize the economy and reduce the power of bureaucrats and interest groups. His charisma and ample parliamentary support made for significant progress, but his LDP and DPJ successors have been too weak to keep the process moving forward. Japan is therefore stuck in a no man's land, exposed to the dislocations of a globalized economy yet not liberalized or strategic enough to compete effectively.

Bitter Medicine

It is not by chance that the West's crisis of governability coincides with new political strength among rising powers; economic and political vigor is passing from the core to the periphery of the international system. And while the world's most open states are experiencing a loss of control as they integrate into a globalized world, illiberal states, such as China, are deliberately keeping a much tighter grip on their societies through centralized decision-making, censorship of the media, and state-supervised markets. If the leading democracies continue to lose their luster as developing countries chart their rise, the unfolding transition in global power will be significantly more destabilizing. Conversely, a realignment of the international pecking order would likely be more orderly if the Western democracies recouped and provided purposeful leadership.

What is needed is nothing less than a compelling twenty-first-century answer to the fundamental tensions among democracy, capitalism, and globalization. This new political agenda should aim to reassert popular control over political economy, directing state action toward effective responses to both the economic realities of global markets and the demands of mass societies for an equitable distribution of rewards and sacrifices.

The West should pursue three broad strategies to meet this challenge and thus better equip its democratic institutions for a globalized world. First, when up against state capitalism and the potent force of global markets, the Western democracies have little choice but to engage in strategic economic planning on an unprecedented scale. State-led investment in jobs, infrastructure, education, and research will be required to restore economic competitiveness. Second, leaders should seek to channel electorate discontent toward reformist ends through a progressive brand of populism. By pursuing policies that advantage mass publics rather than the party faithful or special interests, politicians can not only rebuild their popularity but also reinvigorate democratic institutions and the values of citizenship and sacrifice. Third, Western governments must lead their electorates away from the temptation to turn inward. As history makes clear, hard times can stoke protectionism and isolationism. But globalization is here to stay, and retreat is not an option.

None of these strategies will be easy to implement, and embracing all of them together will require extraordinary leadership and the political courage to match. But until such an agenda is devised and realized, the democratic malaise will persist.

Critical Thinking

1. What effect has globalization had on developing countries?
2. What factors account for western inability to contend with globalization?
3. What must industrialized countries do to meet the challenges of the global marketplace?

Charles A. Kupchan is Professor of International Affairs at Georgetown University and Whitney Shepardson Senior Fellow at the Council on Foreign Relations. This essay is adapted from his forthcoming book *No One's World: The West, the Rising Rest, and the Coming Global Turn* (Oxford University Press, 2012).

Unit 2

UNIT

Prepared by: Robert J. Griffiths, *University of North Carolina at Greensboro*

Political Economy and the Developing World

Economic issues are among the most pressing concerns of the developing world. Economic growth and stability are essential to tackle the various problems confronting developing countries. Even though the developing world is now playing a larger role in the global economy and there have been significant increases in living standards, many countries still continue to struggle to achieve consistent economic growth. Economic inequality between the industrial countries and much of the developing world also persists. This is especially true of the poorest countries that have become further marginalized due to their limited participation in the global economy. Substantial inequality within developing countries is also obvious. The elite's access to education, capital, and technology has significantly widened the gap between the rich and the poor. Since their incorporation into the international economic system during colonialism, the majority of developing countries have been primarily suppliers of raw materials, agricultural products, and inexpensive labor. Dependence on commodity exports means that developing countries are subject to fluctuating and sometimes declining prices for their exports. At the same time, prices for imports tend to remain constant or increase. At best, a decline in the terms of trade has made development planning difficult; at worst, it has led to economic stagnation and decline. Industrialization in China and India has boosted demand for primary products over the past few years, but the recent global economic decline resulted in falling demand and lower prices. Continued strong demand from China and India helped primary producers, especially in Africa, to recover more quickly and post strong economic growth rates, but dependence on the export of raw materials leaves developing countries vulnerable to demand. This is clearly not an ideal long-term strategy for economic success.

With some exceptions, developing countries have had limited success in breaking out of the primary production trap through the diversification of their economies. Efforts at industrialization and export of light manufactured goods have led to competition with the less efficient industries of the industrialized world. The response of industrialized countries has often been protectionism and demands for trade reciprocity, which can overwhelm the markets of the developing countries. Economic conditions in the developing world are not entirely attributable to colonial legacy and protectionism on the part of industrialized countries. Developing countries have sometimes constructed their own trade barriers. In addition, industrialization schemes involving heavy government direction were often ill-conceived or resulted in corruption and mismanagement. Industrialized countries frequently point to these inefficiencies in calling for market-oriented reforms, but the emphasis on privatization does not adequately recognize the role of the state in developing countries' economies; and privatization may result in foreign control of important sectors of the economy, as well as a loss of jobs. Moreover, developing countries charge that the industrialized countries are selective in their efforts to dismantle trade barriers and emphasize only those trade issues that reflect their interests. Delegates from poor countries walked out of the 2003 WTO ministerial meeting in Cancún, Mexico, protesting the rich countries' reluctance to eliminate agricultural subsidies and their efforts to dominate the agenda. Further talks failed to produce an agreement, largely due to disagreement over agricultural trade. The Doha round of trade negotiations fizzled without producing a broad agreement further liberalizing trade. During the 1970s, developing countries' prior economic performance and the availability of petrodollars encouraged extensive commercial lending. The worldwide recession in the early 1980s left many developing countries unable to meet their debt obligations, and international financial institutions became the lenders of last resort. Access to the World Bank and International Monetary Fund became conditional on the adoption of structural adjustment programs that involved steps such as reduced public expenditures, devaluation of currencies, and export promotion, all geared to debt reduction. The consequences of these programs were painful for developing countries, resulting in declining public services, higher prices, and greater reliance on primary production. However, the global economic crisis has undermined the Washington Consensus, which was the basis for many of these policy prescriptions. As a result, developing countries are much more likely to be skeptical of the Western model of development. China's dramatic growth offers not only demand for primary products but also an alternative economic development model. Unlike the Western-dominated international financial institutions, Chinese investment does not involve human rights or good governance stipulations. At the same time, China's massive exports threaten to overwhelm developing country markets and undermine economic diversification in those countries.

Despite a renewed interest in foreign aid after the September 11th attacks, the effectiveness of this assistance remains uneven. Some are calling for a re-evaluation of aid that takes into account broader goals and the greater number of actors involved and provides better ways to measure effectiveness. Efforts to raise more revenue for development aid have led to innovative financing schemes. The money raised by small taxes on airline tickets and voluntary contributions associated with the sale of certain products can then be channeled to developing countries to help fight disease and boost economic activity.

Appropriate development assistance continues to be a subject of considerable controversy. Contributions of clothing and food, however well-meaning, may actually have detrimental consequences. Microloans have been credited with helping to reduce poverty, but criticism has emerged regarding the cost of these loans and the emergence of large banks and financial institutions as providers of these funds. Technology such as mobile phones is also having a major impact on reducing poverty. Globalization has produced differing views regarding the benefits and costs of this trend for the developing world. Advocates claim that closer economic integration, especially through trade and financial liberalization, increases economic prosperity in developing countries and encourages good governance, transparency, and accountability. Critics respond that globalization favors the powerful nations, imposes difficult and perhaps counterproductive policies on the struggling economies, undermines workers' rights and causes environmental degradation. In the past, most of the benefits of globalization have gone to those countries that are already growing—leaving the poorest even further behind. However, recent developments in Africa have brightened prospects for a region that has struggled with the challenges of economic growth.

Article

The Post-Washington Consensus
Development after the Crisis

NANCY BIRDSALL AND FRANCIS FUKUYAMA

The last time a global depression originated in the United States, the impact was devastating not only for the world economy but for world politics as well. The Great Depression set the stage for a shift away from strict monetarism and laissez-faire policies toward Keynesian demand management. More important, for many it delegitimized the capitalist system itself, paving the way for the rise of radical and antiliberal movements around the world.

This time around, there has been no violent rejection of capitalism, even in the developing world. In early 2009, at the height of the global financial panic, China and Russia, two formerly noncapitalist states, made it clear to their domestic and foreign investors that they had no intention of abandoning the capitalist model. No leader of a major developing country has backed away from his or her commitment to free trade or the global capitalist system. Instead, the established Western democracies are the ones that have highlighted the risks of relying too much on market-led globalization and called for greater regulation of global finance.

Why has the reaction in developing countries been so much less extreme after this crisis than it was after the Great Depression? For one, they blame the United States for it. Many in the developing world agreed with Brazilian President Luiz Inácio Lula da Silva when he said, "This is a crisis caused by people, white with blue eyes." If the global financial crisis put any development model on trial, it was the free-market or neoliberal model, which emphasizes a small state, deregulation, private ownership, and low taxes. Few developing countries consider themselves to have fully adopted that model.

Indeed, for years before the crisis, they had been distancing themselves from it. The financial crises of the late 1990s in East Asia and Latin America discredited many of the ideas associated with the so-called Washington consensus, particularly that of unalloyed reliance on foreign capital. By 2008, most emerging-market countries had reduced their exposure to the foreign financial markets by accumulating large foreign currency reserves and maintaining regulatory control of their banking systems. These policies provided insulation from global economic volatility and were vindicated by the impressive rebounds in the wake of the recent crisis: the emerging markets have posted much better economic growth numbers than their counterparts in the developed world.

Thus, the American version of capitalism is, if not in full disrepute, then at least no longer dominant. In the next decade, emerging-market and low-income countries are likely to modify their approach to economic policy further, trading the flexibility and efficiency associated with the free-market model for domestic policies meant to ensure greater resilience in the face of competitive pressures and global economic trauma. They will become less focused on the free flow of capital, more concerned with minimizing social disruption through social safety net programs, and more active in supporting domestic industries. And they will be even less inclined than before to defer to the supposed expertise of the more developed countries, believing—correctly—that not only economic but also intellectual power are becoming increasingly evenly distributed.

The Foreign Finance Fetish

One of the central features of the old, pre-crisis economic consensus was the assumption that developing countries could benefit substantially from greater inflows of foreign capital—what the economist Arvind Subramanian has labeled "the foreign finance fetish." The idea that the unimpeded flow of capital around the globe, like the free flow of goods and services, makes markets more efficient was more or less taken for granted in policy circles. In the 1990s, the United States and international financial institutions such as the International Monetary Fund (IMF) pushed developing-country borrowers to open up their capital markets to foreign banks and dismantle exchange-rate controls.

Although the benefits of free trade have been well documented, the advantages of full capital mobility are much less clear. The reasons for this have to do with the fundamental differences between the financial sector and the "real" economy. Free capital markets can indeed allocate capital efficiently. But large interconnected financial institutions can also take risks that impose huge negative externalities on the rest of the economy in a way that large manufacturing firms cannot.

One of the paradoxical consequences of the 2008–9 financial crisis may thus be that Americans and Britons will finally learn what the East Asians figured out over a decade ago, namely, that open capital markets combined with unregulated financial sectors is a disaster in the waiting. At the conclusion of the Asian financial crisis, many U.S. policymakers and economists walked back their previous stress on quick liberalization and started promoting "sequencing," that is, liberalization only after a strong regulatory system with adequate supervision of banks has been put in place. But they devoted little thought to whether certain developing countries were capable of enacting such regulation quickly or what an appropriate regulatory regime would look like. And they overlooked the relevance of their new message to their own case, failing to warn against the danger of the huge, unregulated, and overleveraged shadow financial sector that had emerged in the United States.

The first clear consequence of the crisis has thus been the end of the foreign finance fetish. The countries that pursued it the most enthusiastically, such as Iceland, Ireland, and those in eastern Europe, were the hardest hit and face the toughest recoveries. Just as for Wall Street, the strong growth records these countries amassed from 2002 to 2007 proved to be partly a mirage, reflecting the easy availability of credit and high leverage ratios rather than strong fundamentals.

Caring about Caring

The second consequence is a new respect among developing countries for the political and social benefits of a sensible social policy. Before the crisis, policymakers tended to downplay social insurance and safety net programs in favor of strategies that emphasized economic efficiency. U.S. President Ronald Reagan and British Prime Minister Margaret Thatcher had come to power in the late 1970s and 1980s attacking the modern welfare state, and many of their critiques were well taken: state bureaucracies had become bloated and inefficient in many countries, and an entitlement mentality had taken hold. The Washington consensus did not necessarily reject the use of social policy, but its focus on efficiency and fiscal discipline often led to cuts in social spending.

What the crisis did, however, was to underscore the instability inherent in capitalist systems—even ones as developed and sophisticated as the United States. Capitalism is a dynamic process that regularly produces faultless victims who lose their jobs or see their livelihoods threatened. Throughout the crisis and its aftermath, citizens have expected their governments to provide some level of stability in the face of economic uncertainty. This is a lesson that politicians in developing-country democracies are not likely to forget; the consolidation and legitimacy of their fragile democratic systems will depend on their ability to deliver a greater measure of social protection.

Consider how continental Europe has reacted in comparison to the United States. Until now, with the eurozone crisis, western Europe experienced a far less painful recovery, thanks to its more developed system of automatic countercyclical social spending, including for unemployment insurance. In contrast, the jobless recovery in the United States makes the U.S. model even less attractive to policymakers in the developing world, particularly those who are increasingly subject to political pressure to attend to the needs of the middle class.

A good example of the new stress on social policy can be found in China. Reacting to the country's rapidly aging population, its leadership is struggling behind the scenes to build a modern pension system, something that represents a shift from the traditional tactic of concentrating solely on generating new jobs to maintain social and political stability. In Latin America, the same pressures are playing out differently. After experiencing fatigue in the wake of liberalizing reforms in the 1990s that did not seem to produce the growth that was expected, the region has moved to the left in this century, and the new governments have increased social spending to reduce poverty and inequality. Many countries have followed the successful example of Brazil and Mexico and instituted cash transfer schemes targeted to poor households (which require beneficiaries to keep their children in school or meet other conditions). In Brazil and Mexico, the approach has contributed to the first visible declines in income inequality in many years and helped shelter the poorest households from the recent crisis.

The question, of course, is whether programs like these that target the poor (and thus keep fiscal outlays surprisingly low) will have difficulty attracting long-term support from the region's growing middle class, and how these and other emerging economies, including China, will manage the fiscal costs of more universal health, pension, and other social insurance programs. Will they be better at handling the problems associated with these unfunded universal entitlement programs, the kinds of problems now facing Europe and the United States as their populations age?

The Visible Hand

The third consequence of the crisis has been the rise of a new round of discussions about industrial policy—a country's strategy to develop specific industrial sectors, traditionally through such support as cheap credit or outright subsidies or through state management of development banks. Such policies were written off as dangerous failures in the 1980s and 1990s for sustaining inefficient insider industries at high fiscal cost. But the crisis and the effective response to it by some countries are likely to bolster the notion that competent technocrats in developing countries are capable of efficiently managing state involvement in the productive sectors. Brazil, for example, used its government-sponsored development bank to direct credit to certain sectors quickly as part of its initial crisis-driven stimulus program, and China did the same thing with its state-run banks.

However, this new industrial policy is not about picking winners or bringing about large sectoral shifts in production. It is about addressing coordination problems and other barriers that discourage private investment in new industries and technologies, difficulties that market forces alone are unlikely to overcome. To promote an innovative clothing industry in West Africa, for example, governments might ensure a constant supply of textiles or subsidize the construction of ports to avoid export bottlenecks. The idea is that by bearing some of the initial financial or other risks and more systematically targeting public infrastructure, governments can help private investors overcome the high costs of being the first movers and innovators in incipient sectors.

For the last three decades, Washington-based development institutions have taken the view that growth is threatened more by government incompetence and corruption than by market failures. Now that American-style capitalism has fallen from its pedestal, might this view begin to shift? Might the idea that the state can take a more active role get far more traction? The answer depends, for any single developing country, on an assessment of its state capacity and overall governance. This is because the most significant critique of industrial policy was never economic but political, contending that economic decision-making in developing countries could not be shielded from political pressure. Critics argued that policymakers would retain protectionist measures long after they had fulfilled their original purpose of jump-starting domestic industries. Industrial policies such as reducing dependency on imports and promoting infant industries, although later derided in Washington, did in fact produce impressive rates of economic growth in the 1950s and 1960s in East Asia and Latin America. The problem, however, was that governments in the latter region were politically unable to unwind that protection, and so their domestic industries failed to become globally competitive.

Therefore, technocrats in developing countries contemplating the use of industrial policies must consider the politics of doing so. Does a bureaucracy exist that is sufficiently capable and autonomous from political pressure? Is there enough money to sustain such an agenda? Will it be possible to make hard political decisions, such as eliminating the policies when they are no longer needed? Most of the successful uses of industrial policy have been in East Asia, which has a long tradition of strong technocratic bureaucracies. Countries without such a legacy need to be more careful.

Making Bureaucracy Work

If countries are to promote industrial development and provide a social safety net, they will need to reform their public sectors; indeed, the fourth consequence of the crisis has been a painful reminder of the costs of not doing so. In the United States, regulatory agencies were underfunded, had difficulty attracting high-quality personnel, and faced political opposition. This was not surprising: implicit in the Reagan-Thatcher doctrine was the belief that markets were an acceptable substitute for efficient government. The crisis demonstrated that unregulated or poorly regulated markets can produce extraordinary costs.

Leaders in both the developing world and the developed world have marveled at China's remarkable ability to bounce back after the crisis, a result of a tightly managed, top-down policymaking machine that could avoid the delays of a messy democratic process. In response, political leaders in the developing world now associate efficiency and capability with autocratic political systems. But there are plenty of incompetent autocratic regimes. What sets China apart is a bureaucracy that, at its upper levels at least, is capable of managing and coordinating sophisticated policies. Among low-income countries, that makes China an exception.

Promoting effective public sectors is one of the most daunting development challenges that the world faces. Development institutions such as the World Bank and the United Kingdom's Department for International Development have supported programs that strengthen public sectors, promote good governance, and combat corruption for the last 15 years with little to show for it. The fact that even financial regulators in the United States and the United Kingdom failed to use their existing powers or to keep pace with rapidly evolving markets is a humbling reminder that effective public sectors are a challenge to maintain in even the most developed countries.

Why has so little progress been made in improving developing countries' public sectors? The first problem is that their bureaucracies often serve governments that are rent-seeking coalitions acting according to self-interest, instead of an ideal of impersonal public service. Outside donors typically do not have the leverage to force them to change, with the partial exception of mechanisms such as the European Union's accession process. Second, effective institutions have to evolve indigenously, reflecting a country's own political, social, and cultural realities. The development of impersonal bureaucracies in the West was the product of a long and painful process, with factors exogenous to the economy (such as the need to mobilize for war) playing a large part in creating strong state institutions (such as Prussia's famously efficient bureaucracy). Institutions such as the rule of law will rarely work if they are simply copied from abroad; societies must buy into their content. Finally, public-sector reform requires a parallel process of nation building. Unless a society has a clear sense of national identity and a shared public interest, individuals will show less loyalty to it than to their ethnic group, tribe, or patronage network.

Moving to Multipolarity

Years from now, historians may well point to the financial crisis as the end of American economic dominance in global affairs. But the trend toward a multipolar world began much earlier, and the implosion of Western financial markets and their weak recoveries have merely accelerated the process. Even before the crisis, the international institutions created after World War II to manage economic and security challenges were under strain and in need of reform. The IMF and the World Bank suffered from governance structures that reflected outdated economic realities. Starting in the 1990s and continuing into the new century, the Bretton Woods institutions have come under increasing pressure to grant more voting power to emerging-market countries such as Brazil and China. Meanwhile, the G-7, the elite group of the six most economically important Western democracies plus Japan, remained the world's informal steering committee when it came to issues of global economic coordination, even as other power centers emerged.

The financial crisis finally led to the demise of the G-7 as the primary locus of global economic policy coordination and its replacement by the G-20. In November 2008, heads of state from the G-20 gathered in Washington, D.C., to coordinate a global stimulus program—a meeting that has since grown into an established international institution. Since the G-20, unlike the G-7, includes emerging countries such as Brazil, China, and India, the expansion of economic coordination represents an overdue recognition of a new group of global economic players.

The crisis also breathed new life and legitimacy into the IMF and the World Bank. Beforehand, the IMF had looked like it was rapidly becoming obsolete. Private capital markets provided countries with financing on favorable terms without the conditions often attached to IMF loans. The organization was having trouble funding its own activities and was in the process of reducing its staff.

But the outlook changed in 2009, when the G-20 leaders agreed to ensure that the Bretton Woods institutions would have as much as $1 trillion in additional resources to help countries better weather future financing shortfalls. Countries such as Brazil and China were among the contributors to the special funds, which have ended up supporting Greece, Hungary, Iceland, Ireland, Latvia, Pakistan, and Ukraine.

By requesting that emerging markets take on a bigger leadership role in global affairs, the Western democracies are implicitly admitting that they are no longer able to manage global economic affairs on their own. But what has been called "the rise of the rest" is not just about economic and political power; it also has to do with the global competition of ideas and models. The West, and in particular the United States, is no longer seen as the only center for innovative thinking about social policy. Conditional cash transfer schemes, for example, were first developed and implemented in Latin America. As for industrial policy, the West has contributed little innovative thinking in that realm in the last 30 years. One has to turn to emerging-market countries, rather than the developed world, to see successful models in practice. And when it comes to international organizations, the voices and ideas of the United States and Europe are becoming less dominant. Those of emerging-market countries—states that have become significant funders of the international financial institutions—are being given greater weight.

All this signals a clear shift in the development agenda. Traditionally, this was an agenda generated in the developed world that was implemented in—and, indeed, often imposed on—the developing world. The United States, Europe, and Japan will continue to be significant sources of economic resources and ideas, but the emerging markets are now entering this arena and will become significant players. Countries such as Brazil, China, India, and South Africa will be both donors and recipients of resources for development and of best practices for how to use them. A large portion of the world's poor live within their borders, yet they have achieved new respect on the global scene in economic, political, and intellectual terms. In fact, development has never been something that the rich bestowed on the poor but rather something the poor achieved for themselves. It appears that the Western powers are finally waking up to this truth in light of a financial crisis that, for them, is by no means over.

Critical Thinking

1. How did the financial crisis affect attitudes about capital mobility?
2. Why are emerging economies more likely to favor social spending in the aftermath of the crisis?
3. What is the emerging attitude about industrial policy?
4. What will countries need to effectively implement social and industrial policies?
5. How has the financial crisis changed developing countries' influence on international economic policy?

Nancy Birdsall is President of the Center for Global Development. **Francis Fukuyama** is Olivier Nomellini Senior Fellow at the Freeman Spogli Institute for International Studies at Stanford University. They are the editors of *New Ideas in Development After the Financial Crisis* (Johns Hopkins University Press, 2011), from which this essay is adapted.

Article

Role Reversal

Emerging economies are less dependent on debt, less vulnerable to volatile investment sentiment, and are rethinking the role of capital flows.

ESWAR S. PRASAD

Times have changed for emerging economies.

In a break from past patterns, a majority of middle-income emerging market economies have bounced back relatively quickly and sharply from the global economic crisis, while advanced economies continue to experience deep and prolonged downturns.

Moreover, unlike in days past when global financial turmoil would lead domestic and international investors to rush for the exits, precipitating meltdowns, emerging economies today appear more resilient to the volatility of capital flows. Few major emerging markets still depend heavily on foreign financing. Some, like Turkey and a few emerging markets in eastern Europe, still do—and are vulnerable to shifts in foreign investors' sentiments. But they are exceptions rather than the norm. Indeed, even countries like Brazil and India that have more money going out than coming in (that is, are running current account deficits) have large stocks of foreign exchange reserves that help them deal with capital flow volatility. Many emerging markets have in fact faced the curse of plenty—surges in capital inflows in recent years.

Underlying these developments are fundamental changes in the nature of international capital flows that will reverberate for a long time. These changes will reshape the debate about the benefits and risks of global financial integration. For emerging economies, international capital flows had come to be seen as a destructive force, increasing volatility and setting off devastating crises, rather than as promoting growth or helping diversify risk by increasing investment opportunities. The shifts documented in this article suggest that emerging economies may now be in a better position to reap the benefits—but they face a new set of risks—from capital flows.

Tighter Financial Linkages

In a process that started in the mid-1980s, picked up pace over the past decade, and was only briefly affected by the crisis, emerging markets have substantially increased their integration into global financial markets. This is evident from their rising stocks of international assets and liabilities.

Rising stocks portend greater risks even for a country whose assets and liabilities are balanced. If a country has large holdings of international assets and liabilities, currency fluctuations and even modest portfolio rebalancing of international investors can result in greater volatility of net flows (the difference between capital entering and capital leaving a country). If an economy comes under pressure, inflows can stop and outflows rise simultaneously, leading to a double blow in terms of net flows.

The magnitude of these effects depends on the shares of liabilities and assets that are in the form of debt versus those that have an equity component—either direct, where the foreign investor has a durable stake in the asset, or portfolio, where the investor is seeking only a financial return. Where an equity component is involved, there is more sharing of risk between domestic and foreign investors. Although rising total positions clearly have a major impact, a closer examination of the structure of external assets and liabilities is warranted because of its implications for both growth and volatility.

Balance Sheet Transformation

The international investment position (IIP) is essentially a country's balance sheet in relation to the rest of the world. One side of the balance sheet contains a country's total foreign assets, the other its external liabilities. The types of assets and liabilities are broken down on each side of the balance sheet. An analysis of changes in the IIPs of major economies reveals large shifts in the structure of global finance.

The external liabilities of emerging economies once were mainly debt. Now foreign direct investment (FDI) and portfolio equity combined predominate (see Chart 1). In 2010, FDI and portfolio equity accounted for more than half of the total liabilities of emerging economies (see table). This pattern held for the five major emerging markets known as the BRICS (Brazil, Russia, India, China, South Africa). For Brazil, China, and South Africa, FDI and portfolio equity account for about two-thirds of external liabilities. By contrast, in advanced economies, portfolio debt (such as bonds issued by corporations) and bank loans together still constitute the major share of external liabilities.

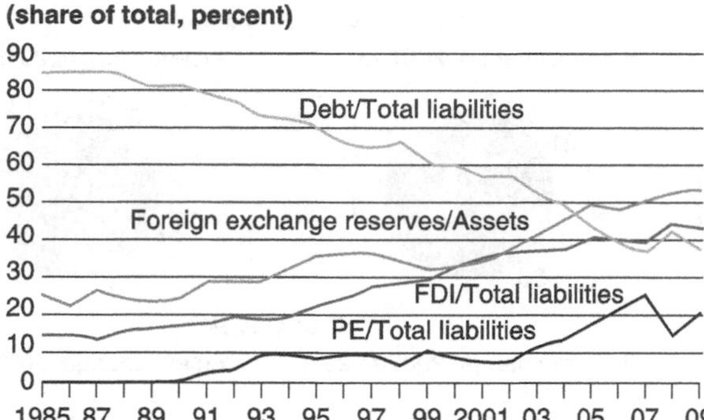

Source: Author's calculations based on the work of Philip Lane and Gian Maria Milesi-Ferretti.

Note: Stocks of foreign direct investment (FDI), portable equity (PE), and debt are shown as a percentage of total external liabilities. Foreign exchange reserves are shown as a percentage of total external assets.

Chart 1

Shifting sources Emerging market liabilities used to be predominantly debt but now foreign direct investment and portfolio equity dominate. Foreign exchange reserves are the major asset.

The changing structure of emerging market balance sheets was striking in the years leading up to the recent financial crisis. Over the period 2000–07, changes in FDI liabilities alone accounted for nearly half of the increase in overall liabilities. FDI and portfolio liabilities together account for about 70 percent of the increase.

Short-term external debt denominated in foreign currencies once was the scourge of emerging markets. These countries faced not only the risk of being unable to refinance the debt if they fell out of favor with international investors but also further trouble if their currencies depreciated, which increased the domestic currency cost of the debt. FDI and portfolio equity are far more desirable forms of capital, and the external debt of these countries is increasingly denominated in their own currencies. When the value of these investments falls either in domestic terms or because of a currency depreciation (or both), foreign investors bear part of the capital and currency risk.

There are interesting developments as well in the asset positions of emerging markets, which are increasingly dominated by foreign exchange reserves. These assets are mostly held in government bonds issued by the four major reserve currency areas (United States, euro area, Japan, United Kingdom). On average, reserves accounted for more than half the total external assets of emerging markets at the end of 2010 (see table). In China and India they accounted for about two-thirds of total external assets.

During 2000–07, reserve accumulation accounted for about half the overall increase in external assets of emerging economies. These results are not driven by China alone. A majority of emerging markets experienced an increase in the share of foreign exchange reserves in total external assets over this period. These countries build up reserves as a by-product of intervention in foreign exchange markets to keep their currencies from appreciating, which would reduce their trade competitiveness. But

Bulked up

At the end of 2010, well over half of emerging market liabilities were in the relatively more stable form of foreign direct investment and portfolio equity.

	FDI/ Liabilities	PE/ Liabilities	FDI&PE/ Liabilities	Foreign exchange reserves/ Assets
Advanced economies				
Median	19.7	9.9	31.4	1.2
Group average	14.9	13.6	28.5	3.0
Emerging economies				
Median	40.5	8.2	56.2	38.8
Group average	6.4	14.6	60.9	52.7
Key emerging economies				
Brazil	36.5	33.3	69.8	47.1
China	63.2	8.8	72.1	69.0
India	32.5	18.5	51.1	67.9
Russia	38.6	17.5	56.1	36.6
South Africa	41.6	35.0	76.6	13.4

Source: Author's calculations.

Note. Median represents the point at which half the group has a higher ratio and half a lower ratio. Foreign direct investment (FDI) occur when an investor has a durable state in an asset. Portfolio equity (PE) represents stock purchases for the purpose of the financial gain. Liabilities and assets refer to a country's external liabilities and external assets.

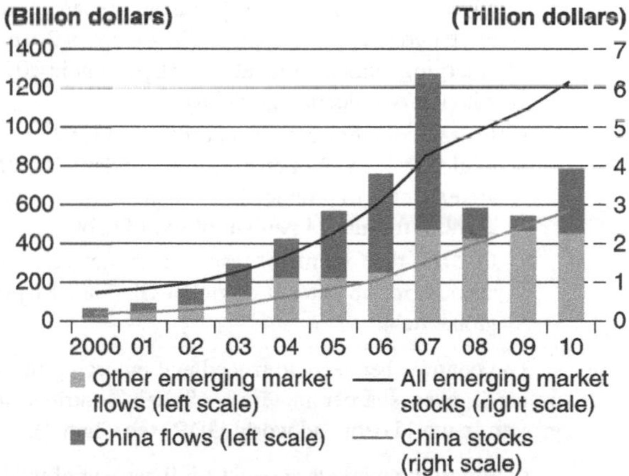

Sources: IMF, Currency Composition of Official Foreign Exchange Reserves database, June 30, 2011; and People's Bank of China.

Note: Flows refer to the annual addition of reserves (left scale); stocks refer to the amount of reserves held by emerging economies at the end of the year (right scale).

Chart 2

Building reserves China and other emerging market economies have been adding foreign exchange reserves rapidly. Reserve accumulation slowed during the recent crisis, but it has picked up again.

reserves also act as a rainy-day fund, providing self-insurance against capital flow volatility.

The recent global financial crisis, along with the rise in total asset and liability positions, has increased emerging economies' demand for precautionary reserves. Indeed, reserve accumulation by these economies peaked in 2007 and slowed during the crisis, but has picked up again (see Chart 2). Meanwhile, the public debt burdens of advanced economies are rising steeply, putting the safety of these assets in jeopardy. As a result, the risk on emerging market external balance sheets has, paradoxically, shifted to the asset side.

Self-insurance Gets Expensive

The accumulation of reserves has been associated with a search by emerging markets for safe assets—typically government bonds of advanced economies. The supply of such bonds is driven by the trajectories of net government debt around the world.

The financial crisis triggered a sharp increase in global public debt levels. Advanced economies account for the bulk of the increase in global net public debt since 2007, both in absolute terms and relative to gross domestic product (GDP). Here are some striking statistics constructed using data and forecasts from the IMF (all at market exchange rates):

- Aggregate debt of advanced economies will grow from $18 trillion in 2007 to $30 trillion in 2011, and rise further to $41 trillion in 2016. The corresponding estimate for emerging markets is $7 trillion in 2016, up $2 trillion from the 2011 level.
- The ratio of aggregate debt to aggregate GDP for advanced economies will rise from 46 percent in 2007 to 70 percent in 2011 and to 80 percent in 2016. For emerging markets, the ratio is 21 percent in 2011, after which it will decline gradually.
- In 2007, emerging markets accounted for 25 percent of world GDP and 17 percent of world debt. By 2016, they are expected to produce 38 percent of world output and account for just 14 percent of world debt.
- In 2011, the four major reserve currency areas together account for 58 percent of global GDP and 81 percent of global debt.

The contrast between advanced and emerging market economies is even sharper in terms of their contributions to the growth in world debt and world GDP (see Chart 3).

- Emerging markets account for 9 percent of the increase in global debt levels from 2007 to 2011 and are expected to account for 13 percent of the increase from 2011 to 2016. Their contributions to increases in global GDP over these two periods are 66 percent and 56 percent, respectively.
- The major advanced economies will make a far greater contribution to the rise in global debt than to the rise in global GDP. The United States will account for 37 percent of the increase in global debt from 2007 to 2011 and 40 percent from 2011 to 2016. Its contributions to the increases in global GDP over those two periods will be 8 percent and 18 percent, respectively.

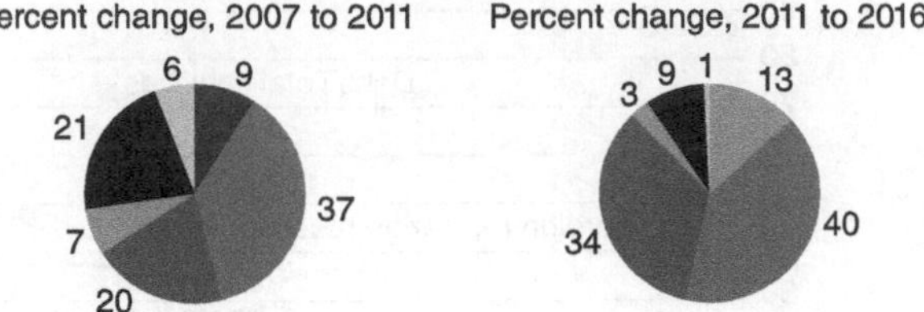

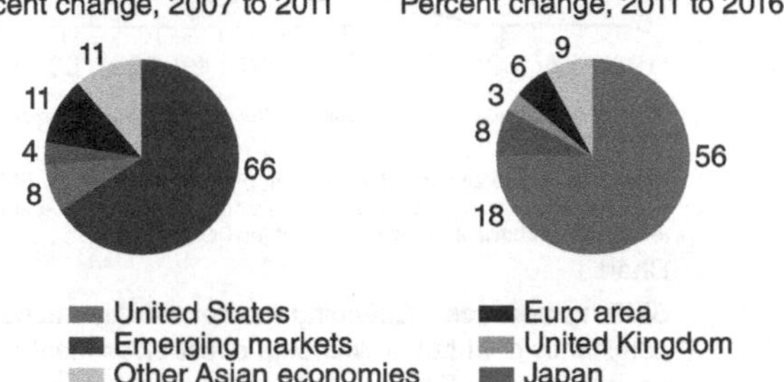

Source: Author's calculations based on the IMF data.

Note: The charts show the percentage contribution of countries or country groups to the changes in the absolute levels of global net government debt and global GDP (measured in a common currency at market rates).

Chart 3

Changing places Emerging markets have replaced advanced economies as the rock of the international financial system.

These figures paint a sobering picture. The major reserve currency economies face daunting trajectories of public debt burdens and weak growth prospects that look worse in light of their low levels of population growth, rapidly aging populations, and rising costs of health care and other entitlement programs.

Reserve currency economies issue sovereign debt in their own currencies, transferring currency risk to the foreign purchasers of their sovereign debt. Moreover, high and rising debt levels imply crowding out of private investment and lower productivity growth in advanced economies relative to emerging markets. These productivity differentials imply that emerging market currencies will eventually appreciate against those of advanced economies, resulting in a significant wealth transfer from poorer to richer countries.

This wealth transfer presents an intriguing paradox—the accumulation of foreign reserves by emerging economies searching for self-insurance is driving up the costs of such insurance, funding advanced economies' fiscal profligacy, and worsening risks worldwide by perpetuating global current account imbalances. In the United States, for instance, foreign investors, both official and private, finance about half of the buildup of net public debt.

Just how safe are advanced economy sovereign assets? Rising debt levels, particularly in "safe haven" economies such as the United States, raise serious concerns about the safety of these bonds from the perspective of emerging market investors. The U.S. Treasury bond market is, of course, very large and has high turnover. That means that the rush into U.S. Treasury bonds in response to instances of global financial turmoil may be more a flight to liquidity and depth than a flight to safety.

The Path Ahead

Traditionally, emerging markets were exposed to risks through their dependence on capital inflows and the structure of their external liabilities. But today, few significant emerging economies depend heavily on foreign financing, and most have large stocks of international reserves. The problem of short-term, foreign currency–denominated debt has diminished substantially. Flexible exchange rate regimes adopted by many emerging markets have also made currency crashes less of a concern (see Kose and Prasad, 2010)

Greater integration of emerging economies into world financial markets does imply that emerging markets are subject to more danger from policy spillover and transmission of shocks from abroad. But these risks are modest relative to domestic ones. Indeed, many emerging economies face a problem of plenty because their strong growth prospects tend to fuel surges in capital inflows and place pressure on domestic inflation, asset prices, and exchange rates.

The major risks emerging economies face as a result of openness to foreign capital are now mainly the tendency for capital flows to magnify domestic policy conundrums. Capital inflows can add fuel to domestic credit booms and asset bubbles that then turn into busts. Inflows and the resulting pressure for currency appreciation also affect income distribution, heightening inequality by feeding into inflation and hurting industrial employment growth.

The solution to a lot of these problems involves financial market development, especially a richer set of financial markets that would improve the ability of emerging economies to absorb capital inflows and manage volatility. For instance, corporate bond markets—which are still minuscule in major emerging markets such as China and India—can provide investment opportunities that would help absorb inflows and effectively channel them into productive rather than speculative activities. The imposition of capital controls, on the other hand, often simply adds economic distortions and is of little lasting value in stemming the tide of inflows.

It is in the self-interest of emerging economies as a group to foster financial market development and broaden domestic access to their formal financial systems. This will allow them to invest more among themselves rather than financing debt buildups in advanced economies. More flexible exchange rate regimes would also reduce reserve accumulation and free up monetary policy to control inflation.

Rather than relying on good policies in advanced economies, emerging economies should focus on managing their own economic destinies. Through their policy choices, they could set an example for advanced economies, which need to swallow the medicine of macroeconomic and structural reforms they have so long prescribed for others.

This article is based on *"Role Reversal in Global Finance," NBER Working Paper No. 17497,* forthcoming in Proceedings of the 2011 Jackson Hole Symposium, from the Federal Reserve Bank of Kansas City.

References

Kose, M. Ayhan, and Eswar S. Prasad, 2010, *Emerging Markets: Resilience and Growth Amid Global Turmoil* (Washington: Brookings Institution).

Lane, Philip R., and Gian Maria Milesi-Ferretti, 2007, "The External Wealth of Nations Mark II: Revised and Extended Estimates of Foreign Assets and Liabilities, 1970–2004," *Journal of International Economics,* Vol. 73, No. 2, pp. 223–50. (Databases are updated regularly by the authors.)

Critical Thinking

1. What has helped developing countries to rebound more quickly from the global recession?
2. How have the assets and liabilities of emerging economies changed?
3. How has the financial crisis affected the industrialized economies?
4. What do emerging markets need to do to continue to strengthen their economies?

Eswar S. Prasad is a Professor at Cornell University, a Senior Fellow at the Brookings Institution, and a Research Associate of the National Bureau of Economic Research.

Article

Is Indonesia Bound for the BRICs?

How stalling reform could hold Jakarta back.

KAREN BROOKS

Indonesia is in the midst of a yearlong debut on the world stage. This past spring and summer, it hosted a series of high-profile summits, including for the Overseas Private Investment Corporation in May, the World Economic Forum on East Asia the same month, and the Association of Southeast Asian Nations (ASEAN) in July. With each event, Indonesia received broad praise for its leadership and achievements. This coming-out party will culminate in November, when the country hosts the East Asia Summit, which U.S. President Barack Obama and world leaders from 17 other countries will attend. As attention turns to Indonesia, the time is ripe to assess whether Jakarta can live up to all the hype.

A little over ten years ago, during the height of the Asian financial crisis, Indonesia looked like a state on the brink of collapse. The rupiah was in a death spiral, protests against President Suharto's regime had turned into riots, and violence had erupted against Indonesia's ethnic Chinese community. The chaos left the country—the fourth largest in the world, a sprawling archipelago including more than 17,000 islands, 200 million people, and the world's largest Muslim population—without a clear leader.

Today, Indonesia is hailed as a model democracy and is a darling of the international financial community. The Jakarta Stock Exchange has been among the world's top performers in recent years, and some analysts have even called for adding Indonesia to the ranks of the BRIC countries (Brazil, Russia, India, and China). More recent efforts to identify the economic superstars of the future—Goldman Sachs' "Next 11," PricewaterhouseCoopers' "E-7" (emerging 7), *The Economist*'s "CIVETS" (Colombia, Indonesia, Vietnam, Egypt, Turkey, and South Africa), and Citigroup's "3G"—all include Indonesia.

The police attempted to frame two of the corruption commission's members for, of all things, corruption.

To be sure, Indonesia's track record has been impressive. In just a few short years following Suharto's 1998 fall from power, Indonesia transformed from a tightly controlled authoritarian system to one of the most vibrant democracies on earth. The elections in 1999 were widely praised as a triumph of democracy; the military stayed on the sidelines, and independent civil-society groups and the media blossomed in the run-up to the polls. With sweeping political and fiscal decentralization, Jakarta devolved real power and resources to the country's hundreds of districts and municipalities. The government created new, independent political institutions to provide for additional checks and balances, including a constitutional court, a judicial commission, and a corruption eradication commission (known by its Indonesian acronym, KPK). An ambitious constitutional reform formalized a presidential system and established a one-man, one-vote process. With no mechanism to filter the results (as the Electoral College does in the United States), Indonesia's voting system is among the most democratic in the world.

The country's economic turnaround has been no less dramatic. In 1998, Indonesia's economy suffered a contraction of more than 13 percent. Since then, it has grown at an average rate of more than five percent per year, including 4.5 percent in 2009, when GDPS in much of the rest of the world shrank. This year, the Indonesian economy is expected to grow 6.5 percent. Indonesia's debt-to-GDP ratio has declined from a high of 100.3 percent in 2000 to 26 percent today, which compares favorably to those of the country's neighbors: Malaysia's is 54 percent, Vietnam's is 53 percent, the Philippines' is 47 percent, and Thailand's is 44 percent. Inflation, which spiked to 77 percent in 1998, now hovers just under five percent. The rupiah, which lost over four-fifths of its value that same year, is the strongest it has been since 2004 and is up 31 percent since 2008 alone. Other ASEAN currencies generally appreciated by between 15 and 20 percent in the same period.

Indonesia has also made great strides in improving its security. In 2004, the government negotiated a peace settlement with Javanese separatists in the region of Aceh, ending a three-decade-long conflict that claimed thousands of lives. Elsewhere, Indonesian security forces have killed or captured hundreds of Islamist militants and have uncovered and shut down major terrorist hideouts and training camps, including one in Aceh in February 2010 that led to a number of high-profile arrests. The government has also implemented important structural reforms, including the creation of a national counterterrorism agency, tasked with forming and enforcing new domestic security laws.

Against this backdrop, Indonesia has started to play a larger role on the international stage. When the G-20 was established in 2008, Indonesia was the only Southeast Asian nation offered membership. That same year, Indonesia launched the Bali Democracy Forum, a yearly regional conference to promote democracy in Asia. In recent months, the forum has become a platform for Indonesia to share lessons from its own democratic transition with some of Egypt's aspiring democrats.

Looming Constraints

Yet despite all the fanfare, the Indonesian score contains some decidedly discordant notes. Indonesia's ports are overstretched, its electrical grid is inadequate, and its road system is one of the least developed in the region. These conditions make the Indonesian economy inefficient and will stifle its future growth. In some regions, the price of basic commodities is up to three times as high as on the main island of Java. Meanwhile, manufacturers are squeezed by exorbitant transportation costs, which are higher in Indonesia than in almost every other ASEAN nation. On the World Bank's 2010 Logistics Performance Index, which is based on a worldwide survey of shippers and carriers combined with data on the performance of each country's supply chain, Indonesia ranked 75 out of 155, well below its neighbors.

Jakarta is well aware of these problems, yet it currently spends only half as much on infrastructure development as it did in the 1990s. Seeking to address almost constant criticism on this issue, in May, Indonesian President Susilo Bambang Yudhoyono issued a new economic "master plan" with an emphasis on infrastructure projects. He also called for higher infrastructure spending in the 2012 budget. But even this budget would cover only about half of the administrations planned development through 2014. Without the new development, Indonesia will not meet its target of 7–8 percent GDP growth by the same year.

Much of the burden of paving roads and providing power and water nationwide will thus fall to the private sector. However, Indonesia's inadequate regulatory framework and weak enforcement of existing regulations have muted private-sector interest. The absence of meaningful eminent domain regulations has proved particularly problematic; the inability to acquire land has prevented many projects from ever getting off the ground. Bureaucratic chaos at the National Land Agency, where plots are often recorded as being owned by multiple parties, has not helped. Yudhoyono has pledged to tackle these problems, but his credibility on the issue is fading.

Endemic corruption further adds to Indonesia's high-cost economy. At the beginning of his first term, Yudhoyono named combating corruption a top priority. Since then, the KPK has sent dozens of politicians and former government officials to jail. Still, corruption runs deep at all levels of government, since the devolution of power after Suharto's fall brought with it the decentralization of graft. Now, officials from Jakarta down to the village level demand bribes and kickbacks, and such payments no longer ensure that things get done.

A number of high-profile scandals during Yudhoyono's second term have showcased the breadth and depth of the problem. Investigations into the 2008 collapse and subsequent $700 million government bailout of Bank Century, a midsize bank with politically connected depositors, revealed that individuals from all elements of law enforcement—senior police officers, officials from the attorney general's office, lawyers, judges—had attempted to profit from the government bailout.

Since then, the police and others have tried to weaken the KPK, including by attempting to frame two sitting members of the commission for, of all things, corruption. The episode paralyzed the KPK for months and made a mockery of Indonesia's judicial system. Although the commission emerged from this episode intact, it has since been focused on lower-profile cases.

Perhaps most damning, the president's own political party has been at the center of an escalating series of corruption scandals in recent months. Muhammad Nazaruddin, the party's former treasurer, and other senior party members stand accused of rigging bids to fulfill government contracts worth more than $1 billion. Nazaruddin fled the country in May and spent three months on the lam before he was arrested in Colombia. Such public drama has undermined domestic and international confidence in the administration's supposed fight against corruption. Perhaps more important, no major political party now credibly carries the anticorruption mantle.

The Yudhoyono administration's promotion of Indonesia as an open, investor-friendly economy is another area in which the gap between rhetoric and reality is particularly large. The government's most recent Investment Negative List, which lays out limitations on foreign investment, is more restrictive than in the past. Indonesia has also backslid on some of its international commitments. The ASEAN-China Free-Trade Area, which came into effect in January 2010, is one such case. As part of the pact, Indonesia and China agreed to reduce or eliminate tariffs on thousands of goods. But since the agreement came into force, Indonesia's domestic industries have pressed for more time to implement its commitments and for the creation of new non-tariff barriers, such as burdensome labeling requirements that would affect a wide range of imports, and not just those from China.

To make matters worse, Yudhoyono announced just days before this year's World Economic Forum in Jakarta that the government would review and revise all its contracts with foreign companies, particularly in the natural resources sector. Underlying the move is an assumption that Indonesia's newly robust economy should give the government the bargaining power to negotiate better terms with foreign firms. Although Indonesian lawmakers applauded the move, foreign investors did not. Indonesia's poor track record on the sanctity of contracts, including, for example, a 2010 regulation that unilaterally changed the economics of previously negotiated oil and gas contracts, helps explain why foreign direct investment in Indonesia lags far behind portfolio inflows to the country.

Indonesia's relative lack of integration with the world economy protected it from the worst of the global financial crisis in 2008. As a result, Yudhoyono's government seems to have concluded that maintaining some insulation from external shocks is more important than allowing rapid growth through foreign investment or through an export-oriented growth strategy. Although the value of Indonesia's exports is up 36.5 percent in 2011 (through July), the increase is overwhelmingly a function of a rise in the price and volume of commodities, namely, gas, coal, palm oil, rubber, and metal. Even with the commodity boom, Indonesia's exports total only around 24 percent of GDP, much less than Malaysia's (96.4 percent), Thailand's (68.4 percent), and the Philippines' (31.7 percent).

The real driver of the country's recent economic growth has been the Indonesian consumer, with consumption accounting for roughly 60 percent of GDP. Indonesian policymakers seem content to keep it that way, and some degree of inward focus may well be appropriate. But Indonesia must strike a balance between protecting itself from external shocks and generating jobs and taking advantage of regional and global growth. If vested business interests continue to drive policies that protect certain sectors from foreign competition, they will create inefficiencies and jeopardize critically needed job creation.

Storm Clouds

Labor and human resource issues are particularly pressing problems for Indonesia, a country of 245 million with five percent of the population now under the age of 30. This means that the proportion that is of working age will rise significantly over the next decade. Indonesian government officials often point to this coming "demographic dividend" as a comparative advantage over aging societies such as China. They argue that a younger generation will consume more and will provide a more productive labor pool. But for the demographic dividend to, in fact, be a dividend, Indonesia would have to create more jobs, including higher-quality and better-paying ones. Extractive industries are capital-intensive, not labor-intensive, and they cannot be counted on to fulfill this role.

Indonesia already faces significant underemployment and poverty, so additional labor force pressures would be a serious concern. According to the most recent official data, in 2011, 6.8 percent of Indonesians were unemployed and 12.5 percent were living under the poverty line. Unemployment and poverty have both decreased since Yudhoyono took office in 2004—unemployment from over nine percent and poverty from over 16 percent. But these numbers do not tell the whole story; over 65 percent of Indonesia's workers are employed informally, most of them in agriculture. Moreover, the number of university-educated unemployed has increased, from 3.6 percent in 2005 to 8.5 percent in 2010. As for poverty, the World Bank estimates that more than half the population lives on less than $2 per day. For upward of 120 million people, then, any disturbance in monthly income could be devastating.

The answer to these challenges is to create jobs. But Indonesia is neither training its work force nor creating the investment climate it needs to attract value-added and labor-intensive industries. Indonesia lags behind both key ASEAN states and all the BRIC countries in access to high-quality education and thus lacks the skilled labor to move up the value-added chain. And even as skilled workers are in short supply, Indonesia maintains one of the most rigid labor regimes in the world, with among the most generous severance packages and most cumbersome layoff procedures. According to the World Economic Forum's 2011-12 *Global Competitiveness Report,* Indonesia scores in the bottom 30 percent of the 142 economies surveyed on labor rigidity.

Meanwhile, Indonesia has seen an increase in the intensity and frequency of ethnic and religious violence in recent years. From communal clashes in Kalimantan to religious violence in Java, the police have been slow to react or unwilling to step in at all, and few perpetrators have been held to account. Yudhoyono has deflected responsibility by calling on local officials to deal with the clashes. His failure of leadership sets a dangerous precedent in a diverse country that is home to at least five different religious traditions and dozens of ethnicities. As its founding fathers understood, Indonesia can survive as a single nation only if tolerance and respect for different ethnicities and religions remain at its core. In addition to casting a shadow over Indonesia's newfound international leadership role, the failure of the state to protect its people and uphold the constitutionally mandated freedom of religion raises the question of whether Indonesia will continue to enjoy the political stability that has allowed for its considerable economic gains.

Yudhoyono's Weak Hand

Indonesia needs a combination of leadership and a renewed push for structural reform to overcome its many challenges. So far, however, both remain in short supply. Yudhoyono was elected with more than 60 percent of the vote in 2004 and again in 2009. Yet despite his strong popular mandate, he has never felt comfortable governing on the basis of popular support. Instead, he has repeatedly tried to use cabinet appointments to create legislative coalitions (as one might in a parliamentary system), despite the absence of any such concept in Indonesia's legal and constitutional framework. This strategy has come at the expense of continued reform, as cabinet appointments are made to gain allies rather than recruit reformers with genuine expertise. Indeed, Indonesia passed all its landmark reforms nearly a decade ago.

To be fair, the fault is not all Yudhoyono's. For a presidential system, Indonesia has an uncommonly large number of political parties—nine in all. The ruling Democrat Party is the single largest in the country's legislature, but it still commands only 26 percent of the seats. As a result, out of the 70 bills proposed at the start of Yudhoyono's second term, only a handful have passed—and largely insignificant ones at that. Indonesia needs fewer parties to overcome this gridlock, but the smaller parties have resisted even modest proposals to increase the threshold of votes required before a party can enter the legislature, and there is little hope of meaningful change before the 2014 legislative elections.

Meanwhile, the Constitutional Court recently lowered the number of votes required to initiate a presidential impeachment process from three-fourths of the legislature to two-thirds. This means that the Democrat Party's 26 percent plurality can no longer protect Yudhoyono from attempts to oust him. The court's ruling seems to have exacerbated his indecisiveness—unsurprising given that Indonesia's first elected president after Suharto, Abdurrahman Wahid, was impeached. Yudhoyono's failure to reshuffle his cabinet, despite making repeated threats to remove nonperforming ministers, has exemplified his paralysis.

As a result, the president is increasingly captive to politicians at odds with his stated reform programs, and Indonesia's competent core of technocrats in government has less room to advance meaningful change. At best, this could portend stasis for the remaining three years of Yudhoyono's term. At worst, Indonesia could see its hard-won gains evaporate. In June, for example, the legislature rolled back key powers of the Constitutional Court—the only court seen as being beyond the reach of corrupt politicians. The legislature is similarly poised to strip the KPK of important authorities.

After decades of authoritarian rule, Indonesians have been reluctant to allow power to concentrate in the hands of any one person or institution. In fact, most of Indonesia's reforms after 1998 were explicitly designed to decentralize power. But the pendulum has swung too far, producing a system with real structural impediments to coherent policy implementation. As Indonesia moves further away from its authoritarian past, reformers need to recalibrate the balance of power. The legislature needs fewer political parties; independent institutions, such as the Constitutional Court and the KPK, need more power; and constitutional reform may be needed to raise the threshold for impeachment of the president. Generational change will hopefully be part of this process. The current political and economic elites are largely a product of the Suharto period. The 2014 electoral cycle might offer an opportunity for new leaders to come to the fore.

As the political restructuring of the Middle East tests whether Islam and democracy can coexist, as pluralism and religious tolerance come under attack in countries from Africa to Europe, and as China's economic rise without political liberalization challenges the Western democratic model, Indonesia's continued success as an open, moderate, tolerant, multiethnic, multireligious democracy with a booming economy is of huge importance as a model for the developing world. Indonesia deserves plaudits for its progress to date, but some gains are under threat, and its continued success requires a new wave of reform. Indonesians proved they were capable of extraordinary things at the turn of this century. Once this fall's summit meetings are over, it will be time for Indonesia's reformers to get back to work.

Critical Thinking

1. What accounts for Indonesia's recent success?
2. What factors constrain Indonesia from becoming a more important international actor?
3. What political reforms are necessary in Indonesia?

Karen Brooks is Adjunct Senior Fellow for Asia at the Council on Foreign Relations.

Article

Prepared by: Robert J. Griffiths, *University of North Carolina at Greensboro*

Broken BRICs: Why the Rest Stopped Rising

RUCHIR SHARMA

Learning Outcomes

After reading this article, you will be able to:

- Identify the factors that will constrain continued high economic growth rates in the BRICs.
- Explain the cyclical nature of economic growth.

Over the past several years, the most talked-about trend in the global economy has been the so-called rise of the rest, which saw the economies of many developing countries swiftly converging with those of their more developed peers. The primary engines behind this phenomenon were the four major emerging-market countries, known as the BRICs: Brazil, Russia, India, and China. The world was witnessing a once-in-a-lifetime shift, the argument went, in which the major players in the developing world were catching up to or even surpassing their counterparts in the developed world.

These forecasts typically took the developing world's high growth rates from the middle of the last decade and extended them straight into the future, juxtaposing them against predicted sluggish growth in the United States and other advanced industrial countries. Such exercises supposedly proved that, for example, China was on the verge of overtaking the United States as the world's largest economy—a point that Americans clearly took to heart, as over 50 percent of them, according to a Gallup poll conducted this year, said they think that China is already the world's "leading" economy, even though the U.S. economy is still more than twice as large (and with a per capita income seven times as high).

As with previous straight-line projections of economic trends, however—such as forecasts in the 1980s that Japan would soon be number one economically—later returns are throwing cold water on the extravagant predictions. With the world economy heading for its worst year since 2009, Chinese growth is slowing sharply, from double digits down to 7 percent or even less. And the rest of the BRICs are tumbling, too: since 2008, Brazil's annual growth has dropped from 4.5 percent to 2 percent; Russia's, from 7 percent to 3.5 percent; and India's, from 9 percent to 6 percent.

None of this should be surprising, because it is hard to sustain rapid growth for more than a decade. The unusual circumstances of the last decade made it look easy: coming off the crisis-ridden 1990s and fueled by a global flood of easy money, the emerging markets took off in a mass upward swing that made virtually every economy a winner. By 2007, when only three countries in the world suffered negative growth, recessions had all but disappeared from the international scene. But now, there is a lot less foreign money flowing into emerging markets. The global economy is returning to its normal state of churn, with many laggards and just a few winners rising in unexpected places. The implications of this shift are striking, because economic momentum is power, and thus the flow of money to rising stars will reshape the global balance of power.

Forever Emerging

The notion of wide-ranging convergence between the developing and the developed worlds is a myth. Of the roughly 180 countries in the world tracked by the International Monetary Fund, only 35 are developed. The markets of the rest are emerging—and most of them have been emerging for many decades and will continue to do so for many more. The Harvard economist Dani Rodrik captures this reality well. He has shown that before 2000, the performance of the emerging markets as a whole did not converge with that of the developed world at all. In fact, the per capita income gap between the advanced and the developing economies steadily widened from 1950 until 2000. There were a few pockets of countries that did catch up with the West, but they were limited to oil states in the Gulf, the nations of southern Europe after World War II, and the economic "tigers" of East Asia. It was only after 2000 that the emerging markets as a whole started to catch up; nevertheless, as of 2011, the difference in per capita incomes between the rich and the developing nations was back to where it was in the 1950s.

This is not a negative read on emerging markets so much as it is simple historical reality. Over the course of any given decade since 1950, on average, only a third of the emerging markets have been able to grow at an annual rate of 5 percent or more. Less than one-fourth have kept up that pace for two decades, and one-tenth, for three decades. Only Malaysia, Singapore, South Korea, Taiwan, Thailand, and Hong Kong have maintained this growth rate for four decades. So even before the current signs of a slowdown in the BRICS, the odds were against Brazil experiencing a full decade of growth above 5 percent, or Russia, its second in a row.

Meanwhile, scores of emerging markets have failed to gain any momentum for sustained growth, and still others have seen their progress stall after reaching middle-income status. Malaysia and Thailand appeared to be on course to emerge as rich countries until crony capitalism, excessive debts, and overpriced currencies caused the Asian financial meltdown of 1997–98. Their growth has disappointed ever since. In the late 1960s, Burma (now officially called Myanmar), the Philippines, and Sri Lanka were billed as the next Asian tigers, only to falter badly well before they could even reach the middle-class average income of about $5,000 in current dollar terms. Failure to sustain growth has been the general rule, and that rule is likely to reassert itself in the coming decade.

In the opening decade of the twenty-first century, emerging markets became such a celebrated pillar of the global economy that it is easy to forget how new the concept of emerging markets is in the financial world. The first coming of the emerging markets dates to the mid-1980s, when Wall Street started tracking them as a distinct asset class. Initially labeled as "exotic," many emerging market countries were then opening up their stock markets to foreigners for the first time: Taiwan opened its up in 1991; India, in 1992; South Korea, in 1993; and Russia, in 1995. Foreign investors rushed in, unleashing a 600 percent boom in emerging-market stock prices (measured in dollar terms) between 1987 and 1994. Over this period, the amount of money invested in emerging markets rose from less than 1 percent to nearly 8 percent of the global stock-market total.

This phase ended with the economic crises that struck from Mexico to Turkey between 1994 and 2002. The stock markets of developing countries lost almost half their value and shrank to four percent of the global total. From 1987 to 2002, developing countries' share of global gdp actually fell, from 23 percent to 20 percent. The exception was China, which saw its share double, to 4.5 percent. The story of the hot emerging markets, in other words, was really about one country.

The second coming began with the global boom in 2003, when emerging markets really started to take OA as a group. Their share of global gdp began a rapid climb, from 20 percent to the 34 percent that they represent today (attributable in part to the rising value of their currencies), and their share of the global stock-market total rose from less than 4 percent to more than 10 percent. The huge losses suffered during the global financial crash of 2008 were mostly recovered in 2009, but since then, it has been slow going.

The third coming, an era that will be defined by moderate growth in the developing world, the return of the boom-bust cycle, and the breakup of herd behavior on the part of emerging-market countries, is just beginning. Without the easy money and the blue-sky optimism that fueled investment in the last decade, the stock markets of developing countries are likely to deliver more measured and uneven returns. Gains that averaged 37 percent a year between 2003 and 2007 are likely to slow to, at best, 10 percent over the coming decade, as earnings growth and exchange-rate values in large emerging markets have limited scope for additional improvement after last decade's strong performance.

Past Its Sell-By Date

No idea has done more to muddle thinking about the global economy than that of the BRICs. Other than being the largest economies in their respective regions, the big four emerging markets never had much in common. They generate growth in different and often competing ways—Brazil and Russia, for example, are major energy producers that benefit from high energy prices, whereas India, as a major energy consumer, suffers from them. Except in highly unusual circumstances, such as those of the last decade, they are unlikely to grow in unison. China apart, they have limited trade ties with one another, and they have few political or foreign policy interests in common.

A problem with thinking in acronyms is that once one catches on, it tends to lock analysts into a worldview that may soon be outdated. In recent years, Russia's economy and stock market have been among the weakest of the emerging markets, dominated by an oil-rich class of billionaires whose assets equal 20 percent of gdp, by far the largest share held by the super-rich in any major economy. Although deeply out of balance, Russia remains a member of the BRICs, if only because the term sounds better with an R. Whether or not pundits continue using the acronym, sensible analysts and investors need to stay flexible; historically, flashy countries that grow at 5 percent or more for a decade—such as Venezuela in the 1950s, Pakistan in the 1960s, or Iraq in the 1970s—are usually tripped up by one threat or another (war, financial crisis, complacency, bad leadership) before they can post a second decade of strong growth.

The current fad in economic forecasting is to project so far into the future that no one will be around to hold you accountable. This approach looks back to, say, the seventeenth century, when China and India accounted for perhaps half of global gdp, and then forward to a coming "Asian century," in which such preeminence is reasserted. In fact, the longest period over which one can find clear patterns in the global economic cycle is around a decade. The typical business cycle lasts about five years, from the bottom of one downturn to the bottom of the next, and most practical investors limit their perspectives to one or two business cycles. Beyond that, forecasts are often rendered obsolete by the unanticipated appearance of new competitors, new political environments, or new technologies. Most CEOs and major investors still limit their strategic visions to three, five, or at most seven years, and they judge results on the same time frame.

The New and Old Economic Order

In the decade to come, the United States, Europe, and Japan are likely to grow slowly. Their sluggishness, however, will look less worrisome compared with the even bigger story in the global economy, which will be the 3 to 4 percent slowdown in China, which is already under way, with a possibly deeper slowdown in store as the economy continues to mature. China's population is simply too big and aging too quickly for its economy to continue growing as rapidly as it has. With over 50 percent of its people now living in cities, China is nearing what economists call "the Lewis turning point": the point at which a country's surplus labor from rural areas has been largely exhausted. This is the result of both heavy migration to cities over the past two decades and the shrinking work force that the one-child policy has produced. In due time, the sense of many Americans today that Asian juggernauts are swiftly overtaking the U.S. economy will be remembered as one of the country's periodic bouts of paranoia, akin to the hype that accompanied Japan's ascent in the 1980s.

As growth slows in China and in the advanced industrial world, these countries will buy less from their export-driven counterparts, such as Brazil, Malaysia, Mexico, Russia, and Taiwan. During the boom of the last decade, the average trade balance in emerging markets nearly tripled as a share of gdp, to 6 percent. But since 2008, trade has fallen back to its old share of under 2 percent. Export driven emerging markets will need to find new ways to achieve strong growth, and investors recognize that many will probably fail to do so: in the first half of 2012, the spread between the value of the best performing and the value of the worst performing major emerging stock markets shot up from 10 percent to 35 percent. Over the next few years, therefore, the new normal in emerging markets will be much like the old normal of the 1950s and 1960s, when growth averaged around 5 percent and the race left many behind. This does not imply a reemergence of the 1970s-era Third World, consisting of uniformly underdeveloped nations. Even in those days, some emerging markets, such as South Korea and Taiwan, were starting to boom, but their success was overshadowed by the misery in larger countries, such as India. But it does mean that the economic performance of the emerging-market countries will be highly differentiated.

The uneven rise of the emerging markets will impact global politics in a number of ways. For starters, it will revive the self-confidence of the West and dim the economic and diplomatic glow of recent stars, such as Brazil and Russia (not to mention the petro-dictatorships in Africa, Latin America, and the Middle East). One casualty will be the notion that China's success demonstrates the superiority of authoritarian, state-run capitalism. Of the 124 emerging-market countries that have managed to sustain a 5 percent growth rate for a full decade since 1980, 52 percent were democracies and 48 percent were authoritarian. At least over the short to medium term, what matters is not the type of political system a country has but rather the presence of leaders who understand and can implement the reforms required for growth.

Another casualty will be the notion of the so-called demographic dividend. Because China's boom was driven in part by a large generation of young people entering the work force, consultants now scour census data looking for similar population bulges as an indicator of the next big economic miracle. But such demographic determinism assumes that the resulting workers will have the necessary skills to compete in the global market and that governments will set the right policies to create jobs. In the world of the last decade, when a rising tide lifted all economies, the concept of a demographic dividend briefly made sense. But that world is gone.

The economic role models of recent times will give way to new models or perhaps no models, as growth trajectories splinter off in many directions. In the past, Asian states tended to look to Japan as a paradigm, nations from the Baltics to the Balkans looked to the European Union, and nearly all countries to some extent looked to the United States. But the crisis of 2008 has undermined the credibility of all these role models. Tokyo's recent mistakes have made South Korea, which is still rising as a manufacturing powerhouse, a much more appealing Asian model than Japan. Countries that once were clamoring to enter the eurozone, such as the Czech Republic, Poland, and Turkey, now wonder if they want to join a club with so many members struggling to stay afloat. And as for the United States, the 1990s-era Washington consensus—which called for poor countries to restrain their spending and liberalize their economies—is a hard sell when even Washington can't agree to cut its own huge deficit.

Because it is easier to grow rapidly from a low starting point, it makes no sense to compare countries in different income classes. The rare breakout nations will be those that outstrip rivals in their own income class and exceed broad expectations for that class. Such expectations, moreover, will need to come back to earth. The last decade was unusual in terms of the wide scope and rapid pace of global growth, and anyone who counts on that happy situation returning soon is likely to be disappointed.

Among countries with per capita incomes in the $20,000 to $25,000 range, only two have a good chance of matching or exceeding three percent annual growth over the next decade: the Czech Republic and South Korea. Among the large group with average incomes in the $10,000 to $15,000 range, only one country—Turkey—has a good shot at matching or exceeding 4 to 5 percent growth, although Poland also has a chance. In the $5,000 to $10,000 income class, Thailand seems to be the only country with a real shot at outperforming significantly. To the extent that there will be a new crop of emerging market stars in the coming years, therefore, it is likely to feature countries whose per capita incomes are under $5,000, such as Indonesia, Nigeria, the Philippines, Sri Lanka, and various contenders in East Africa.

Although the world can expect more breakout nations to emerge from the bottom income tier, at the top and the middle, the new global economic order will probably look more like the old one than most observers predict. The rest may continue to rise, but they will rise more slowly and unevenly than many experts are anticipating. And precious few will ever reach the income levels of the developed world.

Critical Thinking

1. What factors constrain continued high economic growth rates in the BRICs?
2. What is the nature of economic growth?

Create Central

www.mhhe.com/createcentral

Internet References

Center for Third World Organizing
www.ctwo.org

ENTERWeb
www.enterweb.org

International Monetary Fund (IMF)
www.imf.org

TWN (Third WorldNetwork)
www.twnside.org.sg

U.S.Agency for International Development (USAID)
www.usaid.gov

The World Bank
www.worldbank.org

World Trade Organization (WTO)
www.wto.org

Ruchir Sharma is head of Emerging Markets and Global Macro at Morgan Stanley Investment Management and the author of *Breakout Nations: In Pursuit of the Next Economic Miracles.*

Article

Prepared by: Robert J. Griffiths, *University of North Carolina at Greensboro*

Lions, Tigers, and Emerging Markets: Africa's Development Dilemmas

"Much of Africa's wealth is unevenly spread across the continent and tends to be concentrated in resource-rich countries with large populations."

ANNE PITCHER

Learning Outcomes

After reading this article, you will be able to:

- Outline the factors that have contributed to Africa's impressive economic growth rates.
- Evaluate the impact of growing wealth on prospects for democratic stability on the continent.

Four years after it began, the global financial crisis continues to wreak havoc on property values and personal savings in Europe and America, but its effects have not blunted the growing enthusiasm of investors for the so-called "emerging markets" of sub-Saharan Africa. In 2010, the McKinsey Global Institute and the Africa-based offices of McKinsey and Company issued an influential account of Africa's investment potential. Titled "Lions on the Move: The Progress and Potential of African Economies," the report called attention to the continuing risks of conflict and poor governance across the continent, yet its main thrust was decidedly positive—even glowing. McKinsey's analysis trumpeted Africa's "commercial vibrancy," "hard-earned progress and promise," and "growth acceleration," much as previous investment literature had described the Asian "tigers."

At the time, it was tempting to dismiss the report as a marketing move by an international consulting company aiming to attract corporate clients whose patience with the more "reliable" European and American markets was exhausted. But that would have been a mistake. The report proved to be part of a trend of favorable and often hyperbolic accounts in the popular media and among reputable international financial institutions (like the World Bank) proclaiming the rise of Africa. This trend continues today.

For example, the Economist Intelligence Unit, maintaining the characterization of African economies as "lions," issued a January 2012 study that sought to "capture the changing appetite for investing in Africa's frontier and emerging markets" by surveying investors on their perceptions of the continents potential. A majority of investors agreed that markets in Africa offer the world's best prospects for investment growth, and many expected to increase their exposure in the next three to five years. The World Bank for its part speaks often of Africa's "potential." Last year its officials joined heads of private equity firms and investment bankers to discuss the region's prospects at a conference called "Roaring Giant: Africa's Economic Ascent," held at Columbia University.

Although reliance on the trope of the mighty lion to frame Africa's recent growth may be rather trite, its ubiquity in the policy-making literature as well as the popular press suggests that fundamental economic and political shifts have occurred across the continent. But what is the nature of these shifts? Where are they taking place? Who are the beneficiaries? And will African lions replace the Asian tigers? In fact, the complex answers to these questions offer as much cause for caution as for optimism. The continent is definitely changing, but its growth and investment are spatially and socioeconomically uneven, politically contentious, and economically risky.

New Foundations

As a result of conditions imposed on aid by bilateral donors and multilateral financial institutions, countries across Africa in the past two decades have liberalized trade, balanced budgets, established investment centers, created stock markets, and passed privatization laws. Benin, Ghana, Mozambique, Tanzania, and Uganda as well as many other countries have sold the majority of their state-owned enterprises to foreign and domestic investors and sought investment to finance new projects in sectors ranging from mining to consumer goods. Moreover, political changes have accompanied many of these economic shifts. Many governments in Africa now practice some form of democratic electoral politics: Their citizens enjoy basic political rights and civil liberties that were denied to them just 20 years ago.

These policy alterations have provided the foundations for increased investor interest in the continent. Whereas aid from donors such as the United States, the United Kingdom, France, Germany, and the Scandinavian countries has financed large infrastructure projects such as hydroelectric dams and major road corridors, or provided budget support to cash-strapped African governments for education and health care, private investment has surpassed overseas development assistance (ODA) in importance. Despite the recent economic downturn, inflows of foreign direct investment (FDI) were $60 billion in 2009 compared with bilateral and multilateral ODA amounting to $47 billion. In 2010, total FDI and ODA received by African countries were about equal, at $50 billion respectively.

The characteristics of the private investors with an interest in Africa are, in some respects, all too familiar, but in other respects are strikingly different from what they were two decades ago. Large transnational oil corporations such as BP and Chevron continue to be important players in resource-rich countries such as Nigeria and Angola. French companies such as Total, with a long history in Africa, manage oil concessions in Algeria, Gabon, Libya, and Madagascar. Unilever, a British firm whose presence in Africa dates back to the nineteenth century, continues do business in at least 20 African countries, selling a range of items including food, health, hygiene, and beauty products.

But investment in Africa now extends far beyond those companies with roots in the colonial period. International financial institutions have investment arms that help fmance large infrastructural projects along with private capital. They also back private sector-driven investments in retail businesses, office blocks, telecommunications infrastructure, cement factories, and even Coca-Cola bottling plants.

Moreover, most donor countries—including not only the United States, the UK, and France but also Brazil, China, and Saudi Arabia—have created or reorganized development finance institutions with mandates to pursue investments in emerging markets such as in Africa. For example, the Overseas Private Investment Corporation, the development finance arm of the US government established more than 40 years ago, provides financing and support to American companies interested in investing in Africa, among other regions of the world. It also supports projects that will spur private sector growth, such as the expansion of electricity or the provision of loans for small businesses.

Enter Private Equity

Particularly noticeable within the new wave of investors are private equity firms, which have rapidly expanded their presence in Africa over the past five years. These firms typically rely on the capital of institutional investors, such as pension funds and insurance companies, or wealthy individuals to engage in high-risk, high-return investments. The private equity industry grew quickly in the United States during the 1970s, when changes to financial regulations made possible the use of pension funds for investment purposes. The availability of large amounts of capital from these and other funds (such as insurance) facilitated the expansion of the private equity industry into industrialized countries in Europe. But only recently have they extended to the African continent.

Today about 170 global fund managers based in the United States, the UK, France, Saudi Arabia, and China include Africa in their portfolios. Intra-African investment is growing too; with private equity firms registered in Mauritius, Kenya, Ghana, Nigeria, and especially South Africa pursuing opportunities on the rest of the continent. Partial financing of such funds may come from multilateral or bilateral donors, but increasingly much of it comes from institutional investors and individuals of high net worth.

Investments by private equity firms include the provision of venture capital for new projects in consumer goods, health care, agribusiness, corporate and city branding campaigns, and eco-tourism. Private equity firms also engage in leveraged buyouts of existing, usually highly indebted firms in a variety of sectors, from an oil marketing business in Nigeria to a media company in South Africa.

Alternatively, private equity firms rely on so-called "mezzanine capital," a hybrid funding tool that combines debt and equity financing to acquire whole or partial stakes in existing businesses. The use of mezzanine capital in the region has mostly been confined to South Africa, but it is beginning to expand to other countries suph as Botswana and Nigeria. Thus, the complex financing arrangements that are common within developed countries have now spread to Africa.

Commodities and Consumers

As in the past, much capital is allocated to minting and processing Africa's mineral resources. With growing demand for commodities in Brazil, India, and China, private investors are aggressively pursuing the creation or expansion of oil production in Ghana, Angola, Nigeria, and Algeria. Copper mining in Zambia and the Democratic Republic of Congo, gold and platinum mining in Zimbabwe, and natural gas exploration and coal mining in Mozambique are in great demand, although in the latter case, production has barely begun.

Governments have promoted industrial development initiatives, export processing zones, and development corridors in the hope of luring additional investors to the continent. However, with the exception of the Maputo Corridor, which links Johannesburg and its environs to the port of Maputo in Mozambique, few of these proposed nodes of manufacturing, commercial operations, tourism, and transport have actually taken off.

Global demand for food and biofuels has risen—as have prices—and thus investments in agriculture are popular. This has environmental and conservation groups worried. A number of them, including the international nongovernmental organization Oxfam and an independent think tank, the Oakland Institute, view with alarm the growing investor interest in agriculture across Africa. Decrying corporate "land grabs," the Oakland Institute has issued a series of reports detailing the allocation of hundreds of thousands of hectares of land to Swedish, American, British, Dutch, Indian, Chinese, Saudi Arabian, and other companies for biofuels, rice, corn, sugar, soybeans, and forestry products in Tanzania, Ethiopia, Mozambique, and Mali.

The reports raise concerns about the environmental impact of commercial farming and the threats to domestic food production posed by growing agribusiness and biofuel production. Should these threats materialize, they would increase existing food deficits in rural areas and exacerbate the environmental damage already caused by the mining, processing, and transport of extractive resources.

Political and economic liberalization has stimulated investments in consumer goods, financial services, and agriculture.

As long as demand and prices remain high, interest in minerals and agricultural goods will continue but investors seem to be most excited about the potential long-term opportunities in financial services, consumer goods, and the provision of urban housing for Africa's rising middle class.

Virtually ignored since Europeans colonized Africa in the nineteenth century, the African consumer suddenly became visible to investors when sales of cell phones began to explode across the continent a decade ago. Whereas in 1998 just 4 million Africans had access to cell phones, by 2011 there were nearly 500 million subscribers. Two South African cellular telecommunications companies, MTN and Vodacom, both less than 20 years old, dominate the market in countries such as Ghana, Tanzania, the Democratic Republic of Congo, Nigeria, and Uganda. According to their own reports, MTN and Vodacom have more than 116 million and 40 million subscribers respectively across the continent. Foreign telecommunications companies from India, France, and the UK are also prominent players.

The prospect of enormous profits to be made from tapping into the pent-up demand of a hitherto ignored group of mostly urban consumers drives a host of other initiatives. Some are eminently practical and long overdue, in areas such as housing, retail banking services, processed food, ready-to-wear clothing, and cosmetics. Others are grandiose and utopian such as dozens of city building projects that are either imagined, under way, or completed in countries such as Zambia, Kenya, Ghana, Tunisia, Angola, and South Africa.

With half of the population of Africa projected to inhabit cities by mid-century, it makes sense to anticipate where they are going to live and work, and what they are going to do. According to McKinsey, the continent already has 52 cities with over 1 million people, and housing conditions, even for the affluent in many of these cities, are poor.

Elite Retreat

What makes current urban development efforts in Africa so unusual is their financing, their character, and their scale. They are often not publicly conceived or publicly financed, nor are they piecemeal, ad hoc additions to existing cities. Rather, with the blessing of the state, the private sector often spearheads the planning, financing, management, marketing, and construction not only of self-contained, heavily guarded, walled residential areas, but also of much larger mixed-use developments that include housing, office complexes, recreation facilities, schools, and health clinics.

In *Newsweek* in March 2011, the Nigerian author and playwright Wole Soyinka alluded to the grandiose vision behind one of these planned private cities, when he ironically described Eko Atlantic in Nigeria as "rising like Aphrodite from the foam of the Atlantic." Eko Atlantic will be built on nine square kilometers of land being reclaimed from the Atlantic off the coast of Lagos. Although the Lagos state government has played an important role in the project by granting the developer a 78-year lease, syndicated loans and private equity funds from domestic and international banks together with private investors are financing it. A subsidiary of the Chagoury Group, a conglomerate with 30 years of experience in Nigeria, is planning and developing it.

Referred to by some commentators as a "sister city" to Lagos, its imagined tree-lined streets and uninterrupted ocean views could not be more different from the sprawling, overcrowded areas of Nigeria's largest city. In contrast to Lagos, Eko Atlantic aspires to be a green-conscious "world class city" that attracts the top transnational corporations and runs 24 hours a day, with the workday shifting seamlessly to entertainment at night. Moreover, it promises to be free of traffic jams, which is nothing short of miraculous considering that idling in stalled traffic is practically a way of life in densely populated Lagos. Although construction has barely begun, the use of innovative reclamation techniques to halt coastal erosion and flooding has already garnered the development team a Clinton Global Initiative Commitment Certificate.

Private Spaces

Eko Atlantic has attracted an inordinate amount of media hype, but other city building projects such as Waterfall City in South Africa, King City in Ghana, Tatu City in Kenya, Levy Junction in Zambia, and several city building and urban revitalization projects in Angola are either under way or have been completed. Almost all of these are located near existing and highly congested urban areas, but several such as Waterfall City and Tatu Gity are self-contained, stand-alone projects. They are not grafted onto existing urban agglomerations and they are not extensions of public space. They are (or will be) privately run cities in private spaces.

Smaller gated communities and shopping malls are also cropping up across the continent from Tunisia to South Africa. And like the investors in Eko Atlantic, the private sector has mostly led the way on these initiatives, requiring no more or less from their governmental partners than the settlement of land disputes and the security of their property rights. Once these issued are resolved, private companies engage in everything from master planning to the sale of plots for residential and commercial uses.

Who will live in these idyllic private cities, shop at upscale malls, watch movies, or play mini-golf? And what impact might the retreat of the elite behind walls and security gates have on efforts to consolidate democracy and build civil society in African countries? What new roles will the state be asked to perform, or to relinquish, if private city managers replace elected or appointed public servants?

In many cases, only a small elite enjoy the benefits from increased investment and global integration.

Since many of these projects are not yet completed, there are no definitive responses to questions about who will benefit from the changing urban and consumer landscape in Africa and what the projects' relationship to the public sphere will be. But partial answers can be provided by extrapolating from gated communities and new urban spaces that already exist.

Certainly foreign businesspeople and diplomats can be expected to move to cleaner and safer neighborhoods, as they have already done in places such as Luanda Sul in Angola and New Cairo in Egypt. In addition, increasing remittances sent back to the continent from the diaspora may help finance the relocation of relatives or the purchase of second homes in mixed-use developments, as is occurring in Cape Verde, Ghana, and Kenya. Africa received about $40 billion in remittances in 2009; remittances to Ghana alone accounted for 10 percent of the total. Research by the World Bank indicates that remittances not only support families but also contribute to the expansion of local real estate markets and land purchases.

Middle Class Values

Investor interest is betting on the acquisitiveness of Africa's growing "middle class" to ramp up purchases of homes, cars, clothes, and other consumer goods. One difficulty with predicting the behavior of this class, however, is that it is hard to determine who is in it and how big it is. If we use an absolute dollar figure for ascertaining who is in the middle class, setting its lower and upper bounds will determine its size. (Fortunately, in his calculation of the global middle class, Martin Ravallion at the World Bank has adopted some plausible upper and lower bounds, and I follow his lead here.)

If we take income of at least two dollars a day per capita as a measure of the middle class, as several studies do, then about 200 million people in sub-Saharan Africa may be considered middle class. This figure represents an increase of about 3 percent since 1990 in the proportion of the population that is middle class. Yet perceptions about the purchasing power of this group may be highly misplaced. An average income of two dollars a day barely covers absolute necessities, even taking into account that a dollar generally goes further in developing countries.

If we raise the bar to, say, $13 a day per capita, which was the poverty line in the United States (based on poverty guidelines for a family of four) in 2005, then the number of people in sub-Saharan Africa who fit this category shrinks considerably to about 10 million people, or less than 2 percent of the total population. Allowing that the data on income levels from Africa are out of date for many countries, likely do not include informally earned income, and exclude wealthier North African countries such as Tunisia and Egypt, these figures on potential membership of the middle class are still depressingly low. They suggest that only a tiny minority of the African population has access to discretionary income of any consequence.

Whether we use a very conservative or a very generous estimate of per capita income, or a relative measure based on income levels in individual countries, or a calculation based on a households material goods to determine who is in the middle class, the point is that the numbers of Africans who are in a position to purchase big ticket items such as new cars or homes is still very small. They are also concentrated in resource-rich countries like Nigeria, Sudan, and Angola, or in relatively well-developed countries such as South Africa and Mauritius.

Many Africans may now own cell phones, but most are excluded from access to adequate shelter, a steady supply of electricity and water, and a decent income. Informal settlements abound while basic services are both insufficient and expensive. Where a middle class can be detected, the data are insufficient to determine whether its members' livelihoods are stable enough or their savings adequate to support the purchase of homes. With the exception of South Africa, most countries in sub-Saharan Africa do not have mortgage markets. Nonetheless, most countries have small elites that will take advantage of opportunities to enjoy the security and the calm of planned charter cities or walled residential areas.

Zones of Luxury

The emergence of these zones of luxury may pose political problems, however. On a continent where the ideals of political pluralism and democracy are still struggling for consolidation, the spatial segregation and the visibility of wealth that characterize gated communities and private urban enclaves can play havoc with efforts to build meaningful democratic participation and to promote social justice.

The distinction between the haves and the have-nots embodied in a security gate or a "Mediterranean-style" villa has the potential to exacerbate perceptions of income inequality and unequal property access among the poor and the vulnerable. In frustration, they may join other sectors of society to bring down authoritarian regimes, as they have done in Tunisia and Egypt. Alternatively, under more democratic conditions, marginalized residents may resort to protests or more violent forms of political action to demand subsidies for food and gasoline or steady supplies of water and electricity, as they have done in Nigeria, Uganda, and Mozambique.

Opposing trends of democratic inclusion and residential exclusion, growing prosperity and persistent insecurity therefore pose considerable dilemmas for national governments. Some, like that of Zimbabwe, are creating a kind of electoral authoritarianism where balloting takes place but political rights, civil liberties, and economic opportunities remain highly restricted and repressed.

Other countries that enjoy varying levels of democracy, such as Senegal, South Africa, Zambia, Mozambique, and Tanzania, have adopted a hybrid approath. They are blending the developmentalism of yesterday with the entrepreneurialism of today. To offer skills development and jobs to the unemployed, they are resuscitating public works projects or providing training workshops. They are also promising to build affordable housing and subsidize basic necessities such as electricity and water in urban areas, or fertilizer and seeds in rural areas.

At the same time, these are entrepreneurial states. They are relying on sovereign wealth funds, the pension funds of government employees, or development finance institutions to invest alongside the private sector in shopping malls, office complexes, banks, and tourist resorts. States are thus engaging in a delicate balancing act between catering to economically vulnerable or historically disadvantaged sectors of the population (who may also be voters) and partnering with capital in potentially lucrative projects.

Reward and Risk

Without a doubt, African countries today have very different economic and political orientations from what they had just 20 years ago. Political and economic liberalization, generously supported by donors and international financial institutions, has stimulated pockets of investments in extractive sectors as well as consumer goods, financial services, and agriculture.

But these developments also come with risks. Much of Africa's wealth is unevenly spread across the continent and tends to be concentrated in resource-rich countries with large populations. In many cases, only a small elite enjoys the benefits from increased investment and global integration. A sizeable percentage of Africa's population continues to live below the poverty line, and many young people on the continent may never have access to a decent income.

Moreover, although many analysts observe that African economies have weathered the recent ups and downs of the global market fairly well the private equity firms that are now spreading across the continent encounter even fewer regulations than they faced in developed countries. Clients of such firms as well as the countries and communities in which they invest are likely to be even less shielded from the effects of poor decision-making or unscrupulous behavior than those who did business with the now defunct investment houses Lehman Brothers or Bear Stearns.

Little is known about how private equity firms operate, who invests in them, or how they build their portfolios. As the global financial crisis emphatically demonstrated, these funds' returns are quite volatile in an economic downturn even when investors are fully informed of the risks. For all of these reasons, Africa's lions are unlikely to rival Asia's tigers anytime soon.

Critical Thinking

1. What factors help to account for Africa's recent impressive economic growth?
2. What role has private equity played in this growth?
3. In what sectors has global demand been the strongest?
4. How is urbanization demonstrating the growing gap between rich and poor in Africa?

Create Central

www.mhhe.com/createcentral

Internet References

Center for Third World Organizing
www.ctwo.org

ENTERWeb
www.enterweb.org

International Monetary Fund (IMF)
www.imf.org

TWN (Third World Network)
www.twnside.org.sg

U.S.Agency for International Development (USAID)
www.usaid.gov

The World Bank
www.worldbank.org

World Trade Organization (WTO)
www.wto.org

Anne Pitcher, *a professor of African studies and political science at the University of Michigan, is the author of* Party Politics and Economic Reform in Africa's Democracies' *(Cambridge University Press, 2012).*

Article

The New Mercantilism: China's Emerging Role in the Americas

ERIC FARNSWORTH

Learning Objectives

After reading this article, you will more clearly understand the following:

- China's search for raw materials and export markets
- Latin American development
- Differences in Chinese and United States economic approaches toward Latin America
- Labor, human rights and environmental protection

My first visit to China was in 1986; my second was in 2010. The difference between the two visits was profound. Within one generation, it seemed as if everything except the Forbidden City and the Great Wall had changed. Cars had replaced bicycles, shining office towers had replaced ramshackle tenements, and consumerism had replaced the dreary economic hopelessness that many Chinese previously endured.

Which is not to say all is well there. Newly acquired wealth exists side by side with abject poverty. Stunning natural beauty contrasts with choking pollution. And overseeing the country's dramatic change is the Communist Party leadership, which remains jealous of its 60-year monopoly on political power and is unwilling to tolerate any challenge to its rule.

To maintain legitimacy and power, the government has made a strategic bet—that it can keep political control by allowing and even encouraging economic liberalization. Growth and job creation are the keys to making this strategy work, and have become a virtual obsession of Chinese leaders. According to the International Monetary Fund, China accounted for almost a fifth of world growth in 2010. Exports have been and continue to be critical to this success; China uses an undervalued currency as a tool to keep global demand for its exports high.

Production, however, requires inputs, and exports require raw materials. Thus, over the past 10 years, China has been on a global hunt for the raw materials that it needs to keep its production lines humming and its people employed, including the additional millions who join the work force every year. Coal, oil and gas, ores and minerals, soy and other agricultural goods: Chinese demand for these has caused a secular shift in global commodities markets.

China's leaders, moreover, are not content to leave their procurement efforts to the vagaries of global markets. Rather, they seek long-term, guaranteed access to raw materials, in some cases even looking to control the means of production and in-country infrastructure such as ports and rail. Raw materials are then turned into value-added products and re-exported from China around the world.

This is a transparently mercantilist strategy, with domestic political requirements at its core. It is a strategy designed, fundamentally, to keep the ruling party in power. It is not a strategy to project power or to contribute to the development of the impoverished abroad. Nor is it a strategy primarily to build political alliances, though political influence will naturally increase with enhanced trade linkages. (China has asked trading partners, for instance, to support the diplomatic isolation of Taiwan.)

It is a strategy, however, that is changing the world. In Latin America, in particular, the impact has been significant, with game-changing implications for economic growth, long-term development, governance, and US policy.

THE DRAGON ENTERS

Traditionally, China had virtually no footprint in Latin America or the Caribbean. It was a region that Chinese leaders considered the "backyard" of the United States and were reluctant to enter. Similarly, Latin American and Caribbean leaders gave almost no thought to China, the exceptions being smaller nations that recognized Taiwan as a result of Taiwanese financial incentives, and extralegal groups like Peru's Shining Path that purposefully fashioned themselves after Maoist revolutionaries.

Latin American and Caribbean trade and investment generally flowed on a north-south axis, with European connections also playing an important role, particularly in economic relations with Brazil and South America's Southern Cone. Japan, too, played an important, though tertiary, trade role.

In recent years, however, China has entered the region forcefully. Between 2000 and 2009, China's imports from Latin America and the Caribbean ballooned from approximately $5 billion to $44 billion. Exports to the region have followed a similar trajectory, rising from $4.5 billion to $42 billion over the same time period. China is now Brazil and Chile's largest trade partner, and may soon be Peru's as well. The United Nations Economic Commission for Latin America and the Caribbean estimates that China will displace the European Union as the second-largest regional trading partner by 2015, and will trail only the United States.

The US share of regional trade, meanwhile, is declining. From 2002 to 2008, the US share of exports to the region fell from 48 to 37 percent, while China's grew from 4 to 10 percent. This trend is likely to continue, especially as China locks in trade arrangements for the long term.

Bilateral free trade agreements are now in force between China and Chile, Costa Rica, and Peru. Additional agreements are just a matter of time. China buys primarily raw materials from Latin America. In fact, commodities make up fully 80 percent of Chinese purchases—driven, again, by China's domestic development needs. As a result of China's dash for growth, cyclical commodities markets have stabilized and prices have remained at historic highs. Conversely, most of what China sends back to Latin America and the Caribbean is in the form of competitively priced manufactured goods, actually threatening the manufacturing base of countries like Mexico, the Central American states, and even Brazil.

This is the very definition of mercantilism. China buys raw materials from the region, engages in value-added production at home, and then re-exports the finished products to Latin America and the Caribbean, thereby undercutting the region's own efforts at value-added production.

At the same time, Latin America and the Caribbean have clearly benefited from selling to China over the past decade. Weak economic growth, averaging little more than 1 percent per year in the 1980s and 1990s, has given way to regional growth rates in the range of 4 to 6 percent. Brazil's growth alone has risen from an average of 1.7 percent annually in the 1998–2003 period to 4.2 percent since 2004. In 2010, Brazil's economy grew an estimated 7.5 percent; projections suggest a sustainable rate of 5.5 percent through 2014. Much of this is a result of trade with China. And the rest of the commodities-exporting nations in the region have experienced similar growth.

TAKING ADVANTAGE

Those countries without much in the way of commodities sales to China, including Mexico and nations in Central America and the Caribbean Basin, have not done as well. In addition to having only limited commodities to sell in the first place, these countries are truly dependent on the US economy as their primary export market for both goods and services, and also the primary economy from which remittances are sent.

Sluggish recovery in the United States will continue to limit Mexican, Central American, and Caribbean Basin growth rates for the foreseeable future, especially as manufactures from the region come under continuing pressure from Chinese imports.

On the other hand, for those nations, primarily in South America, that have been in a position to take advantage, exports of primary goods to China have been one of the key factors keeping their economies out of the depths of the recent recession and leading them to rapid recovery.

It has also had the effect, however, of shielding such countries from the need to reform their economies to promote broad-based development and to position themselves more competitively for the long run. When nations are able to sell as much as they can produce of any particular product, the thinking is generally to continue doing so and reap the rewards. When economies are growing, there is little political imperative or incentive for reform.

China promises only a commercial relationship without political or policy interference.

Yet Latin America continues to lack knowledge-based, value-added innovation and production. Education rates remain comparatively low. Workforce development and the liberalization of labor codes have lagged. Investment in research and development barely registers in most countries. And national development strategies are virtually nonexistent.

Of course, China has aggressively and successfully promoted its own value-added production, in part by insisting on technology transfer and other capacity-building measures whenever Western companies look to gain access to the Chinese marketplace. It is a strategy that has paid off handsomely for the Chinese, who are starting to compete head to head with others on highly sophisticated products.

There is no reason at all why Latin America should not replicate this model (abstaining, of course, from obviously negative aspects of Chinese practices, such as theft of intellectual property). Brazil is beginning to take this approach, insisting on in-country investments, technology transfer, and joint research and development platforms that help to develop local valued-added capabilities and expertise. Others should, too. For example, Bolivia, South America's poorest nation, should refuse to give Beijing access to its massive deposits of lithium unless the Chinese first agree to joint research and development of the technology needed to build the car batteries for which the lithium is intended. Rather than merely mining lithium, Bolivia might then aspire to become a developer of battery technology, reaping rewards from a potentially huge demand for clean energy transportation alternatives.

The ability to promote labor and environmental protections, human rights, and the rule of law is being commensurately reduced.

LET'S MAKE A DEAL

Expanding trade always attracts attention, but headlines are drawn by investment deals—including blockbuster announcements by Chinese officials detailing massive regional investments that they intend to make. The reality of China's investments in the region is, however, somewhat more complex than the headlines would indicate. The actual flow of money has been limited despite announced figures, as China takes steps to learn about and understand markets before actually committing funds. Even so, investments and acquisitions have begun to surge.

Oil and gas deals have been leading the charge, hitting over $13 billion in 2010, up from zero in 2009. China's oil giant Sinopec has been particularly active, announcing in December 2010 that it would acquire Occidental Petroleum Corporation's assets in Argentina for $2.45 billion. This followed hard on Sinopec's October announcement that it would buy 40 percent of the Spanish company Repose's Brazilian assets for $7.1 billion, the biggest acquisition by a Chinese firm in Latin America to date. Additional significant announcements are on the horizon, as Sinopec, China National Offshore Oil Company, and others vie for assets.

Oil and gas are not the only sectors involved, of course. Mining, power generation, fishing, and agriculture deals have also recently occurred and will continue to occur given China's strategic play to lock in access to raw materials. Because they are commodities producers, Argentina, Brazil, Chile, and Peru have benefited handsomely, while Colombia is also on track to benefit and is currently negotiating a free trade agreement with China.

Infrastructure projects are next in line, given Latin America's significant underinvestment in the infrastructure required to take advantage of its emerging role in the global economy. Roads, bridges, railways, ports, and information technology and telecommunications, for example, will all require huge investments in the near term to help make the region more competitive. As well, signature projects in Brazil, as that nation gets ready to host the World Cup in 2014 and the Olympic Summer Games in 2016, will soon come on line.

The Chinese government is supportive of overseas projects generally, and the Bank of China offers attractive finance. With such backing, Chinese companies have been known to make above-market offers on infrastructure projects and for assets such as oil and gas and mineral deposits that otherwise have attracted little attention, guaranteeing that China will be in position to bid successfully.

China has also done investment deals with Venezuela, Ecuador, Cuba, and Bolivia—leftist-run countries that one would predict, if ideology were an overriding factor in Chinese decisions, might attract the lion's share of investment. To date, however, China's commercial relations with Ecuador have been rocky. An April 2010 promise by Beijing to loan $20 billion to Venezuela in order to lock in access to that country's heavy oil remains pending. And Bolivia's takeover of its gas fields did not impress the Chinese, who are looking for long-term certainty in their investments.

In fact, Chinese companies have no problem dealing with populist or authoritarian leaders, but neither are they unduly attracted to doing business in countries ruled by them. With them, it is strictly business. If a decent, risk-adjusted return can be made, and access to a necessary resource guaranteed, the investment will likely be made. Otherwise, it will not. This is a matter not of charity or ideology, but of China's need to meet its domestic demands in the most efficient and effective manner possible.

It must be said that total Chinese foreign direct investment (FDI) in Latin America and the Caribbean is dwarfed by the stock of US investment in the region, and will be for some time. But Chinese investment is increasing rapidly. In 2009, for example, some 17 percent of total Chinese FDI went to Latin America. And Chinese investment is just at the beginning of the curve as the nation pursues its strategy of locking in access to raw materials.

China appears to be less interested in majority control of enterprises than in taking significant minority stakes, which allow Chinese investors to learn the ins and outs of a heretofore unknown marketplace while guaranteeing long-term access to raw materials. Chinese portfolio investment, on the other hand, has only just begun, but it will play an increasingly important role in the region as Chinese investors, like their Western counterparts, seek higher returns in emerging markets in an era of slow growth elsewhere.

RETURNS ON INVESTMENT

As investment increases, the quality of FDI is important to consider. Not all investment is the same. For example, US investors and corporations operating abroad generally follow anticorruption provisions codified in the Foreign Corrupt Practices Act. They abide by corporate governance and reporting requirements. They comply with US and local labor laws and human resources requirements. They transfer technology and management expertise to local markets. They provide access to the global marketplace for local production. They source locally. They pay taxes, even when tax laws, as in Brazil, are complex and impenetrable.

US businesses often pursue corporate social responsibility activities, including humanitarian relief, thereby contributing to local economies and social development.

They hire from the local economy, using a limited number of expatriates to manage operations while building businesses from local hires. And they abide by US government foreign policies—for example, when countries like Myanmar (formerly Burma), Cuba, or Iran are sanctioned.

Of course, not every company is perfect, and nongovernmental organizations have aggressively highlighted instances in which they believe corporate malfeasance has occurred. To the extent it has, wrongdoers should be held accountable. But in the main, US investors are required by their boards to follow these general guidelines as a matter of course.

Chinese companies, on the other hand, are less likely to abide by these guidelines, though their record is not as lengthy or detailed as that for US investors. One issue that almost universally galls observers of Beijing's investment in the region is China's lack of interest in hiring local workers. Labor forces for construction and operations are routinely brought from China to Latin America and the Caribbean. Many if not most of the jobs that could go to locals are reserved for Chinese nationals.

It is a difficult case to make, as a result, that one of Chinese investment's primary benefits to the region has been job creation. Disgruntlement over this trend can be expected to rise as investment increases, unless active steps are taken to reverse course.

More broadly, the political implications of different investment models are important. The United States and other like-minded nations have traditionally used economic and financial incentives to encourage reforms in Latin America and the Caribbean. Tools have included bilateral and regional trade agreements, market access agreements, defense and security relations, equipment sales and transfer, training and capacity building, and foreign assistance. Areas of interest to US policy makers run the gamut from democracy to human rights, from labor rights to the environment, from investor protections to intellectual property provisions.

The US trade agreement with Colombia, for example, was signed in 2006 but remains pending, given Washington's expressed concerns over labor rights and protections in Colombia. A trade agreement with Peru was held up pending the resolution of environmental concerns. The North American Free Trade Agreement required side agreements on both labor and environmental issues before Congress approved it. A unilateral Andean trade preferences program requires that recipient nations cooperate fully on counternarcotics and also maintain appropriate investment climates. And so on.

China, on the other hand, promises a commercial relationship without political or policy interference in the nations in question. Chinese investors are not hung up on whether a host nation's government is capitalist or populist, authoritarian or democratic, corrupt or not. They certainly do not care if the government is pro-United States or anti-United States.

The Chinese do not care if their investments prop up local bad guys or undercut collective international efforts to enforce norms of behavior. Their emphasis is on doing business effectively and undisturbed. For domestic purposes, they have pursued a strategy of business for business's sake in Latin America and the Caribbean, as they have around the world; they are not attempting to change the world.

CONQUISTADORS

And yet, the world is changing, because by acting in this manner, Beijing offers to the countries of Latin America and the Caribbean the opportunity to forge a path independent of the United States and liberal economic orthodoxy. This is attractive to them, particularly when the US economy is struggling, and to the extent that US leaders at times have been overbearing and self-interested in their actions toward the region. Regional elites have often chafed at what they consider to be the United States' patronizing tendency to use trade and investment to leverage sensitive domestic political changes.

At the same time, the ability of the United States and other Western nations to promote labor and environmental protections, human rights, and the rule of law in Latin America and the Caribbean is being commensurately reduced by the increase in Chinese economic activity. The region is beginning to have other options, a trend cheered by those who most disdain the perceived historic role that the United States has played in the region, and by those who mistakenly view trade itself as an exploitative mechanism that primarily benefits the United States. (This view is particularly pronounced within the human rights and development communities, without the recognition that trade and investment are among the most potent tools that the United States has for promoting the agendas that they themselves hold dear.)

This is ironic. For years, Latin American and Caribbean elites and observers have railed against the United States for its alleged exploitation of Latin America's natural resources, claiming that the North Americans came to conquer, despoil the landscape, impoverish the region, and make off with the riches of the continent.

An entire literature has arisen around these themes, the most famous example of which, perhaps, is Uruguayan journalist Eduardo Galeano's *Open Veins of Latin America: Five Centuries of the Pillage of a Continent.* Though it was written in 1971, the book remains popular with a new generation of leaders, including Venezuelan President Hugo Chávez, who mischievously presented a copy to President Barack Obama at the Summit of the Americas in Trinidad and Tobago in April 2009.

Even Hollywood has gotten into the act. Filmmaker Oliver Stone's 2010 documentary "South of the Border" purports to show that the United States, global capitalism, and the corporate media have caused the ills of the Western Hemisphere. The primary explanation for a lack of development and opportunity in Latin America is the predatory and exploitative behavior of the developed world, with the private sector at the vanguard, supported by the raw military, financial, and political muscle of a hegemonic United States.

This line of thinking is a tired and tiresome approach to analyzing the Americas, and has been widely and repeatedly debunked. At the same time, one often hears across Latin America—including from populist, anti-US leaders—that building relations with China and welcoming Chinese trade and investment are national priorities.

China is now Brazil and Chile's largest trade partner, and may soon be Peru's as well.

For countries such as Brazil, Chile, and Peru, links with China are intended to help build economies. For the new administration of President Juan Manuel Santos in Colombia, China links provide a means to develop a healthier, less dependent relationship with the United States. For others, they are seen as a means of diversifying relations away from traditional trade and investment patterns and the political connections that develop alongside them, while providing new economic options that will allow greater flexibility in governing.

Venezuela's Chávez is the best example of this latter category, particularly regarding the president's desire to diversify the markets for his country's heavy crude away from the United States. Accomplishing this will require massive investments in infrastructure, including specially built refineries, along the Venezuela-to-China supply chain. Economically, this makes zero sense. Politically, it makes a great deal of sense to Chávez. And if it guarantees the Chinese access to Venezuelan crude over the long term, it is win-win, even though the arrangement may take years to materialize fully.

HARD THINKING

At a time when Latin American economies are growing, and when many countries are gaining a new sense of confidence and of a direction apart from the United States, the region is running headlong into an economic embrace of China. This is not to suggest that China will supplant the United States in investment any time soon, or that Chinese economic linkages will lead to political meddling or adventurism from Beijing.

In fact, neither the pronouncements nor the behavior of the Chinese to this point support the contentions of conservative US commentators that Beijing entertains strategic political or military designs on the Western Hemisphere. There is no evidence that China aspires to take over the Panama Canal or otherwise project power into the region. The United States will remain the strongest nation in the Western Hemisphere, albeit less able over time to determine the outcome of regional events.

Still, as economic links with China proliferate, it must be asked whether China is good for the Americas beyond the short-term economic gain it provides, no matter how beneficial this has been and will continue to be for the foreseeable future. One wonders why regional leaders and observers, so quick to condemn the United States for its alleged pillaging of the continent, have not seen fit to raise their voices to question the Chinese approach—an approach that is straightforwardly mercantilist and is lacking in any of the benevolent or pro-development impulses that can be found in US engagement with the region, including the promotion of international norms and Western values.

China's involvement in the region is not illegitimate, illegal, or even necessarily threatening, despite being economically unbalanced. But people in the region do need to think hard about the best means to ensure that Chinese engagement benefits the region over the long term, and not just in the short run.

Correspondingly, the United States needs to meet its own obligations in the hemisphere—from passing pending trade agreements to engaging with the people of the region in a manner that is conducive to cooperation and mutual respect. Perhaps then the silly idea so frequently heard in policy circles and around the region—that Chinese economic engagement is unquestionably positive for the Americas, while US economic engagement is exploitative and should be resisted—can be put to rest. The outcome of this debate will, in any event, help determine Latin America and the Caribbean's political direction, as well as its development prospects, for many years to come.

Challenge Questions

After reading this article, you will be able to answer the following questions:

1. What might be the consequences of the Chinese economic penetration of Latin America and the position of the United States in the region?
2. What dangers does Chinese economic policy pose for Latin American development?
3. What is the connection between Chinese domestic politics and its foreign trade and investment policies?
4. What is meant by the term "mercantilism"?

Article

A Few Dollars at a Time

How to Tap Consumers for Development

PHILIPPE DOUSTE-BLAZY AND DANIEL ALTMAN

Starting in this quarter, hundreds of millions of people will have an unprecedented opportunity to help the world's most unfortunate inhabitants. When purchasing airline tickets through most major reservation websites or through a travel agent, consumers will be asked if they want to make a direct contribution to the fight against the world's three deadliest epidemics: HIV/AIDS, malaria, and tuberculosis. Part of a movement called innovative financing, the project is a new kind of aid that could fundamentally change the relationship between the rich and the poor throughout the world, a few dollars at a time.

Awareness about the epidemics that rage throughout the developing world occasionally crests in the international media when there is an outbreak, as there was of the Ebola virus in the 1990s and of dengue fever in the first years of this century. These periodic outbreaks usually subside within a year or two, or at least are contained before they become pandemics. The HIV/AIDS, malaria, and tuberculosis epidemics have shown more staying power, however, and even now, after years of attention and treatment, each of these diseases still causes more deaths in developing countries than any other single disease, according to the World Health Organization. In 2004, the last year for which statistics were available at the time of this writing, together these three diseases caused one in eight deaths in low-income countries.

Part of the reason these diseases are so harmful is that they reinforce one another. Hundreds of millions of people around the world have latent tuberculosis infections. In most cases, tuberculosis never becomes active, but the disease is much more likely to explode into a full-blown infection, and the infection tends to be much more severe, in people who also have HIV/AIDS. Even those without latent tuberculosis are more susceptible to getting the disease if they already have HIV/AIDS. This is partly because HIV/AIDS suppresses the immune system—which also means that it is harder for people with HIV/AIDS to fight off malaria. And completing the vicious circle, malaria seems to make HIV/AIDS worse: studies by researchers at the Centers for Disease Control suggest that the body encourages HIV to replicate when it creates antigens to fight malaria. Not surprisingly, patients in the developing world—especially in the tropical zones of Latin America, the Caribbean, Africa, and Southeast Asia—are often diagnosed with two or three of these diseases. It makes sense, then, to fight all three together.

Why make them a priority? Worldwide, the mortality rate for heart disease and cancer combined is five times as high as the mortality rate for HIV/AIDS, malaria, and tuberculosis combined. But unlike HIV/AIDS and tuberculosis, heart disease and cancer are not contagious. Heart disease and cancer also tend to prey on the aged, whereas HIV/AIDS, malaria, and tuberculosis kill millions of young adults, children, and babies every year. The World Health Organization estimates that HIV/AIDS and malaria together kill more children under the age of five than all forms of cancer and heart disease combined. By contrast, the American Heart Association reports that 83 percent of people who die from coronary heart disease in the United States are 65 or older. Tuberculosis kills across all ages, but the average age at death is dropping in many countries because of the disease's association with HIV/AIDS.

Stopping HIV/AIDS, malaria, and tuberculosis does not just add a few years to someone's life; it adds a lifetime. Moreover, these lifetimes add real value to the world, and not just in moral terms. Every life lost to infectious disease represents lost economic activity and lost economic development. For example, the death of all the world's poorest people—those destined to earn just $2 a day for 30 working years (with weekends off)—would mean a loss to the world's future economic output of more than $50 billion every year. And that is not counting the loss to overall economic development in poor countries ravaged by these infectious diseases.

There are economic costs to rich countries, too. Disease-stricken states cannot afford to import as much from wealthier ones as they otherwise would. In addition, the desperation caused by these diseases is a source of instability that can devolve into conflict, sometimes pulling neighboring countries and even global powers into difficult situations. As early as 1987, a CIA report discussed how HIV/AIDS could exacerbate conflict in sub-Saharan Africa. A 2006 study by the Institute for the Theory and Practice of International Relations at the College of William and Mary showed that the prevalence of HIV/AIDS in developing countries was strongly associated with higher levels of civil conflict and more human rights abuses. Recent research by Andrew Price-Smith of Colorado

College has suggested that epidemics can distort demographics by reducing the working-age population, weaken governments, and reduce the state's ability to take care of its people, all effects that in turn can breed conflict. If the world could better control these diseases, the benefits—economic, social, and otherwise—would be remarkable.

The good news is that HIV/AIDS, malaria, and tuberculosis are completely controllable diseases; successful treatments are available for all three. The hard part is purchasing and delivering the treatments. The United Nations took up this challenge when its members set the Millennium Development Goals and committed themselves to reversing the spread of these three diseases and to making treatments available to everyone who needed them by 2015. In 2002, the UN's members founded the Global Fund to Fight AIDS, Tuberculosis and Malaria as a central source of financing. The deadline is only five years away, however, and the effort is running tragically behind schedule.

This is largely for lack of money. In 2007, according to the Organization for Economic Cooperation and Development, 22 wealthy countries on its Development Assistance Committee gave $118 billion in direct aid to the developing world but earmarked only $5.3 billion of this for health programs. (Much greater sums went to education, infrastructure, industrial assistance, and debt restructuring.) At the beginning of 2007, according to the World Health Organization, more than five million HIV-positive people in developing countries needed antiretroviral treatment but were not receiving it. To treat all of them every day for a year with just the most basic regimen of drugs would have required raising global aid for health by 20–30 percent. To treat them with the latest generation of antiretroviral drugs would have required more than doubling health-related aid—and that would have been for just HIV/AIDS. There is an enormous gap in the funding for the fight against infectious diseases. The pressing question of how to close it is a matter of life or death for hundreds of thousands of people every year.

A Penny for Your Tickets

One of the most promising methods for closing the gap is innovative financing. The goal of this kind of development aid is to harness markets in an intense effort to quickly raise hundreds of millions, perhaps even billions, of dollars—the kind of money that can make a real difference in the development, purchasing, and delivery of life-saving treatments. Starting big and front-loading investments creates incentives for researchers to look for new treatments, encourages pharmaceutical companies to design the resulting drugs so that they are easy to distribute and administer in poor countries, and reduces the drugs' prices by guaranteeing bulk orders.

A handful of such programs have sprung up in the past several years. For example, the International Finance Facility for Immunization, a charitable corporation set up in 2006 under the auspices of the British government, issues bonds guaranteed by the governments of wealthy countries to raise hundreds of millions of dollars a year for vaccines. The governments repay the bonds over time. So far, the International Finance Facility for Immunization has collected $1.6 billion in up-front cash. Another initiative, (Red), collects donations from companies that sell goods and services under its (Product) Red brand, which is advertised to consumers as a charitable endeavor. Participating brands include household names such as American Express, Apple, Converse, Gap, and Hallmark. Together, they have raised $130 million in three years.

And then there is UNITAID. The program, under the auspices of the World Health Organization, stands apart for collecting money directly from consumers and businesses through the worldwide market for airline tickets. The idea is to share a tiny fraction of globalization's enormous economic gains with sick people in poor countries. UNITAID does not require consumers to buy any particular brand. In 13 countries, whenever consumers purchase an airline ticket, a small tax—sometimes as little as $1—is set aside for the fight against the three major epidemics. With this simple model, UNITAID raised $1.2 billion in the first three years of its existence. And it has begun to finance the antiretroviral treatments of three out of four children who receive treatment for HIV/AIDS, help treat over one million people for tuberculosis, buy 20 million bed nets to protect against malaria-carrying mosquitoes, and more.

Innovative financing sprang from the recognition by former French President Jacques Chirac, Brazilian President Luiz Inácio Lula da Silva, and former Chilean President Ricardo Lagos that the Millennium Development Goals could not be met with official aid alone. A commission of academics and policy experts established by Chirac to investigate other options released scores of ideas in late 2004. The one that grabbed Chirac's attention called for collecting revenue from a tiny tax on transactions in some major industry—currency exchange, carbon-emissions trading, cars, air travel—and committing it to one or more of the Millennium Development Goals.

The three leaders eventually settled on the idea of an airline-ticket tax, and one of us, Philippe Douste-Blazy, then the French foreign minister, proposed that he and his staff turn the idea into reality. The genius of the tax was not only that it would be a tiny levy on a very broad base but also that it would not significantly affect the flow of travelers to the countries that instituted it. If the French government implemented the tax, for example, it would apply only to tickets purchased in France. As a result, French people might be marginally discouraged from flying, but not foreigners traveling to France, unless they bought their tickets in countries that also had the tax. It would be the first time in modern history that countries would be levying a tax on their own citizens exclusively for the benefit of citizens of other countries.

The French and Chilean governments began collecting the tax within a year. South Korea and nine African countries soon followed suit. Before Chirac left office in 2007, the program was housed at the World Health Organization under the name UNITAID, derived from the French "tous unis pour aider" (everyone united to help). The board of UNITAID was composed of representatives from its founding countries—Brazil, Chile, France, Norway, and the United Kingdom—with additional seats for representatives from Africa, Asia, international health groups, and nongovernmental organizations, including patients' rights groups.

Soon, the organization began to receive direct contributions from a few European governments and from the Bill and Melinda Gates Foundation. These were motivated not just by UNITAID's pioneering role in innovative financing but also by its novel approach to spending. UNITAID's board remains committed to financing programs that will have a major impact on HIV/AIDS, malaria, and tuberculosis all at once: creating the first child-sized doses of antiretroviral medicines, lowering the prices of the most cutting-edge malaria treatments to match those of old-fashioned quinine pills, and commercializing the first child-specific drug for tuberculosis. It has also undertaken to finance these treatments as long as the patients need them, something that governments, which allot foreign aid on a yearly basis through an onerous political process, can rarely do. UNITAID can achieve these things because its immense spending power allows it to purchase hundreds of millions of dollars' worth of treatments. Pharmaceutical companies thus have an incentive to reformat medicines—creating, for example, pediatric doses and transforming difficult-to-measure syrups into pills—and to reprice them for underserved populations in the developing world.

One by one, countries began adopting the tax. By the end of 2007, 17 states had passed a law that would implement it and 17 more were considering doing so.

Good Travels

But there was limited enthusiasm in the world's biggest market for airline tickets, the United States. And so it seemed clear that if UNITAID was to become truly global, it would need a complementary approach: voluntary contributions. This idea was the brainchild of Jean-François Rial, a French entrepreneur who heads Voyageurs du Monde, France's leading tourism agency. Realizing that only three companies (Sabre, Amadeus, and Travelport) controlled the reservation systems for two billion plane tickets issued each year—roughly 80 percent of the world's total—he reasoned that if those three companies incorporated a voluntary-contribution mechanism into their reservation software, travelers around the world would have a chance to directly fund the fight against HIV/AIDS, malaria, and tuberculosis.

After two years of development, the mechanism is expected to launch on all three systems this quarter. Travelers from any country who book a trip with Expedia, Opodo, or Travelocity, among many other websites, will be asked during checkout whether they would like to contribute two dollars, two euros, or two pounds to save the lives of poor people. The prompt will be seamlessly integrated into the booking experience—a pop-up window on the computer screen, a box for the travel agent to check. Within weeks, it will become a routine part of life for millions of travelers around the globe—a routine with the potential to help save as many as three million lives every year and prevent the loss of tens of billions of dollars annually in new economic activity, increasing opportunities for growth in poor countries and limiting some of the causes of instability and conflict. The contributors will also have a chance to interact with one another and possibly with the people they are helping through an associated online social initiative called Massive Good. Such communication will enable participants to make the program even more effective: they will be able to encourage businesses where they live to opt for the voluntary contribution when those businesses book travel, and they will be able to check that the treatments arrived at their destinations.

A preliminary study conducted by McKinsey & Company in 2007 suggested that the new mechanism could raise $1 billion in its first four years, almost doubling UNITAID's budget from the airline-ticket tax and other contributions. With this money, UNITAID is now helping manufacturers of generic drugs roll the various medicines needed to treat an epidemic into a single pill. To achieve this, UNITAID is trying to persuade the pharmaceutical companies that developed those medicines to pool their intellectual property and offer it as a package to generic-drug manufacturers. Creating a single pill would greatly simplify the treatment of all three major epidemics—an unprecedented move in public health. UNITAID also hopes to launch a satellite tracking mechanism so that contributors can follow the journey of the treatments they purchase from the factories to the patients, thereby reinforcing solidarity between the world's rich and the world's poor.

Supplements, Not Replacements

Voluntary contributions come with some downsides, however. Most notably, if the program succeeds, the governments of wealthy countries might feel less obligated to send official aid overseas. This possibility could become especially likely during an economic downturn, when governments might be looking for excuses to cut foreign aid—even as they hand out hundreds of billions of dollars to save their troubled banks and insurance companies. Conversely, if the voluntary-contribution scheme were to founder, these governments might take that as a popular verdict against the Millennium Development Goals and use it as a pretext to reduce their official aid.

Some of the nongovernmental organizations that fight HIV/AIDS, malaria, and tuberculosis also might have reason for concern. These groups depend on official aid, in addition to private donations, for a large part of their funding, and they might resent seeing heads of state celebrate the launch of a voluntary-contribution scheme while they freeze or trim that support. Because UNITAID and the other innovative financing mechanisms channel most of their spending through a few big delivery organizations, such as UNICEF and the Clinton HIV/AIDS Initiative, they cannot replace the efforts of hundreds of smaller groups working on locally targeted programs.

This concern is of paramount importance for all innovative financing mechanisms, which were intended as supplements, not replacements, to help close the gap between official aid and the huge sums necessary to turn the tide against the three big epidemics once and for all. If governments invoke these financing schemes as substitutes for official aid, then those funds' very purpose will be defeated. To avoid this, the Millennium Foundation for Innovative Finance for Health, which is a UNITAID partner, and other independent or quasi-independent entities will have to hold governments to account, by shaming them publicly for cutting aid budgets when they do and by holding them to their promises that they will increase aid at least enough to keep up with inflation. The backers of innovative financing mechanisms, such as UNITAID, have two main responsibilities: to help fight diseases through novel ways of raising money and also to ensure that their success does not undermine the existing efforts they set out to strengthen.

Critical Thinking

1. What is helping to finance the campaign against HIV/AIDS, malaria, and tuberculosis?
2. Why are these diseases so harmful? Why target them in particular?
3. What are the potential costs to the rich states of these diseases?
4. What is the goal of innovative financing?
5. What are the downsides of voluntary contributions?

Philippe Douste-Blazy, who served as France's Foreign Minister from 2005 to 2007, is currently the United Nations' Special Adviser for Innovative Financing for Development and Chair of UNITAID. **Daniel Altman** is President of North Yard Economics, a not-for-profit consulting firm serving developing countries. This article is adapted from their book on innovative financing, which will be published in January 2010 by PublicAffairs.

Article

Haiti Doesn't Need Your Old T-Shirt

The West can (and should) stop dumping its hand-me-downs on the developing world.

CHARLES KENNY

The Green Bay Packers this year beat the Pittsburgh Steelers to win Super Bowl XLV in Arlington, Texas. In parts of the developing world, however, an alternate reality exists: "Pittsburgh Steelers: Super Bowl XLV Champions" appears emblazoned on T-shirts from Nicaragua to Zambia. The shirt wearers, of course, are not an international cadre of Steelers die-hards, but recipients of the many thousands of excess shirts the National Football League produced to anticipate the post-game merchandising frenzy. Each year, the NFL donates the losing team's shirts to the charity World Vision, which then ships them off to developing countries to be handed out for free.

Everyone wins, right? The NFL offloads 100,000 shirts (and hats and sweatshirts) that can't be sold—and takes the donation as a tax break. World Vision gets clothes to distribute at no cost. And some Nicaraguans and Zambians get a free shirt. What's not to like?

Quite a lot, as it happens—so much so that there's even a Twitter hashtag, #SWEDOW, for "Stuff We Don't Want," to track such developed-world offloading, whether it's knit teddy bears for kids in refugee camps, handmade puppets for orphans, yoga mats for Haiti, or dresses made out of pillowcases for African children. The blog *Tales from the Hood,* run by an anonymous aid worker, even set up a SWEDOW prize, won by Knickers 4 Africa, a (thankfully now defunct) British NGO set up a couple of years ago to send panties south of the Sahara.

Here's the trouble with dumping stuff we don't want on people in need: What they need is rarely the stuff we don't want. And even when they do need that kind of stuff, there are much better ways for them to get it than for a Western NGO to gather donations at a suburban warehouse, ship everything off to Africa or South America, and then try to distribute it to remote areas. World Vision, for example, spends 58 cents per shirt on shipping, warehousing, and distributing them, according to data reported by the blog *Aid Watch*—well within the range of what a secondhand shirt costs in a developing country. Bringing in shirts from outside also hurts the local economy: Garth Frazer of the University of Toronto estimates that increased used-clothing imports accounted for about half of the decline in apparel industry employment in Africa between 1981 and 2000. Want to really help a Zambian? Give him a shirt made in Zambia.

Perhaps the most embarrassing moment was when the United States airdropped 24 million Pop-Tarts on Afghanistan.

The mother of all SWEDOW is the $2 billion-plus U.S. food aid program, a boondoggle that lingers on only because of the lobbying muscle of agricultural conglomerates. (Perhaps the most embarrassing moment was when the United States airdropped 2.4 million Pop-Tarts on Afghanistan in January 2002.) Harvard University's Nathan Nunn and Yale University's Nancy Qian have shown that the scale of U.S. food aid isn't strongly tied to how much recipient countries actually require it—but it does rise after a bumper crop in the American heartland, suggesting that food aid is far more about dumping American leftovers than about sending help where help's needed. And just like secondhand clothing, castoff food exports can hurt local economies. Between the 1980s and today, subsidized rice exports from the United States to Haiti wiped out thousands of local farmers and helped reduce the proportion of locally produced rice consumed in the country from 47 to 15 percent. Former President Bill Clinton concluded that the food aid program "may have been good for some of my farmers in Arkansas, but it has not worked.... I had to live every day with the consequences of the lost capacity to produce a rice crop in Haiti to feed those people because of what I did."

Bottom line: Donations of cash are nearly always more effective. Even if there are good reasons to give stuff rather than money, in most cases the stuff can be bought locally. Economist Amartya Sen, for example, has conclusively shown that people rarely die of starvation or malnutrition because of a lack of food in the neighborhood or the country. Rather, it is because they can't afford to buy the food that's available.

Yet, as Connie Veillette of the Center for Global Development reports, shipping U.S. food abroad in response to humanitarian disasters is so cumbersome it takes four to six months to get there after the crisis begins. Buying food locally, the U.S. Government Accountability Office has found, would be 25 percent cheaper and considerably faster, too.

In some cases, if there really is a local shortage and the goods really are needed urgently, the short-term good done by clothing or food aid may well outweigh any long-term costs in terms of local development. But if people donate SWEDOW, they may be less likely to give much-needed cash. A study by Aradhna Krishna of the University of Michigan, for example, suggests that charitable giving may be lower among consumers who buy cause-related products because they feel they've already done their part. Philanthrocapitalism may be chic: The company Toms Shoes has met with considerable commercial success selling cheap footwear with the added hook that for each pair you buy, the company gives a pair to a kid in the developing world (it's sold more than a million pairs to date). But what if consumers are buying Toms instead of donating to charity, as some surely are? Much better to stop giving them the stuff we don't want—and start giving them the money they do.

Critical Thinking

1. What is wrong with donating unneeded clothing to poor countries?
2. How does U.S. food aid affect recipient countries?
3. What do poor countries need most?

Charles Kenny, a Schwartz fellow at the New America Foundation, is the author of *Getting Better: Why Global Development Is Succeeding and How We Can Improve the World Even More*.

Article

Prepared by: Robert J. Griffiths, *University of North Carolina at Greensboro*

Please, Don't Send Food

A new study suggests that food aid could actually prolong conflict rather than resolve it.

JOSHUA E. KEATING

Learning Outcomes

After reading this article, you will be able to:

- Describe the connection between food aid and civil conflict.

There's been plenty of debate in recent years about whether humanitarian aid actually helps rid the world of extreme poverty. The inability of developed countries to make a dent in the problem, despite spending billions of dollars each year, is what economist and noted aid skeptic William Easterly calls the "second tragedy" of global poverty. But a recent study takes this skepticism to a whole new level, suggesting that food aid not only doesn't work, but also can prolong the violent conflicts it's meant to help resolve.

Looking at a sample of developing countries between 1972 and 2006, economists Nancy Qian of Yale University and Nathan Nunn of Harvard University found a direct correlation between U.S. food aid and civil conflict. For every 10 percent increase in the amount of food aid delivered, they discovered, the likelihood of violent civil conflict rises by 1.14 percentage points.

The results confirm anecdotal reports that food aid during conflicts is often stolen by armed groups, essentially making international donors part of the rebel logistics effort. According to some estimates, as much as 80 percent of the food aid shipments to Somalia in the early 1990s was looted or stolen. In her book *The Crisis Caravan,* journalist Linda Polman reported how Hutu rebels who fled Rwanda after the 1994 genocide appropriated aid given out in refugee camps in neighboring Democratic Republic of the Congo, further fueling conflict in the region. Polman also estimated that Nigeria's 1967–1970 Biafran war—one of the first African humanitarian crises to get global media attention—may have lasted 12 to 16 months longer than it otherwise would have because of the international aid seized by rebel groups.

More recently, during the war in Afghanistan, there have been widespread reports of everything from Pop-Tarts to staple goods being resold at local markets. Even more worryingly, up to one-third of the aid to Uruzgan province has reportedly fallen into Taliban hands.

Does this mean we shouldn't give any aid at all? Of course not, say the study's authors, who hope instead that the United States, which is the world's largest supplier of food aid, shipping out 2.5 million metric tons in 2010, will reconsider just how this aid is given out. Qian points to the often arbitrary way the United States increases aid during times of domestic agricultural surplus as particularly dangerous. When American farmers grow more food, Washington tends to give away more, regardless of need.

Qian argues that it's time we all get a little more selective about giving. "If you randomly assign aid to countries without considering what's going on, that's going to increase conflict," she says. The main takeaway is if you want to stop civil wars, you've got to stop feeding the warriors.

Critical Thinking

1. How does food aid help to prolong conflict?
2. What factors often determine whether food aid is provided?

Create Central

www.mhhe.com/createcentral

Internet References

Center for Third World Organizing
www.ctwo.org

ENTERWeb
www.enterweb.org

International Monetary Fund (IMF)
www.imf.org

TWN (Third World Network)
www.twnside.org.sg

U.S.Agency for International Development (USAID)
www.usaid.gov

The World Bank
www.worldbank.org

World Trade Organization (WTO)
www.wto.org

Article

Prepared by: Robert J. Griffiths, *University of North Carolina at Greensboro*

It's Economics, Stupid

Mobile Technology in Low-Income Countries

IQBAL Z. QUADIR

Learning Outcomes

After reading this article, you will be able to:

- Outline the links between mobile phones, economic opportunity, and government accountability.
- Explain how the mobile phone business represents an alternative development approach.

In a recent article in *Time,* former United States president Bill Clinton lists five global phenomena as causes for optimism, beginning with the assertion that "phones mean freedom." Clinton explains that mobile phones "foster equality" and have "revolutionized the average person's access to financial opportunity," citing a 2010 UN study that found that mobile phones are "one of the most effective advancements in history to lift people out of poverty." To expand on Clinton's important observations, it is notable that the device that "fosters equality" and "lift[s] people out of poverty" is by and large provided by entrepreneurs and businesses seeking to make a profit.

In other words, a largely commercial phenomenon has brought about remarkable "social progress" in low-income countries. Mobile phones were developed in the United States, eventually deployed to low-income countries through commercial processes and, because of certain qualities, embraced in these countries, where they have had tremendous impact. I estimate that mobile phones have been responsible for a quarter-trillion US dollars in the economies of the world's so-called poverty belt—South Asia and Sub-Saharan Africa—alone, to say nothing of the impact in the rest of the world. Mobiles also have enormous potential as a platform for other businesses in areas such as banking and healthcare and can help otherwise voiceless citizens to organize politically, but that is beyond the scope of this piece. Here, I focus instead on mobiles as one example of a productivity tool—and on their global spread as a model for promoting other such tools.

A New Approach to Development

Given the magnitude of their economic impact, the example of mobiles should spur us to revisit the nature of economic development and related US foreign policy, which generally focus on the governments of low-income countries in any approach to development. In this context, the attention to mobiles by a US president, a leading executor of foreign policies for a period of up to eight years, is particularly noteworthy.

US foreign policy over the last seven decades has regarded governments as the key actors in solving the pressing issues of low-income countries—poverty, bad governance, cultural impediments to democratic progress, and demagoguery among many others, but such a focus may actually exacerbate these problems. Instead, we must look at what actually improves the economic lives of ordinary people. Economically strong citizens, in turn, make their governments more accountable and friendly to worthy causes, including a peaceful and prosperous world. If the effort to economically strengthen the citizenry becomes our endeavor, then mobiles certainly are a striking example. Mobiles have demonstrated that the key to progress—both for low-income countries and in the context of US global interests—is the advancement of commerce as the antidote to many of the ills beleaguering low-income countries.

The commercial nature of mobiles and their potential for broad-ranging social impact are fundamentally intertwined. First, mobiles help ordinary low-income people make economic gains, enabling them to pay for the services; this is particularly apparent in the spread of mobiles in areas where people would not have otherwise been able to afford such devices. Simultaneously, businesses profit from the sale of phones and associated services. Low-income economies advance, while high-income economies enjoy increased exports of equipment to low-income ones. Mobiles have demonstrated that billions of people who fall far short of Western standards in terms of their consumption of basic goods—food, water, medicine, shelter, and education—will purchase a commercial product to make economic gains, in effect voting with their hard-earned money on what actually advances their lives. It all works because someone can spend a little to make a call that advances her economic situation a lot by saving time, money, labor, transportation, and opportunity costs.

From Luxury Item to Mass Product

Mobile phones, powered by microchips that also power computers, can be seen as a model for other devices or technologies; they are simply tools for bolstering productivity, which allow ordinary people, businesses, and economies to advance in tandem. Mobiles have been somewhat unusual, however, in the radical pace at which their prices declined, and the consequences of this particular set of circumstances point to important lessons for economic development.

Mobiles' rapid decline in price is explained by a phenomenon known as Moore's Law, named after Gordon Moore, the founder of Intel. Moore observed in the mid-1960s that the processing power on a microchip can be doubled every 18 months for ongoing scientific and engineering advancements, implying a thousand-fold increase in processing power over 15 years and a million-fold increase in 30 years. Indeed, Moore's Law stands today. The astronomical rise in processing power and precipitous drop in price for mobile phones in the 1990s created an unusual situation whereby a luxury product became a mass product over the short course of a decade.

In the early 1990s, when only a few percent of the US population used mobile phones, governments in low-income countries were not interested in getting involved in the sector nor could justify soliciting "aid" for such involvement. The subsequent rapid transformation in accessibility of mobile phones thus led to the accidental ceding of the mobile industry to entrepreneurs and businesses.

It is important here to comprehend the magnitude of challenges faced by innovators and entrepreneurs in low-income countries under typical circumstances. In most low-income countries, either because of government ownership of economic assets or through extensive red tape, entrepreneurs and businesses are often unable to innovate and grow. Disproportionate state power manifests in undue interventions. Anne Krueger, former World Bank Chief Economist, explained in her 1974 paper on rent seeking that "government interventions [are] frequently all-embracing" in low-income countries. Aid from other countries only magnifies the issue; in a 2004 study, Karen Remmer found that aid money expands the receiving governments and encourages centralized planning and rule-making, leading to extensive bureaucratic red tape.

If mobile phones indeed escaped typical governmental control in low-income countries due to the unusual speed with which they shifted from luxury to mass product, one would expect the governments of countries that introduced mobiles after they had become mass products to keep the sector under state control. That is exactly what happened in Ethiopia and Eritrea; while mobiles were emerging elsewhere in the world, they were embroiled in war. These two countries did not adopt mobiles until 1999, when they were introduced as a state-controlled sector. By that time, the initial success of mobiles in other parts of the world was visible, which probably contributed to the Ethiopian and Eritrean governments' decisions to keep the sector within state control instead of ceding it to private interests; this outcome was most likely bolstered by the relative strength of governments in countries at war.

Mobile Phones Spurring Growth

A Quarter-Trillion Dollar Impact on South Asia and Sub-Saharan Africa

The following is a rough economic calculation of the impact of mobile phones on South Asia and Sub-Saharan Africa, the so-called "poverty belt" of the world and home to 2.3 billion people:

- According to a study of 120 countries by Christine Zhen-Wei Qiang at the World Bank, a 10 percent increase in mobile phone penetration results in a 0.8 percent increase in economic growth. Though Qiang's study did not define the time frame for the 0.8 percent increase, it can be assumed that the impact lasts for more than a year.
- From 1996 to 2011, mobile phone penetration in South Asia and Sub-Saharan Africa combined rose from 0 percent to 63 percent.
- From the above, I roughly—and conservatively—estimate that during this 15-year period the poverty belt experienced on average an additional 1 percent economic growth rate due to mobile phones.
- Within this same period, the combined GDP of South Asia and Sub-Saharan Africa grew, in constant 2000 US dollars, from $811 billion to $1.87 trillion—an average annual growth rate of 5.72 percent.
- Without the impact of mobile phones, I therefore estimate that this economy would have grown at an annual rate of one percentage point fewer (that is, 4.72 percent), and the economy of the poverty belt by 2011 would be only US$1.62 trillion.
- We can, therefore, attribute to mobile phones US$250 billion (constant 2000 US dollars) of the collective GDP of South Asia and Sub-Saharan Africa.

All data from the World Bank.

A Recalibrated Focus

Of greater import than how mobiles ended up in the private sector is the effect of these circumstances: comparing the results of private versus public operation of the mobile phone industry indicates that the former produces markedly better results. To compare, let us continue to study the example of Ethiopia and Eritrea, taking into account the additional case of Afghanistan, which adopted mobiles at a late stage in 2002. However, under

US influence, Afghanistan issued licenses to private companies. Today, Ethiopia, Eritrea, and Afghanistan are comparable countries in terms of income; their GDPs per capita are US$1,100, US$700, and US$1,000, respectively. Yet, Ethiopia and Eritrea have some of the lowest mobile penetration rates in the world (8 percent and 4 percent, respectively), while Afghanistan has achieved a penetration rate of 38 percent. The ability to flourish in the private sector evidently had substantial impact. While governments by definition have the responsibility to provide certain public goods, they do not face pressure to innovate and expand markets. The private sector, on the other hand, motivated by profits, attracts competition. Under competitive pressure, the sector is driven to offer better services, lower prices, greater scale, and relevant innovations.

Despite technological and investment-related differences, a clear pattern emerges in the state-based provision of mobile services and electricity. In most low-income countries, the government controls electricity—and to this day, 87 percent of the rural populations and 56 percent of the urban populations in these countries do not have access to this important resource. State control, in large part, explains these low levels of access. While the mobile sector may have escaped from state control due to unusual circumstances, the fact of the matter is that billions of lives have been improved for a simple lack of state control. If mobiles have advanced the lives of these billions, one might assert that state control of electricity and other resources has held people back.

Like all countries, low-income countries need good governance. Therefore, instead of continuing to pursue prevailing development policies, we should pause to re-examine the thinking that has provided the foundation of the United States. The Founding Fathers of the United States, who reflected on the accumulated wisdom about political economies and thought comprehensively about what makes a stable and prosperous republic, offered pertinent insights on the importance of commerce for such ends. The thinking of the Founding Fathers espoused in the Federalist Papers, which has served the United States well to this day, had economics and commerce at its heart. Alexander Hamilton, who recognized that the United States was "not very opulent" at the time, made it abundandy clear in the Federalist Papers that the main purpose of the Constitution was to secure the commercial success of the United States and to arrange the resources necessary for that commercial success. James Madison considered "the rights of property. . .[as]. . .the first object of government."

Corresponding with the thinking of the Founding Fathers, I argue that just as Clinton focused his presidential campaign with the famous pithy phrase "It's the economy, stupid," US international development policy needs a recalibrated focus on "It's economics, stupid." The greatest contribution of mobile phones to progress, beyond the conveniences they bring, is in helping low-income countries move towards greater commerce. If the example of mobiles can now succeed in moving US foreign policies towards healthier global commercial progress, they will become an even more influential force in society.

Expansion and Unintended Results

When government gains power independent of its citizens, as is the case through aid, it becomes overbearing and intervening. This is not a criticism of specific governments, but rather an observation of the nature of entities that are unchecked by countervailing or interlocking interests from the rest of their societies.

While Krueger and Remmer's observations have shed light on contemporary government interventions in low-income countries, this is a classic observation. Alexander Hamilton emphasized that "in the usual progress of things, the necessities of a nation, in every state of its existence, will be found at least equal to its resources." In other words, governments have resources, they will find ways to use them: necessities are found to match resources, not the other way around. Melancton Smith, an anti-federalist delegate at the Constitutional Convention who disagreed with Hamilton on many fronts, was nonetheless in accordance with Hamilton on this issue, arguing that "all governments find a use for as much money as they can raise." The drive toward expansion occurs even within governments; for example, James Madison repeatedly used language of war (like "attack," "encroach," and "invasion") in the Federalist Papers to describe the potential tendency of one governmental department to intrude into territories of other departments. The desire to expand one's sphere of activities is inherent in human nature and the expansion of the state in low-income countries has been the natural consequence of resources available to the state, including through "aid" money from abroad. Instead of acting as referee for commercial processes, the government becomes a player in a game. In the commercial game, players are properly checked by competition and by governmental supervision; when the government becomes a player instead, these checks fail and, moreover, the government is distracted from governing.

Cultural Impediments and Bad Governance

Many would say that low-income countries are plagued by poor governance, as well as apparent cultural impediments to their economic and social progress. Arguments follow that if a productive, commercial society is to take form, first governments must be reorganized and the mindsets of the citizenry altered. I contend that the process must instead take place in the opposite direction: the progress in Western societies was an effect of commerce, not a precondition for it. Western intellectuals—Adam Smith, Georg Simmel, and Max Weber, among others—have recognized that commerce has positively transformed cultures and behavior, by making people more rational and mutually accountable.

While many development professionals have deduced from the failures of commerce in low-income countries that other avenues need to be found to meet these challenges, these alternatives—state control and interventions—have actually impeded commerce. The solution thus is not implementing an alternative to commerce, but rather the removal of obstacles that stifle its growth.

Mobiles for People of All Walks of Life

Mobiles are:

- *Affordable.* Mobiles are affordable even for ordinary people in low-income countries. Digital technologies—both hardware and software—take billions of dollars to develop but only a few dollars to copy, and prices accordingly have been cascading downward. At the same time, engineering and scientific advancements over decades have made it possible to squeeze increasingly astronomical amounts of processing power into simple devices at a low cost.
- *Easy to use.* Unlike computers, which can be used only by the literate and adequately trained, voice-communication is utilized by virtually everyone in the world. The enormous processing power of mobiles, coupled with their ease of use, makes mobiles profoundly useful to the unskilled and untrained.
- *Universally appealing.* People need to communicate for every imaginable purpose every day, and they are eager to ease that process. In short, mobiles have mass appeal.

In Europe, for example, commerce developed despite opposition from the state and the church. Authorities and other powerful people in pre-modern Europe, like today's governments in low-income countries, imposed various obstructions that caused people to remain poor. These obstructions were gradually removed as people increased their incomes, enticing authorities to align themselves with citizens and thus creating mutually beneficial economic arrangements. For example, members of the British Parliament during the 13th through 17th centuries, knowing that the monarch required their approval to levy taxes, succeeded in extracting various liberties in exchange for higher taxes—money that was generated from commercial processes—and the King's power consequently declined. Similarly, as productivity-enhancing mechanisms and innovations like mobiles allow ordinary people in low-income countries to gain economic clout today, the interests of citizens, businesses, and government come into alignment. This is why Woodrow Wilson, who was a professor of political economy, summarized his reading of history as follows: "The history of liberty is the history of limitations of government power, not the increase of it." In other words, liberty has evolved though citizens' increase of income and their ability to constrain and align with government power.

One of the forms of bad governance plaguing low-income countries today is demagoguery. Countries with regular elections but disproportionate state power often face populist leaders who promise various ways of improving the lives of citizens—banking on political history, personal attacks on other leaders, or how one's character is better or worse than those of others—with little attention to systemic problems. The economically weak citizenry are often unable to hold these governments accountable and can only choose one demagogue over another. Citizens accept this as their fate; they have little time or ability under the circumstances of living in poverty to reflect on how those circumstances can be changed.

Commerce is an antidote to demagoguery. It anchors individual citizens into different groups of economic interests that cannot then be amalgamated by demagogues. In order to prevent potential demagoguery in the United States, James Madison, and other framers of the US Constitution put various checks on the House of Representatives, such as presidential veto and judicial review.

In addition to the constitutional checks, Madison saw that commercial progress gives rise to various different interests groups—"[a] landed interest, a manufacturing interest, a mercantile interest, a moneyed interest, with many lesser interests"—that can prevent demagogues from coalescing people into a common mass. In other words, the Founding Fathers saw commerce not only as an end but also as a means toward good governance. In many low-income countries, in the absence of checks and balances within the government, commerce thus becomes even more crucial to preventing demagoguery.

Fueling the Economy through Mobiles

Mobiles Are Tools for Economic Advancement

There are fundamental economic reasons why ordinary people make meaningful gains through mobiles:

- *Mobiles save time, money, and labor.* Two people can connect to do business in seconds, eliminating the need for expensive travel and transport. The saved time, money, and labor then can be applied for other purposes and contribute to a more complex and diversified economy.
- *Mobiles disperse information beyond local contexts.* Frederick Hayek pointed out in the 1930s that dispersed bits of information, available locally but useful beyond the local setting, are essential ingredients for an economy to gain greater efficiency. For instance, a farmer who notices an oversupply of mangos in his village profits meaningfully if he can discover that a distant town has a shortage of mangos. The ability of mobiles to distribute the local information of many different locations makes the economy more efficient, while individuals profit.
- *Mobiles push the envelope.* With mobiles, people can accomplish things they could not otherwise imagine. Skills, imagination, time, and human contacts now reach further—cheaply and instantaneously. For example, a doctor working in an urban setting had to abandon his ancestral farm to practice medicine. With mobiles, he can practice medicine in town while supervising the manager of his farm.
- *The benefits of mobiles compound.* As mobiles proliferate, all mobiles become more useful because each user can reach a greater number of people.

Interlocking Relationships

Mobiles have not simply flourished commercially, independent of governments; they have started with explicit governmental permissions. The spread of mobiles has successfully created the interlocking economic relationships among citizens, businesses, and governments that have widely proven to be a key to accountability. First, as I have written earlier, citizens pay for a service that generates greater economic value to them, giving them a net gain. Companies that provide the service depend on citizens for their revenues. Through this mutually dependent connection, these companies advance in revenues and profits, enabling them to expand their investment and consumer base. At the same time, these companies pay a substantial amount of taxes to governments: customs duties on imported equipment, value-added taxes on services provided, corporate taxes, and personal taxes paid by people employed by the industry.

These taxes give rise to an interlocking relationship between these companies and governments and, moreover, are collectively much higher than the profits mobile phone companies make. These taxes are also higher than the revenues made by state-owned fixed telephone operators, which usually had a tiny fraction of the subscriber base of today's mobile industry. Governments and their employees become dependent on the mobile industry not only for its services, but also for its revenues. The interlocking relationships between citizens and companies and between industry and government contribute to interrelated accountability and greater governmental dependence on citizens' productivity, a key factor in good governance. Aid impedes rather than builds these beneficial networks of relationships; revenues that are not tied to citizens' productivity generally lead to divergence of interests between governments and their people. Citizens then cannot hold governments accountable, and commerce is stifled.

The story of mobile phones in low-income countries [. . .] is as fundamentally commercial as it is socially impactful.

Unsurprisingly, a process as complex as commerce can give rise to certain problems. Nonetheless, commerce has many self-correcting features. The problems engendered by commerce generally can be addressed by competition among businesses and governmental supervision of businesses. Competition among businesses is rooted in profits; governmental accountability is rooted in citizens' empowerment, which arises through the jobs, training, products and services created through commerce.

Conclusion

Clinton's observation that mobile phones constitute a new kind of freedom reminds us of what John F. Kennedy, in his inauguration speech in 1961, told his "fellow citizens of the world"—that they should "ask not what America will do for [them], but what together we can do for the freedom of man." While Kennedy may have been idealistic, mobiles have actually achieved this goal, decades after being born in US laboratories. Through scientific and engineering breakthroughs, largely in the United States, and many refinements due to global economic forces, mobiles have gone from laboratories to the hands of poor people in developing countries. Because people in low-income countries hold these devices in their hands through their own earnings, they have genuinely given meaning to Kennedy's word "together" in his vision for the creation of freedom. We should also note that Kennedy directed his words to the "citizens of the world," because it is the citizens who must advance economically and politically, and it is they who must produce governments and hold them accountable.

The story of mobile phones in low-income countries, a phenomenon that is as fundamentally commercial as it is socially impactful, offers an important model for continued economic and social progress in low-income countries. Instead of providing aid to governments, why not redirect funds toward the invention of new productivity tools? The possibilities for new instruments of economic empowerment to be held in people's hands are endless. Mobiles have only provided one spectacular example.

Critical Thinking

1. In what ways do mobile phones improve the lives of the poor?
2. How do mobile phones increase government accountability?
3. Why have mobile phone companies prospered from a lack of government involvement in the market?

Create Central

www.mhhe.com/create central

Internet References

Center for Third World Organizing
www.ctwo.org

ENTERWeb
www.enterweb.org

International Monetary Fund (IMF)
www.imf.org

TWN (Third World Network)
www.twnside.org.sg

U.S.Agency for International Development (USAID)
www.usaid.gov

The World Bank
www.worldbank.org

World Trade Organization (WTO)
www.wto.org

IQBAL Z. QUADIR is a professor of practice at MIT, and founder and director of its Legatum Center. In the early 1990s, he realized that mobiles could transform low-income countries and founded Grameenphone, Bangladesh's largest mobile phone company.

Unit 3

UNIT

Prepared by: Robert J. Griffiths, *University of North Carolina at Greensboro*

Conflict and Instability

Conflict and instability in the developing world remain major threats to regional and international peace and security. Conflict stems from a combination of sources, including ethnic and religious diversity, nationalism, the struggle for state control, and competition for resources. In some cases, colonial boundaries either encompass diverse groups or separate people from their ethnic kin, creating the circumstances that can lead to conflict. A state's diversity can increase tension among groups competing for scarce resources and opportunities. When some groups benefit or are perceived as enjoying privileges at the expense of others, ethnicity can offer a convenient vehicle for mobilization. Moreover, ethnic politics lends itself to manipulation both by regimes that are seeking to protect privileges, maintain order, or retain power and those that are challenging existing governments. In an atmosphere charged with ethnic and political tension, conflict and instability often arise as groups vie to gain control of the state apparatus in order to extract resources and allocate benefits. While ethnicity has played a role in many conflicts, competition over power and resources may sometimes be mistaken for ethnic warfare. Weak and failing states with limited capacity are unable to adequately address the poverty and deprivation that often lead to instability and conflict. Failed states also permit the emergence of warlords and may also offer a haven for terrorists and criminals. The spillover from the conflict in these states can also cause wider instability.

Although evidence suggests a decline in violence worldwide, there is no shortage of conflict and instability around the developing world, although the causes may differ from region to region. While the Arab Spring has brought political change to countries where regimes were ousted, the contours of these changes and their effects have yet to be fully determined. Moreover, in some countries the upheaval is still under way. In Syria, the Assad regime's determination to hang onto power has plunged the country into a brutal civil war. Turmoil in the region has also ratcheted up tensions between Iran and Saudi Arabia, only made more dangerous by Iran's nuclear program. On the Korean peninsula, recent provocations by the North, the ascendance to power of Kim Jong-un, and the North's bellicose rhetoric highlight the long-standing security challenges in the region. In Latin America, drug violence is a serious threat to the Mexican government and the effects of the drug trade have spread more broadly to Central America.

Widespread human rights abuses often accompany conflict and instability in the developing world. Humanitarian intervention to prevent such abuses has frequently been hampered by considerations of sovereignty, cost of the operations, and a lack of political will. Although recent experience has better equipped the international community to engage in humanitarian intervention, obstacles to the effectiveness of these efforts and concerns about the cost of these operations remain.

Threats to peace and stability in the developing world remain complicated, dangerous, and clearly have the potential to threaten international security.

Article

World Peace Could Be Closer Than You Think

Joshua S. Goldstein

The World Is a More Violent Place Than It Used to Be—*No Way*

The early 21st century seems awash in wars: the conflicts in Afghanistan and Iraq, street battles in Somalia, Islamist insurgencies in Pakistan, massacres in the Congo, genocidal campaigns in Sudan. All in all, regular fighting is taking place in 18 wars around the globe today. Public opinion reflects this sense of an ever more dangerous world: One survey a few years ago found that 60 percent of Americans considered a third world war likely. Expectations for the new century were bleak even before the attacks of Sept. 11, 2001, and their bloody aftermath: Political scientist James G. Blight and former U.S. Defense Secretary Robert McNamara suggested earlier that year that we could look forward to an average of 3 million war deaths per year worldwide in the 21st century.

So far they haven't even been close. In fact, the last decade has seen fewer war deaths than any decade in the past 100 years, based on data compiled by researchers Bethany Lacina and Nils Petter Gleditsch of the Peace Research Institute Oslo. Worldwide, deaths caused directly by war-related violence in the new century have averaged about 55,000 per year, just over half of what they were in the 1990s (100,000 a year), a third of what they were during the Cold War (180,000 a year from 1950 to 1989), and a hundredth of what they were in World War II. If you factor in the growing global population, which has nearly quadrupled in the last century, the decrease is even sharper. Far from being an age of killer anarchy, the 20 years since the Cold War ended have been an era of rapid progress toward peace.

If the world feels like a more violent place than it actually is, that's because there's more information about wars—not more wars themselves.

Armed conflict has declined in large part because armed conflict has fundamentally changed. Wars between big national armies all but disappeared along with the Cold War, taking with them the most horrific kinds of mass destruction. Today's asymmetrical guerrilla wars may be intractable and nasty, but they will never produce anything like the siege of Leningrad. The last conflict between two great powers, the Korean War, effectively ended nearly 60 years ago. The last sustained territorial war between two regular armies, Ethiopia and Eritrea, ended a decade ago. Even civil wars, though a persistent evil, are less common than in the past; there were about a quarter fewer in 2007 than in 1990.

If the world feels like a more violent place than it actually is, that's because there's more information about wars—not more wars themselves. Once-remote battles and war crimes now regularly make it onto our TV and computer screens, and in more or less real time. Cell-phone cameras have turned citizens into reporters in many war zones. Societal norms about what to make of this information have also changed. As Harvard University psychologist Steven Pinker has noted, "The decline of violent behavior has been paralleled by a decline in attitudes that tolerate or glorify violence," so that we see today's atrocities—though mild by historical standards—as "signs of how low our behavior can sink, not of how high our standards have risen."

America Is Fighting More Wars Than Ever—*Yes and No*

Clearly, the United States has been on a war footing ever since 9/11, with a still-ongoing war in Afghanistan that has surpassed the Vietnam War as the longest conflict in American history and a pre-emptive war in Iraq that proved to be longer, bloodier, and more expensive than anyone expected. Add the current NATO intervention in Libya and drone campaigns in Pakistan, Somalia, and Yemen, and it's no wonder that U.S. military spending has grown more than 80 percent in real terms over the last decade. At $675 billion this year, it's now 30 percent higher than what it was at the end of the Cold War.

But though the conflicts of the post-9/11 era may be longer than those of past generations, they are also far smaller and less lethal. America's decade of war since 2001 has killed about 6,000 U.S. service members, compared with 58,000 in Vietnam and 300,000 in World War II. Every life lost to war is one too many, but these deaths have to be seen in context: Last year more Americans died from falling out of bed than in all U.S. wars combined.

And the fighting in Iraq and Afghanistan has taken place against a backdrop of base closures and personnel drawdowns elsewhere in the world. The temporary rise in U.S. troop numbers in South Asia and the Middle East, from 18,000 to 212,000 since 2000, contrasts with the permanent withdrawal of almost 40,000 troops from Europe, 34,000 from Japan and South Korea, and 10,000 from Latin America in that period. When U.S. forces come home from the current wars—and they will in large numbers in the near future, starting with 40,000 troops from Iraq and 33,000 from Afghanistan by 2012—there will be fewer U.S. troops deployed around the world than at any time since the 1930s. President Barack Obama was telling the truth in June when he said, "The tide of war is receding."

War Has Gotten More Brutal for Civilians—*Hardly*

In February 2010, a NATO airstrike hit a house in Afghanistan's Marja district, killing at least nine civilians inside. The tragedy drew condemnation and made the news, leading the top NATO commander in the country to apologize to Afghan President Hamid Karzai. The response underscored just how much has changed in war. During World War II, Allied bombers killed hundreds of thousands of civilians in Dresden and Tokyo not by accident, but as a matter of tactics; Germany, of course, murdered civilians by the millions. And when today's civilians do end up in harm's way, more people are looking out for them. The humanitarian dollars spent per displaced person rose in real terms from $150 in the early 1990s to $300 in 2006. Total international humanitarian assistance has grown from $2 billion in 1990 to $6 billion in 2000 and (according to donor countries' claims) $18 billion in 2008. For those caught in the crossfire, war has actually gotten more humane.

Yet many people insist that the situation is otherwise. For example, authoritative works on peacekeeping in civil wars (Roland Paris's award-winning *At War's End* and Michael Doyle and Nicholas Sambanis's *Making War and Building Peace*), as well as gold-standard reports on conflict from the World Bank and the Carnegie Commission on Preventing Deadly Conflict, tell us that 90 percent of today's war deaths are civilian while just 10 percent are military—the reverse of a century ago and "a grim indicator of the transformation of armed conflict" in the late 20th century, as political scientist Kalevi Holsti put it.

Grim indeed—but, fortunately, untrue. The myth originates with the 1994 U.N. Human Development Report, which misread work that Swedish researcher Christer Ahlström had done in 1991 and accidentally conflated war fatalities in the early 20th century with the much larger number of dead, wounded, and displaced people in the late 20th century. A more careful analysis done in 1989 by peace researcher William Eckhardt shows that the ratio of military to civilian war deaths remains about 50–50, as it has for centuries (though it varies considerably from one war to the next). If you are unlucky enough to be a civilian in a war zone, of course, these statistics are little comfort. But on a worldwide scale, we are making progress in helping civilians afflicted by war.

Wars Will Get Worse in the Future—*Probably Not*

Anything is possible, of course: A full-blown war between India and Pakistan, for instance, could potentially kill millions of people. But so could an asteroid or—perhaps the safest bet—massive storms triggered by climate change. The big forces that push civilization in the direction of cataclysmic conflict, however, are mostly ebbing.

Recent technological changes are making war less brutal, not more so. Armed drones now attack targets that in the past would have required an invasion with thousands of heavily armed troops, displacing huge numbers of civilians and destroying valuable property along the way. And improvements in battlefield medicine have made combat less lethal for participants. In the U.S. Army, the chances of dying from a combat injury fell from 30 percent in World War II to 10 percent in Iraq and Afghanistan—though this also means the United States is now seeing a higher proportion of injured veterans who need continuing support and care.

Nor do shifts in the global balance of power doom us to a future of perpetual war. While some political scientists argue that an increasingly multipolar world is an increasingly volatile one—that peace is best assured by the predominance of a single hegemonic power, namely the United States—recent geopolitical history suggests otherwise. Relative U.S. power and worldwide conflict have waned in tandem over the past decade. The exceptions to the trend, Iraq and Afghanistan, have been lopsided wars waged by the hegemon, not challenges by up-and-coming new powers. The best precedent for today's emerging world order may be the 19th-century Concert of Europe, a collaboration of great powers that largely maintained the peace for a century until its breakdown and the bloodbath of World War I.

What about China, the most ballyhooed rising military threat of the current era? Beijing is indeed modernizing its armed forces, racking up double-digit rates of growth in military spending, now about $100 billion a year. That is second only to the United States, but it is a distant second: The Pentagon spends nearly $700 billion. Not only is China a very long way from being able to go toe-to-toe with the United States; it's not clear why it would want to. A military conflict (particularly with its biggest customer and debtor) would impede China's global trading posture and endanger its prosperity. Since Chairman Mao's death, China has been hands down the most peaceful great power of its time. For all the recent concern about a newly assertive Chinese navy in disputed international waters, China's military hasn't fired a single shot in battle in 25 years.

A More Democratic World Will Be a More Peaceful One—*Not Necessarily*

The well-worn observation that real democracies almost never fight each other is historically correct, but it's also true that democracies have always been perfectly willing to fight non-democracies. In fact, democracy can heighten conflict by amplifying ethnic and nationalist forces, pushing leaders to appease belligerent sentiment in order to stay in power. Thomas Paine and Immanuel Kant both believed that selfish autocrats caused wars, whereas the common people, who bear the costs, would be loath to fight. But try telling that to the leaders of authoritarian China, who are struggling to hold in check, not inflame, a popular undercurrent of nationalism against Japanese and American historical enemies. Public opinion in tentatively democratic Egypt is far more hostile toward Israel than the authoritarian government of Hosni Mubarak ever was (though being hostile and actually going to war are quite different things).

Why then do democracies limit their wars to non-democracies rather than fight each other? Nobody really knows. As the University of Chicago's Charles Lipson once quipped about the notion of a democratic peace, "We know it works in practice. Now we have to see if it works in theory!" The best explanation is that of political scientists Bruce Russett and John Oneal, who argue that three elements—democracy, economic interdependence (especially trade), and the growth of international organizations—are mutually supportive of each other and of peace within the community of democratic countries. Democratic leaders, then, see themselves as having less to lose in going to war with autocracies.

Peacekeeping Doesn't Work—*It Does Now*

The early 1990s were boom years for the blue helmets, with 15 new U.N. peacekeeping missions launched from 1991 to 1993—as many as in the U.N.'s entire history up to that point. The period was also host to peacekeeping's most spectacular failures. In Somalia, the U.N. arrived on a mission to alleviate starvation only to become embroiled in a civil war, and it quickly pulled out after 18 American soldiers died in a 1993 raid. In Rwanda in 1994, a weak U.N. force with no support from the Security Council completely failed to stop a genocide that killed more than half a million people. In Bosnia, the U.N. declared "safe areas" for civilians, but then stood by when Serbian forces overran one such area, Srebrenica, and executed more than 7,000 men and boys. (There were peacekeeping successes, too, such as in Namibia and Mozambique, but people tend to forget about them.)

In response, the United Nations commissioned a report in 2000, overseen by veteran diplomat Lakhdar Brahimi, examining how the organization's efforts had gone wrong. By then the U.N. had scaled back peacekeeping personnel by 80 percent worldwide, but as it expanded again the U.N. adapted to lessons learned. It strengthened planning and logistics capabilities and began deploying more heavily armed forces able to wade into battle if necessary. As a result, the 15 missions and 100,000 U.N. peacekeepers deployed worldwide today are meeting with far greater success than their predecessors.

Overall, the presence of peacekeepers has been shown to significantly reduce the likelihood of a war's reigniting after a cease-fire agreement.

Overall, the presence of peacekeepers has been shown to significantly reduce the likelihood of a war's reigniting after a cease-fire agreement. In the 1990s, about half of all cease-fires broke down, but in the past decade the figure has dropped to 12 percent. And though the U.N.'s status as a perennial punching bag in American politics suggests otherwise, these efforts are quite popular: In a 2007 survey, 79 percent of Americans favored strengthening the U.N. That's not to say there isn't room for improvement—there's plenty. But the U.N. has done a lot of good around the world in containing war.

Some Conflicts Will Never End—*Never Say Never*

In 2005, researchers at the U.S. Institute of Peace characterized 14 wars, from Northern Ireland to Kashmir, as "intractable," in that they "resist any kind of settlement or resolution." Six years later, however, a funny thing has happened: All but a few of these wars (Israel-Palestine, Somalia, and Sudan) have either ended or made substantial progress toward doing so. In Sri Lanka, military victory ended the war, though only after a brutal endgame in which both sides are widely believed to have committed war crimes. Kashmir has a fairly stable cease-fire. In Colombia, the war sputters on, financed by drug revenue, but with little fighting left. In the Balkans and Northern Ireland, shaky peace arrangements have become less shaky; it's hard to imagine either sliding back into full-scale hostilities. In most of the African cases—Burundi, Rwanda, Sierra Leone, Uganda, the Democratic Republic of the Congo, and Ivory Coast (notwithstanding the violent flare-up after elections there in late 2010, now resolved)—U.N. missions have brought stability and made a return to war less likely (or, in the case of Congo and Uganda, have at least limited the area of fighting).

Could we do even better? The late peace researcher Randall Forsberg in 1997 foresaw "a world largely without war," one in which "the vanishing risk of great-power war has opened the door to a previously unimaginable future—a future in which war is no longer socially-sanctioned and is rare, brief, and small in scale." Clearly, we are not there yet. But over the decades—and indeed, even since Forsberg wrote those words—norms about wars, and especially about the protection of civilians caught up in them, have evolved rapidly, far more so than anyone would have guessed even half a century ago. Similarly rapid shifts in norms preceded the ends of slavery and colonialism, two other scourges that were once also considered permanent features of civilization. So don't be surprised if the end of war, too, becomes downright thinkable.

Critical Thinking

1. Is America fighting more wars than ever?
2. Have wars gotten more brutal for civilians?
3. Will a more democratic world be a more peaceful one?

Joshua S. Goldstein is professor emeritus of international relations at American University and author of *Winning the War on War: The Decline of Armed Conflict Worldwide*.

Article

Uprisings Jolt the Saudi-Iranian Rivalry

Saudi and Iranian meddling aggravates a divisive, dangerous form of identity politics in fragile, vulnerable states.

FREDERIC WEHREY

Saudi Arabia and Iran, long-standing rivals for influence in the Middle East, confront a strategic landscape under rapid transformation by forces largely beyond their control. The old distinctions of Sunni versus Shiite and Arab versus Persian, always somewhat malleable and fuzzy, have been overshadowed by a long-dormant but suddenly more salient dimension of Middle Eastern politics: the people against their rulers. Thrust into this terra incognita, Riyadh and Tehran are now scrambling to prop up wobbly clients and allies (respectively, Bahrain and Syria), vying for influence over Egypt's relations with Israel and the United States, and stepping up their involvement in long-simmering conflicts in Gaza, Lebanon, and Iraq—all while trying to insulate their own populations from the spillover effects of the revolts.

The Saudi and Iranian approaches to the Arab uprisings cannot broadly be labeled revolutionary or counterrevolutionary; instead, realpolitik considerations carry the day. Thus, both states buttress friendly regimes that face protest movements, but they also find themselves in the uncomfortable position of fanning opposition when it threatens their adversaries. In Bahrain, Iran is on the side of political change as a path to Shiite empowerment and a blow to its Saudi rival, while in Syria, Tehran stands firmly against change. In Riyadh's case, the reverse is true. Saudi Arabia sent troops to Bahrain to quash the revolt there, but in Syria it has called for the fall of Bashar al-Assad's regime.

Hypocrisy aside, Saudi and Iranian meddling aggravates a divisive, dangerous form of identity politics in fragile, vulnerable states. Local groups that receive Iranian and Saudi financial support and other forms of aid become more emboldened to press their claims, perhaps through militancy, while the regimes backed by the two powers grow more unyielding and violent in their crackdowns.

The stakes for each player are enormous. The octogenarian rulers in Riyadh and Tehran, beset by domestic debates and looming succession crises, have hitched their sagging domestic legitimacy to their countries' regional roles as patrons of Arabism, Islam, populism, and "rejectionism." For leaders in Tehran, the revolts represent an opportunity to escape their strategic loneliness and help shape a new order in their favor.

For the newly awakened masses in Cairo, Tunis, and Tripoli, however, the charade carried out by Iran and Saudi Arabia has been laid bare. Recent polling reveals that Arab popular opinion regarding both countries is at an all-time low. Crowds who cheered in 2006 for Hezbollah leader Hassan Nasrallah and Iranian President Mahmoud Ahmadinejad, or who lauded the economic benevolence in Lebanon of Saudi Arabia's King Abdullah, now carry banners praising Facebook, French President Nicolas Sarkozy and, most significantly, Prime Minister Recep Tayyip Erdogan of Turkey. Indeed, the most profound and long-term effect of the Arab Spring on the regional balance of power may not relate to Saudi Arabia and Iran at all. Rather, the scales might tip in Turkey's favor, hastening Ankara's entrée onto the Arab stage.

Roots of Rivalry

Iran and Saudi Arabia were engaged in competition long before the Arab Spring. They maintain radically different visions of regional order, and they both aspire to leadership of the Islamic world. Tehran regards Riyadh as America's henchman and as an obstacle to Iran's taking its rightful place as the region's preeminent power. Saudi Arabia harbors a deep distrust of Iran, stemming from the 1979 revolution and from Iran's attempts to overturn the Sunni Arab monarchical order. The 2003 collapse of Saddam Hussein's regime in Iraq, which empowered that country's Shiites, only intensified Saudi fears about an Iranian bid for region-wide dominance, as did jingoistic posturing in 2005 by Iran's "new conservatives" led by Ahmadinejad. Another concern for the Saudis, though a more distant one, is that any Iranian-US rapprochement could jeopardize the privileged position that Riyadh has long enjoyed vis-à-vis the United States due in part to its role in containing Iran.

The regimes in Riyadh and Tehran are divided not just by their well-known sectarian and ethnic differences, but also by divergent political ideologies. The rule of the al-Saud family rests on a careful symbiosis with the clerical establishment, but accords ultimate primacy to the monarchy. Iran's Khomeinist ideology is vehemently antimonarchical and formalizes clerical authority in politics.

In addition, the two states have differing agendas at the Organization of the Petroleum Exporting Countries (OPEC), stemming from their disparate economic needs and demography. Saudi Arabia has the largest proven oil reserves in the world and is a major supplier to East Asia, the United States, and the rest of the world. Therefore it is willing to take a long-term view of the oil market. Iran, with its lower oil reserves and larger population, shows far less concern about the long-term stability of the oil market, and its immediate requirements are more pressing than Saudi Arabia's.

Despite these fundamental differences, tensions between the two states have ebbed and flowed, often depending on the character of the regimes in Riyadh and Tehran, the price of oil, and—most importantly—conflicts in the region. For both states, 2005 saw the emergence of leaders who adopted more activist, muscular foreign policies, which markedly changed the tone of the bilateral relationship. Added to this, the fall of Hussein's regime in Iraq opened a power vacuum that both states sought to fill—though admittedly, Riyadh came late to the game, falling far short of Tehran in cultivating Iraqi partners or even in developing a coherent strategy. The 2006 Lebanon War and the 2011 Arab revolts marked further turning points in the rivalry, opening up new theaters of contestation in each state's near and far abroad.

The sensational disclosure in October 2011 of an alleged Iranian plot to assassinate the Saudi ambassador in Washington is only the latest chapter in the unfolding saga of deteriorating relations. Whether valid or not, news of the plot was a boon for the Saudis—it helps repair the kingdom's previously rocky relationship with the Americans, casts the Saudis as victims, and perhaps most important, refocuses Washington's attention back toward the containment of Iran, rather than encouraging democratic reforms sparked by the Arab Spring. It will also have a galvanizing effect on the states of the Gulf Cooperation Council (GCC), hardening their already confrontational position toward Iran.

Riyadh is alarmed at the warming of relations between post-Mubarak Egypt and Iran.

Red Lines in the Gulf

Speaking in 2007, a Saudi official described the kingdom's strategy toward Iran as "engage in the Gulf, roll back in the Levant, and contain in Iraq." The broad contours of this approach still hold true, with the stark exception of Bahrain, whose uprising was cast by the Saudis and their Bahraini clients as an unprecedented encroachment by Iran into Gulf affairs. On March 14, 2011, Saudi and Emirati troops, ostensibly operating under the banner of the GCC's "Peninsula Shield," rolled into Bahrain to shore up its security forces.

This intervention met with surprising support from the smaller states of the GCC, which have usually resented Saudi Arabia's overbearing approach to Gulf affairs. For its part, Iran warned that it would not "stand with arms crossed" while Riyadh intervened in Bahraini affairs. And the Saudi foreign minister warned that the Saudis would "cut off the finger" of any state threatening their interests.

Evidence of Iranian involvement in the Bahraini unrest, however, has been slim to nonexistent. Bahrain's Shiite actors, both in the parliamentary bloc of the opposition group Al Wefaq and in the rejectionist Al Haq movement, have from time to time threatened to seek Iranian patronage if their demands for reform are not met. But such warnings are mostly bluster, intended as leverage over the ruling al-Khalifa family.

That said, the bogeyman of Shiite fifth columns operating on behalf of Iran has been frequently trotted out by jittery Gulf regimes and their allies among the Sunni clerical establishment. This was especially evident in early 2008, when Saudi Arabia's restive Shiites clashed with morality police in Medina, and in late 2010, when Kuwait and Bahrain arrested members of an alleged Iranian spy ring and Shiite oppositionists. Fear of Iranian influence had reached a fever pitch by the time the Arab Spring broke—and this proved useful for the Saudis in their efforts to discredit as sectarian and Iranian-inspired some scattered protests in Saudi Arabia's Eastern Province.

But whether or not Saudi Arabia actually perceived Iran to be pulling strings in the Gulf is beside the point. The Saudi government saw its intervention in Bahrain—a country often described as Saudi Arabia's Cuba or Puerto Rico—as necessary to restore a modicum of prestige in the wake of setbacks it had suffered at Iran's hands in Lebanon and Iraq. The intervention was also calculated as a shot across the bow of the United States after the overthrow of Egypt's Hosni Mubarak, Riyadh's ally against Iran, whom King Abdullah had accused America of discarding. A third audience may have been Saudi Arabia's own Shiite population and, more broadly, its domestic opposition.

For its part, Iran has played a clever game by limiting its support to rhetoric. It has carefully avoided falling into Saudi Arabia's trap of "sectarianizing" the revolts. Tehran can claim the moral high ground simply by pointing to Riyadh's military intervention in Bahrain (and also Yemen) as evidence of Saudi (and American) opposition to the Arab masses' aspirations. At the same time, it reaps benefit from having its clout over Bahrain greatly exaggerated by Gulf regimes, without having to expend any real capital. All of this occurs while Iran's real influence is exerted quietly, and much more malignly, in Lebanon, Syria, and Iraq.

Rollback in the Levant

The Levant, though far removed from each state's oil resources and lines of communication, has long existed as a sort of strategic prize for Riyadh and Tehran and an arena of violent proxy conflict. Both Iran and Saudi Arabia have deep historical and cultural roots in the region. It is in Lebanon where Iran came closest to exporting its revolution among disenfranchised Shiites, while Saudi Arabia enjoys long-standing links with Lebanon's Sunnis, epitomized by its support for the late prime minister Rafik Hariri. Symbolically, Iran and Saudi Arabia also derive enormous prestige and legitimacy—both domestically and regionally—from being seen as patrons of the Palestinian cause.

Iran has long benefited from upstaging the Saudis through its support for rejectionist groups like Hamas and Hezbollah. The 2006 Lebanon War was a turning point on this front. Hezbollah, a Shiite organization backed by Saudi Arabia's strategic rival, scored a stunning battlefield success against the vaunted Israel Defense Forces—a spectacle that electrified Arab publics while unsettling Sunni Arab regimes that had long opposed Israel but had little to show for it. Inside Saudi Arabia, Hezbollah's audacity stirred significant debate among the Salafist clerics and the royalty about whether to support Hezbollah, exposing deep tensions between the Saudis' rhetorical embrace of pan-Arab causes and the doctrinal rigidity of the country's Salafist establishment.

Turkey is effecting far-reaching changes that simultaneously weaken Iran and upstage Saudi Arabia.

The war occasioned a new activism in Saudi policy toward Iran; much of this activism also coincided with the formal ascension to the throne of King Abdullah in 2005. A central target of this effort was Syria, Tehran's only state ally in the Arab world and its principal conduit into Levantine affairs. The Saudis have headed the Arab effort to reconcile with the Syrians, to coax them away from Iran and back into the Arab fold. To accomplish this, Saudi Arabia has pursued multiple initiatives—ranging from soliciting Turkish leverage over President Assad as a form of "circular diplomacy"; to supporting an international tribunal investigating Hariri's assassination; to cautiously engaging Damascus in 2009 and 2010 on the management of Lebanon in an effort to weaken Iran's control.

The results of these approaches have been mixed, and ultimately unsatisfying. Riyadh saw its Sunni clients humiliated when Hezbollah forces rolled into West Beirut in May 2008, and it suffered a further blow with the ascension of the pro-Syrian Najib Miqati as Lebanon's prime minister in 2011—an event that signaled Hezbollah's effective dominance over the government.

When the Arab Spring finally arrived in Syria, Abdullah was quick to lead a concerted GCC effort to isolate and undermine Assad. Further dissolution in Syria could provoke yet greater Saudi intervention as part of a region-wide proxy war. The kingdom enjoys long-standing links to Sunni tribes in eastern Syria (King Abdullah's own tribe, the Shammar, has branches in Syria) and historically has been a patron to Salafist and Muslim Brotherhood groups in Aleppo and Homs.

The protests in Syria and the subsequent crackdown there have stirred significant debate inside Iran about whether Assad is a strategic asset worth rescuing or a liability to be jettisoned. Meanwhile, Iran's standing in the Levant has taken a battering. As the violence in Syria escalated, reports and rumors circulated that Iranian and Hezbollah advisers were involved in the crackdown, and the protesters increasingly associated Tehran with the despised Assad regime.

In an apparent volte-face, Iran's foreign minister began calling for dialogue within Syria, but Tehran has continued abetting the crackdown through Revolutionary Guards and Hezbollah advisers—acting, in effect, as both arsonist and fireman. This is a timeworn Iranian tactic and one that Tehran has played to great effect elsewhere in the region, particularly in Iraq.

Unease over Iraq

Saudi Arabia views Iraq as a contested arena in its larger geostrategic rivalry with Iran—that is, political gains by Iraqi Shiite groups are viewed as wins for Tehran and losses for Riyadh. Saudi officials have long accused the United States of handing Iraq to Iran, but the Saudis themselves have been surprisingly passive in countering Iranian influence. Privately, Saudi interlocutors bemoan the kingdom's lack of a strategy for post-Hussein Iraq; one former official conceded that "Iran had a plan and got the influence it deserves." Others speak of having written Iraq off as a sphere of Iranian control since at least 2006, and of having pursued containment and damage control since then.

Even so, in late 2008 through 2009, a debate appeared to emerge within Saudi policy circles about the need for a more muscular Saudi approach in Iraq—a response both to the impending US military drawdown and to growing signals that Iraqi Prime Minister Nuri Kamal al-Maliki's government was less an Iranian proxy than previously assumed.

These signals included Maliki's resolve in quashing Iranian-backed militant groups starting in mid-2008; parliamentary ratification of the US-Iraq Status of Forces Agreement, despite extensive Iranian lobbying against it; and the decline in power within the government of the pro-Iran Islamic Supreme Council of Iraq, after a poor showing in January 2009 provincial elections and March 2010 national elections. Riyadh appears to have realized that its policy of undermining Maliki was actually pushing him further into Iran's orbit and that the time was opportune to woo him back into the Arab fold.

In late 2010, King Abdullah extended an invitation to Maliki and his entire parliamentary coalition to meet in Riyadh to discuss the formation of the Iraqi government. Nevertheless, Riyadh is hedging its bets by backing an array of Sunni groups; it has long-standing links to the Iraqi Islamic Party, the former officer corps of Iraq's army, and Salafist groups. Regarding Shiite parties, Riyadh has seen the utility of backing nationalist actors in the south, such as Fadhila, as a counterweight to Iran, and of using tribal intermediaries who have both Shiite and Sunni branches, such as the Shammar.

From Iran's perspective, Iraq is a means to offset its reliance on an increasingly unstable Syria and, for many in the Iranian leadership, a natural, nonnegotiable sphere of influence. Given Tehran's extensive and robust influence over the country, Iran does not worry about Saudi involvement there to the extent that Riyadh worries about Iran's. Still, Iranian commentators are quick to denounce Al Qaeda attacks against Iraqi Shiite pilgrims as a consequence of Saudi Arabian involvement and frequently point to anti-Shiite fatwas of Saudi clerics as further evidence of this.

Iranian voices have also worried that the Saudi- Jordanian strategy of backing the Sunni tribes of Anbar province (the so-called "Anbar Awakening") and Iraqi Sunni militias (the "Sons of Iraq") against Al Qaeda militants could be replicated in southern and central Iraq, where nationalist Shiite tribes are pitted against pro-Iranian elements of the Sadrists and other Shiite groups.

Wild Cards

Among the new variables produced by the Arab revolts, the increasing assertiveness of Turkey and the shifting orientation of Egypt are the most salient to the Saudi-Iranian relationship. Turkey under Ahmet Davutoglu, its visionary foreign minister, has articulated a proposed new order in the Middle East, one in which Ankara's former allies Syria and Israel fall into isolation and the Saudi-Iranian dyad is replaced by a new Turkish-Egyptian axis of influence stretching from the Black Sea to the Nile.

In addition, many observers have hailed Turkey as the Arab Spring's ultimate winner because its ruling Justice and Development Party offers a balance of liberalism and Islam that is attractive to a broad swath of actors across the Arab world, particularly youth. It is too early to tell how much of this praise and admiration will translate into actual changes on the ground. Nevertheless, Turkey is effecting far-reaching changes to the regional landscape, changes that simultaneously weaken Iran and upstage Saudi Arabia.

In Syria, Turkey had previously cultivated ties with Assad, possibly believing that, like the Saudis, it could woo him away from Iran. After Assad's repeated rebukes and his unfulfilled promises to halt his crackdown, Turkey has now begun hosting Syrian opposition groups and defectors from the country's officer corps. Further breakdown and civil war in Syria could spell Turkish intervention intended to safeguard its borders and staunch the flow of refugees.

In part because of Iran's stance toward Syria, Turkish-Iranian relations have deteriorated sharply, compared to a warming trend that began around 2007. Since the onset of the 2011 revolts, Iran's state and conservative media portrayals of Turkey have shifted markedly, with some outlets lambasting Ankara, ironically, as an "executor of Zionist policy." Meanwhile, Erdogan's mounting criticism of Israel and Turkey's suspension of military cooperation with Tel Aviv have earned accolades from Arab publics, in contrast to the apparent paralysis of the Saudis.

The dynamic state of Egypt's domestic and foreign policy is another new variable in the Saudi-Iranian struggle. Riyadh saw Mubarak as a helpful partner against Iran and, starting in 2008, there was growing coordination between the two Arab states on countering Tehran in Iraq and the Levant. Riyadh, now deprived of this ally, is alarmed at the warming of relations between post-Mubarak Egypt and Iran and at Cairo's more favorable disposition toward Iran-backed Hamas in the Palestinian occupied territories.

To counter this drift and to deny Iran any openings to exploit, Saudi Arabia has spent $4 billion to shore up the provisional military government in Cairo, while at the same time reportedly bolstering the country's Salafists through aid to charitable networks. Signs are emerging that this checkbook diplomacy is paying dividends. Many analysts saw more than a coincidence when Nabil al-Arabi, an Egyptian foreign minister who called for normalizing relations with Iran, was replaced (after the brief tenure of Mohamed el Orabi) with Mohamed Kamel Amr, who was the former Egyptian ambassador to Riyadh and who adheres closely to the Mubarak-era status quo.

In addition to staving off any Egyptian-Iranian rapprochement, a crucial goal for Riyadh is diluting the power of the Muslim Brotherhood. From Riyadh's perspective, an ascendant Brotherhood would empower Hamas: Soon after the Brotherhood broke through in 2005 Egyptian parliamentary elections and won 20 percent of the seats in the lower house, Hamas eclipsed Fatah in the 2006 Palestinian vote. Riyadh is wary of Hamas not only because it is an Iranian ally but also because it presents an alternative to the kingdom's more dogmatic and anti-electoral version of Salafist Islamism.

A caveat regarding these Saudi concerns is the actual part that Egypt played in the Saudi-Egyptian "bloc" against Iran. Even at the peak of Egypt's tensions with Iran—after the 2008 Gaza-Egypt border opening alerted policy makers in Cairo to the extent of Iran's involvement at their doorstep—Egypt played a limited role in helping Saudi Arabia counter Iran. Moreover, latent and unresolved tensions between the two Arab powers were exposed; these remain from their struggle for pan-Arab leadership in the 1950s and 1960s, and may emerge yet again.

Egyptian analysts privately concede that Mubarak had played up the Iranian threat to maintain Cairo's relevance in Arab affairs and they criticize Saudi Arabia for its heavy-handed approach toward Iran. For their part, Saudi officials in 2010 described Cairo as a junior partner that was too distracted by its internal problems and succession crisis to play an effective regional role. Now, despite likely shifts in Cairo's posture toward both Iran and Israel, domestic issues will probably consume Egypt's new rulers for quite some time.

The Geometry of Power

In light of the Saudi-Egyptian tensions brought on by the Arab Spring, it is tempting to cast the kingdom as the centerpiece of a US containment strategy against Iran, with Riyadh deploying its vast financial resources and its diplomatic weight to rally local and global actors against Tehran. But such an assumption is problematic for several reasons.

First, it overstates Saudi Arabia's capacity to act as an Arab balancer and it understates the risks associated with such a proxy strategy—namely, increased sectarianism and the possible growth of Sunni extremism throughout the Middle East.

Second, it posits a degree of regional consensus regarding Riyadh's leadership that has never really existed, including within the GCC. Any such consensus that did exist has now been overshadowed by Turkey's new prominence.

Third, it reads Riyadh's current rivalry with Tehran as immutable, and glosses over periods when the two powers have coordinated and collaborated on such issues as Lebanon and the Gulf.

In short, the Saudi approach to Iran is more multidimensional than a Manichean cold war analogy would suggest. This complexity is rooted in Riyadh's perception of Iran as a strategic rival but also a neighbor and a fellow Islamic power.

In light of such nuance, US policy makers would do well to take the long view of the Saudi-Iranian relationship, recalling in particular the pre-1979 era—when Saudi Arabia and Iran were part of a "twin pillars" strategy and shared de facto leadership in the region—and also the mid-1990s, when reformers made inroads in Iranian politics and relations between the two countries warmed. These eras are instructive for what they reveal about the two nations' capability to minimize ideological and structural tensions so as to reach an accommodation on regional order.

At the same time, they highlight two perennial truths about power relations in the Gulf, which apply regardless of US policy preferences and no matter the character of the regime in Tehran: Saudi Arabia maintains a deeply ingrained preference for some external power to balance Iran, and Iran desires a more indigenous Gulf security system whose acceptance by Saudi Arabia would imply a de facto recognition of Iranian primacy.

Within this geometry of power, another enduring fact is that weak and poorly governed polities in the region—whether Iraq, Gaza or, increasingly, Syria—invariably invite interference from Riyadh and Tehran as the two powers vie for supremacy in a zero-sum game.

Nukes and Nerves

Underpinning the rivalry is the looming specter of an Iran with nuclear capability. Saudi Arabia views Iran's nuclear program in several ways: as a potential existential threat, as an enabler of greater Iranian militancy across the region, as a coercive tool in Gulf diplomacy, and as an affront to Saudi leadership of the Islamic world.

Much has been made of Saudi Arabia's aspirations to acquire its own nuclear deterrent; it is beyond the scope of this article to address Riyadh's political calculations or technical capacity regarding this option. What is clear is that such a step would signal a drastic break with Saudi Arabia's principal security patron, the United States, thus upending 50 years of fruitful cooperation. If the Saudis grow dissatisfied with the assurances they receive from Washington, the nuclear option is a risk they might be willing to take.

For now, Saudi leaders support a variation of the US approach toward proliferation in the region, calling for a nuclear-free zone in the Persian Gulf—a departure from their previous insistence on a Middle East free of weapons of mass destruction, which implicitly included Israel. Still, Washington must account for the possibility that Riyadh could pursue a more unilateral path.

The protests in Syria have stirred debate inside Iran about whether Assad is a strategic asset worth rescuing.

Thus far, the United States has employed diplomacy and security cooperation to assuage the Saudis' unease about Iranian nuclearization and preempt any push by Riyadh to acquire its own nuclear deterrent. Washington agreed in 2010 to a $60 billion package that will expand the Saudis' arsenal of advanced fighter jets, attack helicopters, and missile defenses.

Among the levers that could potentially aid the United States in pressuring or isolating Iran, the so-called "oil weapon" is the most discussed. American officials appear hopeful that Riyadh's energy resources will be leveraged to solicit China (which counts Saudi Arabia as its biggest supplier of oil) for its support of tougher United Nations sanctions against Tehran. According to this line of thinking, Saudi Arabia could offer China better commercial opportunities in the petroleum sector than it currently finds in Iran. However, many analysts have downplayed this idea, citing differences between Beijing and Riyadh over joint-venture Saudi refineries in China and Riyadh's desire to maintain a monopoly in oil exploration within its territory.

Similarly, it is unlikely that the Saudis would use their excess production capacity (estimated at 4 million barrels a day) to depress oil prices, constrict Iran's cash flow, and undermine the Iranian regime's ability to satisfy an already discontented population. This option ignores Riyadh's historical preference for maintaining solidarity with fellow OPEC members and its desire to avoid overtly provoking Tehran for fear of Iranian retaliation.

Meanwhile, the Saudi regime's hasty announcement of $35 billion in subsidies to address domestic dissent in the wake of the Arab revolts has created a budgetary constraint on the regime's ability to deploy the oil weapon. That said, if it were faced with the imminent prospect of an Iranian nuclear weapon, Riyadh might be willing to withdraw these subsidies and accept the risk of domestic dissent—as long as it believed that the oil weapon stood a chance of halting Iran's nuclear program or altering Tehran's behavior.

Critical Thinking

1. What are the differences between Iran and Saudi Arabia?
2. How do the two countries differ on Syria, Iraq, and the Gulf?
3. What role does Egypt play in this rivalry?
4. What country in the region is most likely to benefit from this rivalry and why?

Frederic Wehrey is a senior policy analyst at the RAND Corporation and the author of *Saudi-Iranian Relations Since the Fall of Saddam* (RAND, 2009).

Article

A New Kind of Korea

Building Trust Between Seoul and Pyongyang

PARK GEUN-HYE

On August 15, 1974, South Korea's Independence Day, I lost my mother, then the country's first lady, to an assassin acting under orders from North Korea. That day was a tragedy not only for me but also for all Koreans. Despite the unbearable pain of that event, I have wished and worked for enduring peace on the Korean Peninsula ever since. But 37 years later, the conflict on the peninsula persists. The long-simmering tensions between North and South Korea resulted in an acute crisis in November 2010. For the first time since the Korean War, North Korea shelled South Korean territory, killing soldiers and civilians on the island of Yeonpyeong.

Only two weeks earlier, South Korea had become the first country outside the G-8 to chair and host a G-20 summit, welcoming world leaders to its capital, Seoul. These events starkly illustrated the dual reality of the Korean Peninsula and of East Asia more broadly. On the one hand, the Korean Peninsula remains volatile. The proliferation of weapons of mass destruction by North Korea, the modernization of conventional forces across the region, and nascent great-power rivalries highlight the endemic security dilemmas that plague this part of Asia. On the other hand, South Korea's extraordinary development, sometimes called the Miracle on the Han River, has, alongside China's rise, become a major driver of the global economy over the past decade.

These two contrasting trends exist side by side in Asia, the information revolution, globalization, and democratization clashing with the competitive instincts of the region's major powers. To ensure that the first set of forces triumphs, policymakers in Asia and in the international community must not only take advantage of existing initiatives but also adopt a bolder and more creative approach to achieving security. Without such an effort, military brinkmanship may only increase—with repercussions well beyond Asia. For this reason, forging trust and sustainable peace on the Korean Peninsula represents one of the most urgent and crucial tasks on Asia's list of outstanding security challenges.

Introducing Trust

A lack of trust has long undermined attempts at genuine reconciliation between North and South Korea. What little confidence did exist between the two countries virtually disappeared last year, after North Korea destroyed the South Korean naval ship *Cheonan* in March and brazenly attacked Yeonpyeong Island in November. North Korea also revealed that it had constructed a sophisticated uranium-enrichment facility, directly contravening commitments it had undertaken, most recently in the September 19, 2005, joint statement of the six-party talks, to forbid uranium enrichment and abandon its nuclear weapons program.

As one Korean proverb goes, one-handed applause is impossible. By the same token, peace between the two Koreas will not be possible without a combined effort. For more than half a century, North Korea has blatantly disregarded international norms. But even if Seoul must respond forcefully to Pyongyang's provocations, it must also remain open to new opportunities for improving relations between the two sides. Precisely because trust is at a low point these days, South Korea has a chance to rebuild it. In order to transform the Korean Peninsula from a zone of conflict into a zone of trust, South Korea should adopt a policy of "trustpolitik," establishing mutually binding expectations based on global norms.

"Trustpolitik" does not mean unconditional or one-sided trust without verification. Nor does it mean forgetting North Korea's numerous transgressions or rewarding the country with new incentives. Instead, it should be comprised of two coexisting strands: first, North Korea must keep its agreements made with South Korea and the international community to establish a minimum level of trust, and second, there must be assured consequences for actions that breach the peace. To ensure stability, trustpolitik should be applied consistently from issue to issue based on verifiable actions, and steps should not be taken for mere political expediency.

Building trust between competing nations has been accomplished before. The United States and China overcame deep mutual suspicions to establish relations in the 1970s. Egypt and Israel signed a peace accord in 1979 after a gradual process of trust-building between the two sides, and the agreement remains a linchpin of stability for the entire Middle East, even after the change in regime in Egypt earlier this year. In the 1950s, European nations overcame a half century of warfare to create what would later become the European Union.

Although Asia's cultural, historical, and geopolitical environment is unique, the continent can learn from these precedents, particularly Europe's experience. To begin with, Asian states must slow down their accelerating arms buildup, reduce military tensions, and establish a cooperative security regime that would complement existing bilateral agreements and help resolve persistent tensions in the region. In addition, they should strengthen existing multilateral regimes—such as the ASEAN Regional Forum, a formal dialogue among 27 nations on East Asian security issues; the trilateral summits through which China, Japan, and South Korea coordinate their shared policy concerns; and the Asia-Pacific Economic Cooperation. Together, these efforts would help form a more resilient Asian security network and build trust and security on the Korean Peninsula. Such endeavors will undoubtedly take time. But if North and South Korea and other Asian countries can institutionalize confidence-building measures, they will bolster the odds that economic and political cooperation can overcome military and security competition.

Bringing Pyongyang into the Fold

To establish trustpolitik on the Korean Peninsula, South Korea should adapt its past strategies toward North Korea. Previous governments in Seoul have alternatively attempted to engage and deter Pyongyang. The ones that have emphasized accommodation and inter-Korean solidarity have placed inordinate hope in the idea that if the South provided sustained assistance to the North, the North would abandon its bellicose strategy toward the South. But after years of such attempts, no fundamental change has come. Meanwhile, the governments in Seoul that have placed a greater emphasis on pressuring North Korea have not been able to influence its behavior in a meaningful way, either.

A new policy is needed: an alignment policy, which should be buttressed by public consensus and remain constant in the face of political transitions and unexpected domestic or international events. Such a policy would not mean adopting a middle-of-the-road approach; it would involve aligning South Korea's security with its cooperation with the North and inter-Korean dialogue with parallel international efforts. An alignment policy would entail assuming a tough line against North Korea sometimes and a flexible policy open to negotiations other times. For example, if North Korea launches another military strike against the South, Seoul must respond immediately to ensure that Pyongyang understands the costs of provocation. Conversely, if North Korea takes steps toward genuine reconciliation, such as reaffirming its commitment to existing agreements, then the South should match its efforts. An alignment policy will, over time, reinforce trustpolitik.

To implement such an alignment policy, South Korea must first demonstrate, through a robust and credible deterrent posture, that it will no longer tolerate North Korea's increasingly violent provocations. It must show Pyongyang that the North will pay a heavy price for its military and nuclear threats. This approach is not new, but in order to change the current situation, it must be enforced more vigorously than in the past.

In particular, Seoul has to mobilize the international community to help it dismantle Pyongyang's nuclear program. Under no circumstances can South Korea accept the existence of a nuclear-armed North Korea. North Korea's nuclearization also poses a major threat to the international community because Pyongyang could develop long-range missiles with nuclear warheads or transfer nuclear technologies and materials abroad. Through a combination of credible deterrence, strenuous persuasion, and more effective negotiation strategies, Seoul and the international community must make Pyongyang realize that it can survive and even prosper without nuclear weapons. If North Korea undertakes additional nuclear tests, South Korea must consider all possible responses in consultation with its principal ally, the United States, and other key global partners.

Even as Seoul and its allies strengthen their posture against North Korea's militarism and nuclear brinkmanship, they must also be prepared to offer Pyongyang a new beginning. Trust can be built on incremental gains, such as joint projects for enhanced economic cooperation, humanitarian assistance from the South to the North, and new trade and investment opportunities. When I met the North Korean leader Kim Jong Il in Pyongyang in 2002, we discussed a range of issues, including a Eurasian railway project that would reconnect the Trans-Korean Railway, which has been severed since the Korean War, and link it to the Trans-Siberian and Trans-China lines. Reconnecting the Korean railway would be a testament to mutual development and inter-Korean peace. And if that line were then tied to other regional lines, the effort could help develop China's three northeastern provinces and Russia's Far East—and, in turn, perhaps transform the Korean Peninsula into a conduit for regional trade. Although tensions have delayed further discussions about the railway project in recent years, these could be restarted as a means of building trust on vital security matters.

The rest of the world can help with these efforts. To begin with, strengthening the indispensable alliance between South Korea and the United States should send unequivocal signals to North Korea that only responsible behavior can ensure the regime's survival and a better life for its citizens. The EU is not a member of the six-party nuclear talks, but the model of regional cooperation that Europe represents can contribute to peace building on the Korean Peninsula. Asian countries can devise ways to adopt a cooperative security arrangement based on the model of the Organization for Security and Cooperation in Europe, the world's largest intergovernmental security organization. The OSCE process of fostering security and economic cooperation could be adapted to Northeast Asia: offering guarantees that North Korea would receive substantial economic and diplomatic benefits if it changed its behavior would reassure its leaders that the regime can survive without nuclear weapons.

Given its role as North Korea's principal economic benefactor and ally, China can play a critical part in prompting Pyongyang to change. Chinese efforts to encourage reforms in North Korea could be spurred by a more cooperative U.S.-Chinese relationship. As that relationship deepens, Pyongyang's outlier status will increasingly undermine Beijing's desire to improve its ties with Washington. Conversely, tensions between China and the United States might only increase North Korea's intransigence, allowing it to play the two countries off each other.

Because South Korea maintains both a critical alliance with the United States and a strategic partnership with China, confidence building on the Korean Peninsula would also improve trust between Beijing and Washington, creating a virtuous cycle in which a more cooperative U.S.-Chinese relationship would bolster more positive inter-Korean relations and vice versa. Although North Korea continues to depend heavily on China's economic and diplomatic protection, China's growing global stature and interest in improving its ties with the United States may limit its support for North Korea if Pyongyang continues to threaten the region's stability. North Korea may finally join the family of nations if it realizes that assistance from China cannot last forever.

Making the Right Choice

The dual realities of the Korean Peninsula—prosperity and military tension—have coexisted for the past 60 years. In the midst of war and the bleakest of circumstances, South Korea received critical assistance from the United States and the international community that propelled its economic development and its democratization. Its progress was so fast, in fact, that in 2009 it became the first underdeveloped, aid-recipient country to become a member of the Organization for Economic Cooperation and Development's Development Assistance Committee. South Korea adheres to denuclearization, participates in countering the proliferation of other weapons of mass destruction, and increasingly contributes to global initiatives, such as reconstruction efforts in Afghanistan and antipiracy naval operations around the Horn of Africa.

Enduring trust between the international community and South Korea was instrumental to Seoul's development. To achieve the same outcome with North Korea, South Korea should adopt a principle of trustpolitik and an alignment policy. Once the vestiges of the harsh confrontation between Seoul and Pyongyang are overcome, the Korean Peninsula could emerge as a hub for cooperation and economic prosperity. Should the North relinquish its nuclear weapons and behave peacefully, it could work with the South to enhance economic cooperation between the two countries through special economic zones and the free movement of goods and people, gain development assistance from institutions such as the World Bank, and attract foreign investment. Such developments would contribute significantly to the establishment of a more enduring peace on the Korean Peninsula, and they might expedite the peninsula's unification as well as encourage the gradual institutionalization of economic and security cooperation in Northeast Asia. A democratic, unified Korea would be an economic and security asset to the region.

Many assert that in the coming years the Korean Peninsula will face growing uncertainty. But Koreans have shown that they can turn challenges into historic opportunities. In the 1960s and 1970s, South Korea chose to develop itself through rapid industrialization. In the 1990s, it expanded and deepened ties with countries and regions with which it had shared little during the Cold War, such as China, eastern Europe, and Russia. Over the last decade, it has emerged as one of Asia's most vibrant democracies. Today, South Korea stands ready to work with the United States and other members of the international community to ensure that North Korea follows the same path.

Critical Thinking

1. What is the main reason for the failure of reconciliation on the Korean Peninsula?
2. How should South Korea adapt its past strategies toward the North?
3. How can the rest of the world help with the efforts to diffuse tensions?

Park Geun-hye is a Member of the National Assembly of the Republic of Korea.

Article

Central America's Security Predicament

MICHAEL SHIFTER

Learning Objectives

After reading this article, you will more clearly understand the following:

- The sources of instability in Central America
- The problems caused by drug-trafficking
- The impact of increased criminal activity and violence

In retrospect, it was probably naïve to expect that, with the signing of the last of the Central American peace accords (Guatemala, 1996), the heightened civil strife that beset the region for decades would give way to a greater measure of social peace. Although Central America can celebrate the virtual end of political violence over the past 15 years, the five countries of the isthmus that in the 1980s were in the international spotlight on account of instability—Guatemala, El Salvador, Honduras, Nicaragua, and Costa Rica— are, to varying degrees, still notably troubled.

That this is true even of Costa Rica—the Central American nation most known for (relative) tranquility, social progress, and democratic performance—speaks to the depth of the problems in the region. Indeed, at the end of 2010 Costa Rica found itself increasingly contending with drug-fueled violence and also experiencing a tense standoff with neighboring Nicaragua over a disputed border area. Yet, despite Costa Rica's difficulties, the country's position remains comparatively advantageous. It is better equipped institutionally than its more vulnerable neighbors to withstand the global pressures and strains that contribute to societal disintegration.

The region has registered, to be sure, some impressive economic, political, and social gains in recent years, including higher levels of political competition within countries. These achievements have mostly been eclipsed, however, by an overall deterioration in security conditions and by continuing economic stagnation. Unfavorable external conditions and internal decay and fragmentation have produced societies with increasingly urgent problems.

Central America has been squeezed by rising energy costs—the region has little choice but to import its oil and gas—and has suffered disproportionately from the financial and economic crisis that originated in the United States in 2008 and continues to be acutely felt. Remittance flows from the United States, which are critical to sustaining the region's economies, have sharply dropped as a result of the economic downturn.

Meanwhile, precarious political institutions and endemic poverty and inequality have rendered governance challenges daunting. The results of the 2010 Latinobarómetro report, a region-wide public opinion survey, reveal that Central Americans are particularly tepid in their support of democracy.

Such ambivalence is understandable in light of the ominous tendencies of both organized and common crime in the subregion. Pervasive fear often corresponds to objective data on violence. According to a study carried out in 2008 by the Latin American Public Opinion Project, high crime levels significantly erode interpersonal trust and tend to fray the social fabric on which democracies are constructed. The study found that, in the five Central American countries, roughly 14 percent to 19 percent of citizens said they had been victims of crime during the preceding 12 months.

Other research has highlighted the explosive growth of private security companies that often outstrip official police forces and typically function without controls or regulation. A 2009 United Nations Development Program report showed that in Guatemala and Honduras private security personnel outnumber police forces by five to ten times. No Central American country has more police than private security officers. Economic costs associated with anti-crime measures absorb an increasing share of national budgets throughout the subregion.

Regrettably, Central America is often overlooked compared with other regions within Latin America. While

South America, led by Brazil, has drawn praise for its remarkable ascent, and Mexico has dominated headlines because of its unrelenting and particularly brutal criminality, Central American nations have been off the international radar and are at best treated as an afterthought.

Yet what is taking place both north and south of Central America is contributing to the deepening predicament of the region, which has become a hub for drug trafficking routes. Only recently has concern substantially increased in Washington and elsewhere regarding a set of countries that occupied center stage—and generated moderately high hopes and expectations—just two decades ago.

GUATEMALAN GANGLAND?

Recent developments in Guatemala have especially alarmed observers and policy officials. Guatemala is Central America's largest country and also the one where a decades-long civil war took the greatest toll, with 200,000 dead. Long-standing inequities highlighted by sharp ethnic divisions—Guatemala's population is majority indigenous—have posed formidable challenges for governing the country. Guatemala has among the region's lowest tax rates, with notoriously fierce resistance from wealthy sectors to contributing their fair share, and this has made it even more difficult to redress the glaring disparities.

However, while political violence and old-fashioned militarism have subsided, there has been a striking surge in the penetration of organized crime in all spheres of the nation. Analysts often refer to dark forces and parallel structures that engage in illicit activities and operate with nearly assured impunity. Judicial and police institutions are riddled with corruption. The country's governance structures are too weak and ineffective to cope with such powerful pressures. In this context, the International Commission Against Impunity in Guatemala (CICIG) performs a fundamental role. A special judicial body assembled in cooperation with the United Nations, the CICIG began its work in 2007 with the aim of supporting efforts by the country's flawed criminal justice system to root out criminal networks operating inside government bodies.

A succession of murky and complicated incidents in recent years has highlighted disturbing trends in the country. In May 2009, the killing of a Guatemalan lawyer, Rodrigo Rosenberg, became a major political controversy after a video was made public in which Rosenberg, before he died, blamed President Alvaro Colom for his assassination. The CICIG investigated the Rosenberg case and in January 2010 announced detailed findings concluding that Rosenberg staged his own murder in an attempt to call attention to the killing of his son, in which Rosenberg believed Colom had had a hand.

The CICIG investigations also led to the arrest of a former president, Alfonso Portillo, on corruption charges and in response to an extradition request from the United States on money laundering charges. And the commission contributed to the arrest in March 2010 of a former national police chief, Baltazar Gómez, for involvement with drug trafficking and blocking an investigation of corrupt police officers.

In June 2010, however, the head of CICIG, a Spanish lawyer named Carlos Castresana, resigned out of frustration, complaining that the Guatemalan government had not been following the commission's recommendations and that there was an active campaign to discredit the CICIG among groups with an entrenched interest in continued impunity.

The resignation was provoked by the Colom government's appointment of Conrado Reyes as attorney general—after the CICIG had identified Reyes as having ties to drug trafficking and illegal adoption rings. Castresana's decision created a political firestorm, and the country's Constitutional Court ultimately rejected Reyes's appointment on grounds that the selection process may have been influenced by organized crime. The UN then appointed Costa Rican Attorney General Francisco Dall'Anese, a renowned advocate against organized crime, to succeed Castresana as the CICIG's head.

Another illustration of the sort of convoluted intrigue that increasingly characterizes Guatemala occurred in early December 2010, when a Guatemalan court sentenced eight people to prison for lengthy terms for involvement in the February 2007 murders of three Salvadoran members of the Central American Parliament and their driver. The CICIG had worked closely with Guatemalan prosecutors on the case, and among those sentenced was a former Guatemalan congressman charged with masterminding the killing. The court ruled that the four men had been murdered at the behest of a Salvadoran legislator who had been expelled from his party over allegations of criminal activity. The murders were actually carried out by four Guatemalan police officers, who were slain in a high-security prison just days after being arrested.

And in January 2011, a bomb attack on a bus in Guatemala City claimed seven lives. In recent years, the country's public transport has been increasingly subjected to extortion by organized crime groups (a member of the Mara 18 gang was charged in the January attack). In 2010, according to Guatemalan police, bus drivers paid out over $1.5 million in extortion money. Local rights groups report that 119 of the country's bus drivers and 51 other transport workers were murdered last year.

As if the security situation and the fragility of political institutions were not serious enough, Guatemala has been profoundly affected by the brutal and bloody cartel battles being waged in Mexico. Fighting among Mexican drug cartels and the aggressive response by the government of Felipe Calderón not only have resulted in more than 30,000 deaths since the start of the Calderón administration. They also have pushed the cartels further south, into northern Guatemala, where they increasingly wreak havoc in an already battered nation that has few defenses.

Members of Los Zetas, a Mexican drug trafficking group, and the Sinaloa drug cartel now routinely attack local law enforcement officials and control substantial swaths of territory, according to a US State Department report. As the journalist Steven Dudley has written in *Foreign Policy,* "as Mexico and Colombia cracked down on their own drug trafficking problems, the criminals sought new refuge, and Guatemala fit the bill: a weak government, a strategic location, and a bureaucracy whose allegiance came cheap." At present the homicide rate in Guatemala is four times that in Mexico.

On December 19, 2010, the Guatemalan government, worried that the situation was spiraling out of control, declared a state of siege in the northern province of Alta Verapaz, large areas of which had reportedly been taken over by Mexican drug traffickers. As an *Associated Press* dispatch observed two days later, "Gangs roamed the streets with assault rifles and armored vehicles, attacking whomever they pleased and abducting women who caught their eye. Shootouts became so common residents couldn't tell gunfire from holiday fireworks." Local leaders from the province, which had become a prime corridor for drug trafficking from Honduras to Mexico, said they had been requesting the intervention of federal authorities for two years.

Undisciplined and fractured political parties aggravate the dire situation in a country that the International Crisis Group has called a "paradise for criminals." Colom's party, for example, holds barely a fifth of the seats in the legislature. This has made promises of greater social inclusion nearly impossible to achieve. According to the World Bank, more than half the population lives in poverty.

While it still may not be accurate (or constructive) to depict Guatemala as a "failed state" or "narco-state," mounting evidence points to conditions of rampant lawlessness that warrant considerable alarm. The real risk is that, with a presidential election scheduled for the fall of 2011, unchecked criminality could trigger reflexes for more authoritarian approaches that evoke what was widely thought to be a bygone era.

HONDURAS IS MURDER

Together with Guatemala and El Salvador, Honduras forms part of the so-called "Northern Triangle," a doorway for cocaine traffic into Mexico. The World Drug Report of 2010, published by the UN Office on Drugs and Crime, documents that this territory has the highest murder rates of any region in the world, with more than 50 homicides each year per 100,000 people. *The Economist* notes that Honduras currently has the highest murder rate in the world, at 67 per 100,000; the murder rate in the United States, by contrast, is 5.4 per 100,000.

According to the UN report, Honduras is the Central American country that is most affected by the drug trade. With dense jungle territories and the longest Caribbean coastline, Honduras is positioned as the first corner of the triangle, leading into trade routes that eventually reach Mexico and the United States. The Mexican cartels have penetrated Honduras, as have expanding criminal gangs with readily accessible firearms. The Sinaloa cartel is reported to have assassinated Honduras's top counter-drug official in December 2009 over the seizure of a pseudoephedrine shipment. A plot by the Zetas to kill the minister of security was thwarted in early 2010.

Honduras's highly unsettling security situation has been exacerbated by a still-unresolved political crisis that has undermined governance and, in turn, has tended to benefit drug trafficking organizations and criminal gangs. More than a year and a half after Honduras suffered a military coup that dislodged the constitutionally elected government of Manuel Zelaya (who is in exile in the Dominican Republic), the country remains profoundly polarized between Zelaya's supporters and those associated with the de facto government that took control in June 2009, led by Roberto Micheletti.

In accordance with previously scheduled elections, a new government headed by Porfirio Lobo of the National Party took office in January 2010 and has struggled to navigate and overcome the country's sharp divisions. Conciliatory measures to defuse tensions have borne scant fruit. Distrust and bitterness on both sides compound the difficulties of addressing the country's daunting policy agenda, which includes not just expanding criminality but also high levels of unemployment and deepening social and economic distress.

A truth commission directed by Guatemala's former foreign minister and vice president Eduardo Stein has sought to pursue a balanced approach and heal the wounds, but the undertaking has not garnered broad support and has been criticized from both sides. A clear measure of the country's polarization can be seen in the reaction to a July 2009 diplomatic cable by US ambassador Hugo Llorens, which was leaked by Wikileaks, in which Llorens clearly called the ouster of Zelaya unconstitutional. Whereas coup supporters were upset that the United States adopted a critical stance toward a move they regarded as justified, coup opponents were puzzled that Washington failed to respond to such a depiction with more forceful action against the de facto government.

Honduras continues to be a significant source of discord and strain in inter-American relations. The coup caused member states of the Organization of American States (OAS), the hemisphere's chief political body, to expel Honduras—only the second country, after Cuba (1962), to have met such a fate. Despite substantial pressure to recognize the Lobo government that has been exerted by the United States and all but one of Honduras's Central American neighbors (Nicaragua), key players in regional political affairs still deem the government illegitimate—including Venezuela (Zelaya was an ally of Venezuela's president, Hugo Chávez) and, most crucially, Brazil (Zelaya took refuge in Brazil's embassy in Tegucigalpa, the capital of Honduras, before going into exile). The continued ostracism of the country from regional forums has complicated Honduras's ability to secure needed funds from multilateral financial institutions and has slowed down the government's attempts to ameliorate the nation's acute socioeconomic ills.

Indeed, the economic impact of the political crisis since June 2009 has been quite significant. It is estimated that 200,000 jobs were lost as a direct result of it. Some 36 percent of the workforce was unemployed or underemployed in 2009. Not surprisingly, foreign investment also suffered, with the Honduran central bank reporting a drop of almost 50 percent from 2008 levels, though the global economic downturn surely played a part in that as well. More recently, access to international capital has eased.

One particularly troubling phenomenon in Honduras, which reflects the confluence of security and political crises, has been the killing of journalists (which is also a serious problem in Mexico, though less so in other Central American nations). In 2010, eight journalists in Honduras were murdered. Several of them reported on organized crime, whereas others, according to rights groups, may have been targets of political crimes. In any case, all of the murders have gone unpunished.

In a July 2010 report, the Committee to Protect Journalists accused the Honduran government of "fostering a climate of lawlessness that is allowing criminals to kill with impunity." Buttressing that assessment was a December 2010 report issued by Human Rights Watch, entitled "After the Coup: Ongoing Violence, Intimidation, and Impunity in Honduras." The report documented some 47 attacks or threats against journalists, human rights defenders, and political activists during Lobo's first year in office.

EL SALVADOR TESTED

El Salvador, since the two sides to the country's bitter and bloody civil war signed a peace agreement in 1992, has seen a huge upsurge in gang violence. There are an estimated 30,000 gang members in a country of just over 6 million. This phenomenon, which has become more associated with El Salvador than with other countries in Central America, has to some degree offset the welcome peace dividends that accompanied the end of political violence. The legacies of the armed conflict—along with a proliferation of firearms, enduring socioeconomic woes, and transnational contacts with US-based gangs (an element of which is increased deportations from the United States back to El Salvador)—have resulted in a toxic mix.

Many observers were hopeful that, with the election of President Mauricio Funes in 2009, El Salvador would be better able to develop the institutional capacity to cope with its monumental security and social problems. After nearly two decades of rule by the rightist Arena party, Funes is El Salvador's first elected president from the FMLN (Farabundo Martí National Liberation Front), the party of the demobilized guerrilla movement that fought in the civil conflict (1979–92). Funes's election carried enormous symbolic significance and heightened expectations for a region seeking to bridge longstanding ideological chasms.

Funes, governing largely as a moderate pragmatist, has tried to model his government after that of Luiz Inácio Lula da Silva, Brazil's hugely successful former president. Operating within significant constraints, Funes has accorded more emphasis to poverty-alleviation strategies than his predecessors, presiding over important advances in education and health care. His administration's foreign policies have been notably centrist. El Salvador's posture toward the United States has been accommodating, and regarding the Honduras controversy the Funes administration has been supportive of President Lobo, strongly urging other Latin American governments to recognize his elected government.

According to public opinion surveys, Funes's political approach has wide appeal in a country weary of partisan rancor. Yet the president faces fierce resistance from his FMLN party, which is pressing for a more radical agenda, as well as from factions of the opposition Arena, and he has yet to build a solid governing structure. To do so will require considerable political skill and a measure of luck, but most importantly concrete results in improving El Salvador's security and economic conditions. This will not be easy, especially in light of declining remittances coming from the United States to a country that relies heavily on such flows.

In confronting the security challenge, Funes has moved to criminalize gang membership and has also tried to appeal to Central American neighbors to pursue more coordinated efforts to reduce the spread of criminality, which poses the greatest threat to rule of law in the region. It is far from clear, however, that such measures, however well intentioned, will succeed in arresting the overall deterioration. The growing presence of Mexican drug trafficking organizations in El Salvador could well overwhelm efforts to deal with the gang phenomenon, which has been around since the 1990s.

NICARAGUA'S STRONG MAN

Beyond and beneath the Northern Triangle, one finds a greater measure of tranquility. With 14 murders per 100,000 citizens, Nicaragua is almost a model of social peace compared to Guatemala, Honduras, and El Salvador. Part of the explanation for this is the country's more consistently professional police force, which has been maintained since the transition from Sandinista revolutionary rule to democratic, elected government in 1990.

While crime is less rampant, however, the perpetuation in power of Daniel Ortega remains a concern. Ortega, who has led the Sandinista National Liberation Front since 1979 and was president of Nicaragua from 1985 until his defeat at the polls in 1990, was elected president in 2006 after a number of failed runs for the office. Now he is scarcely disguising his intention to stay on as president: He plans to run again in 2011 despite the fact that doing so is unconstitutional. Through shrewd manipulation of institutions (for example, illegally extending the terms of two Sandinista judges); frequent use of decree authority; cynical and convenient political pacts with prominent opposition figures (especially the former president Arnoldo Alemán); and some moderately successful social programs, Ortega appears to be in a strong position to pull it off.

This is particularly so because there is no guarantee the voting process will be free and fair. Local elections in 2008, in which no outside observers were permitted, were widely deemed to be fraudulent. Ortega's brand of strongman rule, marked by the steady erosion of checks and constraints on executive authority, recalls certain features of the dictatorship of Anastasio Somoza (1967–1979), against which Ortega and his fellow Sandinistas fought in the 1970s. To date, Ortega has been able to proceed with his blatant power grab with little response from the rest of the hemisphere, which is politically fragmented and is not focused on the Nicaraguan situation.

Despite Ortega's alliance with President Chávez, and despite Nicaragua's participation in the Chávez-led regional group ALBA (Bolivarian Alliance for the Americas), ideology has for Ortega clearly taken a back seat to sheer power politics. He appears ready to do whatever is necessary to remain in power. Ortega has, for example, been quite accommodating with international financial institutions and even parts of Nicaragua's private sector. And, occasionally harsh rhetoric notwithstanding, he has been open to dealing with the United States, even fully honoring the 2005 Central American Free Trade Agreement.

In October 2010—in a move few regard as unrelated to Ortega's quest to remain in power—some 50 Nicaraguan troops were sent to a disputed zone on the country's border with Costa Rica, presumably to help dredge the San Juan River. That led Costa Rica to mobilize some of its police force (Costa Rica abolished its military in 1948), resulting in a tense standoff. The OAS has intervened but, despite the adoption of several resolutions, has so far been unable to get Ortega to withdraw the soldiers. The Costa Rican government has also appealed to the International Court of Justice in The Hague for a resolution of the conflict.

Not surprisingly, the dispute has aroused nationalist sentiment in both countries, and has thus boosted Ortega's political standing as he prepares for the 2011 race amid intense controversy over a 2009 Supreme Court ruling that exempted him from the constitutional ban on consecutive reelection. In alliance with Alemán, Ortega also has successfully turned to the national assembly to support legislation that would provide a new framework for the country's defense and security policies, including the formation of an intelligence-gathering network.

Critics warn of further erosion of the rule of law and the prospect of growing militarization of Nicaraguan society. Some observers are also worried about the politicization of the country's police forces, which so far have been an important factor in guarding against the rise and penetration of organized crime that have afflicted Guatemala, Honduras, and El Salvador.

VULNERABLE COSTA RICA

Although Costa Rica on nearly all institutional and social measures is more advanced than its Central American neighbors, it is far from immune to some of the wider phenomena creating security problems in the region. At the end of 2010 the government of President Laura Chinchilla of the center-left National Liberation Party was clearly preoccupied with the tense impasse with Nicaragua.

By resorting to the OAS and the International Court of Justice, Chinchilla, Costa Rica's first woman president and a noted expert on public security matters, was pursuing diplomatic and legal options to keep the situation from getting out of control. Further, as the only Central American country with relations with China (established under the previous administration of Oscar Arias), Costa Rica is focused on attracting investment and boosting trade.

Chinchilla's professional background and expertise may turn out to be useful in addressing the problem of drug-related violence, which is putting a strain on Costa Rican institutions. Unlike its neighbors, Costa Rica does not have armed forces, so it cannot deploy military units as other countries have done to bolster police presence and combat spreading criminality. Thus, while Costa Rica does not face the risk of "militarizing" what is fundamentally a law enforcement issue, it is vulnerable to a problem that its police forces may not be fully equipped to handle.

As a result, in accordance with a Joint Maritime Agreement, the United States military, with some 46 warships and 7,000 troops off the coast, has been granted permission to enter the country should the need arise. Although the decision has generated some minor controversy in the country, for the most part the bilateral deal has not so far posed a serious political problem. For Costa Ricans, along with other Central Americans, security has become an increasingly salient concern.

CENTRAL AMERICA'S TRAVAILS

Survey after survey point to the same finding: Security is the overriding issue for most Central Americans. Available data tend to bear out the widespread perception: The end of political, armed conflict 15 years ago has not been accompanied by higher levels of social peace. On the contrary, fear and lawlessness today are rampant in the region. This situation is the product of precarious governance structures, including ineffective judicial institutions and incoherent political parties, along with a far from propitious external environment. High energy costs and the consequences of the severe economic downturn in the United States—particularly in sectors of the economy in which Hispanics are disproportionately active—have hit Central America with unusual force.

Mechanisms of integration, both within the Central American subregion and across the hemisphere, have to date not responded adequately to the worsening problems—particularly the organized crime in Guatemala, Honduras, and El Salvador, and the authoritarianism in Nicaragua. The US-backed Mérida Initiative, started under the George W.Bush administration and extended under President Barack Obama, has essentially sought to assist Mexico, through the provision of various kinds of equipment and training, in its enormously difficult fight against drug-fueled violence and organized crime. Within that package of some $1.6 billion over three years, however, relatively few resources have been directed further south, to Central America, despite the problems aggravated by drug trafficking and the war on drugs.

To its credit, the Obama administration has become increasingly concerned with the deteriorating security situation in Central America. In August 2010, the State Department launched the Central American Regional Security Initiative, which lists a set of laudable aims and proposes to devote $165 million to supporting law enforcement and judicial institutions in the region as well as an array of social and economic programs. In September the administration added Honduras, Nicaragua, and Costa Rica to the United States' list of countries with major drug trafficking or producing problems.

Given the magnitude of the challenge and the high stakes involved, however, it is not clear whether such efforts, however worthwhile, will be sufficient to deal effectively with problems that require sustained, high-level political attention and a more robust and energized multilateral system. For Washington, a broader strategy would, for example, focus seriously on stemming continuing flows of arms and money from the United States to the region; fostering more genuine cooperation among Central American governments and other Latin American countries, particularly Mexico; and rethinking an antidrug policy that has yielded such disappointing results.

Although Central America's crime problem cannot be reduced to drugs—illicit activities flourish in a number of different areas—it is a key factor in the overall situation and, if properly addressed, would help mitigate the worst consequences of criminality.

SHARED RESPONSIBILITY

The urgent need for a comprehensive approach was highlighted in August 2010, when 72 migrants—most of them from Central America—were executed by the Zetas, the Mexican drug trafficking group. In pursuit of profit, the Zetas help migrants from Guatemala, Honduras, and El Salvador cross the border into Mexico on the way to the United States, then hold some of them hostage and force their families to pay ransom or insist that they help with drug smuggling. If they refuse, they are often executed, as happened in this case.

Such extortion practices and human trafficking, in addition to other tragic stories associated with the narcotics trade and gang violence, are all too common among the United States' closest neighbors, whose citizens make up an increasing share of the US population. For reasons of national interest—not to mention out of a sense of shared responsibility—Washington should seek to catalyze a broader hemispheric effort, marshalling both economic and political resources to address a colossal problem, one that shows no signs of abating and indeed threatens to metastasize.

Challenge Questions

After reading this article, you will be able to answer the following questions:

1. Why is security of paramount importance for Central Americans?
2. Why are the levels of violence and criminal activity lower in Nicaragua and Costa Rica than in the other three Central American states?
3. How are the global economic crisis and high energy costs related to national security concerns in Central America?
4. What might be some possible solutions to the region's instability?

Article

Humanitarian Intervention Comes of Age

Lessons from Somalia to Libya

JON WESTERN AND JOSHUA S. GOLDSTEIN

No sooner had NATO launched its first air strike in Libya than the mission was thrown into controversy—and with it, the more general notion of humanitarian intervention. Days after the UN Security Council authorized international forces to protect civilians and establish a no-fly zone, NATO seemed to go beyond its mandate as several of its members explicitly demanded that Libyan leader Muammar al-Qaddafi step down. It soon became clear that the fighting would last longer than expected. Foreign policy realists and other critics likened the Libyan operation to the disastrous engagements of the early 1990s in Somalia, Rwanda, and Bosnia, arguing that humanitarian intervention is the wrong way to respond to intrastate violence and civil war, especially following the debacles in Afghanistan and Iraq.

To some extent, widespread skepticism is understandable: past failures have been more newsworthy than successes, and foreign interventions inevitably face steep challenges. Yet such skepticism is unwarranted. Despite the early setbacks in Libya, NATO's success in protecting civilians and helping rebel forces remove a corrupt leader there has become more the rule of humanitarian intervention than the exception. As Libya and the international community prepare for the post-Qaddafi transition, it is important to examine the big picture of humanitarian intervention—and the big picture is decidedly positive. Over the last 20 years, the international community has grown increasingly adept at using military force to stop or prevent mass atrocities.

Humanitarian intervention has also benefited from the evolution of international norms about violence, especially the emergence of "the responsibility to protect," which holds that the international community has a special set of responsibilities to protect civilians—by force, if necessary—from war crimes, crimes against humanity, ethnic cleansing, and genocide when national governments fail to do so. The doctrine has become integrated into a growing tool kit of conflict management strategies that includes today's more robust peacekeeping operations and increasingly effective international criminal justice mechanisms. Collectively, these strategies have helped foster an era of declining armed conflict, with wars occurring less frequently and producing far fewer civilian casualties than in previous periods.

A Turbulent Decade

Modern humanitarian intervention was first conceived in the years following the end of the Cold War. The triumph of liberal democracy over communism made Western leaders optimistic that they could solve the world's problems as never before. Military force that had long been held in check by superpower rivalry could now be unleashed to protect poor countries from aggression, repression, and hunger. At the same time, the shifting global landscape created new problems that cried out for action. Nationalist and ethnic conflicts in former communist countries surged, and recurrent famines and instability hit much of Africa. A new and unsettled world order took shape, one seemingly distinguished by the frequency and brutality of wars and the deliberate targeting of civilians. The emotional impact of these crises was heightened by new communications technologies that transmitted graphic images of human suffering across the world. For the first time in decades, terms such as "genocide" and "ethnic cleansing" appeared regularly in public discussions.

Western political elites struggled to respond to these new realities. When U.S. marines arrived in Somalia in December 1992 to secure famine assistance that had been jeopardized by civil war, there were few norms or rules of engagement to govern such an intervention and no serious plans for the kinds of forces and tactics that would be needed to establish long-term stability. Indeed, the marines' very arrival highlighted the gap between military theory and practice: the heavily armed troops stormed ashore on a beach occupied by only dozens of camera-wielding journalists.

Although the Somalia mission did succeed in saving civilians, the intervention was less successful in coping with the political and strategic realities of Somali society and addressing the underlying sources of conflict. U.S. forces were drawn into a shooting war with one militia group, and in the October 1993 "Black Hawk down" incident, 18 U.S. soldiers were killed, and one of their bodies was dragged through the streets of Mogadishu while television cameras rolled. Facing domestic pressures and lacking a strategic objective, President Bill Clinton quickly withdrew U.S. troops. The UN soon followed, and Somalia was left to suffer in a civil war that continues to this day.

Meanwhile, two days after the "Black Hawk down" fiasco, the UN Security Council authorized a peacekeeping mission for Rwanda, where a peace agreement held the promise of ending a civil war. The international force was notable for its small size and paltry resources. Hutu extremists there drew lessons from the faint-hearted international response in Somalia, and when the conflict reignited in April 1994, they killed ten Belgian peacekeepers to induce the Belgian-led UN force to pull out. Sure enough, most of the peacekeepers withdrew, and as more than half a million civilians were killed in a matter of months, the international community failed to act.

Around the same time, a vicious war erupted throughout the former Yugoslavia, drawing a confused and ineffective response from the West. At first, in 1992, U.S. Secretary of State James Baker declared that the United States did not "have a dog in that fight." Even after the world learned of tens of thousands of civilian deaths, in May 1993, Clinton's secretary of state, Warren Christopher, described the so-called ancient hatreds of ethnic groups there as a presumably unsolvable "problem from hell." Unwilling to risk their soldiers' lives or to use the word "genocide," with all of its political, legal, and moral ramifications, the United States and European powers opted against a full-scale intervention and instead supported a UN peacekeeping force that found little peace to keep. At times, the UN force actually made things worse, promising protection that it could not provide or giving fuel and money to aggressors in exchange for the right to send humanitarian supplies to besieged victims.

The UN and Western powers were humiliated in Somalia, Rwanda, and the former Yugoslavia. War criminals elsewhere appeared to conclude that the international community could be intimidated by a few casualties. And in the United States, a number of prominent critics came to feel that humanitarian intervention was an ill-conceived enterprise.

The political scientist Samuel Huntington claimed that it was "morally unjustifiable and politically indefensible" to put U.S. soldiers at risk in intrastate conflicts, and he argued at another point that it was "human to hate." Henry Kissinger saw danger in the United States becoming bogged down in what he later called "the bottomless pit of Balkan passions," and he warned against intervening when there were not vital strategic interests at stake. Other critics concluded that applying military force to protect people often prolonged civil wars and intensified the violence, killing more civilians than otherwise might have been the case. And still others argued that intervention fundamentally altered intrastate political contests, creating long-term instability or protracted dependence on the international community.

Nonetheless, international actors did not abandon intervention or their efforts to protect civilians. Rather, amid the violence, major intervening powers and the UN undertook systematic reviews of their earlier failures, updated their intervention strategies, and helped foster a new set of norms for civilian protection.

A key turning point came in 1995, when Bosnian Serb forces executed more than 7,000 prisoners in the UN-designated safe area of Srebrenica. The Clinton administration quickly abandoned its hesitancy and led a forceful diplomatic and military effort to end the war. The persistent diplomacy of Anthony Lake, the U.S. national security adviser, persuaded the reluctant Europeans and UN peacekeeping commanders to support Operation Deliberate Force, NATO's aggressive air campaign targeting the Bosnian Serb army. That effort brought Serbia to the negotiating table, where U.S. Assistant Secretary of State Richard Holbrooke crafted the Dayton agreement, which ended the war. In place of the hapless UN force, NATO sent 60,000 heavily armed troops into the "zone of separation" between the warring parties, staving off renewed fighting.

The "problem from hell" stopped immediately, and the ensuing decade of U.S.-led peacekeeping saw not a single U.S. combat-related casualty in Bosnia. Unlike previous interventions, the post-Dayton international peacekeeping presence was unified, vigorous, and sustained, and it has kept a lid on ethnic violence for more than 15 years. A related innovation was the International Criminal Tribunal for the Former Yugoslavia (ICTY), a court that has indicted 161 war criminals, including all the principal Serbian wartime leaders. Despite extensive criticism for ostensibly putting justice ahead of peace, the tribunal has produced dramatic results. Every suspected war criminal, once indicted, quickly lost political influence in postwar Bosnia, and not one of the 161 indictees remains at large today.

Buoyed by these successes, NATO responded to an imminent Serbian attack on Kosovo in 1999 by launching a major air war. Despite initial setbacks (the operation failed to stop a Serbian ground attack that created more than a million Kosovar Albanian refugees), the international community signaled that it would not back down. Under U.S. leadership, NATO escalated the air campaign, and the ICTY indicted Serbian President Slobodan Milosevic for crimes against humanity. Within three months, the combined military and diplomatic pressure compelled Serbia to withdraw its forces from Kosovo. And even though many observers, including several senior Clinton administration officials, feared that the ICTY's indictment of Milosevic in the middle of the military campaign would make it even less likely that he would capitulate in Kosovo or ever relinquish power, he was removed from office 18 months later by nonviolent civil protest and turned over to The Hague.

Outside the Balkans, the international community continued to adapt its approach to conflicts with similar success. In 1999, after a referendum on East Timor's secession from Indonesia led to Indonesian atrocities against Timorese civilians, the UN quickly authorized an 11,000-strong Australian-led military force to end the violence. The intervention eventually produced an independent East Timor at peace with Indonesia. Later missions in Sierra Leone, Liberia, and Côte d'Ivoire used a similar model of deploying a regional military force in coordination with the UN and, on occasion, European powers.

Correcting the Record

Despite the international community's impressive record of recent humanitarian missions, many of the criticisms formulated in response to the botched campaigns of 1992–95 still guide the conversation about intervention today. The charges are outdated. Contrary to the claims that interventions prolong civil wars and lead to greater humanitarian suffering and civilian casualties, the most violent and protracted cases in recent history—Somalia, Rwanda, the Democratic Republic of the Congo, Bosnia before Srebrenica, and Darfur—have been cases in which the international community was unwilling either to intervene or to sustain a commitment with credible force. Conversely, a comprehensive study conducted by the political scientist Taylor Seybolt has found that aggressive operations legitimized by firm UN Security Council resolutions, as in Bosnia in 1995 and East Timor in 1999, were the most successful at ending conflicts.

Even when civil wars do not stop right away, external interventions often mitigate violence against civilians. This is because, as the political scientist Matthew Krain and others have found, interventions aimed at preventing mass atrocities often force would-be killers to divert resources away from slaughtering civilians and toward defending themselves. This phenomenon, witnessed in the recent Libya campaign, means that even when interventions fail to end civil wars or resolve factional differences immediately, they can still protect civilians.

Another critique of humanitarian interventions is that they create perverse incentives for rebel groups to deliberately provoke states to commit violence against civilians in order to generate an international response. By this logic, the prospect of military intervention would generate more rebel provocations and thus more mass atrocities. Yet the statistical record shows exactly the opposite. Since the modern era of humanitarian intervention began, both the frequency and the intensity of attacks on civilians have declined. During the Arab Spring protests this year, there was no evidence that opposition figures in Tunisia, Egypt, Syria, or Yemen sought to trigger outside intervention. In fact, the protesters clearly stated that they would oppose such action. Even the Libyan rebels, who faced long odds against Qaddafi's forces, refused what would have been the most effective outside help: foreign boots on the ground.

Two decades of media exposure to genocide have altered global attitudes about intervention.

Recent efforts to perfect humanitarian intervention have been fueled by deep changes in public norms about violence against civilians and advances in conflict management. Two decades of media exposure to mass atrocities, ethnic cleansing, and genocide have altered global—not simply Western—attitudes about intervention. The previously sacrosanct concept of state sovereignty has been made conditional on a state's responsible behavior, and in 2005, the UN General Assembly unanimously endorsed the doctrine of the responsibility to protect at the UN's World Summit. NATO's intervention in Libya reflects how the world has become more committed to the protection of civilians. Both UN Security Council resolutions on Libya this year passed with unprecedented speed and without a single dissenting vote.

In the wake of conflicts as well, the international community has shown that it can and will play a role in maintaining order and restoring justice. Peacekeeping missions now enjoy widespread legitimacy and have been remarkably successful in preventing the recurrence of violence once deployed. And because of successful postconflict tribunals and the International Criminal Court, individuals, including national leaders, can now be held liable for egregious crimes against civilians.

Collectively, these new conflict management and civilian protection tools have contributed to a marked decline in violence resulting from civil war. According to the most recent *Human Security Report,* between 1992 and 2003 the number of conflicts worldwide declined by more than 40 percent, and between 1988 and 2008 the number of conflicts that produced 1,000 or more battle deaths per year fell by 78 percent. Most notably, the incidence of lethal attacks against civilians was found to be lower in 2008 than at any point since the collection of such data began in 1989.

Still, although international norms now enshrine civilian protection and levels of violence are down, humanitarian interventions remain constrained by political and military realities. The international community's inaction in the face of attacks on Syrian protesters, as of this writing, demonstrates that neither the UN nor any major power is willing or prepared to intervene when abusive leaders firmly control the state's territory and the state's security forces and are backed by influential allies. Furthermore, the concept of civilian protection still competes with deeply held norms of sovereignty, especially in former colonies. Although humanitarian intervention can succeed in many cases, given these constraints, it is not always feasible.

Getting Better All the Time

It is against this backdrop that the international community should evaluate the two most recent interventions, in Cote d'Ivoire and Libya. In Côte d'Ivoire, a civil war that began in 2002 led to the partition of the country, with a large UN force interposed between the two sides. After years of peacekeeping, the UN oversaw long-delayed elections in 2010 and declared the opposition leader victorious. The incumbent, President Laurent Gbagbo, refused to leave, causing a months-long standoff during which Gbagbo's forces killed nearly 3,000 people. As another civil war loomed, France sent in a powerful military force that, in tandem with the UN peacekeepers, deposed Gbagbo and put the legitimate winner in the presidential palace.

Two decades ago, a similar situation in Angola led to disaster. After the UN sent a mere 500 military observers to monitor elections in 1992, the losing candidate resorted to war and the international community walked away. The crisis in Côte d'Ivoire ended much differently, partly because the mission was broadly seen as legitimate. Supporters of the action included not just the UN Security Council and Western governments but also the African Union, neighboring West African countries, and leading human rights groups. Moreover, the intervention in Côte d'Ivoire applied escalating military force over the course of several months that culminated in overwhelming firepower. The operation's planners allowed for, but did not count on, diplomacy and negotiation to dislodge Gbagbo. When those paths proved fruitless, the international community hardened its resolve.

More important than an exit strategy is a comprehensive transition strategy.

Although the final chapter of the Libya mission has yet to be written and serious challenges remain, it has enjoyed several of the same advantages. The international response began in February when, as Qaddafi's security forces intensified their efforts to crush the protests, the UN Security Council unanimously passed Resolution 1970, which condemned the violence, imposed sanctions on the regime, and referred the case to the International Criminal Court. Three weeks later, Qaddafi's forces moved toward the rebel capital of Benghazi, a city of more than 700,000, and all signs pointed to an imminent slaughter. The Arab League demanded quick UN action to halt the impending bloodshed, as did major human rights organizations, such as the International Crisis Group and Human Rights Watch. In response, the Security Council passed Resolution 1973, which demanded a suspension of hostilities and authorized NATO to enforce a no-fly zone to protect civilians. Although five members of the Security Council—Brazil, China, Germany, India, and Russia—expressed reservations, none of them ultimately opposed the resolution. The subsequent intervention has been a genuinely multinational operation in which the United States at first played a central combat role and then stepped back, providing mostly support and logistics.

The intervention has accomplished the primary objective of Resolution 1973. It saved civilian lives by halting an imminent slaughter in Benghazi, breaking the siege of Misratah, and forcing Qaddafi's tank and artillery units to take cover rather than commit atrocities. And despite the initial military setbacks and some frustration over the length and cost of the operation, the intervention contributed to the end of the civil war between Qaddafi and the rebels, which otherwise might have been much longer and more violent.

Lessons Learned

Ever since U.S. marines stormed the Somali coast in 1992, the international community has grappled with the recurring challenges of modern humanitarian intervention: establishing legitimacy, sharing burdens across nations, acting with proportionality and discrimination, avoiding "mission creep," and developing exit strategies. These challenges have not changed, but the ways the international community responds to them have. Today's successful interventions share a number of elements absent in earlier, failed missions.

First, the interventions that respond the most quickly to unfolding events protect the most lives. Ethnic cleansing and mass atrocities often occur in the early phases of conflicts, as in Rwanda and Bosnia. This highlights the necessity of early warning indicators and a capacity for immediate action. The UN still lacks standby capabilities to dispatch peacekeepers instantly to a conflict area, but national or multinational military forces have responded promptly under UN authority, and then after a number of months, they have handed off control to a UN peacekeeping force that may include soldiers from the original mission. This model worked in East Timor, Chad, and the Central African Republic, and it guided the international community's response to the impending massacre in Benghazi.

Second, the international community has learned from Somalia, Rwanda, and Bosnia that it needs access to enough military power and diplomatic muscle to back up a credible commitment to protecting civilians and to prevail even if things go wrong along the way. Lighter deployments may also succeed if members of the international community have additional forces close at hand that can be accessed if needed. When UN peacekeepers ran into trouble in Sierra Leone in 2000, for example, the United Kingdom rushed in with 4,500 troops to save the government and the peacekeeping mission from collapse.

Third, intervening governments must be sensitive to inevitable opposition from domestic constituencies and must design interventions that can withstand pressure for early exits. As Libya has demonstrated, protecting civilians from intransigent regimes often requires persistent and sustained action. In all likelihood, seemingly straightforward operations will turn out to be much less so. In past, failed missions, the international community was unwilling to accept coalition casualties and responded by withdrawing. Successful interventions, by contrast, have been designed to limit the threat to the intervening forces, thus allowing them to add resources and broaden the dimensions of the military operations in the face of difficulties.

Fourth, legitimate humanitarian interventions must be supported by a broad coalition of international, regional, and local actors. Multilateral interventions convey consensus about the appropriateness of the operations, distribute costs, and establish stronger commitments for the post-intervention transitions. But multilateralism cannot come at the expense of synchronized leadership. War criminals usually look to exploit divisions between outside powers opposing them. Interventions need to avoid having multiple states and organizations dispatch their own representatives to the conflict, sending mixed signals to the target states.

Finally, perhaps the most daunting challenge of a humanitarian intervention is the exit. Because violence against civilians is often rooted in deeper crises of political order, critics note that once in, intervenors confront the dilemma of either staying indefinitely and assuming the burdens of governance, as in Bosnia, or withdrawing and allowing the country to fall back into chaos, as in Somalia.

Some observers, then, have demanded that any intervention be carried out with a clearly defined exit strategy. Yet more important than an exit strategy is a comprehensive transition strategy, whereby foreign combat forces can exit as peacekeepers take over, and peacekeepers can exit when local governing institutions are in place and an indigenous security force stands ready to respond quickly if violence resumes. The earliest phases of an intervention must include planning for a transition strategy with clearly delineated political and economic benchmarks, so that international and local authorities can focus on the broader, long-term challenges of reconstruction, political reconciliation, and economic development.

Successful transition strategies include several crucial elements. For starters, negotiations that end humanitarian interventions must avoid laying the groundwork for protracted international presences. The Dayton peace accords, for example, created a duel-entity structure in Bosnia that has privileged nationalist and ethnic voices, and Kosovo's final status was left unresolved. Both of these outcomes unwittingly created long-term international commitments.

Intervening powers must also proceed with the understanding that they cannot bring about liberal democratic states overnight. Objectives need to be tempered to match both local and international political constraints. Recent scholarship on post-conflict state building suggests that the best approach may be a hybrid one in which outsiders and domestic leaders rely on local customs, politics, and practices to establish new institutions that can move over time toward international norms of accountable, legitimate, and democratic governance.

Humanitarian interventions involve an inherent contradiction: they use violence in order to control violence. Setbacks are almost inevitable, and so it is no surprise that the operations often attract criticism. Yet when carried out thoughtfully, legitimately, and as part of a broader set of mechanisms designed to protect civilians, the use of military force for humanitarian purposes saves lives. Mass atrocities, ethnic cleansing, and genocide are truly problems from hell, but their solutions—honed over the course of two decades of experience from Mogadishu to Tripoli—are very much of this world.

Critical Thinking

1. What incidents prompted skepticism about the effectiveness of humanitarian intervention?
2. What are the criticisms of humanitarian intervention and how valid are they?
3. What has strengthened the willingness of the international community to intervene?
4. What are the lessons of recent humanitarian interventions?

Jon Western is Five College Associate Professor of International Relations at Mount Holyoke College. **Joshua S. Goldstein** is Professor Emeritus of International Relations at American University and the author of *Winning the War on War: The Decline of Armed Conflict Worldwide*.

Article

The True Costs of Humanitarian Intervention

The hard truth about a noble notion.

BENJAMIN A. VALENTINO

As forces fighting Libyan leader Muammar al-Qaddafi consolidated control of Tripoli in the last days of August 2011, many pundits began speaking of a victory not just for the rebels but also for the idea of humanitarian intervention. In Libya, advocates of intervention argued, U.S. President Barack Obama had found the formula for success: broad regional and international support, genuine burden sharing with allies, and a capable local fighting force to wage the war on the ground. Some even heralded the intervention as a sign of an emerging Obama doctrine.

It is clearly too soon for this kind of triumphalism, since the final balance of the Libyan intervention has yet to be tallied. The country could still fall into civil war, and the new Libyan government could turn out to be little better than the last. As of this writing, troubling signs of infighting among the rebel ranks had begun to emerge, along with credible reports of serious human rights abuses by rebel forces.

Yet even if the intervention does ultimately give birth to a stable and prosperous democracy, this outcome will not prove that intervention was the right choice in Libya or that similar interventions should be attempted elsewhere. To establish that requires comparing the full costs of intervention with its benefits and asking whether those benefits could be achieved at a lower cost. The evidence from the last two decades is not promising on this score. Although humanitarian intervention has undoubtedly saved lives, Americans have seriously underappreciated the moral, political, and economic price involved.

This does not mean that the United States should stop trying to promote its values abroad, even when its national security is not at risk. It just needs a different strategy. Washington should replace its focus on military intervention with a humanitarian foreign policy centered on saving lives by funding public health programs in the developing world, aiding victims of natural disasters, and assisting refugees fleeing violent conflict. Abandoning humanitarian intervention in most cases would not mean leaving victims of genocide and repression to their fate. Indeed, such a strategy could actually save far more people, at a far lower price.

The Intervention Consensus

As the Cold War ended, many foreign policy analysts predicted that the United States would return to isolationism. Without the need to counter the Soviet Union, it was argued, Americans would naturally turn inward. It hardly needs saying that these predictions have not been borne out. Throughout the 1990s, the United States continued to play the leading role in global affairs, maintaining military bases around the world and regularly intervening with military force. The 9/11 attacks only reinforced this pattern. Politicians from both parties today regard the deployment of military forces as a routine part of international relations.

It was not always this way. Although isolationism among conservatives went virtually extinct in the 1950s, during the Cold War, and especially after Vietnam, liberals almost always opposed the use of military force, even for humanitarian purposes. But after the Soviet Union collapsed, many on the left began to embrace the idea that the vast military capabilities assembled to check its influence could now be used to save lives rather than destroy them. The evaporation of Soviet power also made it easier to use those forces, lifting one of the most important constraints on the deployment of U.S. troops abroad. The astonishing success of the U.S. military in the Persian Gulf War of 1990–91, meanwhile, convinced many people that Americans had finally lost their aversion to intervention abroad, kicking the "Vietnam syndrome" once and for all. The costs of using force appeared to have fallen dramatically.

The end of the Cold War also touched off a bloody civil war in Yugoslavia, the first major conflict in Europe in almost 50 years. Although the United States had few national security interests at stake there, the brutal nature of the fighting prompted many calls for intervention, mostly from the left. These calls did not move President George H. W. Bush to intervene in the Balkans, but his decision to send forces to Somalia in 1992 was partially an effort to demonstrate that he was willing to use the military for humanitarian missions if the conditions were favorable. Under President Bill Clinton, the United States went further, undertaking major humanitarian interventions in Bosnia, Haiti, and Kosovo.

A surprising number of opinion-makers on the left, including Peter Beinart, Thomas Friedman, Christopher Hitchens, Michael Ignatieff, and Anne-Marie Slaughter, later lent their support to the 2003 invasion of Iraq out of the conviction that it would end decades of human rights abuses by Saddam Hussein.

Prominent Democrats also called on the United States to use military force to end the mass killings in Darfur, Sudan. In 2007, then Senator Joe Biden told the Senate Foreign Relations Committee, "I would use American force now. . . . I think it's not only time not to take force off the table. I think it's time to put force on the table and use it." During the 2008 Democratic presidential primary race, Hillary Clinton repeatedly called for the imposition of a no-fly zone in Sudan. Most recently, in March, Obama defended the intervention in Libya, saying, "There will be times . . . when our safety is not directly threatened, but our interests and values are. . . . In such cases, we should not be afraid to act." The public agreed: a poll conducted days after NATO began air strikes against Libya found that, even with two other ongoing wars, majorities of both Democrats and Republicans supported the military action. Only self-described independents were more likely to disapprove than approve.

Tallying the Costs

Proponents of such interventions usually make their case in terms of the United States' moral responsibilities. Yet perhaps the most important costs incurred by military interventions have been moral ones. On the ground, the ethical clarity that advocates of human rights have associated with such actions—saving innocent lives—has almost always been blurred by a much more complicated reality.

Aiding defenseless civilians has usually meant empowering armed factions claiming to represent them.

To begin with, aiding defenseless civilians has usually meant empowering armed factions claiming to represent these victims, groups that are frequently responsible for major human rights abuses of their own. Although advocates of humanitarian intervention in the 1990s frequently compared the atrocities of that period to the Holocaust, the moral calculus of intervening in these conflicts was inevitably more problematic. The Tutsi victims of Hutu *génocidaires* in Rwanda and the Bosnian Muslim and Kosovar Albanian victims of Serbian paramilitaries in the former Yugoslavia were just as innocent as the Jewish victims of the Nazis during World War II. But the choice to aid these groups also entailed supporting the less than upstanding armed factions on their side.

In Bosnia, for example, the United States eventually backed Croatian and Bosnian Muslim forces in an effort to block further aggression by Serbian President Slobodan Milosevic. These forces were far less brutal than the Serbian forces, but they were nevertheless implicated in a number of large-scale atrocities. In August 1995, for example, Croatian forces drove more than 100,000 Serbs in the Krajina region of Croatia from their homes, killing hundreds of civilians in what *The New York Times* described as "the largest single 'ethnic cleansing' of the war." It was later revealed that the U.S. State Department had allowed private U.S. military consultants to train the Croatian army in preparation for the offensive. In April of this year, two Croatian military leaders in charge of the campaign were convicted of crimes against humanity at The Hague.

Similarly, after the NATO bombing campaign in 1999 helped evict Serbian forces from Kosovo, the Kosovo Liberation Army turned on the Serbian civilians remaining in the province and in neighboring Macedonia, killing hundreds and forcing thousands to flee. Since the end of the war, human rights groups and the Council of Europe have repeatedly called for investigations of high-ranking KLA officials suspected of engaging in executions, abductions, beatings, and even human organ trafficking.

Another set of moral costs stems not from the unsavory behavior of the groups being protected but from the unavoidable consequences of military intervention. Even if the ends of such actions could be unambiguously humanitarian, the means never are. Using force to save lives usually involves taking lives, including innocent ones. The most advanced precision-guided weapons still have not eliminated collateral damage altogether. Many Americans remember the 18 U.S. soldiers who died in Somalia in 1993 in the "Black Hawk down" incident. Far fewer know that U.S. and UN troops killed at least 500 Somalis on that day and as many as 1,500 during the rest of the mission—more than half of them women and children.

In Kosovo, in addition to between 700 and several thousand Serbian military deaths, Human Rights Watch estimates that NATO air strikes killed more than 500 civilians. NATO pilots, ordered to fly above 10,000 feet to limit their own losses, found it difficult to distinguish between friend and foe on the ground. Sixteen civilians were also killed when NATO bombed a Serbian television station that it accused of spreading pro-government propaganda. These and other incidents led Human Rights Watch to conclude that NATO had violated international humanitarian law in its conduct of the war. Amnesty International accused NATO of war crimes.

Although military interventions are calculated to increase the costs of human rights abuses for those who commit them, perhaps interventions' most perverse consequence has been the way they have sometimes actually done the opposite. If perpetrators simply blame the victims for the setbacks and suffering inflicted by the intervention, the incentives to retaliate against victim groups, and possibly even popular support for such retaliation, may rise. Foreign military interventions can change victims from being viewed as a nuisance into being seen as powerful and traitorous enemies, potentially capable of exacting revenge, seizing power, or breaking away from the state. Under these conditions, even moderates are more likely to support harsh measures to meet such threats. And with most humanitarian missions relying on airpower to avoid casualties, potential victims have little protection from retaliation.

In Kosovo, for example, the NATO bombing campaign hardened Serbian opinion against the Kosovar Albanians and rallied public support behind Milosevic, at least initially. Many Serbs donned T-shirts with a bull's-eye and attended anti-NATO rock concerts to express their solidarity against the West and for Milosevic's regime. One Serb told a reporter, "When Milosevic thought he could do whatever he wanted with us, I was against him. Now I am against NATO because they are strong and we are weak." Still worse, the bombing may have actually provoked a major upsurge in the violence, or at least given Milosevic the excuse he needed to implement a long-held plan to ethnically cleanse the region. Either way, when Serbian attacks on Kosovars escalated, NATO planes were flying too high and too fast to protect civilians on the ground.

The prospect of foreign military intervention also may encourage victims to rise up—a perilous course of action if the intervening forces are not equipped to protect them or if the intervention arrives too late or not at all. Perhaps the most clear-cut example of this perverse dynamic occurred in the aftermath of the Persian Gulf War. During the war, Bush said the Iraqis should "take matters into their own hands and force Saddam Hussein, the dictator, to step aside." Many Iraqi Kurds and Shiites responded to this call, believing that the United States would send military forces to assist them or at least protect them from retaliation by Saddam. It was not to be. Wishing to avoid a quagmire, Bush decided to end the war just 100 hours after the ground invasion had begun. Saddam responded to the domestic uprisings with extreme brutality, killing perhaps 20,000 Kurds and 30,000–60,000 Shiites, many of them civilians.

Another set of costs associated with humanitarian interventions are political. The United States' humanitarian interventions have won the country few new friends and worsened its relations with several powerful nations. The United States' long-term security depends on good relations with China and Russia, perhaps more than any other countries, but U.S.-sponsored interventions have led to increasing distrust between Washington and these nations. Both countries face serious secessionist threats and strongly opposed U.S. intervention in Bosnia and Kosovo out of fear of setting an unwelcome precedent. The accidental bombing of the Chinese embassy in Belgrade in 1999, which killed three Chinese citizens, resulted in major demonstrations outside the U.S. embassy in Beijing and an acute deterioration of relations between the two countries that lasted almost a year. Conflict with Russia over Kosovo continues to this day.

The political strains have not been limited to relations with potential U.S. adversaries. Brazil and India, two of the United States' most important democratic allies in the developing world, also opposed the intervention in Kosovo and have refused to recognize its independence. More recently, both countries sided with China and Russia and condemned the intervention in Libya, arguing that NATO's actions significantly exceeded what the UN Security Council had authorized.

A less tangible political cost of these interventions has been their corrosive effect on the authority of international organizations such as the UN. In regard to Kosovo, the threat that China and Russia would veto a resolution to intervene in the UN Security Council forced proponents of intervention to insist that the mission did not require UN authorization. A few years later, however, many of these one-time advocates found themselves arguing against U.S. intervention in Iraq, at least in part on the grounds that Washington had failed to obtain UN approval. Having ignored the UN when it came to Kosovo and Iraq, it will be more difficult for the United States to condemn the use of force by other states that fail to obtain UN approval.

Opportunities Lost

Perhaps the most frequently ignored costs of humanitarian interventions, however, have been what economists call opportunity costs—the forgone opportunities to which the resources for a military mission might have been put. These costs are considerable, since military intervention is a particularly expensive way to save lives.

Each of the more than 220 Tomahawk missiles fired by the U.S. military into Libya, for example, cost around $1.4 million. In Somalia, a country of about 8.5 million people, the final bill for the U.S. intervention totaled more than $7 billion. Scholars have estimated that the military mission there probably saved between 10,000 and 25,000 lives. To put it in the crudest possible terms, this meant that Washington spent between $280,000 and $700,000 for each Somali it spared. As for Bosnia, if one assumes that without military action a quarter of the two million Muslims living there would have been killed (a highly unrealistic figure), the intervention cost $120,000 per life saved. Judging the 2003 Iraq war—now a multitrillion-dollar adventure—primarily on humanitarian grounds, the costs would be orders of magnitude higher.

The lesson that many human rights advocates have drawn from these calculations is not that intervention is too costly but that it is no substitute for prevention. A careful study commissioned by the Carnegie Corporation of New York, for example, concluded that early but robust efforts at conflict prevention were almost always more cost-effective than reactive interventions. If only the math were so simple: this argument seriously underestimates the full costs of preventive efforts by assuming that the international community will correctly identify catastrophes long before they occur and intervene only in those cases. In reality, predicting which hot spots will turn violent is extremely difficult. As then UN Secretary-General Boutros Boutros-Ghali told reporters in Sarajevo in 1992, although the situation there seemed dire, his job was to think about all the conflicts around the world that might benefit from intervention. "I understand your frustration," he said, "but you have a situation that is better than ten other places in the world. . . . I can give you a list." Thus, although the costs of prevention in any given conflict would surely be much lower than the costs of a purely reactive intervention, these costs must be multiplied many times over because forces would end up intervening in crises that were never going to rise to a level that would have justified military intervention.

What is more, the record of low-cost preventive missions has been at least as bad as the record of interventions reacting to atrocities. One of the most tragic aspects of the genocides in Bosnia, Rwanda, and Darfur was that international peacekeepers were present during some of the worst episodes of violence, such as the slaughter of some 8,000 Bosnian Muslims in Srebrenica in 1995, which was witnessed by 400 UN peacekeepers. The problem in these cases was not that no one was sent to prevent the violence; it was that the forces that were deployed were not given the resources or the mandates to stop the violence breaking out around them. In some cases, they could not even protect themselves. More robust preventive deployments might have been more effective, but they would not have been cheap.

More for the Money

To be sure, $120,000 or even $700,000 does not seem like an unreasonably high price to pay to save a life; developed countries routinely value the lives of their citizens much more highly. Although these costs may seem low in absolute terms, in comparison to the other ways the United States' scarce resources might have been spent to save lives abroad, humanitarian intervention begins to look almost extravagant. Three strategies offer the prospect of helping more people with a much lower moral, political, and economic cost: investing in international public health initiatives, sending relief aid to victims of natural disasters and famines, and assisting refugees fleeing violent conflict. Millions more lives could be saved if the billions of dollars spent on humanitarian interventions were instead spent on these efforts.

In comparison with the other ways to save lives abroad, military intervention begins to look almost extravagant.

International public health programs are almost certainly the most cost-effective way to save lives abroad. The World Health Organization estimates that every year at least two million people die from vaccine-preventable diseases alone (millions more die from other easily treatable infectious diseases, such as malaria or infectious diarrhea). This is an annual toll more than twice as large as the Rwandan genocide and more than 200 times the number of civilians who died in Kosovo. Measles alone killed more than 160,000 people in 2008, almost all of them children. It costs less than $1 to immunize a child against measles, and since not every unvaccinated child would have died from measles, the cost per life saved comes out to an estimated $224. Even using the exceedingly generous estimates above of the number of lives saved by military intervention, this means that on a per-life basis, measles vaccination would be 3,000 times as cost-effective as the military intervention in Somalia and more than 500 times as cost-effective as the intervention in Bosnia. The provision of antimalarial bed nets may be more efficient still—costing only between $100 and $200 per life saved. The final bill may be even lower, since preventive public health expenditures such as these often more than pay for themselves in averted medical costs and increased productivity.

The lifesaving potential of such public health programs is enormous. Indeed, because of intensive vaccination initiatives, measles deaths have dropped by almost 80 percent since 2000, probably saving well over four million lives in the last ten years. And of course, vaccinating children for measles did not require killing anyone, violating international laws, or damaging important relationships with powerful countries.

A second way that the United States can save lives without the use of force is through disaster-relief efforts. The International Red Cross estimates that more than one million people were killed between 2000 and 2009 in natural disasters such as earthquakes, floods, and hurricanes. It is difficult to estimate how many lives were saved by international relief efforts in these disasters or how many more might have been saved had even greater resources been devoted to disaster preparedness and response. Disaster-relief programs are almost certainly less economically efficient in saving lives than the most effective public health programs, but like public health efforts, they avoid many of the moral and political costs of military intervention. Few forms of intervention are more deeply appreciated by recipients. After the U.S. military sent rescue and medical teams and emergency supplies to Indonesia in the wake of the devastating 2004 tsunami, the proportion of Indonesians who held favorable views of the United States, which had plummeted following the invasion of Iraq, more than doubled—an important gain in the world's largest Muslim country.

Outside powers need to keep their borders open to victims fleeing violence.

A third set of strategies focuses on aiding potential victims of violent conflict and repression, including genocide and mass killing. Although using military forces to halt perpetrators and protect victims on the ground is usually very expensive, it is possible to assist victims of violent conflict at much lower cost by helping them escape to safer areas. Large refugee flows are rightly seen a humanitarian emergency in themselves, but refugees of violence are also survivors of violence. In practice, measures designed to help victims reach safety across international borders and to care for refugee populations once they arrive have probably saved more lives from conflict than any other form of international intervention.

History provides numerous examples that illustrate the potential of providing safe havens for refugees. Although the Nazis clamped down on emigration after World War II began, between 1933 and 1939 Germany actively encouraged it, a process that ultimately resulted in the exodus of approximately 70 percent of Germany's Jews. Had Western nations put up fewer barriers to Jewish immigration or actively sought to assist Jewish emigration, they would surely have saved many more lives. The ability of potential victims to escape likely played an even greater role in limiting the toll from repressive governments during the Cold War. Following the communist takeover in North Korea, for example, more than one million people, around ten percent of the population living above the 38th parallel, made their way to the South between 1945 and 1947. Had they been unable to flee, many would surely have been labeled enemies of the state and executed or sent to the North Korean gulag. Similarly, roughly 3.5 million Chinese refugees, mostly supporters of Chiang Kai-shek who would have been prime targets of Mao Zedong's subsequent campaigns against political enemies, escaped to Taiwan and Hong Kong following the communist victory in the Chinese Civil War in 1949. Today, many of the 250,000 Sudanese refugees surviving in camps in eastern Chad likely would have joined the 300,000–400,000 victims of the mass killing in Darfur had they not fled the fighting.

The first order of business, then, should be for outside powers to keep their borders open to victims fleeing violence. The large numbers of refugees who managed to escape the bloodshed in North Korea, China, and Kosovo were able to do so only because they could flee across open borders into neighboring states. Many victims are not so fortunate. For example, Iraqi Kurdish refugees attempting to flee the crackdown following the Gulf War initially faced closed borders as they tried to go to Iran and Turkey. Diplomatic pressure and economic assistance from the United States and NATO, however, ultimately prompted these countries to open their borders, at least temporarily.

Even when neighboring states are willing to open their doors, perpetrators often try to block victims' escape. Such was the case in Rwanda, where Hutu *génocidaires* set up roadblocks to prevent Tutsis from crossing into Burundi, Congo, Tanzania, and Uganda. In cases like these, the use of limited military force may make sense. In Rwanda, a relatively small military intervention, perhaps with airpower alone, could have destroyed roadblocks and secured key escape routes, helping tens of thousands reach safety. By one estimate, this strategy might have saved 75,000 lives.

The international community should also ensure the survival of refugees once they reach their destinations. The conditions awaiting most refugees of mass violence seldom provide much better odds of survival than do those faced by victims who remain behind. Not only are food, water, and shelter in short supply, but refugees are also frequently subject to violence and thievery at the hands of other refugees or local populations. Few refugees would survive for long without substantial external assistance. As a result, when the options for potential refugees are unattractive, many will prefer to stay and fight, even when their chances of success are slim. When refugees can expect more hospitable conditions across the border, however, more will choose to flee and more will survive when they arrive.

Humble Humanitarianism

Proponents of humanitarian intervention may object that the calculus laid out here understates its effectiveness by neglecting the other U.S. interests that these military missions serve. Even the most ardent advocates of intervention in such places as Kosovo, Sudan, or Libya, however, usually concede that the United States' safety was never directly threatened by the crises there. At the same time, helping refugees and saving lives through public health programs and disaster relief also serve a variety of secondary U.S. interests—improving relations with other countries, promoting economic development, and increasing regional stability. A full accounting cannot neglect these benefits, either.

Some may also protest that the United States cannot give up on humanitarian intervention since it is the only country with the capability to project power around the globe. This may be true, but it would be a relevant concern only if other countries or nongovernmental organizations were already devoting sufficient resources to nonmilitary forms of humanitarian aid. The millions of easily preventable deaths that still occur every year are evidence that much more is needed. Still others may assert that the United States has a special responsibility to oppose governments that are engaged in massive human rights violations, even at much greater cost, because doing so sends a message that the world will not tolerate crimes against humanity and despotism. But that message need not be sent with bombs. A stronger message, in fact, should be sent to governments that fail to provide even inexpensive health care or essential services to save the lives of their own citizens. Finally, some will argue that the United States does not need to choose between military intervention and humanitarian aid since it can afford both. This is correct, but given the number of people who could benefit from increased humanitarian aid, the country will have to vaccinate many more children and assist many more refugees before military intervention begins to look affordable in comparison.

The strategies suggested here are not without their own dilemmas, of course. Large refugee populations can foster instability if the refugees attempt to fight their way home or fall into conflict with local populations. And humanitarians have learned the hard way that relief aid and medical supplies can be hijacked by corrupt governments or violent rebel groups. Fortunately, these problems are less severe than the problems of military intervention, and there are ways to mitigate them, even if they cannot be eliminated altogether. The provision of humanitarian aid should be more closely monitored, the aid should be linked to other forms of aid that recipients desire, and the aid should be targeted to those countries and local groups that demonstrate that they can use it most effectively. Strategies to assist refugees must be combined with diplomatic coercion and tough economic sanctions designed to end the conflicts that forced the refugees out in the first place. With defenseless victims out of harm's way, international pressure on perpetrators would be much less likely to provoke further crackdowns.

As with most of the choices in international relations, these strategies are simply the best of a poor set of alternatives. Even so, a foreign policy based on them would not mean simply standing by in the face of atrocity and injustice. Indeed, efforts such as helping refugees could save thousands of lives even when a major military intervention is out of the question. Equally important, these strategies would do much to allow Americans to wholeheartedly embrace a less militarized foreign policy, restoring the United States' image as a force for good in the world and providing Americans with an alternative perspective on the use of force, something that has been absent from U.S. foreign policy debates. U.S. foreign policy has always sought to promote the values of its citizens, as well as protect their material and security interests abroad. The country should not abandon that noble impulse now. It simply needs a better way to act on it.

Critical Thinking

1. What are the drawbacks of humanitarian intervention?
2. What are the alternatives to intervention?
3. How could humanitarian aid be made more effective?

Benjamin A. Valentino is Associate Professor of Government at Dartmouth College.

Unit 4

UNIT

Prepared by: Robert J. Griffiths, *University of North Carolina at Greensboro*

Political Change in the Developing World

Democracy and human rights remain an elusive goal in many parts of the developing world. The history of authoritarian colonial rule and the failure to prepare colonies adequately for democracy at independence helps to account for the fragility of democracy and human rights in many developing countries. Even when there was an attempt to foster parliamentary government, the experiment often failed, largely due to the lack of a democratic tradition and political expediency. Independence-era leaders frequently resorted to centralization of power and authoritarianism, either to pursue ambitious development programs or simply to retain power. In some cases, leaders experimented with socialist development schemes that emphasized ideology and the role of party elites. The promise of rapid, equitable development proved elusive, and the collapse of the Soviet Union further discredited this strategy. Other countries had the misfortune to come under the rule of tyrannical leaders who were concerned only with enriching themselves and who brutally repressed anyone with the temerity to challenge their rule. Although there are some notable exceptions, the developing world's experiences with democracy since independence have been uneven.

Given that history, the results of democracy's "third wave" have been mixed so far. While democracy has increased across the world, the pace of democratic change has slowed recently, and in some instances democratic reform has regressed. The Arab Spring brought political change to a few countries in the Middle East while discontent simmers in several others. Progress toward democracy in Tunisia, Egypt, and Libya remains uncertain. The Egyptian military's compliance with democratic norms, the role of Islam and its compatibility with democracy, and sectarian divisions are among the factors that make the outcome of this upheaval uncertain. There is some evidence that Islamic political parties have moderated their message and that those that have not do not fare well in elections. Prospects for broader democratic reform in the region will depend on the success of efforts to reframe the political debate and the willingness of ruling elites to accept change. In Asia, there has been a surprising political opening in Myanmar/Burma and Singapore's one-party dominance is facing increasing challenge.

Africa's experience with democracy has also been varied since the third wave of democratization swept over the continent beginning in 1990. Although early efforts resulted in the ouster of many leaders, some of whom had held power for decades, and international pressure forced several countries to hold multiparty elections, the political landscape in Africa includes consolidating democracies and authoritarian states. South Africa, the continent's biggest success story, held its fourth round of democratic elections in April 2009, but the elections took place amid allegations of corruption against the new president, Jacob Zuma, and featured a nasty split in the ruling African National Congress. The ANC recently celebrated its 100th anniversary and continues to enjoy overwhelming majority support, but South Africa still faces major challenges.

While there has been significant progress toward democratic reform around the world, as the recent trend suggests, there is no guarantee that these efforts will be sustained. Although there has been an increase in the percentage of the world's population living under democracy, nondemocratic regimes and human rights abuses persist. Promoting democracy and human rights remains an uphill battle.

Prepared by: Robert J. Griffiths, *University of North Carolina at Greensboro*

Article

One Step Forward, Two Steps Back

Democracy is in retreat. And there's a surprising culprit.

JOSHUA KURLANTZICK

Learning Outcomes

After reading this article, you will be able to:

- Describe the trends in the spread of democracy.
- Explain the connection between economic prosperity and support for democracy.

Over the past two years, the world's attention has been captured by previously unimaginable—even rapturous—changes throughout parts of the Arab world, Africa, and Asia, where political openings have been born in some of the most repressive and unlikely societies on Earth. In Burma, where only six years ago a thuggish junta ordered the shooting of red-robed monks in the streets, the past two years have seen a formal, and seemingly real, transition to a civilian democratic government. In Tunisia, Egypt, and Libya, longtime autocrats were toppled by popular revolutions, and citizens in these states seemed at last to be enjoying the trappings of freedom.

"The Arab Spring is the triumph of democracy," Tunisian President Moncef Marzouki, a former human rights activist, told the Guardian in 2012. The Arab peoples "have come up with their own answer to violent extremism and the abusive regimes we've been propping up. It's called democracy," wrote New York Times columnist Thomas Friedman.

Don't believe the hype. In reality, democracy is going into reverse. While some countries in Africa, the Arab world, and Asia have opened slightly in the past two years, in other countries once held up as examples of political change democratic meltdowns have become depressingly common. In fact, Freedom House found that global freedom dropped in 2012 for the seventh year in a row, a record number of years of consistent decline.

The Arab Spring has not only led to dictators like Syria's Bashar al-Assad and Bahrain's ruling Al Khalifa family digging in across the region, but it has also pushed autocrats around the world to take a harder line with their populations—whether it's China censoring even vague code words for protest or Russia passing broad new treason laws and harassing human rights NGOs. As Arch Puddington, Freedom House's vice president for research, put it, "Our findings point to the growing sophistication of modern authoritarians". Especially since the Arab Spring, they are nervous, which accounts for their intensified persecution of popular movements for change."

But it's not the Arab Spring alone that's to blame. According to Freedom House, democracy's "forward march" actually peaked around the beginning of the 2000s. A mountain of evidence supports that gloomy conclusion. One of the most comprehensive studies of global democracy, the Bertelsmann Foundation's Transformation Index, has declared that "the overall quality of democracy has deteriorated" throughout the developing world. The index found that the number of "defective" and "highly defective democracies"—those with institutions, elections, and political culture so flawed that they hardly resemble real democracies—was up to 52 in 2012.

In another major survey, by the Economist Intelligence Unit, democracy deteriorated in 48 of 167 countries surveyed in 2011. "The dominant pattern globally over the past five years has been backsliding," the report says. We're not just talking about the likes of Pakistan and Zimbabwe here. Thirteen countries on the Transformation Index qualified as "highly defective democracies," countries with such a lack of opportunity for opposition voices, such problems with the rule of law, and such unrepresentative political structures that they are now little better than autocracies.

Even countries often held up as new democratic models have regressed over the past decade. When they entered the European Union in 2004, the Czech Republic, Hungary, Poland, and Slovakia were considered success stories. After nearly a decade as EU members, however, all of these bright lights have dimmed. Populist and far-right parties with little commitment to democratic norms gained steady popularity; public distaste for democracy increased; and governments showed more willingness to crack down on activists. Hungary has deteriorated so badly that its press freedoms rate barely better than they were under the communists.

Meanwhile, as European democracy falters, old-fashioned coups are returning elsewhere. In Africa, Asia, and Latin

America, coups had become rare by the late 1990s. But between 2006 and 2012, militaries grabbed power in Bangladesh, Fiji, Guinea, Guinea-Bissau, Honduras, Madagascar, Mauritania, Mali, Niger, and Thailand, among others. In places like Ecuador, Mexico, Pakistan, and the Philippines, where the military did not launch an outright coup, it still managed to restore its power as a central actor in political life.

This is also true across the Middle East, where the Arab uprisings appear to be entrenching the power of militaries, sparking massive unrest, scaring middle-class liberals into exodus, and empowering Islamist majorities. Protesters may have bravely challenged leaders from Yemen to Egypt, but it's the loyalty of the military that has determined whether these rulers stay in power.

So WHAT WENT wrong? Let's start by blaming an unlikely culprit: the middle class. Contrary to the modernization theories of Samuel Huntington, Seymour Martin Lipset, and most Western world leaders, who have long argued that the growth of the middle class in developing countries is a boon to democratization, it hasn't worked out that way.

In theory, as the middle class expands, men and women should become more educated and more demanding of greater economic, social, and ultimately political freedoms. And once a country reaches the per capita GDP of a middle-income country, it should rarely if ever return to authoritarian rule. "In virtually every country [that has democratized] the most active supporters of democratization came from the urban middle class," Huntington wrote. Or consider the words of Russian economist Sergei Guriev, who declared just this past January that his country's booming middle class has become "too well-educated and too determined to enjoy increases in their quality of life" not to force an end to President Vladimir Putin's creeping authoritarianism. "They will demand that the Russian government is less corrupt and more accessible," Guriev said.

But they're not succeeding. Sure, it's true that the middle class globally is exploding; the World Bank estimates that between 1990 and 2005, the middle class tripled in size in developing countries in Asia, and in Africa it grew by a third over the past decade, according to the African Development Bank Group. Today, roughly 70 million people worldwide each year begin to earn enough to join the middle class.

It seems, however, that this new global middle is choosing stability over all else. From Algeria to Zimbabwe, the rising middle class has often supported the military as a bulwark against popular democracy, fearing that it might empower the poor, the religious, and the less-educated. In research for my book, I studied every coup attempt in the past 10 years in the developing world and then analyzed a comprehensive range of local polls and media. I found that in 50 percent of cases, middle-class men and women either agitated in advance for coups or subsequently expressed their wholehearted support for the army takeover. This is a shockingly high percentage, given that in many of these countries, such as Pakistan and Thailand, the middle class had originally been at the forefront of trying to get the army out of politics.

And in many countries, middle classes have increasingly come to disdain norms of democratic culture such as using elections, not violent demonstrations, to change leaders. From Bolivia to Venezuela to the Philippines, middle classes have turned to street protests or appeals to the judiciary to try to remove elected leaders.

And the trend is only growing stronger. Opinion polling from many developing countries shows that not only is the quality of democracy declining, but public views of democracy are deteriorating. The respected Globalbarometer series uses extensive questionnaires to ask people about their views on democracy. It has found declining levels of support for democracy throughout much of sub-Saharan Africa. In Central Asia and the former Soviet Union, the story is the same. In Kyrgyzstan, which despite its flaws remains the most democratic state in Central Asia, a majority of the population did not think that a political opposition is very or somewhat important. And recent polls show that only 16 percent of Russians surveyed said that it was "very important" that their country be governed democratically. Likewise, in Colombia, Ecuador, Honduras, Guatemala, Nicaragua, Paraguay, and Peru, either a minority or only a tiny majority of people thinks democracy is preferable to any other type of government.

Global economic stagnation since the 2008 crash has only weakened public support for democracy. New middle classes have been hit hard by the malaise, particularly in Eastern Europe. A comprehensive study of Central and Eastern Europe by the European Bank for Reconstruction and Development released in 2011 found that the crisis severely lowered support for democracy in all 10 of the new EU countries. "Those who enjoyed more freedoms wanted less democracy and markets when they were hurt by the crisis," the report noted.

Even in Asia, one of the world's most economically vibrant and globalized regions, polls show rising dissatisfaction with democracy—what some researchers have termed "authoritarian nostalgia." Indonesia, for example, is considered by many to be the democratic success story of the 2000s. Yet vote-buying and corruption among elected politicians have begun to wear. In a 2011 study, only 13 percent of respondents thought that the current group of democratic politicians was doing a better job than leaders during the era of Suharto's authoritarianism.

Even where democracy has deeper roots, disillusionment with the political process has exploded in recent years. From hundreds of thousands of Indians demonstrating against corruption to Israelis camping in the streets of Tel Aviv to protest their leaders' lack of interest in basic economic issues to the French pushing back against government austerity measures, middle classes are increasingly turning to street protests to make their points. "Our parents are grateful because they're voting," one young woman told a reporter in Spain, where unemployment now tops 50 percent for young people. "We're the first generation to say that voting is worthless."

In his second inaugural address, U.S. President Barack Obama, like every U.S. president for decades, spoke of America's role in helping promote democracy around the globe. "We will support democracy from Asia to Africa, from the Americas to the Middle East, because our interests and our conscience compel us to act on behalf of those who long for freedom," he declared. Obama may have the best of intentions, but in reality there is little he can do. The sad, troubling regression of democracy in developing countries isn't something that America can fix—because it has to be fixed at home too.

Middle classes have come to disdain norms of democratic culture such as using elections, not violent street protests, to change leaders. And the trend is only growing stronger.

Critical Thinking

1. What are the trends in democracy worldwide?
2. What are the sources of disillusionment that account for this backlash against democracy?

Create Central

www.mhhe.com/createcentral

Internet References

Center for Research on Inequality, Human Security, and Ethnicity
www.crise.ox.ac.uk

LatinAmericanNetworkInformationCenter—LANIC
www.lanic.utexas.edu

ReliefWeb
www.reliefweb.int/w/rwb.nsf

Joshua Kurlantzick, fellow for Southeast Asia at the Council on Foreign Relations, is author of Democracy in Retreat: The Revolt of the Middle Class and the Worldwide Decline of Representative Government.

Article

Good Soldier, Bad Cop

The Nasser model set the ground rules for Africa's post-colonial regimes: authoritarian, nationalist, single-party, and underwritten by the military.

Egypt matters as an economic power and a political exemplar. That is why the scenes from Tahrir Square resonated across Africa so powerfully. Now, Egypt's revolutionaries are asking whether the military can be trusted to manage the transition to democracy.

It was the military high command that finally pushed Hosni Mubarak and Zine el Abidine Ben Ali out, but Tunisians and Egyptians are ambivalent about whether the soldiers will promote or steal the revolution. Civilian politicians have taken centre stage in Tunisia, but the military waits in the wings. In Egypt, the military keeps control at the head of the Supreme Military Council. Field Marshal Mohamed Hussein Tantawi has issued decrees paving the way for free elections and independent political parties.

The late distinguished Egyptian diplomat Mahmoud Kassem traced the origins of authoritarian rule in Africa to the Free Officers' revolution that toppled King Farouk in 1952 and ushered in Gamal Abdel Nasser. The Nasser model, said Kassem, set the groundrules for Africa's post-colonial regimes: authoritarian, nationalist, single-party and underwritten by the military.

Tunisia and Egypt put such regimes on notice. A million-strong security apparatus in Egypt, the generals calculated, could not hold back the aspirations of a large proportion of the 80 million other Egyptians. Under Nasser's model, the secret (and unsecret) police did the spying and torturing while the army and air force stayed away from daily repression, burnishing credentials as guardians of the national interest.

Those lines blurred in Libya under Colonel Muammar Gaddafi's Jamahiriya. Fearing coups, Gaddafi weakened the military, constrained it with revolutionary committees alongside an omnipresent secret police and set up armed units run by his sons outside the formal command structure. That is why regiments in eastern Libya joined the opposition and turned on their nominal commander-in-chief.

Will Africa's other armies go the Egyptian or Libyan route? In West Africa, home to more military coups than any other region, the soldiers are back in the barracks, for now. The Ghanaian and Nigerian militaries had followed Nasser's model, but as they grew as corrupt and dysfunctional as their civilian counterparts, the generals handed over power to elected regimes.

Different dynamics are at work in states such as Algeria, Angola, Mozambique and Zimbabwe, where the national army grew out of forces that had fought colonial rule. Such armies earned kudos as national liberators but have become fused to ruling parties that are running corrupt and repressive regimes.

The question haunting presidents Abdelaziz Bouteflika and Robert Mugabe is how their militaries would react to people power on the streets of Algiers and Harare. Bouteflika looks the more worried. As a key apparatchik in the post-colonial regimes in the 1960s and 1970s, Bouteflika returned to power in the 1990s determined to reduce the strength of the military. Some scores have yet to be settled. Should opposition to the regime gather momentum in the streets, the generals would not hesitate to suggest that Bouteflika go into retirement.

Mugabe gets on with the military, whose top brass get lucrative contracts and top jobs in government. Soldiers generally stay out of the hurly-burly while the police and special units such as the Green Bombers do the political killings and torture. Mugabe, one of Africa's canniest tacticians, is lucky that few of the generals trust his main opponent, Morgan Tsvangirai.

Realists in the officers' corps see that the 87-year-old Mugabe has now reached the endgame. Like their Egyptian counterparts, they will want to steer the coming transition without losing political influence, and they will not necessarily ask Comrade Mugabe for his advice.

Critical Thinking

1. What role did the military play in the political changes in the Middle East?
2. How can rulers weaken the armed forces' ability to force political change?
3. What are the prospects that armed forces in other African countries will play a role in political reform?

Article

Islamism after the Arab Spring

It makes no sense today to divide Arab politics into neatly crafted opposites, the 'Islamist' versus the 'civil democratic' blocs.

ASHRAF EL SHERIF

During the early euphoria of the Arab Spring, the secular disposition of the uprisings led some to argue, incorrectly, that Islamism is becoming an anachronism in North Africa. In fact, alongside the goals of democracy and social justice, religious symbolism was evident in the revolts. Demonstrations began after Friday prayers at mosques. In Egypt, the Muslim Brotherhood (MB) played a prominent role in the protests, as did Al Nahda activists in Tunisia. The Libyan Islamic Fighting Group (LIFG) was closely involved in Tripoli's liberation.

Today, the coin has been flipped and many observers emphasize the Islamists' organizational competence as an advantage in the postrevolutionary context. Apprehensive secular political activists in Egypt, Libya, and Tunisia now worry: How can we protect the Arab Spring's incipient democracies from Islamist takeover? After all, other countries that have undergone revolutionary turmoil have experienced moments when the fruits of rebellion fell into the hands of the most organized and determined political factions.

Yet Islamism in North Africa is neither receding nor about to strangle democratic aspirations in their cribs. Secularist/Islamist dichotomies thrived under the long rule of Egypt's Hosni Mubarak and Tunisia's Zine el-Abidine Ben Ali—but it makes no sense today to divide Arab politics into neatly crafted opposites, the "Islamist" versus the "civil democratic" blocs.

Two trends shed light on possible trajectories for Islamist politics in North Africa after the Arab Spring. The first is a growing factionalism among moderate mainstream Islamists. Various Islamist parties are emerging, particularly in Egypt, manifesting class and generational divisions in addition to differences in social outlook, cultural sensibilities, and approaches to Islamic texts.

Many Islamist liberals are full-fledged democrats who are establishing ingenious new approaches to Islamist politics. However, the proliferation of new parties could hurt them electorally. And the incumbent mainstream—still peaceful and not extremist, yet more conservative—remains hesitant or unready to join reformist democratic Islamism.

We must wait for the current transition period to end before we can see this factionalism play out on a grand scale, as the parties engage questions of socioeconomic policy and issues of democratic state building. And it remains to be seen which of the new Islamist parties will forswear contention over the Islamist/secularist divide, and where they will situate themselves within these countries' incipient democratic transitions in the battle between democratic and authoritarian politics.

The second trend is the participation of ex-radical Islamist groups in the democratic transition process. Such groups have established political parties to stand in Egyptian elections, engaged in peaceful political contestation and debate in Tunisia, and played an important role in the political and military war effort of the Libyan revolution.

Ex-militant Islamists are moderating politically and ideologically—and their conventional, dogmatic doctrine of total regime rejection, which led groups in Egypt and Libya toward a course of armed confrontation with governments, is gone with the wind. Today these groups are championing an Islamist discourse of opposition to political, economic, or social policies that, in their view, contradict Islamic law or do not serve the public.

Their commitment to democracy as a system, and to its concomitant pluralist political culture, remains questionable. This problem is of greater significance in Libya than in Egypt, given the role played by the LIFG in the revolutionary effort against Muammar el-Qaddafi, and the fact that this group has emerged from the civil war with considerable military strength and social influence.

Some analysts portray the 83-year-old MB as disconcerted about Egypt's unexpected political reconfiguration. But even if they were latecomers to the uprising, both the MB in Egypt and Al Nahda in Tunisia remain key beneficiaries of it. Both movements emerged from the upheaval with state recognition, and both have built bridges with other opposition forces. Decades-old ideological animosities were eclipsed somewhat by collaboration against a common enemy—the former regimes.

To be sure, a long-awaited secular democratic politics is in the making in North Africa. The middle-class youth who headed the protest movement are playing a greater role in Egyptian and Tunisian politics. Their ingenuity, secular sensibilities, and longing for good governance, democracy, and human rights may well prove the backbone of an emerging non-Islamist bloc.

The youthful activists could coalesce around reformist factions within the state, as might liberal business groups, both of which will be keen on distancing themselves from the outdated oligarchic practices that characterized state-business relations under the old regimes. A surge in Egyptian labor militancy may also engender a center-left political bloc anchored in the trade union movement.

The Salafists' eagerness to establish hegemony over the Islamic public sphere is undercut by their political incompetence.

Democratization, however, could also enable democratic reformist Islamists to reach their longterm goals. In Egypt, competition for votes could prompt organizational and ideological reforms within the MB, which has often shown a savvy ability to adapt to changing circumstances. The use of Islamism as a bogeyman could finally be rendered ineffective, provided that Islamist factions recognize and adust to the new political conditions.

Islamism in North Africa may be undergoing a dramatic transformation that will become more visible in coming years. Political struggle to defend countries' "Islamic identity" against secularists and Westernizers is becoming increasingly irrelevant to people's needs. Popular demands for good governance, economic development, and social empowerment are compelling Islamist politics to adapt and transcend its traditional concern with safeguarding Islamic identity. Or at least the identity discourse is being supplemented with socioeconomic and civic agendas that relate to the daily life and welfare of the people instead of talismanic ideologies of an "Islamic political order" and an "Islamic state."

Islamists in Disarray

Islamism is a broad category that includes diverse actors converging on the goal of creating a sociopolitical, legal, and economic order based on interpretations of Islam not only as a religion but also as a social and legal system. In Egypt today, in the wake of the revolt that toppled Mubarak, Islamists are splitting into incongruous sociopolitical and ideological factions. In fact, some Islamists can more easily find political bedfellows among non-Islamist movements than among their Islamist brethren. We can speak today of Islamist rightist movements, Islamist leftists, Islamist libertarians, Islamist communitarians, Islamist liberalism, and Islamist conservatism.

The MB itself has spawned multiple parties. In addition to the official MB party (the Freedom and Justice Party), three other MB parties are being established: Al Nahda (Renaissance), Al Reyada (Pioneers), and Al Tayar al-Masri (Egyptian Current) parties. Salafists, who pursue a literalist and puritanical approach to Islamic theology, have their own parties. Differences among these factions are genuine and reflect not just old distinctions in ideological outlook but also variations along a new spectrum of Islamist politics.

MB factional politics, long viewed as pitting conservatives against reformists, is developing in new directions. Before the January uprising, major points of contention between the old guard and new guard primarily involved internal organization: decision-making rules, transparency and accountability, bylaws, grassroots representation, rotation of leadership figures, freedom of debate, and participation by women and youth. Since the regime's teeth were pulled, organizational contention still matters in the MB, but not as much.

Conservatives controlling the group's Guidance Bureau originally threw their lot behind Egypt's new rulers—that is, the Supreme Council of Armed Forces (SCAF)—in the hope that an orderly transition would grant the MB kingmaker status in parliamentary elections. The Islamist reformists have been more inclined to share with the secularist revolutionaries a politics of relentless pressure on the SCAF to implement reforms.

The Reformists

Reformists in the MB are a loosely defined category consisting of Islamist political pundits, public activists, civil society workers, student movement leaders, social media consumers, and community service workers. Differences in age, socioeconomic status, and occupation—often overlooked by analysts—are muted by a joint commitment to the values and processes of political modernity as reconciled with an open-minded approach to Islam.

The restless MB reformist youth are part of the "youth bulge" in Egyptian politics. It was they who drove older leaders to take part in the uprising, after an initial period of indeterminacy. Then a "we-did-it" euphoria encouraged many MB youths to join the ranks of the "permanent revolution" camp, which is pushing for comprehensive political and social transformation. Reformists believe that such youth fervor can be successfully incorporated into a modern Islamist party.

After the January revolt and the movement toward democracy, MB reformists, already discouraged by the leadership's indifference to their organizational concerns in recent years, started showing signs of discontent with the MB and its official Freedom and Justice Party's (FJP's) political profile. Key differences had to do with the FJP's less-than-revolutionary standpoint on questions of state reform, police and judiciary restructuring, deconstructing the regime's political networks and resources and, finally, the combustive issue of labor rights and strikes.

The MB Guidance Bureau and the FJP were reluctant to exert pressure on the SCAF or join forces with the disgruntled secular revolutionary forces that started taking to the streets again in popular demonstrations as early as April. Apparently, the MB old guard's conservatism prevented it from matching the revolutionary fervor of the organization's youthful reformist activists. In addition, the reformists criticized the top-down, elitist organization of the FJP. It was logical for disaffected MB voices to start looking for new political venues.

MB reformists are not very likely, despite various ideological commonalties with it, to join the veteran Islamic party Al Wasat (also known as the Center, formed in 1996 by a group of ex-MB activists), which has finally been licensed by court decision after 11 years of legal struggle. Still as elitist as ever, Al Wasat is more a highbrow cultural salon than a political party. Ten years of legal prohibition wrought damage to it that is reparable but nevertheless daunting, and it suffers from intellectual stagnancy, a peculiar problem considering the party's supposedly "modernist" posture. In the eyes of MB reformist youth, a more attractive solution is to establish their own MB reformist parties.

Striving to fashion themselves after the Moroccan Justice and Development Party, the MB reformist parties (Al Nahda, Pioneers, and Egyptian Current) are already formulating online and in print an advanced Islamist discourse on citizenship, good governance, development, human rights, gender, and civic participation. And they are insisting on keeping political activism entirely separate from the workings of proselytizing and religious groups.

MB reformists are tapping into the socioeconomic demands of a sullen, youthful labor force as well as wired and middle-class but relatively deprived yuppies—while drawing on their own good-governance ambitions (which were at the heart of the January revolt). They may shift toward a center-left position out of a desire for political feasibility and ideological reassessment.

In their platforms, MB reformist parties claim they would support community development, human rights, and civil society organization, instead of the talismanic metapolitics of the "Islamic state" and sharia. This would necessitate an all-encompassing ideological revision and imaginative rupture with traditions of Islamic learning, an already ongoing process launched by Islamist intellectuals in the 1980s. No less importantly, bridges with non-Islamist liberal and leftist political actors could help create a democratic front transcending identity politics demarcations.

The Old Guard

The Freedom and Justice Party, the "official" MB party dominated by conservatives, is attempting to preserve the organizational and political dominance of the group's leadership (the Guidance Bureau) over the party. This replicates the model of the Jordanian Islamic Action Front. The MB leadership claims that it wishes to maintain functional separation of the party and the parent organization. Nonetheless, it is widely expected that the MB will devise institutional devices to maintain control over the FJP. Informal and patriarchal power relations will be key. Party bylaws, still not officially endorsed, are expected to dodge issues of dual membership and leadership.

This is consequential. The MB Guidance Bureau is more than reluctant to alter its doctrine regarding the "totality" of Islam. The MB's self-image as "greater than a party and less than a state" remains a stubborn article of faith among its immovable leadership and also much of its grassroots. Functional differentiation between the MB and the political party can be achieved if tactically advantageous, which is evidently the case right now. But to dissolve all ties is raising the bar too high. MB conservatives remain faithful to the Leninist traditions of vertical organization and iron discipline. The party today is acting like the MB's auxiliary or simply its political department.

The FJP needs the MB for its ability to add demographic depth and religious clout, while the MB needs the party to run the day-to-day political business and back the religious group politically. MB conservatives, in light of the Guidance Bureau's composition and financial machinations, are attentive to the worldview of the business oriented conservative bourgeoisie. Demands for a rationalized and pious market economy comport well with comparable agendas among business classes nationwide. Are we watching the rise of the Egyptian form of Turkey's Justice and Development Party (a coalition of pro-European Islamists, Anatolian businesspeople, and nationalist liberals escaping the calamities of the old center-right parties)?

Such a rise would prove action-packed. But MB conservatives, still representing the mainstream of this key political group, are held back by tactical considerations. They preferred compromising with the SCAF during most of the transitional period, to the dismay of other revolutionary partners. They opted to appease the SCAF with an eye toward an expected big win in parliamentary elections—a classic example of tactics replacing strategy. Focused on temporary political gains, the MB and its FJP are apparently not prioritizing the democratizing of state structures and state-society relations even though political wisdom suggests institutional reforms are prerequisites for the long-term success of a democratic transition.

MB leaders are reluctant to stake their position along lines of contention between democratic and authoritarian forces. A more familiar and easier battlefield for them is ideological polarization between Islamists and non-Islamists. This is a misfortune for the revolutionary process and for Islamist political development.

The Turkish Justice and Development Party, with its embrace of democratic pluralist politics, governance record, successes in municipalities and community services, and promotion of economic development, is a source of inspiration claimed by both Islamist conservatives and reformists. Controversy arises, however, when the prerequisites and conditions for the Turkish "Islamist success story" are brought up. Given the MB leadership's foot-dragging on issues such as separating politics from proselytizing and foregoing ideology in favor of good governance and economic development—not to mention the glaring contextual differences between Egypt and Turkey—a straightforward copy of the Turkish model by the MB is not likely.

Unprepared for Politics

And what of the Salafists? Their popularity in Egypt has been amply evident over the past two decades. They reflect a deeply rooted religious tendency—a desire to return to a "purer" form of Islam—that has been present on the Egyptian street for a long time. However, their bearing on today's reality should not be exaggerated. Salafists are relegated to troublemaker status, nothing more. They lack the organization, resourcefulness, political expertise, and mindset to translate their doctrinal steadfastness into meaningful political dividends, even within the Islamist camp.

Islamism may be undergoing a dramatic transformation that will become more visible in coming years.

Salafists remain faithful to their original mission to monopolize the Muslim religious public sphere and to deride all religious authorities save their own. For them, politics is operational only in this respect. Their approach is not a matter of artfulness or opportunism as much as a cognitive screen that does not permit comprehension of politics except in terms of spreading or conserving hegemony over the religious sphere.

The confident Salafists underestimate how confused they seemed in the aftermath of the revolt. The uprising contravened their teachings on ignoring politics and focusing on preaching, and it included substantial participation by members of the Salafist grassroots, in defiance of their clerics' fatwas. The revolt's politicization of wide segments of society shook the Salafists' once unshakable belief that their moment is yet to come.

In the final analysis, the Salafists' key rivals are the Islamist reformists. Salafists are aware of the greater clout that reformists might enjoy under a more democratic political system. Indeed, the balance of power within the all-important religious public sphere is subject to reconfiguration now in light of the newly empowered Islamist reformist actors. And Islamist reformist politics rests partially on challenging orthodox and conservative Islamic interpretations. Hence, after a decade of prolific proselytizing in the mass media, mosques, online social media, and on the ground, restructuring the religious sphere is the Salafists' worst nightmare.

Whatever can stop a reformist-led religious structural readjustment is tolerable to the Salafists. This would include deceitful politics, half-hearted support of revolutionary goals, compromising with the SCAF's style of rule, forming alliances with the counterrevolutionary forces of business oligarchies and the security establishment, and certainly exploiting their Saudi connections.

Since the revolt, the Salafists through both their political parties and religious networks have disseminated a mix of scorching propaganda and populist ideas designed to reinvigorate identity politics and foment sectarian strife. Concurrently, they have acted as provocateurs, decrying secular liberalism as blasphemous and alien, and its Egyptian adherents as "cultural stooges of the West."

Salafism nevertheless is gradually losing ground to politicized Islam, whether in its reformist or conservative versions. As political actors, Salafists have hardly any experience with electoral politics: cadre building, resource mobilization, and interest aggregation techniques. Their mobilizing capabilities are hyped, but their past successes have relied less on sound organization than on exploiting public emotions and prejudices. Egypt's new political atmosphere is pushing the Salafists into unfamiliar territory, and their eagerness to establish hegemony over the Islamic public sphere is undercut by their political incompetence.

Islamist reformists are establishing ingenious new approaches to politics.

Militants' Makeover

The loud voices of the MB and Salafist movements amid the Egyptian revolt have drawn attention away from another Islamist movement that bests any other local Islamist actor in terms of achieving ideological revisions and organizational remodeling. This is the Gama'a Islamiyya, or Islamic Group—an organization traditionally dedicated to the forcible overthrow of the government and its replacement with an Islamic state.

Though relatively small, the Islamic Group is an interesting experiment in the Islamist laboratory, one in which an ex-violent movement is naturalized socially and politically, albeit while trying to keep its organizational and ideological character intact. For the sake of analysis one can identify two factions: revisionists and militants.

The revisionists, led by Nageh Ibrahim, are writing new chapters in Islamist self-critique and reorientation. Ibrahim believes that Islamists do not monopolize representations of Islam and argues that self-critique is a forgotten Islamist duty. Literalist scripturalism is dismissed. He calls for reforming state religious institutions, long subjugated by the Mubarak regime, to promote peaceful and non-coercive proselytizing, preaching, and dialogue. He wants the institutions to lobby the government, to make sure Islamic cultural and social values are respected in the state media and in educational and artistic discourse. But on questions of cooperation with liberals, peaceful action versus violence, and the role of the state and rule of law, Ibrahim and his followers are Islamist pioneers.

The militants are led by Mohammed Essam Derbala, the new head of the Islamic Group. Their theoretical discourse on political participation may not be very distant from that of the revisionists, but they have positioned themselves in the authoritarian camp that disavows further radicalization in protests and further confrontation with the SCAF. However, whether they are proud of their violent past or not, the militants do expressly repudiate violence now. And while they ridicule party activism in the past, they have established a party called Building and Development, which will participate in legislative and local elections.

No Call to Arms

In Tunisia, the Al Nahda Party leadership has historically had a more liberal outlook than Egypt's MB. In 1981, Al Nahda was the region's first Islamist movement to declare its full commitment to the values of democracy, multiparty politics, and pluralism. It cannot afford ideological intransigence in a society that is among the most modern, literate, and educated in the Arab world. As a result, the party does not face the prospect of splintering that the MB does.

No less important, secularist political forces in Tunisia are far more potent than in Egypt. Traditions of political and civil society organization in secular forums such as the Tunisian labor movement have proved effective, not just during the mass mobilization of the revolt but also in the transition period. Unlike in Egypt, Tunisians created a transitional civilian administration to prepare for the election of a constituent assembly to write a new constitution. Secularist political forces are present and vocal in the administration and their voices will be heard in crafting a national charter. Egyptian secularists, by contrast, fear that Islamists will write the new constitution by virtue of their expected strength in the new parliament, which will appoint a constitution writing committee.

Al Nahda has rebuilt an extensive and efficient party organization nationwide, which in October elections helped it win a plurality of seats in the constituent assembly. But party leaders, while articulating Islam-inspired values, have highlighted their commitment to Tunisia's modernist achievements, as well as their willingness to work in coalition governments with the secularist center-leftist parties.

Islamists in Tunisia, most notably Salafists and the jihadist Islamic Liberation Party, are not likely to make much noise—they are past their prime. Tunisian Salafists, influenced through strong Saudi connections, will probably retain the ultraconservatism that has brought them into alliances with the most unscrupulous factions of the former regime, including the security agencies and oligarchic businessmen. In a healthier political system, this would be an invitation to irrelevancy. As for jihadist groups, their already limited base of support is expected to shrink further with the dwindling popularity of jihad and Islamist militancy as a model of change in the Middle East.

Libya's Revisionists

In Libya, the Libyan Islamic Fighting Group has implemented important doctrinal and organizational revisions over the past decade, after the model of Islamist counterparts in Egypt. Lengthy books have explicated the new doctrine, dismissing violence against innocent people as religiously forbidden and politically immoral and unconstructive. Excommunicating people and apostatizing regimes are wrong, according to the new religious interpretations. Instead, the LIFG emphasizes gradualism, renewal, realistic concerns, good manners, high demeanor, jurisprudence, flexibility, and escaping rigid scripturalism.

Among the key promoters of these revisions was Abdel Hakim Belhaj, who emerged later as one of the Libyan revolutionary war leaders—he was in charge of the Tripoli liberation operation. Other Islamist groups, most notably the Libyan MB and Salafists, maintained an active profile during the revolution. The Salafists, particularly popular in Libya's eastern cities, manned most of the armed groups that carried out the bulk of the revolutionary fighting. The MB placed two members in Libya's National Transitional Council.

Many fear that the liberal façade of the transitional council is irrelevant in light of Islamist domination on the ground. This explains Belhaj's incessant messages of appeasement both to the Libyans and the West. He worked on the LIFG's latest revisions and was quick to deny holding any grudges against the West, despite his own rendition during the US-led war against terror after 9/11. According to Belhaj, the LIFG's "new Islamism" is a democratic popular project in contradistinction to elitist secularism. He has highlighted the national character of the Libyan revolution, Islamic legitimacy, and the feasibility of party activism under a new, fair, and just political system.

It is unclear yet whether the LIFG will operate as a political party in post-Qaddafi Libya. For any integration of Islamism into the political process to succeed, Islamists would need to endorse republicanism, democracy, pluralism, and constitutional rule. But no less important is the willingness and ability of the LIFG, the Salafists, and the MB to develop their discourses and act in accordance with political realities in Libya, which are very different from the situation in Egypt and Tunisia.

Libyan peculiarities include a deep tribal structure, a failed state, crippled bureaucracy, regional animosities, Western influence resulting from aid to the revolutionaries, and the all-important issue of oil-revenue allocation. The first adaptability test is coming soon. Once the state-building process starts, will the LIFG and other armed groups disarm and incorporate their militias into the national army? This is only one of many questions facing Islamic movements in Libya and elsewhere as they redefine themselves, summon new strategies, and set out on new courses in the aftermath of the Arab Spring.

Critical Thinking

1. What two trends are likely to affect Islamist politics after the Arab Spring?
2. What are the various trends within the Islamist movement?
3. What are the prospects for Islamic radicalism?

Ashraf El Sherif is a lecturer in politics at the American University of Cairo.

Article

Prepared by: Robert J. Griffiths, *University of North Carolina at Greensboro*

Between Democracy and Militancy: Islam in Africa

"[T]he effort to try to distinguish between good and bad Muslim ideologies may be much less important than the need to support functional political institutions."

LEONARDO A. VILLALÓN

Learning Outcomes

After reading this article, you will be able to:

- Classify the range of political actors contending for influence in the aftermath of the Arab Spring.
- Identify the obstacles to a greater role for Salafist groups in post-Arab Spring countries.

Long peripheral in both government and scholarly considerations of the Muslim world, Islam in sub-Saharan Africa now finds itself center stage in policy discussions of acute international concern, most notably due to fears of a seemingly enhanced terrorist threat. While the trajectory of the Al Shabab movement in Somalia is complicated by schisms in its ranks and its handling of widespread famine, two other militant movements in western Africa have recently expanded their activities. In the past year Al Qaeda in the Islamic Maghreb has penetrated much further south into the Sahel—notably into central Mali—in carrying out kidnappings and ambushes from its Saharan bases.

And the shady Nigerian movement widely known as Boko Haram ("Western schooling is forbidden") launched its first direct attack on an international target with the August 2011 bombing of the United Nations headquarters in Nigeria's capital, Abuja. This was followed by a number of attacks on Nigerian government targets across the northeastern parts of the country provoking virulent government reprisals, and causing extensive death and destruction. The movement of people and arms southward following the collapse of Muammar el-Qaddafi's regime in Libya raised further concerns that militant movements across the region will benefit from the ensuing chaos. These fears proved well founded with the rapid expansion of a new militant group, Ansar Dine, in northern Mali following a March 2012 coup.

It is now clear that militant movements in Muslim Africa present larger challenges than seemed likely until very recendy, and their disruptive potential in the region must be emphasized. At the same time, however, such movements represent only a tiny sliver of the contemporary dynamics of Islam in African politics. Fully understanding both the threat they present and their limitations requires that we consider radical Islamists in a broader context of religious trends south of the Sahara. There is a wide—and increasing—diversity to Muslim movements and organization in the region. These are in large part shaped by highly varying contexts, and the variety of regimes and political systems as well as very different patterns of religious demography are fundamental bases of this diversity. A narrow focus on militancy can cause us to lose sight of Islam's complex—and often quite positive—participation in African debates about democratization.

The Muslim Third

Census data in Africa are scarce and not always reliable, but the continent as a whole is at least half Muslim, and a conservative estimate would put the percentage of Muslims in sub-Saharan Africa at one third of the population, perhaps more. The common analytic distinction made between the five North Africa countries—usually lumped with the Middle East, given their mostly Arab and Muslim populations—and the rest of the continent is an increasingly blurry one. Mauritania, and now Sudan (having been amputated of its primarily non-Arab and non-Muslim south) in many ways share more in common with their neighbors to the north than those to the south. And indeed social, political, and religious dynamics across the Sahel, from Senegal to Chad, bridge the Saharan divide. I will nevertheless focus the discussion here on the region classically described as sub-Saharan, thus excluding the Arab Spring dynamics of North Africa.

Fully 32 of the 48 countries in the region today have significant Muslim populations, ranging widely from 10 percent to 100 percent. The demographic context in itself is often central in shaping national dynamics. In the 10 countries with Muslim majorities of some 85 percent or more (Comoros, Djibouti, Gambia, Guinea-Conakry, Mali, Mauritania, Niger, Senegal, Somalia, and Sudan), the core question has often centered on the extent to which the state should be shaped by the religion of the vast majority. In what we might label the divided countries, with likely Muslim populations between 30 percent and 60 percent (Burkina Faso, Chad, Ivory Coast, Eritrea, Ethiopia, Guinea-Bissau, Nigeria, Sierra Leone, and Tanzania), the relative influence of different religious communities in the state and the economy has an inherent potential for presenting a serious political fault line, though there is wide variation in the extent to which this has been the case.

And in the 13 countries with significant Muslim minorities of perhaps 10 percent to 20 percent (Benin, Cameroon, Central African Republic, Ghana, Kenya, Liberia, Madagascar, Malawi, Mauritius, Mozambique, South Sudan, Togo, and Uganda), periodic debates center on the rights of religious minorities within national legal and political frameworks. It merits noting that another 10 African countries have small but at times politically significant Muslim minorities, South Africa and Gabon among them.

Within these very different demographic variations, Muslims in Africa also live across the highly varied range of political systems on the continent. The domestic environments of individual countries comprise the principal arenas for Islam and politics. At the same time, African Muslim societies find themselves caught up in global debates on Islam and tied to transnational Muslim dynamics. The trajectories of national religious communities are thus situated at the intersection of international trends with the local structures and organization of religious authority, as played out within the context of the political systems of specific states.

Religious Ferment

Doctrinally, Islam in Africa is overwhelmingly Sunni, with the Maliki legal school followed across the northwestern parts of the continent, and the Shafi'i school followed by the majority in the east. Across the region the dominant practice of Islam has been shaped by the Sufi tradition, which emphasizes mysticism over legalism and assigns particular importance to saintly religious guides (sheikhs). There is significant variation in what this has meant in practice, in terms of both social organization and religious observance. Nevertheless, Sufism was key to the spread of Islam in Africa, and historically quite accommodating to local cultures and realities.

This has led to a long history of attempting to distinguish a supposedly more "peaceful" or "tolerant" African Islam from a more "rigid" or "fundamentalist" Arab Islam, an effort that marked much of colonial discourse and is still reflected in contemporary analyses. In fact, the very process of accommodating Islam to local cultures and societies has long fed debates about correct religious practice among Muslims in Africa. For example, West African jihads of the late eighteenth- and nineteenth centuries were in large part reformist movements aimed at purifying Islam, but squarely within Sufi traditions. The distinction between Sufis and puritanical reformists must thus be nuanced.

The adoption of sharia has helped empower social groups critical of the political class, thus increasing support for democracy.

Nevertheless, Muslim societies in much of Africa have indeed been marked by the gradually increasing importance of explicitly anti-Sufi religious movements, often calling themselves simply "Sunnites," but frequendy labeled by others as "Wahhabis" or "Salansts." In most cases, organized reformist movements had their genesis in the late colonial period. Frequently they appealed to Africans with Western educations in modern sectors, often as an alternative to the perceived quiescence of traditional Sufi leaders in relation to colonial rule, and in reaction to the perceived "backwardness" of rural religious practice.

Throughout most of Africa these movements stayed small and had very limited popular appeal until the 1980s, directing their attention primarily to critiques of religious practice for an audience of urban intellectuals. In the context of the apparent worldwide "Islamic revival" of the 1970s and 1980s, however, reformist movements began to exhibit a new dynamism and to take on more explicidy political orientations. Given the disillusionment both within the Muslim world and in Africa about the failure of the promises of independence, there was a new receptivity to arguments about the need for local alternatives to Western models of "modernization."

Economic stagnation and the implementation of structural adjustment programs that marked the end of assured state employment for university graduates also fed demands for change, stimulating new reflections on the social and political role of Islam. Although its impact in Africa was limited and in retrospect rather brief, the Iranian revolution of 1979 sparked some unprecedented efforts to organize explicitly political movements based on religion in some parts of the continent. In the effervescence of the period, various new religious movements emerged, and small inroads were made by Muslim groups from outside the region, including Shiite Islam and the South Asian Ahmadiyya movement.

Increased contacts between sub-Saharan Africa and the Arab world following independence accelerated in the wake of the oil booms of the 1970s, and across the region private schools teaching at least partially in Arabic proliferated as alternatives to official state schools teaching in the colonial languages. The new schools gradually channeled some students into the Arab world for advanced studies, and the oil wealth of Saudi Arabia and the Gulf states expanded scholarship opportunities. Returning home after years in the Arab world, these *"arabisants"* as they are known in the Francophone countries, tended to be less respectful of local authorities and to preach against what they perceived as the corrupt practices of local Islam.

The Wahhabi-inspired austerity and individualism that the arabisants often promoted found particular resonance with urban youth, as well as with merchants and the new business classes. In a number of African countries, this led to organized and ideologically motivated reform movements with increasing importance in the public sphere. Perhaps the most significant of these was a Nigerian movement founded in 1978, which came to be known as *Izala* (from its full name: *Jama't Izalat al Bid'a Wa Iqamat as Sunna,* or Society for the Removal of Innovation and the Reestablishment of the Sunna), but parallel dynamics have been documented in Muslim communities in such far-flung countries as Ethiopia, Mozambique, and the Democratic Republic of Congo.

The diversification of religious voices and ideologies was to expand rapidly with the wave of democratization that began in Africa in the early 1990s. Regardless of the fate of given democratic transitions, the substantive liberalization of politics on the continent that began in this period produced a flourishing of social movements and organizations, ranging from an emergent "civil society" to new ideological and identity-based movements.

The consequent opening of a Muslim public sphere in many countries gave rise to intense debates about the authority to speak for Islam or for Muslim communities, and led in many ways to a real democratization of religion. New social actors, not only among those with Arabic or Islamic educations, but often from professional and modern sectors, formed Islamic associations claiming the right to speak on religious matters. Importantly, the emergence of Muslim women's voices added a new dimension to the religious public sphere.

With their authority under challenge, traditional religious leaders have often reinvented themselves in various ways, prompting further change. In the context of this plurality of religious voices, the attacks against America on September 11, 2001, and the subsequent wars in Iraq and Afghanistan provoked significant internal debate—in Africa as elsewhere—regarding the relationship of Islam to politics in the modern world.

The result is that Muslim Africa today encompasses a broad diversity of religious ideologies, fully engaged in debates about the appropriate role for Islam and about the social and political organization of Muslim communities. While the old dichotomies—traditional versus reformist, or Sufis versus Salafists—maintain some relevance, the range of ideologies and religious postures in the African public sphere is much broader and varied, and often highly fluid.

In The Square

Despite the globalization of Muslim discourse, and the possibilities provided by new communications technologies for actors in widely dispersed locales to engage in debates on religion and modernity, the major arena for Islamic politics in Africa, as elsewhere, remains the state context. It is within the domestic political sphere that issues of deep concern to religious actors—rights and duties of religious communities, religious education the regulation of marriage and family life, and more—are debated and shaped. The state context thus remains central to the vast majority of Muslim political actions.

Historically the nondemocratic governments of Africa after independence had only limited interest in religion. To the extent that they did so in Muslim Africa, however, their actions were shaped by dual imperatives: first, trying to control religious, organizations so as to preempt potential challenges to rule, and second, seeking legitimation of the regime through symbolic efforts in support of religion. With the increased mobilization of religion in the 1970s, a common strategy for governments was to create official Islamic organizations that could be controlled via state sponsorship while simultaneously demonstrating government solicitude toward Islam.

Examples of this strategy can be found in both Muslim majority and minority contexts: the Malian Association for the Unity and Progress of Islam or the Islamic Association of Niger in the francophone Sahel, and the Supreme Council of Kenyan Muslims or the Supreme Council of Tanzanian Muslims in anglophone East Africa. In each of these cases the state-sponsored organizations were the only legally recognized religious associations.

These corporatist arrangements were to collapse with the liberalization of politics in the 1990s. Although the old official Islamic associations often survived, they quickly found themselves rivaled by an explosion of new religious groups, part of a boom of voluntary association in Africa in the 1990s. These diverse groups' entry into politics in an attempt to influence new state structures prompted some fears of a religious "backlash" against democratization.

But in fact there were very few, if any, efforts to impose religiously based systems as an alternative to democracy. The rise of religion in the public sphere, while it has brought tensions, might best be seen as a normal and predictable consequence of liberalization. And the primary political activities of such groups have been directed at democratic politics. Most efforts have centered on demands for states to ensure the rights of religious communities, and to take religious values, into account in determining public policies.

In minority or divided cases of religious demographics, questions of communal rights are often linked to constitutional issues, and hence create a potential for politicizing the religious divide, Kenya and Tanzania; home to the largest populations of Swahili speaking Muslims, present especially important cases. Kenya in the 1970s and 1980s witnessed various efforts to limit special legal provisions for the Muslim community that had been enshrined in the constitution at independence. With the beginning of liberalization in the 1990s, the Supreme Council of Kenyan Muslims found itself rivaled by many new Muslim civil society groups, and together these religious actors took a central role in debates about the country's political institutions.

Most notably, a core issue in the decade-long struggle to write a new constitution for Kenya was the question of whether to maintain special *Kahdi* courts with jurisdiction for Muslim personal law. The issue proved to be one of the constitution's more controversial provisions, but in the end the new charter approved in a referendum, in August 2010 maintained the courts, winning strong support from Kenya's large Muslim minority.

Similar debates have occurred in Tanzania, centering in part on whether legal provisions for Muslims on the mainland should parallel those on Zanzibar, the almost completely Muslim islands of the United Republic. As new Islamic groups have challenged the Supreme Council of Tanzanian Muslims, the country has seen a rise in religious tensions. To date, however, these appear to have been expressed and channeled within institutional politics.

In a wide range of other countries with Muslim minorities—including Benin, Ghana, and the interesting case of South Africa—Muslim politics in democratizing contexts has involved debates about special legal provisions for Muslim minorities within national political institutions. These debates can of course provoke tensions across religious lines, but to date democratic political institutions have managed them rather well. More worrisome in terms of potential religious conflict have been cases where nondemocratic governments in semi-liberal contexts have used claims of "extremism" to control dissent, a tactic that the Ethiopian regime, for example, seems to have embraced.

The Sharia Debate

Arguably the most significant experiment with political Islam in the context of democratization—not only in Africa but indeed anywhere in the Muslim world—was the adoption of the sharia penal code by 12 Muslim-majority states of northern Nigeria in the wake of that nation's 1999 transition to democracy. Nigeria, Africa's most populous country, is roughly equally divided between Muslims and non-Muslims, and the role of sharia courts in Nigeria's federal system has historically been a subject of intense acrimony. When the collapse of the particularly repressive authoritarian regime of Sani Abacha brought a new effort at democratization in 1999, the issue once again arose.

In this context an electoral campaign promise to enact sharia law by a candidate for governor in the small northern state of Zamfara struck a resonant popular chord, and the policy was quickly instituted after his election. Reaction in the other northern states was highly positive, and by 2002 11 others had followed suit, billing the move as a "return" to sharia as it had been practiced in the region before independence.

In the decade since, the implications of this unprecedented adoption of sharia via democracy have been complex and varied, but some trends can be discerned. Several initial harsh legal rulings in criminal cases (sentences of stoning for adultery and such) have not been repeated, and indeed none of the initial ones was ever carried out. The principle of sharia has remained widely popular among northern Nigerian Muslims, and among virtually all social classes. But rather than imposing rigid adherence to an inflexible notion of sharia, the adoption of Islamic law has opened the door to wide-ranging debates about what "true" sharia should entail. These debates have given rise to varied interpretations, including important ones centered on social justice and demands for government accountability.

Strikingly, then, the adoption of sharia has helped empower social groups critical of the political class, thus increasing support for democracy. Many unsettled issues remain, and both the actual practice of politics in these states and other troubling trends could intervene, but the positive correlation between support for democratic development and sharia implementation is a striking aspect of the Nigerian context

In a somewhat different mode, the experiences of three overwhelmingly Muslim countries of the francophone Sahel—Senegal, Mali, and Niger—are also interesting for the question of Islam and democracy in Africa. The political trajectories of the three nations have varied, and the tragic collapse of the Malian regime in the spring of 2012 under pressures sparked by the post-Qaddafi chaos in Libya leaves the future of the region in question. But in all three countries there are lessons to be drawn from two decades of experimentation with democracy in the context of liberalized public spheres with widespread religious participation.

To be sure, the agenda of democratization as embraced in the early 1990s brought initial clashes between Islamic actors and secular civil society groups. And intense and sometimes angry debates have continued since then, notably on such issues as the meaning of secularism in public life, the adoption of family law, and the role of religion in education. Increasingly however, religious actors of widely varying ideologies have moved from protesting that democracy as initially presented was not "compatible" with Islam, to embracing democracy and arguing that its practice in Muslim societies should mean policies that reflect Muslim values.

Support for democracy has been strengthened precisely because it has allowed religious groups to advocate for policies that are more accommodating of local cultural values than has ever been possible in postcolonial Africa. This of course is not to the liking of secular actors, and religious activism at times is presented as a sign of threats to democracy. Yet this tendency to debate policy issues in religious terms might well be considered a normal part of democracy in religious societies.

There is a wide—and increasing—diversity to Muslim movements and organization in the region.

Much of the religious influence on Sahelian politics resembles nothing more than the religious involvement in many current American debates—about gay marriage, for example, or prayer in public schools. The Sahelian countries of West Africa thus present fertile ground for examining both the potential and the likely course of democratic debates in Muslim societies, with important lessons for Tunisia, Egypt, and other countries of the Arab Spring.

It is highly significant, in this context, that participation in democratic politics is not the purview of "moderate" Muslims alone, but in fact of Muslim citizens of widely varying ideologies. Future debates doubtless will be intense, but public opinion surveys by Afrobarometer and the Pew Forum on Religion and Public Life show broad and apparently strengthening support for both democracy *and* religion among Muslims across Africa. And considerable evidence suggests that democratic politics has proved a rather effective means of channeling Muslims' political concerns, whether as majorities or minorities, via institutional avenues. This is the case even though, in Africa as in the United States, the impact on public policies may not be the liking of secular citizens.

Born in Chaos

In addition to the new dynamic of Muslim politics in Africa's liberalized state arenas, the past decade has also witnessed the rise of militant religious groups, which though small in number have managed to carry out violent activities with very high impact. In fact, terrorism in the name of an Islamic ideology began in Africa well before the events of 9/11, most dramatically with the simultaneous bombings of the American embassies in Kenya and Tanzania in August 1998. All indications are that those early Al Qaeda actions were planned to take advantage of vulnerable targets, with no clear connections to Kenyan or Tanzanian politics or social groups.

Recently, however, some militant Islamic movements in Africa have appeared to be more rooted in local contexts, raising fears and questions about Africa as a potential new "front" in the "war on terror." The issue is deeply vexed and subject to competing interpretations. It is difficult to discern the extent to which various policy initiatives—not the least of which was the creation of AFRICOM, the US military command for Africa—are reactions to a rising threat or are responsible for creating the perception of increased threats.

If we consider the most worrisome cases, it is clear that the real dangers of militant religious movements are deeply embedded in very specific political contexts, even while they draw on global connections. In addition, though the forms of these movements can certainly be labeled as manifestations of militant or "extremist" Islam, there is no consensus on how to sort out the religious origins of militancy from other factors. To the extent that ideologies are at the base, how to explain the rise of such pockets of militancy in the context of the broad and diverse range of religious positions we have noted above? Or if poverty, underdevelopment, and disaffected youth are the ingredients for militant action, as often asserted, how are we to understand the rarity of such movements in some of the poorest and least-developed countries, such as those of the Sahel?

If we have no clear answers to these and other critical questions, one important commonality does appear to emerge from a consideration of the militant religious movements currently of deepest concern: Each of them has arisen in highly fraught political environments and seems to feed on ongoing and long-standing conflicts.

Al Shabab, the Somali militant organization, is rooted in the chaos that followed the collapse of the Somali state in the early 1990s. But in many ways what is most striking in this 100 percent Muslim society is the fact that religious dynamics were for so long marginal to the effort to rebuild a political system. When religion did emerge as central to politics more than a decade after the state's collapse, it was in the form of the Islamic Courts Union (ICU), the closest the country has come to a functional government in two decades, and now widely seen by Somalis as a moment of real promise and hope. The US-backed Ethiopian invasion of Somalia in late 2006 ended the rule of the ICU, and helped spawn a series of radical jihadist movements, as well as other threats to the international community, such as the rise of piracy.

Militant movements in Muslim Africa present larger challenges than seemed likely until very recently.

Al Shabab, until then a small group linked to one particular court in Mogadishu, and with no known link to Al Qaeda at the time, was well placed to capitalize on the opportunity. Reinventing itself as an insurgency against the Transitional Federal Government, which was supported by outside powers, Al Shabab adopted terrorist tactics and saw its influence rise until 2008 or so. Since then the movement's trajectory has been complicated by its contentious relationship with Al Qaeda, and by its mishandling of the famine situation in 2011 (for example, by blocking humanitarian aid). Although the group clearly attempts to draw on transnational resources, it is striking that Al Shabab's very existence and its likely fate are intricately linked to the fate of Somalia.

Homegrown Militants

There are many more questions than answers about the Boko Haram movement in Nigeria, and in the conspiracy-prone culture of Nigerian politics rumors abound about its origins, connections, and goals. There are questions about the extent of the movement itself, and reports that many acts claimed in its name are actually the work of ordinary criminals. Possible links to other organizations, including Al Qaeda, are far from clear and hotly debated. And competing accusations point fingers at both government and opposition politicians as supporters of the movement for political aims.

If we silt through the debate, Boko Haram appears to build on a reaction to the moderation of the sharia implementation process, and to feed on an extremely difficult socioeconomic context, in a country with a long history of militant minority religious movements. Boko Haram has focused its attacks primarily on Nigerian government targets, and Nigerian security forces have badly managed their reaction, almost certainly fanning the flames of the movements militancy. YouTube videos of summary executions of the Boko Haram leader and other alleged members, sometimes with very tenuous or no evidence, have been widely circulated and have undermined support for the security forces. Although the movement is likely building ties to transnational organizations, its impact has to date remained very limited across national borders. The group clearly is deeply rooted in the Nigerian context, a new manifestation of the violent face of the country's historical religious politics.

And finally, in the Sahara and posing a particular threat to Niger, Mali, and Mauritania, the movement now known as Al Qaeda in the Islamic Maghreb (AQIM) has provoked significant international reaction. AQIM's genealogy can be traced to the Algerian civil war that followed the aborted effort at a transition to democracy in 1991–92. Islamist militants who challenged the military regime at the time eventually renamed themselves AQIM in 2007.

The organization's tactics have focused primarily on kidnapping Western hostages for ransom, which raises questions about its ultimate goals. As opposed to the Somali and Nigerian groups discussed above, AQIM has had no apparent success in becoming a social movement, having found almost no ideological traction with local populations. Indeed, it is striking that despite massive poverty and misery in the countries where it is active, AQIM has so far found little popular resonance and apparently managed only the rare recruit.

The fear remains, however, that the movement will spread its influence in the region, with the most significant concern being that it will draw support from the nomadic Tuareg populations of the Sahara, in the wake of the extreme disruption to Tuareg society that resulted from the fall of Qaddafi in Libya. Indeed, the rise of the Ansar Dine group in Mali this spring appears to reflect precisely this dynamic. The adoption of AQIM's current name of course points to an ideological link with the transnational jihadism of Al Qaeda, but its operations to date and its potential for future transformation are rooted squarely in the difficult political contexts of the Sahara, and continue to be largely shaped by the cleavages of Algerian politics.

Drawing Distinctions

Islamism in the sense of an ideological commitment to shape political systems to Muslim values is a global movement, and globalization produces some commonalities in the forms it takes in different locales. But important variations are rooted in local contexts. The shape and form of Muslim political action are largely determined by specific political systems, even when claiming inspiration from elsewhere. Indeed, ideological resources for a wide range of "Islamic" political options are available in the international realm.

Muslim societies in sub-Saharan Africa have open to them the full diversity of options, including the significant resources available from Muslim history and tradition, for participating constructively in democratic politics in both majority and minority settings. While the threat of militant interpretations cannot be ignored, we must also not allow fears of militancy to detail or obscure the underlying wealth of this diversity.

Much of the concern about Islamic terrorism in Africa is expressed in terms of worries about the "spread of extremist ideologies," and efforts to combat it are often framed around promoting Muslim "moderates" and suppressing "extremists." But taking into consideration the broad variation in religious beliefs and forms of political participation across the continent, the effort to try to distinguish between good and bad Muslim ideologies may be much less important than the need to support functional political institutions.

Critical Thinking

1. What is the range of political actors contending for influence in the aftermath of the Arab Spring?
2. What obstacles do Salafist groups face in post-Arab Spring countries?

Create Central

www.mhhe.com/createcentral

Internet References

Center for Research on Inequality, Human Security, and Ethnicity
www.crise.ox.ac.uk

LatinAmericanNetworkInformationCenter—LANIC
www.lanic.utexas.edu

ReliefWeb
www.reliefweb.int/w/rwb.nsf

Leonardo A. Villalón is an associate professor of political science and African studies at the University of Florida.

Article

The Awakening

Inside the Burmese Spring.

EMMA LARKIN

One evening recently in Rangoon, my friend Ko Ye (not his real name) arrived at the apartment where I was staying, brandishing the latest issue of the weekly newspaper he runs. It was, he announced with great fanfare, a landmark edition: For the first time ever, government censors had allowed him to run a photo of Aung San Suu Kyi, the country's most prominent dissident, on the cover. The edition also included other previously banned topics: political analysis of U.S. relations with Burma and an article about Martin Luther King that contained the taboo phrase "human rights" in the headline. "And here," said Ko Ye, jabbing another headline, "is the first time I've been able to write about the 2.2 trillion *kyat* budget deficit. This is *real* news!"

I first met Ko Ye ten years ago, and his tireless struggle to squeeze the truth past government censors has taught me much about life under a military dictatorship. If you want to understand Burma, he told me then, "you must look for what's missing and learn how to find the truth in these absences." The advice seemed counterintuitive, but it worked. In the curtailed reality of an authoritarian state, the truth of events is rarely out in the open for everyone to see; rather, it can be found in the sentences and stories excised by the censor's pen or in the voices of people silenced by imprisonment or intimidation. I used to love listening to Ko Ye's tales about sneaking elements of the truth past the censors by burying contraband facts deep within seemingly innocuous articles or constructing florid sentences with double meanings.

These days, however, Ko Ye has less need for such antics. Ever since the country's longtime dictator, Than Shwe, stepped aside early last year, a remarkable thaw has appeared to be underway in Burma—and journalists have been among the prime beneficiaries. In June 2011, the government announced that magazines focusing on sports, technology, entertainment, health, and children's topics no longer had to be submitted for censorship. Later, publications covering business, economics, law, or crime were also exempted. In October, U Tint Swe, head of the Press Scrutiny and Registration Department, made a mind-boggling statement during a rare interview with Radio Free Asia (RFA). "Press censorship," he said, "is nonexistent in most other countries as well as among our neighbors, and, as it is not in harmony with democratic practices, press censorship should be abolished in the near future." For the head of the censorship board to say this at all was astonishing, but for him to say it to a news organization like RFA, which is funded by the U.S. government and has been banned in Burma, was unthinkable. (Until recently, state media spouted melodramatic slogans about RFA and other external radio services running Burmese-language programs, calling them "killers in the airwaves" and accusing them of producing a "skyful of lies.")

This media openness has extended to foreign journalists as well. Previously, to report on Burma, one almost always had to sneak into the country on a tourist visa, but recently a number of prominent foreign reporters have been granted official journalist visas. While watching the BBC news one afternoon in Rangoon, I saw a British correspondent reporting beneath the tagline "LIVE FROM NAYPYIDAW," the once strictly off-limits capital. He had no particular news to report; the fact that he had been allowed in Naypyidaw for the first time was news enough to make the day's top stories.

Indeed, from the moment I arrived in November, it was clear things were different. When I opened up my laptop to use the Internet, I noticed that the websites of exile Burmese media, which used to be blocked by firewalls, were now accessible; gone was the standard admonishment, displayed in a stern red font across my screen, "ACCESS DENIED." For the first time, I changed my dollars in a real bank at a rate slightly higher than what was available on the black market—a sign that efforts are being made to adjust the ludicrous gap between the official rate (6 *kyat* to the dollar) and the black market rate (around 800 *kyat* to the dollar).

But by far the most visible difference was the reappearance of Aung San Suu Kyi, who had spent most of the past two decades under house arrest while her image and name were fastidiously erased from the public arena. To display or sell pictures of her was once to risk a jail sentence; her followers kept her photo tucked away in wallets or hung on the walls of family rooms where strangers did not enter. Now, a wide variety of posters depicting Suu Kyi are being openly sold on the streets of Rangoon.

"It feels like everyone in the city has just heaved a collective sigh of relief," a friend in Rangoon told me. People are talking more freely; they no longer lower their voices when discussing politics; and one hears alarm-bell words—democracy, elections, dictatorship—bandied about with an uncharacteristic ease. My Burmese friends even spoke more openly on the telephone—once considered dangerous due to potential wiretaps.

In my experience, there are no people more justifiably distrustful of government initiatives than the Burmese, who have been betrayed many times over by their rulers. So I found this new insouciance utterly surprising, even a little alarming. And I was not alone in my discomfort: Many dissidents, activists, and academics outside the country are understandably wary. They suspect the generals who have long ruled Burma of trying to pull off an elaborate hoax to lure the West into lifting sanctions and investing in the country's ailing economy. Is it really possible, they ask skeptically, that Burma is changing? But many of the Burmese citizens I spoke to during my recent trip no longer have any interest in this question. They are already persuaded that the answer is yes.

When I first visited Burma in the mid '90s, it was a country that appeared to have been locked in time: a sad and secretive land, filled with untold stories and hidden histories. In 1962, just 14 years after Burma's independence from Britain, a military dictator had seized control and sealed it off from the outside world, transforming a country rich in natural resources into one of the poorest in Asia. In 1988, after soldiers killed an estimated 3,000 demonstrators, the ruling generals were nominally replaced by a new military dictatorship that called itself, first, the State Law and Order Restoration Council and, later, the State Peace and Development Council.

Contrary to its name, the State Peace and Development Council was a brutal military junta with one of the worst human rights records in the world. To flush out guerrilla fighters from minority ethnic groups, Burmese soldiers razed whole villages, commandeered civilians as human minesweepers, and, in some regions, practiced systematic rape. Elsewhere in the country, a vast network of spies and informers operated, ensuring that anyone who did or said anything that might threaten the regime was swiftly punished.

In the wake of the quashing of the 1988 demonstrations, and after the military stepped up efforts against minority ethnic armies in the '90s, many Burmese fled into exile. Members of this diaspora, joined by Western activists, have worked hard to raise awareness of Burma's oppressive politics. They have successfully called for a tourism boycott and economic sanctions. But Burma's generals have seemed impervious to these efforts. In 2007, the regime violently put down a widespread protest led by Buddhist monks. In May 2008, when Cyclone Nargis thundered across the country, killing an estimated 138,000 people, the junta was unable to provide adequate relief for the millions of people affected, but stubbornly refused, and even scuppered, assistance from other governments and the international humanitarian community. It is safe to say that few people expected this oppressive regime to ever instigate political reform.

It is even safer to say that few people thought it would happen *this* way. In the popular narrative of revolution and political transformation, dictators are expected to meet grim ends: They are brutalized by furious crowds or stand ridiculous and unrepentant against the bland backdrop of a court of law. They don't, as a rule, shuffle quietly off center stage having set in place the mechanisms for reform. Yet this is exactly what appears to have happened in Burma.

In November 2010—with Shwe planning to retire—the generals held an election. It was, by all accounts, an unpromising event. Suu Kyi was still under house arrest (she was released a few days after the election took place), and her party refused to participate. The only party with the infrastructure to contest all 1,157 parliamentary seats was the Union Solidarity and Development Party (USDP), led by politicians who had recently retired from the army so they could run as civilians. A popular joke had it that the only change the election would herald was a change of clothes: The ruling generals had done little more than exchange their uniforms for civilian attire in order to act out their roles as would-be politicians in a mock democracy.

Unsurprisingly, the USDP "won" the vast majority of seats, and, in January last year, a new parliament was convened in a brand new building in the capital. The unremarkable first session focused primarily on administrative matters, such as the selection of a president and two vice presidents. But soon, there were hints that change might be afoot. The new president, Thein Sein, gave an inaugural speech to parliament on March 30 that, while filled with the usual praise for the military, also referred to real problems that were not acknowledged by the previous regime. Among other topics, he spoke of "the hell of untold miseries" in ethnic areas, rights for workers, and the need to improve education and health care with the assistance of international nongovernmental organizations and the United Nations.

Then, during the second sitting of parliament, which began last August, events started to move in truly unexpected directions. The parliamentary sessions were televised, and local journalists were invited to sit in a press gallery. Numerous legislative proposals were debated, among them a labor organization bill that has since been enacted. This new law allows for the formation of trade unions (banned in Burma since 1962) and has been described by the International Labor Organization as "a massive move for the country." Also in August, Suu Kyi met with Sein. As all earlier efforts at high-level dialogue had failed miserably, everyone was astounded when Suu Kyi declared she was happy with the meeting, even adding that she thought the president was "honest" and "sincere."

For Ko Ye, and many others I spoke with, the key turning point came the following month, in September 2011, when the government put a stop to the construction of the Myitsone Dam. Backed by the Chinese, the Myitsone Dam was to be a major hydropower station situated in northern Burma. Despite Burma's chronic power shortages, 90 percent of the electricity generated by the dam was slated for China, and an environmental impact assessment leaked last year cited all sorts of potential problems, including the possible endangerment of Burma's major river, the Irrawaddy. As part of a "Save the

Irrawaddy" campaign, Burmese intellectuals and celebrities spoke out against the dam. On September 30, Sein announced that, in accordance with "the will of the people," he had suspended the project. Though Ko Ye is sure that broader, geopolitical factors influenced the decision, he acknowledges it as an unprecedented instance of the Burmese government responding to popular sentiment. "I was shocked when I heard the news," he said. "Really, really shocked."

As if to prove the point about Burma's abysmal power shortages, my conversation with Ko Ye and another friend who had joined us was interrupted by one of Rangoon's frequent power cuts. Looking out the window, we could see that electricity was down across the entire city; even the powerful floodlights that illuminated the massive, golden Shwedagon Pagoda were off. The result was a blackness so complete that we could barely see each other across the dining room table. Within a few minutes, we heard the roar of the building's generators kicking into action, and the lights flickered back on. Just as our eyes had readjusted to the light, another power cut plunged us back into darkness. We all laughingly agreed that it was an apt metaphor for the Burmese condition: The political developments we had charted over the course of the evening had come so far, but they could just as easily disappear at the flick of a switch.

Hovering over the flurry of reforms and the general air of optimism is the difficult question of why: Why did the generals, who had closely guarded their power for so long, suddenly decide to step back?

Analysts point to geopolitical and economic incentives as one likely possibility. Ostracized by the West for so many years, Burma turned to neighboring China for support. China provided Burma with a valuable defender in the U.N. Security Council and became a heavyweight political ally, but there has been a price to pay: Chinese investment in Burma has tended toward large-scale infrastructure projects such as dams, deep-sea ports, and natural gas pipelines—the products and proceeds of which go mostly to China. Burma may now be looking to open new markets and establish international relationships that will help counterbalance China's overbearing presence. That strategy might be working: Hillary Clinton arrived in Burma on November 30, the first time in over half a century that Washington had dispatched such a high-level emissary to the country.

There may also be a more personal motivation for the generals. Burmese military rulers often meet with untimely or ignominious demises. The founder of the Burmese army, General Aung San (father of Aung San Suu Kyi), was assassinated in 1947 just months before the independence from Britain he had fought so hard to achieve. General Ne Win, who seized power in 1962 and ruled Burma for more than a quarter of a century, saw his family charged with plotting to overthrow the government in 2002. Though the aged ruler had officially retired, his son-in-law and three grandsons were imprisoned, and he and his favorite daughter were placed under house arrest. Other top generals have had similarly miserable fates and few have been able to retire peacefully. The Burmese use the phrase *wut leh deh*—which means something akin to "what goes around comes around"—to explain this inescapable cycle of karmic retribution.

It is highly possible that Shwe is using liberalization as an exit strategy so that he, his family, and his close colleagues can survive with their wealth and freedom intact. This, too, may be working out according to plan: A campaign for a U.N. commission of inquiry into crimes committed by the junta that was gathering momentum last year has been put on the back burner since Clinton's visit.

Perhaps because the generals' motivations are hard to discern, not everyone I met in Rangoon was optimistic about the recent changes. "This is nothing more than a game," a friend told me. "I can never think of this government as a new one. Make no mistake: It's the same government as before. It has not changed. This so-called progress is just a trick, nothing more than mind games."

Indeed, there are valid reasons for pessimism. Chief among them are the country's large number of political prisoners. Last year, amnesties were granted to more than 310 political prisoners, but some 1,000 still remain in jail, according to the Assistance Association for Political Prisoners (Burma). The release of all remaining political prisoners would be a powerful demonstration of the government's sincerity, and this was one of the key points emphasized by Clinton in her meeting with Sein. Yet a much-anticipated amnesty earlier this month proved disappointing when only 34 prisoners were released.

More potentially destabilizing is the problem of ethnic conflict in Burma. At the same time as positive developments have taken place in Naypyidaw, renewed fighting has broken out between the Burmese army and ethnic forces. In Shan state, a cease-fire signed with the Shan State Army-North in 1989 recently fell apart after more than 20 years of uneasy peace. Further north, in Kachin state, the Kachin Independence Army has resumed its struggle after 17 years of relative peace; the fierce fighting has already displaced some 30,000 civilians.

Even for those who believe that the changes in Burma are likely to proceed, there is no doubt that the situation is precarious. While Sein appears willing to cooperate with the opposition, he still must pacify the hard-line generals whose power would be threatened by change. Nay Win Maung, a passionate leader of civil society in Burma who died of a heart attack on January 1 of this year, maintained that recalcitrant generals were already plotting to derail the process. In a press interview before he died, he said, "Thein Sein means change, but it's just as likely the situation ends in a military coup."

All it takes is a simple paradigm shift to see the cup as half empty. At first glance, the relaxation in censorship rules appears categorically positive; yet many subjects still remain off limits. Similarly, there is much room for skepticism when looking at the new legislation promulgated by Sein. For instance, though the new law that allows protest is a welcome development, it may prove meaningless while the existing Emergency Provisions Act and State Protection Law enable authorities to arrest anyone perceived to be a threat to state security. Even Suu Kyi's newfound freedom can be seen as a plot to neutralize her power. Though her party has decided to run in the upcoming election, only 48 seats will be available—which means that, even if her party wins every single seat, it will still be only a minority in parliament. And, if Suu Kyi herself wins a seat, it could become diplomatically challenging for Western governments to channel their policy toward Burma through a single member of parliament, who is just one among many.

And yet, despite all these serious caveats, I found it impossible to spend time in Rangoon and not be swept up by the city's newfound energy. In anticipation of the possible lifting of sanctions and an expected gold rush of foreign investment, there is much talk of new business ventures. Tourist arrivals have increased by more than 25 percent during the past year, flights into Burma are full, and hotels that were once empty are now filled with guests. News reports tell of foreign companies and organizations scoping out possibilities. George Soros was in Burma over New Years and Standard Chartered Bank has expressed interest in reestablishing a branch in the country (during the British colonial period, the bank had a handsome art deco headquarters; it still stands, much dilapidated, in the heart of downtown Rangoon). There are also hints that Burmese exiles living abroad will start to come home; the government has extended invitations to them, and, in Burma-related circles, much gossip revolves around which high-profile dissidents are cutting deals with the government for favorable conditions and protection should they decide to return.

While I was in Rangoon, I met up with a young Burmese friend who was home on holiday from a university in Bangkok. "When I finish my studies, maybe I can come back here and get a job," she said, visibly excited at the prospect. The country's education system deteriorated so severely under decades of military rule that most young Burmese with the means to travel abroad for further education choose to do so; and many have ended up staying abroad, as the country's decimated economy offers few sustainable career paths. "Before, my only chance to get a proper job in Burma might have been with the U.N. or one of the international NGOs," she explained. "But, by the time I've finished my degree, maybe there will be possibilities in the corporate sector, too."

This ability to talk about positive future outcomes is new to Burma. Throughout my years of traveling to the country to research articles and books, I have often returned home smothered by a cloud of depression. Indeed, when I finished writing my first book and sent the draft to my editor in London, she was perturbed by what she called its downbeat tone. "Is this what it's really like?" she asked, urging me to come up with a happier conclusion. I managed to barely appease her by adding a halfway positive sentiment as an ending—but it was nothing like the one I might be able to write today. For the first time in decades, there is a sense of forward momentum in Burma and, rather astonishingly, a profound sense of hope.

Critical Thinking

1. What did Burma's new president do that indicated change?
2. Why was this change unanticipated?
3. What factors may have led to these reforms?
4. What issues remain problematic?

Emma Larkin is the pseudonym for a journalist based in Bangkok. She is the author of *Finding George Orwell in Burma and No Bad News for the King.*

Article

Divergent Paths

The Future of One-Party Rule in Singapore

MENG CHEN

Is democracy always the most fitting model of governance, or can circumstances justify a more authoritarian approach for the sake of securing the country's material wealth? The parliamentary republic of Singapore has been under international scrutiny for its stringent one-party rule by the People's Action Party (PAP) and suppression of the media and minority parties that oppose its control of the government. However, many attribute Singapore's rapid rise to first-world status and economic prosperity to the same set of ideologies the PAP used to build up the state following independence from the United Kingdom. Since 1959, the first Prime Minister Lee Kuan Yew has had an important say in who would govern the country and how. Now, as Lee, the current leader of the PAP, approaches the age of 87 and shows signs of a worsening heart condition, many around the world have begun to question the nation's unclear future, specifically its path of succession. A public conference was even held on April 21, 2009, to discuss Singapore's path after Lee's death. Will the dynastic pattern of succession continue beyond Lee Kuan Yew's son, incumbent Prime Minister Lee Hsien Loong? Will there be changes to government practices pertaining to press freedom and political opposition? As the older Lee eventually leaves the country in the hands of younger generations, Singapore must face the decision of whether to continue Lee's legacy or embrace sociopolitical reform.

The Self-Renewal of the PAP

Although the extraordinary success of the PAP has helped Singapore rapidly grow in the past, the country now stands at a crucial juncture with this new generation. Indeed, the system may be particularly vulnerable to the internal self-renewal of the PAP itself, as Ho Kwong Ping, Chairman of Singapore Management University, suggests. Elections are held every five years in Singapore; the next election in 2011 will test the PAP's ability to maintain its grip on the government in the years to come, but Lee remains unfazed. "I don't see any problem in the next election or probably in the next one after that," he says. However, Lee does express concern that if the younger generation of politicians is unable to form a good team by then, the PAP will be at risk of being overtaken by a well-organized opposition party. Kishore Mahbubani, Dean and Professor of the Lee Kuan Yew School of Public Policy, National University of Singapore, believes that there are three scenarios post-Lee Kuan Yew: first, a smooth transition and continuation of the current political system; second, a significant reversal of Lee's legacy; third, continued domination of the government by the PAP, but with greater opposition. According to Mahbubani, destabilizing change seems unlikely due to seven factors that should perpetuate the patriarch's legacy: a quality education system, national service, strong public institutions, a victory-prone political party, ethnic harmony, meritocracy, and a firm anti-corruption policy.

A key factor pointed out by Mahbubani in the PAP's success in elections is the current lack of opposition. The party's ability to be "victory-prone" acts as a stabilizer against government reform from the outside. As a testament to the party's infallibility, the unicameral parliament currently has 82 of 84 seats occupied by PAP members, the other two held respectively by the Singapore Democratic Alliance and the Worker's Party. The current president, Sellapan Ramanathan, took office in 1999, endorsed by Lee, after all opponents were disqualified by the Electoral Committee; in 2005, the same scenario occurred and the scheduled election was never held.

Although the PAP's governing system is still less than democratic, many Singaporeans say that they do not speak against it, solely out of respect for the contributions of the country's iconic founder. Journalists have noted that even the country's youth, ignorant of the beginnings of Singapore's post-independence transformation, harbor a certain sentiment of gratitude towards Lee, thanks to the country's astonishing economic success and stability and the strength of his personality. Once Lee Kuan Yew can no longer guide the younger ruling generation, the legitimacy of the PAP will diminish without the venerated founder at its helm. Opposition is likely to grow from Singapore's minority parties, such as the Singapore Democratic Party (SDP), whose Secretary-General Chee Soon Juan is a long-standing opponent of the former prime minister. Chee has been imprisoned multiple times for public rallies and protests, among other acts banned by the government. After being sued by Lee and declared bankrupt in 2006 on a charge of slander against the former prime minister, Chee continues his activism domestically and internationally, to Lee's dismay.

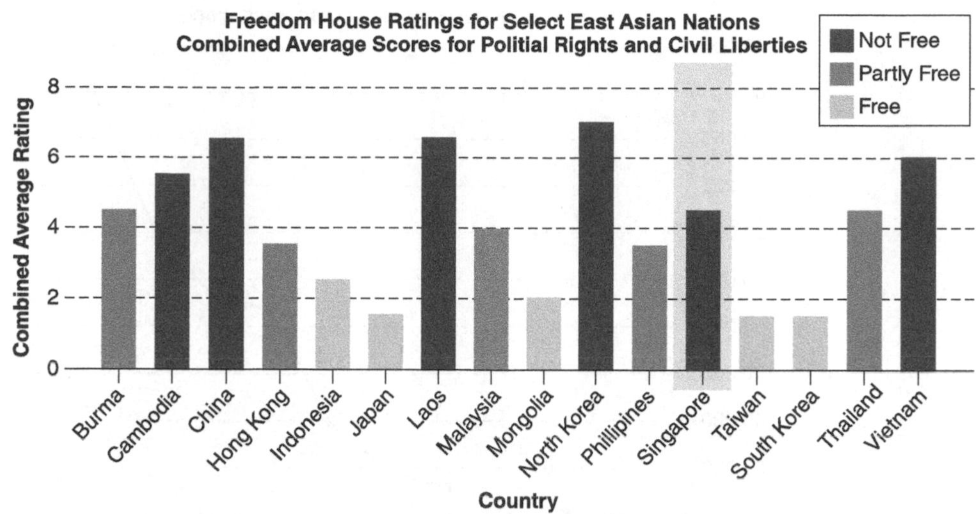

Disparities in Democracy Methodology: Each country and territory is assigned a numerical rating—on a scale of 1 to 7—for political rights and an analogous rating for civil liberties; a rating of 1 indicates the highest degree of freedom and 7 the lowest level of freedom.

Freedom House; 2010

Ingredients of Singapore's Success

In response to critics such as Chee who protest that Singapore's government restricts the press and free speech, imposes over-stringent laws, and acts authoritarian on other accounts, Lee counters that his undemocratic policies were necessary to build the nation up to its current prosperity. The PAP's legitimacy in continuing these practices would be challenged without the attribution of Singapore's success to Lee—it is thus crucial to assess whether his style of heavy government involvement has truly been necessary in state-building. Lee asserts that the sense of vulnerability in the country's foundation is what keeps his fists clenched. He argues that the survival of the country depended on the adoption of his methods of governance and that Singapore's current modernity is the product of these. Without Lee's style, the country would have collapsed, he argues. Indeed, in Singapore there are almost no natural resources and no common culture, only a disharmonious mixture of Chinese, Malays, Indians, and other groups that have yet to create a strong cultural identity. So in some sense, Lee's rule consolidated a population that may otherwise have engaged in ethnic conflict.

It is undeniable that Lee's stringent government policies played a considerable role in guiding the country's rapid development from a British settlement to a city-state of material wealth far exceeding its neighbors' in less than 60 years. In the early stages of Singapore's nation-building, attracting long-term foreign investment was still a concern due to active labor unions and strikes. Such practices have destabilized the workforce of multinational corporations and fueled unsustainable inflation, as currently is the case in Argentina and several other Latin American countries. President Yusof bin Ishak announced in December 1965 that trade unions were "irrespon sible" and called them unaffordable luxuries. Therefore, when the PAP won all 58 parliamentary seats in 1968, Lee's government passed new legislation that allowed longer working hours, cut holidays, and granted employers greater control over hiring, firing, and promoting workers in order to shake the power of unions. At the same time, however, workers were also given sick leave and unemployment compensation. Due to Lee's policies of tightened control and higher employee benefits, productivity soared and 1969 passed without a single strike. The government was then able to implement policies to attract foreign investors, such as tax relief for up to five years and full repatriation of profits in certain industries. Singapore has since continued to attract foreign investment due to such favorable policies.

However, it is questionable whether the nation's success along the purportedly narrow road can be primarily attributed to Lee's "ideology-free" policies. In *Development as Freedom,* Amartya Sen attacks the "Lee thesis" as having little empirical support. Although some say denial of basic civil and political rights helps promote the economy, Sen believes that evidence for this "Lee thesis" is not strong enough.

A pertinent question, then, is which factors drove the small island country's speedy path to economic prosperity. Prior to independence, Singapore was already a crucial British settlement and thus had a head start on its infrastructure development, much as is arguably the case for Hong Kong and India. Although Singapore's neighbor, Malaysia, shared a similar history in that its origin lies in the independence of former British Malaya in 1957, its less strategic geographic location and larger land mass put it at a disadvantage in terms of both organizing the country and trade prosperity. At the eastern end of the Strait of Malacca, between western Malaysia and Indonesian Sumatra, Singapore has been one of the world's busiest ports for many decades, only bypassed by Shanghai in shipping tonnage in 2005. It is also considerably simpler for the government to optimize land use and to devise efficient property taxation laws for the city-state of Singapore with its 268 square miles (693 square km), than it is for its comparatively giant neighbor Malaysia with its 127,350 square miles (329,849 square km). Due to this large disparity in land size, it may be categorically incorrect to compare Singapore's

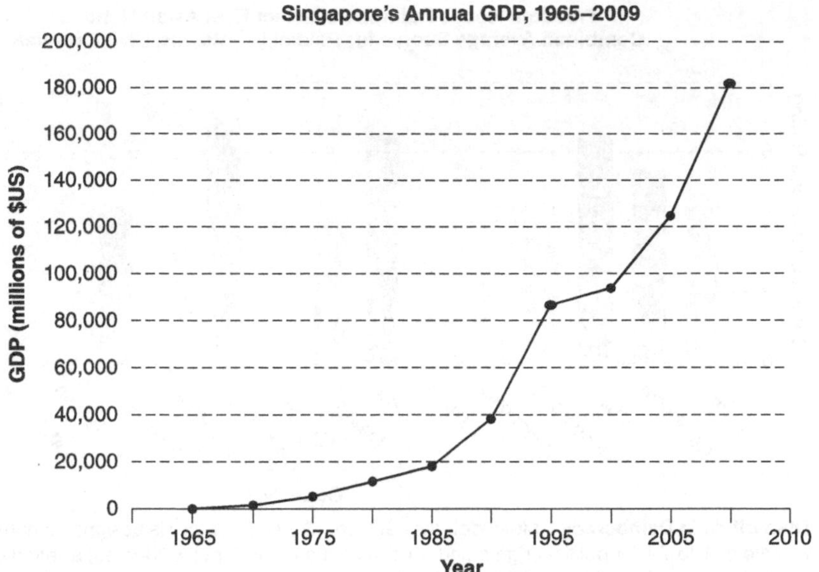

A Startling Spike

Singapore Federal Department of Statistics; 2010

model of development to countries such as Malaysia. In addition, the world economy was experiencing a period of growth during the mid-1960s, and after President Suharto stepped down from power in 1966 in Indonesia, his ban on trade with Singapore was lifted and the neighboring country resumed transactions. Due to the United States' heavy involvement in Indochina at the time, Singapore soon became a major supplier. History might have slightly favored the nation's economic ascendancy.

Reform: Taking It Slow

Even if the "Lee thesis" is true in that authoritarian rule was essential to Singapore's growth, the underlying reason for limiting freedom of the press and political activism no longer seems as convincing as when Singapore was still an underdeveloped, newly independent island. Singapore has since become technologically advanced and economically prosperous.

So what is holding back reform liberalization? It is true that with Singapore's maturation, Lee Kuan Yew has gradually loosened control. In 1990, he stepped down from office and handpicked his deputy and defense minister Goh Chok Tong to succeed him. However, he left himself considerable influence in the government by remaining as Minister Mentor in Goh's cabinet and continuing to lead the PAP. Mr. Goh acknowledges the difficulties that Lee has had in restraining himself from participation in state affairs, but he chooses to accept and welcome such intervention. Under Goh's administration, Lee Hsien Loong, Lee Kuan Yew's son, became Deputy Prime Minister. It came as no surprise when he was appointed the new Prime Minister on August 12, 2004, when Goh Chok Tong switched roles with the younger Lee and became the Chairman of the Monetary Authority of Singapore. Since then, Lee Hsien Loong has slowly been relaxing restrictions on the media and opposition parties, but at what Andrew Loh says is "the speed of a sedated sloth." Loh worries that the government's hesitation to enact socio-political change is "creating a generation of political infants" that may not be able to cope if such a change were to come in a drastic and inescapable form. However, there is little reason to worry because groundbreaking government reform is highly unlikely to occur.

One variable that prevents large scale reform is the series of tactful policies that have been set up to limit the extent to which an opposition government can enact changes. For instance, it would be required by law to gain the president's approval to withdraw from international reserves, suggesting it would not be granted.

The education system and meritocracy in government also tend toward maintaining the status quo, perhaps with minute changes. To bring the country's top scholars into the government and assure that they align themselves with the PAP, the nation's brightest crop of students are selected for generous Public Service Commission Scholarships such as the President's Scholarship, which pays for their tuition in addition to a stipend to attend the world's most prestigious universities. Upon graduation, they are required to return to Singapore and work several years in the government in one of the various tracks of their choice; given a chance to rise to high positions, many stay with the government and perpetuate the system. This is one of the factors listed by Mahbubani that continue Lee Kuan Yew's legacy—meritocracy in a Confucian sense. By educating the smartest students abroad before incorporating them into the government, new perspectives are introduced to the administration even though democratic elections are not held.

In order to compete with the private sector for those with the highest qualifications and to dissuade corruption, Singapore offers one of the highest incomes in the world for the country's political leaders. According to *The Economist,* Singapore's Prime Minister's annual salary was over US$2.1 million in the latest year with data released, which is the highest in the world and second highest in terms of the ratio of political leader's pay to the national GDP per capita. In comparison, the President of the United States earns US$400,000 annually. In the case of China, while the official income of government leaders is average, their "gray income" or undisclosed earnings was reported to be 5.4 trillion yuan (about US$797.1 billion) in 2009, which exceeded a total government revenue of only 3.6 trillion yuan. The theory underlying the Singaporean government's generous compensations is that high salaries will give incentive for officials holding the desired positions to remain in those posts and produce high quality work.

Lee's meritocratic system, which diverges from common Western models of governance, can be both a hindrance and a boon to reform. The way officials are often appointed by the PAP without democratic elections reinforces the dominant party's control in Singapore and bars reform from outside the government. However, this self-selecting process within the PAP allows smooth transition of power, as seen in the past two instants when the prime ministers voluntarily stepped down for the younger generation. In addition, by recruiting the brightest scholars into the PAP after providing them with university education abroad, new ideas are brought into the government. Without a takeover by an opposition party, smaller internal reforms within the PAP, one at a time, is the most effective way to create change. These various factors indicate that minor progress towards increased socio-political freedom in the current administration, despite old political safeguards created by Lee Kuan Yew, is yet promising. The times of strong governmental control of the media and elections are slowly passing away. Ideological changes and liberalization are occurring slowly already and may even be hastened by external opposition if the PAP diminishes in influence.

In the end, it appears that Singapore post-Lee Kuan Yew will continue in his legacy due to his carefully crafted policies that prevent significant change even if an opposition party gains a majority in elections. Just as former prime ministers remain in the cabinet, vestiges of old policies are unlikely to disappear soon. However, as the reasons for Lee's strict guidelines erode due to stable economic growth, more freedom will inevitably be given, whether due to changing ideologies within the PAP or pressure from opposition parties striving to gain legitimacy.

Critical Thinking

1. What role has Lee Kuan Yew played in Singapore's rapid rise?
2. What role has Singapore's location played in its prosperity?
3. What are the obstacles to political reform in Singapore?

Article

How the ANC Lost Its Way

The legendary liberation movement celebrates *its* centenary, but the party of Mandela has done far too little for a still divided South Africa.

ALEX PERRY

It has been exactly 99 years and 11 months since the world's most storied liberation movement, the African National Congress, was born, and I am looking for its birthplace. In Bloemfontein, the old Boer capital on South Africa's central prairie, a white tourist-information officer points me to a building on the edge of town called Maphikela House—after Thomas Maphikela, who built it and who helped found the ANC. "I've never been there myself," the information officer says. "It's a township." Then she pulls out a map and circles another part of town that I am to avoid. "Dangerous," she says. She means "black people."

On Jan. 8, thousands of **ANC** supporters and 46 heads of state descend on Bloemfontein to celebrate the party's centenary. I've come early to explore the origins of the organization that gave the world Nelson Mandela and laid the foundations of modern South Africa—and Africa—by inspiring the overthrow of centuries of colonialism and racist deprivation.

At least that's **ANC** legend. I'm in Bloemfontein to measure that against reality. Because while South Africa has seen steady economic growth in the 17 years after apartheid, it has also experienced an abiding racial divide. That partition is expressed in enduring prejudice on both sides and persistent economic segregation. Remarkably, income inequality rose after apartheid ended: redistribution programs have mainly benefited a politically connected elite. Most whites and a few blacks live in the first world. But out of a total population of 50 million, 8.7 million South Africans, most of them black, earn $1.25 or less a day. Millions live in the same township shacks, travel in the same crowded minibuses (called taxis in South Africa) and, if they have jobs, work in the same white-owned homes and businesses they did under apartheid—all while coping with some of the world's worst violent crime and **its** biggest HIV/AIDS epidemic.

The **ANC** blames apartheid's legacy and, as party spokesman Keith Khoza describes it, "the reluctance of business to come to the party." But 17 years is almost a generation. The government's failure to transform South Africa from a country of black and white into a "rainbow nation," in Archbishop Desmond Tutu's phrase, means black poverty is still the key political issue. A second, related one, however, is the ANC's dramatic loss of moral authority. At 93, Mandela is still among the most admired people on earth. But his party has become synonymous with failure—and not coincidentally, arrogance, infighting and corruption. Tutu, a Nobel Peace Prize laureate and, at 80, still the nation's moral conscience, encapsulated South African political debate last year when he came out of retirement to give two speeches. In the first he asked whites to pay a wealth tax in recognition of their persistent advantage. In the second he called the **ANC** "worse than the apartheid government."

Africa is littered with liberation movements that, upon victory, forgot the people in whose name they fought. That era is coming to an end as the continent becomes more democratic and prosperous. The International Monetary Fund says seven of the world's 10 fastest growing economies are African, despite holdovers like Zimbabwe. Is South Africa, the continent's economic and political powerhouse, a gateway to this bright future or a window on **its** unhappy past?

Across the Tracks

The short drive to Maphikela house crosses South Africa's divide. I start in leafy all-white suburbs, home to cafés, bookstores and the Hobbit Boutique Hotel, modeled on the fantasies of Bloemfontein's most famous son, J.R.R. Tolkien. Then I cross a railway track, and I'm in the township: no trees, full of potholes and all black. Where my tourist map indicates Maphikela House should be is instead an abandoned warehouse, the windows smashed, graffiti by **its** broken door announcing thug mansion.

The local metropolitan authority says unemployment is 56%, and 59% of those with jobs earn $100 or less a month. Hanging out on a corner opposite Thug Mansion is Tumelo Lekhooe, 20, who was out of work for a year after school before finding a job as a street sweeper. "The **ANC** is full of corruption," he says. "There are no good roads here, no parks, good schools or jobs. The **ANC** use connections to win government tenders, then spend the money on themselves."

Lekhooe is describing a phenomenon in postapartheid South Africa: the growth of the tenderpreneur. The term describes those who get rich from government contracts or from dispensing them for kickbacks. Tenderpreneurs have turned government into a business. The national Special Investigating Unit, which targets corruption, reckons that up to a quarter of annual state spending—$3.8 billion—is wasted through overpayment and graft. The Auditor General says a third of all government departments have awarded contracts to companies owned by officials or their families; in December it found that three-quarters of all tenders in one **ANC**-ruled province, the Eastern Cape, rewarded officials in this way. Those being investigated for suspected corruption include two ministers, the country's top policeman and the head of the **ANC's** Youth League, Julius Malema. (All deny the charges.)

Tenderpreneurs are just one chapter in the saga of **ANC** scandals. There are the perks, like the $550 million the opposition Democratic Alliance (DA) claims ministers and their wives have spent on themselves since 2009. There is the state security minister whose wife was convicted of running an international drug ring, and the local government minister who used public money to fly first class to Switzerland to visit his girlfriend, also in prison for narcotics. There is the previous police chief, jailed for 15 years for taking bribes from the mob. And there is a corrupt $4.8 billion European arms deal that has haunted the **ANC** leadership since it was agreed to in 1999.

South African President Jacob Zuma declined to be interviewed for this article, but he can be candid about the **ANC's** poor record. "I have traveled to many parts of the country in recent months, monitoring the performance of government," he said at a business breakfast in Cape Town in November. "I come face to face with the triple scourge of poverty, inequality and unemployment." Zuma has taken action, however. He has sacked two ministers, suspended a raft of top officials, including the police chief, and set up an independent inquiry into the arms deal. He appropriated all the duties of a corrupt and inept **ANC** state government in Limpopo and dispatched his own officials to improve two more. He has already delivered one spectacular success to confound the skeptics: the 2010 soccer World Cup, the world's biggest sporting event, which went off with barely a hitch.

Zuma also has a vision of how to mend the government. In November he published a 19-year national plan that identified the nation's priorities as "corruption, divided communities, too few jobs, crumbling infrastructure, resource intensive economy, exclusive planning, poor education, high disease burden, public service [that is] uneven." By 2030, it pledges to have created 11 million jobs, built two more universities and several railway lines, privatized power, made private business illegal for bureaucrats, deployed up to 1.3 million community health workers and facilitated the installation of 5 million solar heaters. The plan is meant to inspire a party made complacent by a consistent two-thirds electoral majority. "We are too strong," Zuma told TIME in 2009, soon after becoming President. "You take things for granted."

'I don't know why we still vote for them. It's our grandparents. They say we are here only because of the ANC.'

—Tumelo Lekhooe, A 20-Year-Old Street Sweeper in Bloemfontein

It sounds impressive. Worryingly, that may be precisely the idea. "Eleven million jobs by 2030?" asks a Western diplomat in Pretoria. "Great. Excellent. From where?" After all, Zuma has made similar commitments before. In June 2009 he promised 4 million jobs by 2014—ambitious then, unreachable now. He also pledged 80% coverage of antiretroviral treatment by 2011 (unlikely, given UNAIDS's figure of 25% for 2010) and an annual 7% to 10% annual cut in serious crime (against an actual 2011–12 fall of 5.75%). Critics say his purges of officials are less about corruption or ineptness than political vendettas.

Zuma himself is tainted by charges of corruption. He was linked to the arms deal through one of his financial advisers, who was jailed in 2005 for trying to solicit bribes on his behalf. Since Zuma was elected, the DA says the state has spent $50 million on refurbishing his homes. Tellingly, Zuma goes after those who would check his behavior. In November the **ANC**-led Parliament passed a law known as the "secrecy bill," which penalizes whistle-blowers or journalists in possession of secret documents and allows no public-interest defense. He has installed unqualified allies in top positions across the justice system. Meanwhile, internal party politicking, particularly Zuma's rivalry with Malema, has overshadowed government, something that will only increase in the run-up to a party conference in Bloemfontein in December at which Zuma is running for re-election as **ANC** President. "For the next 12 months, nobody will be running the country," says Fiona Forde, author of *An Inconvenient Youth,* about Malema.

Mythmaking

With such an underwhelming record in office, **how** does the **ANC** win elections? By invoking **its** legend. The centenary celebrations, like so many other **ANC** events, hammer home **how** much black South Africans owe the party. Using such a "powerful legacy" only makes electoral sense, concedes DA leader Helen Zille. "When you've fought a liberation struggle and suffered so much and a party is perceived to have given you back your dignity, that party becomes who you are. **How** are you going to turn your back on that?" On his street corner, Lekhooe says, "I don't know why we still vote for them," then corrects himself. "It's our grandparents. They say we are here only because of the **ANC.**"

Zille based her last general election campaign on the message that the **ANC** betrayed Mandela's legacy. But **how** real is that inheritance? The central figure in **ANC** legend is Mandela, who reinvigorated the party in the 1940s and eventually led it to power in 1994. But as Mandela recounts in his autobiography, his transformation from rebel leader to global icon was, in part, a piece of imagemaking by the **ANC**. In 1980, after nearly four decades of fighting a regime that had not moved an inch, the party tried a new publicity strategy: personalizing **its** campaign with the slogan "Free Nelson Mandela." It was wildly effective. The slogan found its way onto T-shirts and posters around the world, even into a pop song. But as it tends to, such mythmaking also distorted reality, not least in regard to Mandela's failing marriage to Winnie. "She married a man who soon left her, that man became a myth, and then that myth returned home and proved to be just a man after all," Mandela wrote in *Long Walk to Freedom.*

His remarkable ability to emerge from prison with forgiveness for his persecutors was a genuine wonder that averted a looming race war—and, for many, validated his myth. But if his reputation was merely enhanced, his party's was whitewashed. At the time that the **ANC** was becoming an international cause célèbre, a 1984 internal party inquiry—the Stuart Commission—found that the **ANC's** training camps in Angola were "autocratic," "corrupt" and sadistic, run through a mix of torture, rape and execution. "There was a lot of corruption, a lot of thuggery," says Forde of the party's years in exile, pointing also to alliances with African leaders such as Zimbabwe's Robert Mugabe and Libya's Muammar Gaddafi. "You see that coming to the fore again."

In Bloemfontein, corruption and mythmaking have combined for the **ANC's** birthday party. When I eventually find Maphikela House—a grand red-brick place with two stories and a porch—the old lady who lives there directs me instead to a second building in another rundown neighborhood closer to town. In 1992, Mandela celebrated the **ANC's** 80th anniversary at Maphikela House. But in 2002, National Museum historian Hannes Haasbroek discovered that the house was built in 1926, 14 years after the **ANC** was formed, and the party's true birthplace was a former Wesleyan church hall a few miles away, since converted into an auto-body-repair shop. Unperturbed by this uprooting and relocating of **its** nativity fable, the **ANC** city authority promptly bought the bare-brick, wood-frame, tin-roof building and began fixing it up—at a total taxpayer cost of $4 million. Bloemfontein DA leader Roy Jankielsohn accuses the party of an "abuse of state resources." **ANC** spokesman Khoza denies corruption and insists the party is paying the bulk of the centenary costs. But he sees nothing wrong with using state money to preserve the party's history. "The **ANC** should be treated as part of our collective heritage as a nation," he says.

With such an underwhelming record in office, how does the ANC win elections? By invoking its legend.

As the Arab Spring showed, ruling parties that fail to distinguish their interests from those of the nation may also not spot their approaching fall. And the signs of the **ANC's** decline are there. The party is fragmented. **Its** support peaked at 69% at elections in 2004 and fell to 61% at local elections in 2011. And in December it lost three previously safe seats in local by-elections. Meanwhile, the DA is growing. **Its** support rose from 1.7% in a general election in 1996 to 16.7% in 2009, when it also took Western Cape province, and to 23.8% in 2011. Zille says her ambition is to take two more provinces in the next general election in 2014 and the government in 2019. Like any other politician, she wants power. But she insists that removing the **ANC** is essential if South Africa is to finally enjoy genuine democracy. "Loyalty is a great trait, but if you are to hold political leaders to account, you can't be loyal to a political party," she says.

In a previous life, Zille was an antiapartheid journalist. Her ultimate goal, she says, is to make good on Tutu's vision of a Technicolor nation. But in South Africa's black-and-white present, Zille is only too aware that she has a "melanin deficit." Hence moves by the DA to recruit to **its** leadership a black-struggle legend of **its** own: Mamphela Ramphele, a former World Bank managing director and long-standing **ANC** critic. If the name is unfamiliar, that's because Ramphele never married her partner: Steve Biko.

Critical Thinking

1. What are the key political issues in South Africa?
2. What are the sources of corruption charges against the ANC?
3. What has been the ANC's response to those charges?
4. What represents a potential challenge to ANC dominance?

Article

Prepared by: Robert J. Griffiths, *University of North Carolina at Greensboro*

Shifting Fortunes: Brazil and Mexico in a Transformed Region

"Just as Mexico has shown signs of an upswing, Brazil seems to be facing mounting difficulties."

MICHAEL SHIFTER AND CAMERON COMBS

Learning Outcomes

After reading this article, you will be able to:

- Describe how the fortunes of Brazil and Mexico have changed recently.
- Contrast the strengths and weaknesses of Brazil's and Mexico's economic and political systems.

Just three years ago, Brazil, the country that long marketed itself as the home of samba and soccer, was all the rage in global affairs. Adorning its cover with Rio de Janeiro's Christ statue shooting up like a rocket, the Economist proclaimed in November 2009 that Brazil was "taking off." The first among the BRICS (Brazil, Russia, India, China, and South Africa), the preeminent power bloc of developing nations, Brazil was, it seemed, realizing its enormous potential. It was enjoying strong economic growth. It was aggressively reducing levels of poverty—and even inequality—while fostering a vibrant democracy. If the twenty-first century was really to be the Century of the Americas, Brazil was poised to lead the way. Its star power had few peers.

While Brazil basked in effusive praise, Mexico, the other Latin American titan, was portrayed in markedly negative, sometimes even macabre, terms. The media described unremitting, drug-fueled violence that, in the most extreme depictions, threatened the very integrity of the Mexican government. Indeed, in a US government report, Mexico was viewed as possibly becoming a "failed state." Spreading criminality was compounded by a severe recession in 2009. The economy contracted by over 6 percent, largely the result of a financial crisis originating in the country to which Mexico was inextricably tied: the United States.

In 2013, the narratives of the two countries that account for over half of Latin America's population and almost two-thirds of its economic output have nearly been inverted. In the past two years, Mexico's economic growth has exceeded Brazil's; its violence, though still severe, declined markedly in 2012; and the onset of a new administration in Mexico City committed to pursuing far-reaching reforms has injected a measure of optimism regarding the country's outlook.

In sharp contrast to Mexico's moderate growth of roughly 4 percent, Brazil's economy expanded by just 1 percent in 2012. Among other constraints, vulnerability resulting from Brazil's heavy dependence on commodity sales—chiefly to an economically slowing China—became increasingly evident. In addition, international media accounts have focused on escalating violence in São Paulo and police raids into the favelas of Rio de Janeiro. And, as the World Bank has reported, it is far more difficult to do business in Brazil: Investors have become increasingly frustrated with a cumbersome public sector.

The ostensibly shifting fortunes of both countries caution against hyperbole and argue for nuance. The dominant characterizations of three years ago were overdrawn, and so are many today. Brazil and Mexico represent distinctive approaches to governance and development, and their positions in the Western Hemisphere and the world are appreciably different. Until now, their separate paths have only rarely intersected.

Brazilians and Mexicans are keenly conscious of each other's performance, making comparisons inevitable. Still, it would be a stretch to describe the relationship as a rivalry in the strictest sense. Brazil and Mexico seldom clash over major economic questions (making a recent dispute over auto sales especially stand out), and their policies are hardly antagonistic. Rather, the two countries often jockey for position, power, and influence in a Latin America that in recent decades has been utterly transformed.

By most measures, both nations have advanced in remarkable ways. But they also face similar, long-term challenges—not unlike those confronting the United States—including high inequality and deficient infrastructure and education systems.

The Brasília Consensus

Latin America has long been a veritable laboratory of political experimentation, yet over the past decade a formula for success embodied by the Brazilian experience has taken hold and exerted broad appeal. The ingredients consist of a commitment to economic growth through fiscal discipline, a significant concern for poverty reduction, and a deepening of democracy. Progress in each sphere can be attributed in part to a succession of effective political leaders, each with a remarkable personal story: Fernando Henrique Cardoso (1995–2002), Luiz Inácio "Lula" da Silva (2003–2010) and, currently, Dilma Rousseff.

All have, under different circumstances, sought to balance and integrate these three ingredients. Cardoso's chief accomplishments were taming Brazil's chronic inflation and initiating a more vigorous social agenda. Under Lula, and especially during his second term, Brazil "took off" in impressive fashion. The combination of strong growth and the expansion of a conditional cash transfer program, *Bolsa Família,* helped lift some 20 million Brazilians out of poverty during Lula's eight years in office. Rousseff has adhered to the broad outlines of her predecessors' approaches, though she has had to confront difficult challenges—both external and domestic—that have led to slower economic growth.

Few, if any, countries can match such competence and continuity in political leadership. Solid macroeconomic management, combined with a profound concern for the social agenda and a penchant for political negotiation, has produced extraordinary results in policy making. Brazil's model was particularly tested by the 2009 financial crisis, which, defying many expert predictions, it weathered remarkably well. Its economy, today the world's seventh largest, grew by 7.5 percent in 2010.

Brazil has also been at the forefront of the development of biofuels (ethanol in particular). And with its new oil finds and large reserves of shale gas, the country appears poised to become a major global energy power. The Brazilian government plays an active, interventionist role in the economy that, coupled with a strong private sector, has resulted in a hybrid, public-private approach toward economic development. This approach is reflected in Brazil's biggest and best-known companies, such as the mining juggernaut Vale, the aerospace conglomerate Embraer, and, of course, the oil giant Petrobras.

Brazil's record on its domestic agenda over the past decade has enabled it to play a more influential, high-profile role in global and regional affairs—fulfilling its long-held feelings of *grandeza* (greatness). The country will surely be in the spotlight in coming years as it hosts the 2014 World Cup and 2016 Summer Olympics. At the global level, Brazil has been notably assertive in forums such as the Group of 20 (Mexico and Argentina are the other Latin American members) and the World Trade Organization.

Its BRICS membership and ambition to become a permanent member of the United Nations Security Council (Brazil has been a non-permanent member 10 times since 1946) have opened doors for its presidents and top officials across the globe. Under Lula, buoyed by progress on the domestic front, Brazil pursued a more aggressive foreign policy, seeking to perform a mediating role in the Middle East while developing a joint proposal with Turkey (much to Washington's displeasure) for dealing with Iran's nuclear program. Showcasing Brazil's commendable HIV/AIDS efforts, Lula also pursued more robust south-south diplomacy, including deeper cooperation with Africa.

Brazil has sought to enhance its global position with greater engagement in regional affairs. Regarding itself much more as a "South American" than a "Latin American" nation, Brazil has principally concentrated on its immediate geographic sphere of influence, while showing limited interest in Central and North America, which are viewed as the United States' strategic prerogative. Indeed, Brazil's distance and independence from Washington have been key to its aspiration to be taken more seriously as a global actor.

In 1991, Brazil jointly spearheaded the effort to create Mercosul (whose original members also included Argentina, Uruguay, and Paraguay), which aimed to eventually become a common market. This organization has since become less credible on trade questions, diverging from its original purpose and acquiring a more political cast. For many, this perception crystallized when Venezuela became a Mercosul member through the back door—the result of a hasty suspension of Paraguay (whose senate had been blocking Venezuela's entry) following President Fernando Lugo's (equally hasty) impeachment in June 2012.

Also on the regional front, building on what Cardoso began years before, Brazil (with Venezuela's backing) in 2008 launched the Union of South American Nations (UNASUL). This organization assumes an explicitly political function; it has, for example, established an affiliated South American Defense Council. In 2011, in a move that partly reflected the evolving Brazil-Mexico relationship, the Community of Latin American and Caribbean States (CELAC) got off the ground, encompassing all of the hemisphere's governments—with the exception of Canada and the United States.

Although Brazil has had little choice but to devote increased attention to hemispheric concerns in recent years, it has accorded even greater precedence to its global priorities.

Mexico's Trajectory

Geography may not be destiny, but Mexico's location just south of the United States has—for better or worse—significantly shaped its economic, security, and demographic situation. Roughly 80 percent of Mexico's exports, chiefly manufactures, go to the United States—compared with less than 20 percent of Brazil's. Two decades ago, the United States, Mexico, and Canada adopted the North American Free Trade Agreement (NAFTA), which has substantially boosted trade and investment among the three countries. Today Mexico is the second-largest trading partner of the United States, slightly ahead of China. Some experts predict that in six to eight years, Mexico could overtake Canada as the United States' principal trading partner, as connections across the Rio Grande continue to deepen on all fronts.

Under the administration of President Felipe Calderón, which ended in December 2012, the main story of the past six years has been Mexico's drug-fueled violence. It has taken some 60,000 Mexican lives. It has also hurt the country's economy (investment and tourism in particular) and, of course, its international image. Major US publications have frequently invoked sensationalist phrases to describe the country: "deepening drug-war mayhem," "reign of terror," "criminal anarchy." When Calderón took office in 2006, he called on the military to play a central role in carrying out the drug war, a move questioned by some Mexican and international observers.

As with trade, the links with the United States in the drug war are profound—but in this case, far less benign. As the world's largest consumer of cocaine and the primary provider of the smuggled arms used in drug-related killings, the United States bears an enormous responsibility for the criminal violence wracking Mexico. The Mérida Initiative, a program of cooperation between Mexico and the United States to combat drug-fueled violence, has been in place since 2008. While security collaboration has never been higher, the level of US support falls short of the magnitude of the challenge, and implementation of the initiative has been plagued by delays and inefficiencies. At the same time, the United States has been unable or unwilling to tackle contentious and difficult domestic reforms related to drug policy and gun control that could help allay the situation.

A major question is the possibility of a more pronounced bifurcation in the hemisphere.

In recent years, Mexico's security crisis and even stronger ties with its northern neighbor have restricted its ability to pursue a more multifaceted foreign policy, as it once did during the Central American civil conflicts of the 1980s through the Contadora Group, a regional initiative. Instead, it has focused on deepening cooperation on a wide-ranging agenda with the United States, and on trade promotion worldwide. Mexico today has free trade agreements with some 40 countries, compared with the United States' 18.

Before 2010, Mexico's trade boom had been accompanied by lackluster economic growth, which encouraged significant out-migration to the north. This was largely the result of failure to pursue long-needed energy, fiscal, and education reforms, together with economic problems in the United States. For many years, the effect of China's rising role in the region was also considerably less helpful than it was in the case of Brazil. China, when its labor costs were lower, dealt a blow to Mexico's manufacturing sector, causing scores of factories to close and many jobs to be lost. Hit hard by the financial crisis and understandably wearied by the frustrating drug war, Mexico dropped to a low point in 2009 as pessimism intensified. At the same time, hype about Brazil was nearing its zenith.

Turning the Tables?

In the last three years of the Calderón administration, the outlook in Mexico began to brighten. Most notably, the economy began climbing out of its deep hole, with growth approaching 4 percent in 2011 and 2012. The US recovery, however anemic, gave Mexico a needed boost. With labor costs increasing in China, foreign investment in Mexico began to increase, and exports became more competitive.

A new narrative has emphasized an expanding middle class (by some estimates, reaching nearly 50 percent of the population); a reduction in poverty levels (the conditional cash transfer program, though often associated with Brazil, actually began in Mexico in the 1990s); a public mood increasingly ready for real reforms; and, according to an April 2012 study produced by the Pew Research Center, net zero migration to the United States.

Further, although the overall security situation may not be on a sustained path of improvement, levels of violence declined in 2012. Some success stories have even begun to emerge: Ciudad Juárez, long a site of unprecedented levels of violence, recently witnessed a sharp drop in homicides.

The election of Enrique Peña Nieto of the Institutional Revolutionary Party (PRI) in July 2012 helped crystallize the perceptions of positive change. Although the PRI had dominated Mexico's political system for more than seven decades—and its highly authoritarian old guard has hardly disappeared—many argue that Mexican society has become far more democratic since the 1990s. There is little prospect of recreating the old PRI model in the context of an increasingly autonomous and assertive Congress, judiciary, civil society, and media.

Since the beginning of the new administration and announcement of the cabinet on December 1, 2012, there have been clear signs that Peña Nieto is moving quickly to undertake a broad reform agenda. Observers are relatively sanguine about the prospects for reform that would open Mexico's energy sector, with its significant endowments of oil and gas, to some form of private sector participation.

Even during the lame duck session of Congress, labor reform designed to create a more flexible and formal workforce was adopted with ample support. And, within the framework of a new political pact among the country's three main parties, Peña Nieto has left little doubt that he plans to introduce badly needed education reforms, which would likely mean a fierce battle with the country's largest and most powerful teachers' union.

Just as Mexico has shown signs of an upswing, Brazil seems to be facing mounting difficulties. A slump in key European markets and the economic slowdown in China, together with indications that its huge domestic market has become overly leveraged, requires significant adjustments in Brazil's economic policy. Some argue, moreover, that Brazil has begun to reach limits on rapid growth unless it pushes through pending reforms to boost productivity across all sectors.

For example, a recent *Foreign Affairs* article entitled "Bearish on Brazil," by Morgan Stanley's Ruchir Sharma, criticized the country for being overly dependent on commodity exports and not investing enough in infrastructure or manufacturing. The World Economic Forum's 2012–2013 Global Competitiveness Report ranked Brazil 107th worldwide in quality of overall infrastructure—far behind Mexico at 65th. Unlike Brazil, Mexico has recently been lauded for diversifying its exports over the past two decades: In the 1980s, 10 percent of Mexico's total exports were manufactures; now that figure stands at over 75 percent.

Tracking the supposed competition to see which one is up and which is down is shortsighted.

The automobile sector starkly illustrates the relative weight each country gives to exports versus serving its internal market. In 2011, the year for which the most updated data are available, Mexico produced 2.6 million vehicles and exported 2.1 million of them. Brazil, meanwhile, produced 3.4 million vehicles, but exported just 0.54 million of them.

Also, though investment is high in both countries, the so-called "Brazil cost" (the additional expense of goods due to insufficient infrastructure, high taxes and interest rates, and an excessively onerous bureaucracy) renders doing business more difficult. According to the World Bank, it takes an average of 119 days to start a new business in Brazil—the fifth-longest wait in the world. Mexico, in contrast, is one of the best countries in the region for conducting business. Although none of these problems is new to Brazil, they were largely eclipsed by more positive features highlighted during its widely touted "takeoff" phase.

Brazil's economic setbacks have begun to constrain the country's foreign policy projection. After a period of frenetic worldwide diplomacy at the end of the Lula period, Rousseff has assumed a more subdued global and regional profile. At the same time, some of Brazil's longstanding problems, such as corruption, criminal violence, and strains on the justice system, are bound to draw even more media scrutiny in the run-up to the World Cup.

After the United States, Brazil is the world's second largest consumer of cocaine, and although there have been improvements and success stories in reducing urban violence, its homicide rate is higher than Mexico's (23 versus 18 per 100,000 people, according to the United Nations). Brazil's stepped-up antidrug policies in relation to cocaproducing neighbors like Bolivia and Peru reveal how worried national authorities are about this problem.

Nevertheless, though Mexico's star has recently brightened—while Brazil's has faded a bit—it is unwise to embrace any sweeping, zero-sum interpretations about the region's two most important countries. Both nations are protean, susceptible to natural economic cycles, shifting global tendencies, and national vicissitudes. Moreover, though continued progress is likely in terms of both countries' national development and global role, their enduring challenges are significant. They are also strikingly similar.

Two Peas in a Pod

The litany of problems facing Brazil and Mexico is by now familiar. While crime and security issues have different manifestations in each country, they remain serious challenges that demand more effective and credible police forces and justice systems. Deteriorating infrastructure remains an obstacle to robust development, though the Rousseff administration has recently undertaken a notable initiative with public and private sector support to address this challenge, especially in advance of the World Cup and Olympics.

Low productivity stems in part from the poor quality of education; although access to schooling in both countries has significantly increased, the amount that students are actually learning remains dismal by global standards. The Program for International Student Assessment, a project of the Organization for Economic Cooperation and Development, in 2009 ranked Brazil 52nd out of 64 countries for reading and 56th for math; Mexico fared only slightly better, ranking 47th for reading and 49th for math.

In terms of fiscal issues, both governments have displayed admirable discipline, yet taxation in Brazil is too high and regressive. Mexico, in contrast, taxes too little and makes up for it by drawing on oil profits, undercutting the vitality of its energy sector.

The problems of inequality and corruption deserve special mention. Although recent studies by the economists Nora Lustig and Luis López Calva show that there have been modest reductions in inequality in both Brazil and Mexico, both countries remain among the worst performers in the Americas.

In 2009, for example, the top 20 percent of Brazilian earners accounted for 59 percent of the nation's income, while the bottom 20 percent's share was merely 3 percent. Mexico is quite similar: That year, the top 20 percent received 54 percent of earnings, compared with the bottom quintile's meager 4.7 percent. The still enormous gaps between rich and poor have important political and economic implications. In coming years, progress on fiscal and education reforms will be critical to achieving a more equitable distribution of income.

There are few rigorous and reliable measures of corruption, though governments in both countries (and throughout much of Latin America) have identified it as a priority. According to the 2012 Corruption Perceptions Index produced by the monitoring group Transparency International, Brazil fares better than Mexico. It placed 9th among the 26 Latin American and Caribbean countries, while Mexico came out 16th. Not surprisingly, the issue has drawn considerable media attention in both countries.

Since Rousseff assumed office, she has wasted no time demonstrating her intolerance for corruption, and has fired seven of her ministers. The so-called mensalão scandal, which involved millions of dollars in bribes to members of Congress during the Lula administration, has resulted in the most significant trial in the country's modern history, even sending the former president's chief of staff to prison. A new "clean slate" law, forbidding individuals with criminal records from running for office in Brazil, barred some 1,200 candidates nationwide in 2012.

In Mexico, meanwhile, *The New York Times* has done much to expose the misbehavior of the giant retailer Wal-Mart, which reportedly offered bribes on a regular basis to Mexican officials for favors such as zoning approvals. The recently installed Peña Nieto administration has already set up a new anticorruption commission.

In sum, while it is tempting to extrapolate from short-term swings in each country, it is more productive to examine longer-term trends. Brazil and Mexico exhibit distinctive policy approaches, largely attributable to their geographical positions and divergent political legacies. On balance, the tendencies in each are heartening and point to more significant influence in global affairs, sustained growth, social progress, and political openness. Dramatic retrogressions in each country seem improbable. Nonetheless, the pending challenges remain serious and, unless effectively tackled, will impede continued progress for both nations and the region as a whole.

Looking Ahead

Forecasts predict Mexico and Brazil to be among the world's top ten economies by 2020; indeed, some projections rank them within the top five by mid-century. Both countries' influence in regional and global affairs is bound to grow in coming decades. In a hemisphere in considerable flux, Brazil and Mexico's decisions about their economic policies and governance models will be critical in shaping the future direction of the Americas.

In the past two years, Mexico's economic growth has exceeded Brazil's.

For Mexico, the strategic alignment with the United States is likely to endure. No matter what strains and tensions emerge over sensitive bilateral questions that invariably arise in a close relationship, the increasingly profound connections between the two countries militate against any significant rupture. Migratory flows over the 2,000-mile border are bound to accelerate, not diminish, though one hopes they will occur under a more sensible and realistic legal framework. Current and subsequent Mexican administrations may well seek to diversify their relationships in the hemisphere and throughout the world, but the bilateral agenda will require continued attention and effort.

To be sure, such close ties carry some risks for Mexico. The country's dependence on the United States for such a large percentage of its exports, remittances, and tourist dollars is of some concern. The costs to Mexico of the 2008–09 financial crisis underscore the hazards of close reliance on a single partner. At the same time, such deep linkages confer clear advantages. Most obviously, the US anchor gives Mexico proximity to the world's largest economy and provides a huge market for its goods and labor. Mexico's solid industrial sector is the result in part of competing with countries such as China for market share in the United States.

If there is serious immigration reform in the United States—and reform of the energy sector in Mexico—the prospects for an even stronger bilateral relationship will increase. These were the most sensitive concerns when NAFTA was negotiated and approved two decades ago. If there is progress on both fronts, the opportunities for deepening integration will multiply.

Also critical will be whether a major new trade initiative, the Trans-Pacific Partnership (TPP), actually takes hold. In addition to Australia, New Zealand, a handful of Asian countries, and Mexico, the TPP prospectively includes the United States, Canada, Peru, and Chile. If such a scheme were to carry weight and prosper, it would have profound implications for cementing economic ties between the more open Latin American and Asian economies and ensuring that the Pacific remains the world's most dynamic market.

It is unclear how Brazil and the more closed Mercosul countries would fit into such a scenario. While the TPP and other initiatives to more formally link Latin American countries with Asia hold enormous commercial promise, they risk further accentuating already discernible strains in hemispheric economic relations. A major question moving forward is the possibility of a more pronounced bifurcation in the hemisphere— with discrete US- and Brazil-led blocs—and the growing challenge of achieving broader hemispheric cooperation on a common agenda.

Brazil does, however, enjoy considerable advantages as it carries out its global and regional strategies. The country is economically diverse (its trade, for instance, is fairly evenly distributed among China, the United States, Europe, and Latin America); its resource endowment is formidable; and it has substantial political initiative and ample room for maneuver.

With almost half of South America's population, Brazil has a massive internal market fostered by extending new lines of credit, which has resulted in an expanding middle class. While many bemoan Brazil's protectionist bent, its robust consumption may allow policy makers to expand the economy—albeit perhaps not as efficiently—with limited exposure to foreign competitors. And Brazil's independence from the United States, as it has historically, will likely enable it to more effectively pursue multiple options on the global stage.

While Brazil and Mexico have forged ahead independently of one another, it would be a mistake to rule out the possibility of greater economic and political cooperation between the two in coming years. Certainly, Brazil's decision in 2012 to impose high tariffs on Mexican automobiles did little to inspire confidence among business leaders. But with the prospect of energy sector reform in Mexico— and given that Peña Nieto has cited Petrobras as a possible model to follow—serious bilateral cooperation on that issue could be in store.

In addition, with Brazil's disappointing growth in 2012, and an increasingly problematic commercial relationship with its neighbor Argentina, the Rousseff government may find Mexico's expanding market attractive.

Strategy and Oscillations

Over the past dozen years, Latin America has undergone dramatic changes. The region has become stronger economically, more independent politically, and more assertive in global affairs. Deepening fiscal problems and debilitating political polarization within the United States have only reinforced this trend by limiting Washington's sway. The result has been a region increasingly emboldened, yet also fragmented and moving in a number of directions at once. In this context, the relative success of Mexico and Brazil likely will influence how other countries choose to navigate an unpredictable global marketplace and the demands of an emergent middle class.

In a hemisphere in such flux, it is scarcely surprising that the apparently changing fortunes of Brazil and Mexico have given rise to commentaries about which will occupy the number one spot. In February 2012, Mexico's former foreign minister Jorge Castañeda claimed in an op-ed in El País, entitled "The Mexico-Brazil Rivalry," that once Mexico's drug war wound down—and Brazil's poor infrastructure and communications were exposed during the World Cup—the Brazilian government's marketing of a twenty-first century miracle would be effectively debunked.

In August 2012, *Forbes* asserted, "Sorry Brazil, Mexico Is Better." The title of a *New York Times* piece on the G-20 meeting held in Los Cabos, Mexico, in June 2012, was telling: "World Leaders Meet in a Mexico Now Giving Brazil a Run for Its Money." The Economist and Financial Times blogs also have noted that Mexico seems to be pulling ahead of Brazil, with the latter instructing readers, "Forget the BRIC countries or even just Brazil . . . it's all about Mexico now."

The so-called "Latin rivalry" provides grist for the media mill and makes for a compelling narrative. But tracking the supposed competition to see which one of the region's twin powers is up and which is down serves as little more than a distraction and is shortsighted. For the United States, the fundamental question is how to build a more productive, long-term relationship with both countries. These relationships demand commitments from Washington as serious and sustained as with any top-tier nation in the world.

Regardless of the choices they make, Brazil's and Mexico's underlying trajectories should be matched with a correspondingly farsighted mindset among senior US policy makers—a mindset that remains focused on strategic considerations, no matter the eye-catching oscillations of the moment.

Critical Thinking

1. How have the fortunes of Brazil and Mexico changed recently?
2. What are the strengths and weaknesses of Brazil's and Mexico's economic and political systems?

Create Central

www.mhhe.com/createcentral

Internet References

Center for Research on Inequality, Human Security, and Ethnicity
www.crise.ox.ac.uk

LatinAmericanNetworkInformationCenter—LANIC
www.lanic.utexas.edu

ReliefWeb
www.reliefweb.int/w/rwb.nsf

MICHAEL SHIFTER, *a* Current History *contributing editor, is president of the Inter-American Dialogue and an adjunct professor of Latin American studies at Georgetown University's School of Foreign Service. Cameron Combs is a program assistant at the Inter-American Dialogue.*

Article

Human Rights Last

China's diplomats have the ear of the world's bad guys. So what are they telling them?

Gary J. Bass

On Feb. 21, 2010, the Chinese Embassy in Harare threw a birthday party for Robert Mugabe, Zimbabwe's heavy-handed and increasingly erratic octogenarian despot, complete with cake, almost 100 guests, and a "Happy 86th birthday" sign. Xin Shunkang, China's dapper ambassador, led the embassy staff in singing the Zimbabwean national anthem in the Shona language. The embassy invited local students to sing Chinese folk songs. "The Chinese people sing the Zimbabwean national anthem in Shona; Zimbabwean people sing Chinese songs in Chinese," recalled Xin when we met in Harare some months later. "It's harmonious." It was the first time Mugabe had visited a foreign embassy since Zimbabwe became independent in 1980. "It's not easy to get a president to come to your embassy," said Xin with a bit of pride. "Not every ambassador can do this, but I could do it."

In Zimbabwe and many other countries far from Beijing, China's hand is increasingly conspicuous these days, and its choice of friends, like the thuggish Mugabe, is increasingly under scrutiny. It used to be that the Western world lectured China most extensively about its poor human rights record at home, for detaining dissenters and silencing free speech. But as China's power and influence grow, the Chinese government now finds itself weathering criticism for its support of cruel regimes around the world—from accusations, as *New York Times* columnist Nicholas Kristof and others have put it, that "Beijing is financing, diplomatically protecting and supplying the arms for the first genocide of the 21st century" in Darfur, to the recent warning by Win Tin, co-founder of Aung San Suu Kyi's National League for Democracy, that if Chinese leaders "praise the [Burmese] regime" without helping the public, then "China will fail to win the hearts of the people." Chinese officials are newly sensitive to such reproaches, if not exactly responsive. As one Foreign Ministry official told me with surprise in the run-up to the 2008 Beijing Olympics, "For the first time, China's foreign position on human rights outweighs the world's concern for China's domestic human rights."

Certainly, as Chinese trade and commerce have exploded over the last decade, they have been an economic boon to many developing countries, correspondingly boosting China's clout in countries as remote from Beijing as Angola, Ethiopia, and Uzbekistan. But in many of those places, China has purchased its clout at the cost of maintaining warm ties with murderous governments, from Burma to North Korea to, perhaps most prominently, Sudan—where two U.S. presidents, George W. Bush and Barack Obama, have accused Omar Hassan al-Bashir's regime of genocide.

Yet it is much less obvious how the Chinese government thinks about these awkward relationships. How does a generation of Chinese who opened up their own country to the world square China's ongoing transformations with such ties to some of the most closed societies on Earth? How does a country haunted by awful memories of the Great Leap Forward and the Cultural Revolution overlook suffering in other countries? Is the Chinese government defending its long-standing principle that national sovereignty should reign supreme, seeking natural resources to fuel its red-hot economic growth, or offering a new model of international development and diplomacy? Is there any way the United States can more effectively engage with China on these issues? Above all, what do China's complex attitudes toward its rogue friends say about the kind of great power China will become?

How does a country haunted by awful memories of the Great Leap Forward and the Cultural Revolution overlook suffering in other countries?

It is almost impossible to report on what China's top rulers think and say behind secure doors in the Zhongnanhai leadership complex. But over the course of multiple trips to Beijing in the last several years, I was able to interview about a dozen Chinese Foreign Ministry officials from various departments, some repeatedly, about China's dealings with outlaw governments. They seemed well briefed that I write about human rights—ordinarily a topic much avoided in Beijing.

Having documented what the historic rise of liberal great powers like Britain and America meant for human rights, I wanted to know how Chinese officials see their own impact.

When asked about human rights, Chinese officials invariably start with a principled defense of national sovereignty. Dating back to the 1949 revolution, this tenet recalls China's own searing experience of colonial oppression by the West and Japan. But defending sovereignty may be Chinese diplomats' only guiding ideology today. Since Deng Xiaoping, China has given up on sponsoring Maoist revolutions, as it did in Africa during the 1960s and 1970s. Chinese officialdom remains deeply wary of most of the tools that Western governments have used to promote human rights, not least because the Chinese state has been on the receiving end of many of them.

Chinese authorities recoil at the prospect of humanitarian military intervention, as the West undertook in Kosovo in 1999. Criticizing the use of force in general, a Chinese official drew a stark contrast toward the end of 2008: "This year we had two big events. China had the Olympic Games; Russia attacked Georgia." Another Foreign Ministry official told me, "Sometimes we think what's caused by intervention could be even more thorny than the reality before, like what [the Americans] have in Afghanistan and Iraq. Out of some emotion, [the Americans] initiated those two wars. But it becomes very difficult to get out." When I raised Rwanda as an example of a terrifyingly fast genocide that the outside world failed to stop, one Chinese official rather lamely suggested that the African Union should have been allowed to mediate. Another, asked about Rwanda, uneasily hinted at personal dissatisfaction with the official line, but wouldn't say anything more.

Chinese officials are equally appalled by economic sanctions, which were imposed on their own country after the June 1989 Tiananmen Square crackdown. "In Myanmar, you give more sanctions, but the leaders have a very happy life," argued a Foreign Ministry official. "Why do you just make people suffer, but you cannot change the regime?" Even the tactic of naming and shaming human rights violators is too much for the Chinese state—itself frequently singled out for its own human rights abuses. "It is maddening to be rebuked by foreign countries in a high-profile way," a Chinese Foreign Ministry official told me. Instead, this official boasted, "We usually convince the other parties in a most subtle manner."

Whatever their private misgivings, Chinese officials can be determinedly unwilling to publicly criticize even their most outrageous partners. When, in an unsubtle manner, I pointed out that North Korea had starved a million of its own people to death, as well as sunk the South Korean corvette *Cheonan* and shelled South Korean civilians on Yeonpyeong Island in recent days, a Chinese diplomat would go no further than saying, "We encourage them to have better living standards for their people." According to this official, when Kim Jong Il visited China recently, his hosts were impressed with his desire to develop the North Korean economy. This official, while questioning whether North Korea had really sunk the *Cheonan,* said, "Generally speaking, North Korea is a normal state. It's a nation that has its own right to choose how to govern."

Reluctant to publicly condemn even the baddest of bad actors, Chinese officials champion a diplomacy based on trade and engagement, rather than on military, political, or economic leverage. As one Chinese diplomat told me in Beijing in October 2008, the North Koreans "want to talk to the U.S. The U.S. won't talk to them. Then they develop nuclear weapons; then the U.S. talks to them." The official added jokingly, "But still the U.S. is reluctant to talk to Myanmar officials, perhaps because they did not develop nuclear weapons."

With the outbreak of violence in Darfur in 2003, even some of the most sophisticated Chinese officials were startled to find themselves facing blistering Western criticism over their support for Bashir's government. In 2007, a puzzled Chinese Foreign Ministry official asked me whether Bush had latched onto Darfur as a potential "legacy issue," like the North Korean nuclear negotiations, on which China and the United States cooperated closely and effectively. The official said, "For many Chinese, it's a surprise. Two years ago, people, even academics, would say, 'What is Darfur? Where is Darfur?' " A Foreign Ministry official told me, "One or two years ago, we didn't realize that Darfur was so important."

Nobody has borne the brunt of foreign outrage over China's Sudan policy more than Liu Guijin, China's first-ever special representative for Darfur. Liu is the model of an old Africa hand: an influential veteran diplomat who served in Kenya and Ethiopia, as ambassador to South Africa, and as director of the Africa department in the Foreign Ministry. He is a sprightly man with owlish glasses, a ready smile, and a gracious manner. He's steeped in Western literature, recommending to me *Saviors and Survivors,* a book by Columbia University professor Mahmood Mamdani that shows, Liu said, how the "Darfur issue has been highly politicized." When he gets going, he has the air of a man who's not used to being interrupted.

Liu, who met with me at the gargantuan stone-and-glass Foreign Ministry building in Beijing in August 2009 and again in December 2010, was unembarrassed about China's economic stake in Sudan. It is, he said, "a matter of fact that China does have a great interest there." He defended the state-owned China National Petroleum Corp.'s $7 billion investments in Sudan's oil sector over protests from human rights campaigners: "I say that to get oil that way is not so rare. Lots of multinational corporations do that too. And not everywhere the multinational corporations go have that good a human rights record. So to have economic dealings in countries like Sudan, that the Western countries do not love, that is something normal." Even Liu, a sophisticated character, doesn't register that this might not be the most winning banner for Chinese foreign policy: as principled as a multinational corporation.

During the worst of the slaughter in Darfur, in 2003 and 2004, China was the Sudanese government's most powerful supporter. It used its U.N. Security Council power to block or water down tough measures against Sudan, like the imposition of sanctions or peacekeeping troops. Western accusations of genocide caused a particular headache because China is a party to the Genocide Convention, which obliges states to prevent and punish killings and persecutions "committed with intent to destroy, in whole or in part, a national, ethnical, racial or religious group." To dodge that obligation, Chinese diplomats deny that Darfur meets the definition. One Chinese official did tell me, "If there is a widely agreed opinion that there is a genocide, I think that the international community has the obligation to prevent or to help end it." But the official then downplayed claims from the likes of Bush and activist Mia Farrow ("the star lady") that Darfur counts as genocide.

During the worst of the slaughter in Darfur, China was the Sudanese government's most powerful supporter.

A Foreign Ministry staffer remembered a colleague returning from a trip to Darfur and giving a PowerPoint presentation about the refugee camps. While admitting that Sudan might have stage-managed the trip, this official said, "We didn't see anyone dying. It's serious, but how serious? We have some doubts." Although credible human rights groups estimate that several hundred thousand people have died in Darfur, Chinese officials and elites are skeptical. "I don't know how many people died," a Chinese Foreign Ministry official told me. Another asked: "There are so many crises that need attention. Why this one? We think it's because of the strategic interest of Western countries."

But as the death toll mounted and the U.S. government repeatedly accused Sudan of genocide, Chinese policy quietly began to shift. Liu, who has met with Darfur activists, told me he was impressed with their effectiveness: "They are so successful, the Save Darfur Coalition and Enough." In a September 2005 speech that got Beijing's attention, Robert Zoellick, then the U.S. deputy secretary of state, urged China to become a "responsible stakeholder" in the world system and specifically rebuked China over its support for Sudan. In February 2007, Hu Jintao became the first Chinese president to visit Khartoum, offering loans, partnership accords, and financing for a new presidential palace. But in a break with past practice, China also privately pressured Bashir to accept new peacekeepers, according to Chinese officials. In public, Hu called for creativity in Darfur peacekeeping, as well as a U.N. role there. In July 2007, China for the first time joined the Security Council in voting to deploy a joint African Union and U.N. peacekeeping mission to Darfur, known as UNAMID. Liu bluntly said, "We played a key role in convincing Khartoum to accept UNAMID," and pointed out that China also sent about 300 Chinese engineers to help the peacekeepers.

In another step aimed at heading off Western criticism, in May 2007 China announced Liu's appointment to his unusual envoy position. Liu, in a remarkable statement by the standards of Chinese officialdom, told me being named as "special envoy for a country which is thousands of miles far away from China—that is something unprecedented, the first time in history. It shows that China feels, though we still adhere to the principle of noninterference in the affairs of a sovereign state, we have a more flexible interpretation than 10 or 20 years before."

After the International Criminal Court (ICC) issued an arrest warrant for Bashir in March 2009, China bristled and tried to neutralize the tribunal's action. Even so, Liu said that behind the scenes, China's "strong advice" to the Khartoum government was "please do not stop your cooperation with UNAMID or expel UNAMID. The consequences will be devastating." He warned the Khartoum government not to retaliate against foreigners living in Sudan, he said. His account is borne out by a confidential U.S. State Department cable released by WikiLeaks, recounting that in September 2008, before the arrest warrant, Zhai Jun, China's assistant foreign minister (as paraphrased by a U.S. diplomat), "expressed grave concern" about ICC charges but "strongly counseled" the government of Sudan to "remain prudent."

Human rights activists argue that China's shift hasn't gone far enough. When I asked Liu about a U.N. request for Chinese helicopters to help more with Darfur peacekeeping, he replied that the Sichuan earthquake had shown China "so seriously lacking in necessary helicopters" of the kind needed in the vast spaces of western Sudan. He noted that, before the sanctions imposed after the Tiananmen Square massacre, a U.S. arms maker had sold Black Hawk helicopters to China, which are now grounded for lack of spare parts. He wryly told a story about a Chinese leader who, visiting the United States, was asked for helicopters for Darfur. The Chinese leader pointedly replied that China didn't have enough helicopters, but "if you could sell us some, we will pay you in cash, and immediately we are going to send them to Darfur."

Today, China is showing flexibility in another part of Sudan: the oil-rich south. As a January referendum on the secession of Southern Sudan approached, which a Chinese official admitted would inevitably mean southern independence, China nimbly built up ties with the southerners. A senior Obama administration official told me that Obama, Secretary of State Hillary Clinton, and other top officials energetically enlisted China's backing for the referendum, with many specific requests. "President Obama is raising it in every meeting with Hu Jintao," said this official, so that Bashir faced united American and Chinese support for the referendum. So long as the referendum was "free, transparent, and credible," Liu told me beforehand, China would accept it—an unusual solicitude about fair voting from a Chinese official.

But China has not abandoned its support of Sudan, only modified it. Beijing remains a powerful backer of Bashir, albeit with fresh reservations. Still, China's changes in Sudan policy lend some credence to those who argue that Western engagement with China can have benefits for human rights even in China's worst client states. "Publicly we are very cautious," acknowledged Liu. "But when we engage with our Sudanese brothers, I am sometimes quite straightforward." Liu said, "One strict principle is that we do not interfere. But we do not regard giving advice, suggestions, as interference." When I pointed out that when a country of 1.3 billion people suggests something, smaller governments are going to listen, he laughed in agreement. Another time, he said flatly, "When we give advice to Sudan, it has to consider it seriously. Because China is one of the few friends of that country."

Sudan was a rare case for China: where international pressure, not least U.S. engagement, was overwhelming. But China is less impressed with American clout today, and most places where China is investing and cultivating friendships, from Burma to Angola, haven't made it onto the Western agenda in the same way. In these neglected places, China is free to stick closer to its own view of its influence. In particular, Chinese officials point to a success story for their softer kind of diplomacy, with a case that would startle many Westerners: Zimbabwe.

"Zimbabwe is a good example for us," said a senior Chinese official. As seen from Beijing, Zimbabwe exemplifies a model of inclusive compromise, with two local rivals coming together without thundering military or economic threats from self-interested superpowers. In September 2008, the dictatorial Mugabe and opposition leader Morgan Tsvangirai made a quiet deal to move forward. The brokers were fellow Africans, not the meddling hegemonists of Washington and London. "It proves once again that it is a good way of countries to solve issues by themselves," said a Chinese official in Beijing. This official suggested that Zimbabwe made a good precedent for other troubled countries: "In light of what happened in Zimbabwe, we should still give time to the Sudanese government and parties in Sudan to make a new accomplishment." But there's an obvious problem with this pleasant vision: Mugabe has repeatedly and brazenly violated the power-sharing pact, maintaining his grip on power while China continues its happy talk.

China has supported Mugabe since his revolutionary struggle against British colonialism and white supremacy. "He led the Zimbabwean people to win their independence," Xin, the Chinese ambassador, told me in May 2010 over dinner at a Hunanese restaurant in a low-density area of crumbling, ravaged Harare. "Just like Chairman Mao."

This friendship endured even as Mugabe drove Zimbabwe into economic collapse after 2000, with at least 80 percent unemployment, hyperinflation reaching 231 million percent, a quarter of the population fleeing, and female life expectancy plummeting to 34 years, the lowest on Earth. Chinese officials admit frankly that, unlike in oil-rich Sudan, they have little economic stake in Zimbabwe; "it's just one drop in the sea," as one put it. But even so, "China did not stop our normal economic relations, as Western countries did," said Liu Guijin, himself a former ambassador to Zimbabwe. Another Chinese official said, "The West is suspicious: Why do you have such good relations with Zimbabwe? Is there a secret deal? I don't know of any secret deal at all."

The key test for China came in March 2008, when the opposition Movement for Democratic Change (MDC), led by Tsvangirai, claimed victory over Mugabe's party in presidential and parliamentary elections. Tsvangirai's movement endured widespread government-backed violence, in which some 200 people died. When I asked Xin about this bloodshed, he replied, "If they say the president beat some people, did you see that with your own eyes? People could believe it or not."

Tsvangirai, shaken by the carnage, pulled out of a second, decisive round of voting scheduled for June 2008. Neighboring African states refused to accept Mugabe's assertions of victory. Finally, South Africa helped broker a power-sharing arrangement, with Tsvangirai becoming prime minister while Mugabe held on as president. Despite loud MDC claims that Mugabe stole the elections, Chinese officials in Beijing are sanguine: "The Zimbabwe issue is by its nature a domestic issue; like in the U.S. you also in 2000 had this controversy."

This, for Chinese officials, stands out as the proper way to handle an African political crisis. A Chinese diplomat told me, "Many people in the West think it's better to intervene in the domestic situation of the Zimbabwean election. We advocated that the Zimbabweans should solve the issue themselves, with what is good for the nation itself in mind. They went through some zigzags on the road, but the result is much better." A Chinese Foreign Ministry official praised Mugabe's statesmanship: "For a hero of the liberation struggle to make such a big compromise is not an easy thing."

A Chinese Foreign Ministry official praised Mugabe's statesmanship: "For a hero of the liberation struggle to make such a big compromise is not an easy thing."

Now, Chinese officials are full of praise for the joint Mugabe-Tsvangirai government. One Foreign Ministry official said (without evident irony), "That agreement is a great leap forward." In Harare, a city that still suffers frequent power and water outages, Xin told me, "Things are getting better and better." The two parties, he claimed, are like siblings: "For ZANU-PF, there is a new brother, so they have to get used to discussing things." As for Tsvangirai's movement, "The MDC is like a younger brother; they don't have experience in running the country. They try to learn how to cooperate with the older brother."

China balks at using its considerable influence to pressure the regime. One Chinese official told me, "We cannot put a gun to Mugabe and say that you have to accept this or accept that." Liu argued that sanctions would be counterproductive: "It's the ordinary people who suffer from sanctions or embargoes. That is not Mugabe."

It was particularly important to China that the deal be done without superpower interference. "We still see it as a domestic affair," said a Chinese diplomat. "It's not something that needs the intervention of the U.N. Security Council." China usually reserves its Security Council veto for core security issues like Taiwan. In Zimbabwe, one Foreign Ministry official told me, "there is no direct [Chinese] interest involved, no vital interest involved."

But on July 10, 2008, just after Mugabe was sworn in for a sixth term as president, China vetoed a U.S.-sponsored Security

Council resolution imposing an arms embargo on Zimbabwe and a travel ban and asset freeze on Mugabe and some of his top aides. Russia joined China, as did South Africa. Liu said that the African Union had asked China to veto the sanctions. "Because China is the only developing country" in the permanent five members of the Security Council, "that veto belongs to the developing countries," said a Chinese Foreign Ministry official, adding, "No matter how serious it is, it is their internal affair. If the U.N. Security Council really adopts a resolution to sanction Zimbabwe, it maybe sets a very bad precedent; it may set a precedent to have the U.N. interfere in the domestic affairs of a sovereign country."

The reality in Zimbabwe—devastating levels of unemployment, infrastructure in collapse, Mugabe squarely in control—is miserably different from China's rosy official version. It's true that Zimbabwe halted its economic free-fall by adopting the U.S. dollar as its base currency, ending hyperinflation. But Mugabe has trampled the power-sharing deal repeatedly. He named loyalists to all 10 of the regional governorships, though they were supposed to be distributed among the rival factions. He grabbed the most important ministries. Without consulting Tsvangirai, Mugabe appointed a stooge as attorney general and reappointed the central bank governor who had presided over the country's economic meltdown. In May 2010, to the MDC's shock, Mugabe appointed the controversial former electoral chief, accused of helping rig the 2008 election, as the president of Zimbabwe's high court. Tsvangirai's finance minister, Tendai Biti, has complained, "ZANU-PF cannot continue to urinate on us."

When I asked Xin about these vehement complaints, he said, "First, I didn't hear such comments from any ministers from the MDC. Second, I want to say that such a thing is just like in the past 30 years ago; there was a lot of not very accurate criticism of China." It's hard to believe that Chinese officials are truly naive about Mugabe. Liu, who knows the old dictator well from his posting as ambassador in Harare, was unsurprised at the thought of Mugabe violating the power-sharing deal: "I could imagine it. He's such a senior leader, well established, controls everything." Still, with Mugabe and Tsvangirai now jockeying over the prospect of new elections, Chinese diplomats seem to be among the last to publicly assert faith in a shotgun marriage that has overwhelmingly benefited Mugabe.

My most recent trip to China coincided with the awarding of the Nobel Peace Prize to Liu Xiaobo, the Chinese writer and democracy activist sentenced in December 2009 to 11 years in prison for inciting subversion. A few days before the prize was placed in Liu Xiaobo's empty chair, an urbane, worldly Chinese official in Beijing, who usually emphasizes his country's peaceful cooperation with the United States, vented some of his government's fury: "If a million or even a hundred million people listened to Liu Xiaobo's call and make moves to overthrow this government, what could happen to China?" This official heatedly warned that Liu Xiaobo risked igniting an "endless quarrel" like the Cultural Revolution, a dreaded memory among reformist Chinese elites: "How can China stand it? China will fall into a chaotic situation. Then China cannot pull people out of poverty. Nobody cares for China but us. The basic law helps us enjoy this kind of stability. We can prevent this country falling into the abyss."

This kind of scorched-earth response makes it tempting to explain China's friendships with dictatorships as a simple affinity with China's own resilient authoritarianism. After all, China has taken a hard line on domestic dissent over the past several years, including Liu Xiaobo's stiff jail sentence. But Chinese officials style themselves as a different kind of government: one that has lifted hundreds of millions of its people out of poverty, reached out to the world, allowed limited openness at home, and played a helpful role on the global stage. They point with pride to their role in pressing North Korea on its nuclear weapons and to China's considerable contributions to U.N. peacekeeping operations.

This self-presentation makes China's support for radical tyrants like Robert Mugabe and Kim Jong Il more than a little awkward. Mugabe drove his economy into the ground, and Kim rages against the international system; Chinese diplomats are proud of doing none of those things. Liu Guijin recalls sitting in on summits with African leaders, where "our paramount leader Deng Xiaoping said, 'I don't wish you to take up socialism.'" Liu, remembering China's own experiences, told me he warns Africans against revolutionary excess: "If you go a more drastic revolutionary way, you will destroy infrastructure; you will undermine what you have achieved. You will have more resistance. And you may be faced with embargoes or sanctions."

That softer kind of thinking may yet leave an opening for people who care about human rights. After all, it's easier for China to engage with the West on the human rights situation—couched in suitably diplomatic terms—in a faraway country like Sudan than within China itself. Even before the Sudan experience, Liu noted, China had become more open in its view of sovereignty: "Twenty years ago, we regard[ed] U.N. peacekeeping as a kind of interference in internal affairs. But now we are active participants." And the Sudan example demonstrates that smart, sustained Western engagement with China can pay off. China's shift, however belated or inadequate, puts the lie to the notion that China will never pressure a friendly government about its domestic abuses.

Yet, getting China to reconsider its rogue relationships takes an enormous amount of effort and skill. Other issues—Taiwan, renminbi undervaluation, Iran—will threaten to crowd out America's concerns about China's record on human rights abroad, just as they do on China's domestic human rights record. "I'd put Sudan in the same category of currency, Iran, and North Korea," a senior Obama administration official told me.

The Chinese government excels at spotting weaknesses in foreign pressure. Chinese officials are full of praise for Scott Gration, Obama's special envoy on Sudan, who prefers offering inducements to Bashir. "There is a new approach of Scott Gration," Liu said after the Obama team took charge. "It's no longer 'You do this; we do that.'" In August 2009, when I told a Chinese Foreign Ministry official that Darfur was an important personal and moral issue for Obama, the official replied, "In the character of President Obama, we not only find his morality but also his pragmatism." (This was meant as a compliment.) But more recently, after a surge of sustained engagement on Sudan from the highest levels of the Obama administration, Liu noted that "not everyone in Washington agrees with [Gration's] moderate policy." A senior Obama administration official told me, "We've seen them step up in surprising ways" on Sudan.

Yet America's influence over a more assertively nationalist China is already on the wane. At a moment when many elites in today's more self-confident China, particularly in the military, believe that the American system is in decline, dragged down by bitterly deadlocked politics and a stagnant economy, it will not be easy for the United States to engage with Beijing on its human rights impact abroad.

But a more responsible Chinese attitude toward its pariah friends would actually benefit China. By cozying up to Mugabe, China stands to alienate generations of ordinary Zimbabweans, not to mention the millions of other Africans looking on helplessly from outside. In April 2008, dockworkers at the South African port of Durban, with the backing of their powerful labor unions, refused to unload weapons bound for Zimbabwe from a Chinese ship. That could be but a taste of enduring African resentment of Chinese influence.

China risks falling into the same trap that America fell into during—and even after—the Cold War. In places like Pakistan and Argentina, Egypt and Tunisia, the United States championed convenient tyrants and thereby embittered ordinary citizens against America for decades. "Even when we are economically stronger, in the middle of this century, I hope China's behavior will not be the same as the superpowers," Liu Guijin said. "We have such a unique history that is so similar with the developing countries." It is an admirable sentiment. There are some reasons to hope that China will get more responsible. But so far, there are few Darfuris or Zimbabweans who would see much to cheer in China's growing global influence. China would not be the first big power to grow both strong and cold.

Critical Thinking

1. How does China justify its reluctance to criticize the human rights records of countries like Zimbabwe and North Korea?
2. What policy decisions show flexibility in China's thinking?
3. How do China's economic interest influence its willingness to criticize human rights violations?

Gary J. Bass, a professor of politics and international affairs at Princeton University, is the author of *Freedom's Battle* and *Stay the Hand of Vengeance*.

Article

Not Ready for Prime Time

Why Including Emerging Powers at the Helm Would Hurt Global Governance

JORGE G. CASTAÑEDA

Few matters generate as much consensus in international affairs today as the need to rebuild the world geopolitical order. Everyone seems to agree, at least in their rhetoric, that the makeup of the United Nations Security Council is obsolete and that the G-8 no longer includes all the world's most important economies. Belgium still has more voting power in the leading financial institutions than either China or India. New actors need to be brought in. But which ones? And what will be the likely results? If there is no doubt that a retooled international order would be far more representative of the distribution of power in the world today, it is not clear whether it would be better.

The major emerging powers, Brazil, Russia, India, and China, catchily labeled the BRICS by Goldman Sachs, are the main contenders for inclusion. There are other groupings, too: the G-5, the G-20, and the P-4; the last—Brazil, Germany, India, and Japan—are the wannabes that hope to join the UN Security Council and are named after the P-5, the council's permanent members (China, France, Russia, the United Kingdom, and the United States). Up for the G-8 are Brazil, China, India, Mexico, and South Africa. The G-8 invited representatives of those five states to its 2003 summit in Evian, France, and from 2005 through 2008, this so-called G-5 attended its own special sessions on the sidelines of the G-8's.

Others states also want in. Argentina, Egypt, Indonesia, Italy, Mexico, Nigeria, Pakistan, and South Africa aspire to join the UN Security Council as permanent members, with or without a veto. But with little progress on UN reform, none of them has been accepted or rejected (although China is known to oppose admitting Japan and, to a lesser degree, India). After the G-8 accommodated the G-5, other states, generally those close to the countries hosting the summits, also started to join the proceedings on an ad hoc basis. When the global economic crisis struck in 2008, matters were institutionalized further. The finance ministers of the G-20 members had already been meeting regularly since 1999, but then the heads of state started participating. Today, the G-20 includes just about everybody who wishes to join it: the P-5 and the P-4, the G-8 and the G-5, as well as Argentina, Australia, the European Union, Indonesia, Nigeria, Saudi Arabia, South Korea, and Turkey. Still, despite the express wishes of some—and because of the tacit resentment of others—the G-20 has not replaced the G-8. Earlier this year, the smaller, more exclusive group met at a luxury resort in Muskoka, a lake district in Canada, while the larger assembly was treated to demonstrations and tear gas in downtown Toronto.

There is some overlap in this alphabet soup. France, Russia, the United Kingdom, and the United States belong to both the P-5 and the G-8; China is in the P-5, the G-5, and the G-20; Brazil and India desperately want to join everything in sight. At the end of the day, the world's inner sanctum will be expanded to include only the few states that possess the ambition to enter it and at least one good reason for doing so—such as geographic, demographic, political, or economic heft. That means the shortlist boils down to Brazil, China, Germany, India, Japan, and South Africa.

Bric-A-Brac

The Chief rationale for inviting these states to join the world's ruling councils is self-evident: they matter more today than they did when those bodies were created. India will soon be the most populous nation on earth, just before China. In current dollars, Japan is the world's second-largest economy, with China and Germany gaining on it rapidly. Brazil combines demographic clout (it has about 200 million inhabitants) with economic power (a GDP of almost $1.6 trillion) and geographic legitimacy (Latin America must be represented), and in fact, it has already begun to play a greater role in international organizations such as the International Monetary Fund and the World Bank. Africa cannot be altogether excluded from the world's governing councils, and only South Africa can represent it effectively.

Germany and Japan are a case of their own. The two defeated powers of World War II already work closely with the permanent members of the UN Security Council (when it comes to policy having to do with Iran, for example, Germany acts together with the P-5, forming the P-6), and both belong to the Nuclear Suppliers Group, which promotes the enforcement of nuclear nonproliferation by monitoring exports of nuclear material, among other things. Germany is participating in the NATO operation in Afghanistan (as it did in the mission in Kosovo in the late 1990s); Japan supported the U.S.-led invasion and occupation of Iraq with logistical assistance on the high seas. The values and general conduct of these two highly developed democracies are indistinguishable from those of the powers already at the helm of international organizations. These states would thus provide additional clout and talent to the Security Council—the only membership at stake for them—if they joined it, but they would hardly transform it. Meanwhile, since including Germany and Japan and not others is unimaginable, for now they will have to accept the status quo: de facto participation in lieu of formal membership.

The argument for admitting Brazil, China, India, and South Africa to the helm rests on the general principle that the world's leadership councils should be broadened to include emerging powers. But unlike the case for Germany and Japan, this one raises some delicate questions. Over the past half century, a vast set of principles—the collective defense of democracy, nuclear nonproliferation, trade liberalization, international criminal justice, environmental protection, respect for human rights (including labor, religious, gender, ethnic, and indigenous peoples' rights)—have been enshrined in many international and regional treaties and agreements. Of course, this system is not without problems. A Eurocentric, Judeo-Christian tint pervades—a flaw one can acknowledge without approving of female circumcision, child soldiers and child labor, or amputation as a punishment for robbery—and the Western powers have often flagrantly and hypocritically violated those values even while demanding that other states respect them.

The United States has been an especially reluctant participant in the current world order. It has opposed the International Criminal Court, the Kyoto Protocol, and the convention to ban antipersonnel land mines, and it has undermined progress in the Doha Round of international trade negotiations by refusing to suspend its agricultural subsidies. Still, the world is a better place today thanks to the councils and commissions, the sanctions and conditions that these values have spawned—from the human rights mechanisms of the UN, the European Union, and the Organization of American States (OAS) to the International Criminal Court; from the World Trade Organization to the Nuclear Nonproliferation Treaty (NPT); from international cooperation on combating HIV/AIDS to the International Labor Organization's conventions on labor rights and the collective rights of indigenous peoples; from UN sanctions against apartheid in South Africa and the African Union's attempt to restore democracy in Zimbabwe to the OAS' condemnation of a military coup in Honduras.

Constructing this web of international norms has been slow and painful, with less overall progress and more frequent setbacks than some have wished for. Many countries of what used to be called the Third World have contributed to parts of the edifice: Mexico to disarmament and the law of the sea; Costa Rica to human rights; Chile to free trade. But now, the possible accession of Brazil, China, India, and South Africa to the inner sanctum of the world's leading institutions threatens to undermine those institutions' principles and practices.

Weak Links

Brazil, China, India, and South Africa are not just weak supporters of the notion that a strong international regime should govern human rights, democracy, nonproliferation, trade liberalization, the environment, international criminal justice, and global health. They oppose it more or less explicitly, and more or less actively—even though at one time most of them joined the struggle for these values: India wrested its independence from the United Kingdom, South Africa fought off apartheid, and Brazilian President Luiz Inácio Lula da Silva (known as Lula) opposed the military dictatorship in Brazil.

Consider these states' positions on the promotion of democracy and human rights worldwide. Brazil, India, and South Africa are representative democracies that basically respect human rights at home, but when it comes to defending democracy and human rights outside their borders, there is not much difference between them and authoritarian China. On those questions, all four states remain attached to the rallying cries of their independence or national liberation struggles: sovereignty, self-determination, nonintervention, autonomous economic development. And today, these notions often contradict the values enshrined in the international order.

It is perfectly predictable that Beijing would support the regimes perpetuating oppression and tragedy in Myanmar (also known as Burma) and Sudan. The Chinese government has never respected human rights in China or Tibet, and it has always maintained that a state's sovereignty trumps everything else, both on principle and to ward off scrutiny of its own domestic policies. Now that China wants to secure access to Myanmar's natural gas and Sudan's oil, it has used its veto in the UN Security Council to block sanctions against those states' governments.

India's stance—to say nothing of Brazil's or South Africa's—is not much better. India once promoted democracy and human rights in Myanmar, but in the mid-1990s, after seeing few results, it started to moderate its tone. In 2007, when the military junta in Myanmar cracked down more violently than usual on opposition leaders, dissenters, and monks, New Delhi issued no criticism of the repression. It refused to condemn the latest trial and conviction of the opposition leader Aung San Suu Kyi and opposed any sanctions on the regime, including those that the United States and the European Union have been enforcing since the mid-1990s. India has its reasons for responding this way—reasons that have little to do with human rights or democracy and everything to do with Myanmar's huge natural gas reserves; with getting the junta to shut down insurgent sanctuaries along India's northeastern border; and, most important, with making sure not to push the Myanmar regime into Beijing's hands. New Delhi's official support for what in 2007 it called "the undaunted resolve of the Burmese people to achieve democracy" has been more rhetorical than anything else.

India has also adopted a problematic approach toward refugees and Tamil Tiger ex-combatants in Sri Lanka. Today, a year after the civil war in Sri Lanka ended, more than 100,000 of the Tamil Tigers' supporters (and, by some accounts, as many as 290,000) remain in displaced persons camps that are virtual prisons. According to Human Rights Watch, India—together with Brazil, Cuba, and Pakistan—blocked a draft resolution by the UN Human Rights Council that would have condemned the situation; instead, it supported a statement commending the government of Mahinda Rajapaksa. New Delhi has been looking the other way, knowing full well that Sri Lanka would have bowed under pressure from India to allow displaced Sri Lankans to return home. There are perfectly logical explanations for India's stance, including the fact that India has its own social and political problems in the southern state of Tamil Nadu; the Indian politician Sonia Gandhi's husband, Rajiv, was assassinated there by a Tamil suicide bomber in 1991. New Delhi prefers to turn a blind eye toward the Sri Lankan government's violations of human rights rather than risk taking a principled stand on an issue too close to home.

One could argue, of course, that this kind of cynical pragmatism is exactly what the Western powers have practiced for decades, if not centuries. France and the United Kingdom in their former colonies, the United States in Latin America and the Middle East, even Germany in the Balkans—all readily sacrificed their noble principles on the altar of political expediency. But the purpose of creating a network of international institutions, intergovernmental covenants, and nongovernmental organizations to promote democracy and human rights was precisely to limit such great-power pragmatism, as well as to ensure that authoritarian regimes do not get away with committing abuses and that civil society everywhere is mobilized in defense of these values. India's stance does nothing more to advance these goals than does China's. In fact, given its prestige as the world's largest democracy and founder of the Non-Aligned Movement, it might be undercutting them even more when it fails to uphold them.

This last point is even truer for South Africa. No other African country enjoys such moral authority as South Africa does, thanks to Nelson Mandela's struggle against apartheid and his work on behalf of national reconciliation. But the African National Congress remains a socialist, anti-imperialist national liberation organization, and Mandela's successors at the head of the party and the country, Thabo Mbeki and Jacob Zuma, still basically endorse those values. Partly for that reason, the South African government opposed censuring the government of President Robert Mugabe in Zimbabwe even after it cracked down especially brutally on the Zimbabwean opposition following the contested elections of March 2008. Mbeki, who was then president, was unwilling to challenge his former national liberation comrade and the principal goal of not intervening in neighbors' affairs. Working through the African Union and the South African Development Community, Pretoria did help broker a power-sharing deal between the government and the opposition in Zimbabwe. But as an April 2008 editorial in *The Washington Post* argued, Mugabe managed to stay in office thanks to the support of then South African President Mbeki.

The South African government, like nearly every regime in Africa, is wary of criticizing the internal policies of other countries, even if they are undemocratic or violate human rights. Unlike other African states, however, South Africa is a thriving democracy that aspires to a regional and even an international role. So which is it going to choose: nonintervention in the domestic affairs of its neighbors in the name of the passé ethos of national liberation and the Non-Aligned Movement or the defense—rhetorical at least and preferably effective—of universal values above national sovereignty, as would befit a new member of the world's ruling councils?

Brazilian Lulabies

And which way will it be for Brazil, for whose leaders the issues of democracy and human rights were once especially dear? Like his predecessor, Lula opposed the military dictatorship that ruled Brazil between 1964 and 1985. At the time, he was an advocate of human rights, free and fair elections, and representative democracy; he often sought out foreign governments to support his cause and censure the people who were torturing members of the Brazilian opposition. But since he has been in office, he has not paid much heed to these issues. Although he has repeatedly flaunted Brazil's entry into the great-power club, he has been dismissive of the importance of democracy and human rights throughout Latin America, particularly in Cuba and Venezuela, and in places as far afield as Iran. He has reinforced the Brazilian Foreign Ministry's tendency to not meddle in Cuba's internal affairs. Earlier this year, he traveled to Havana the day after a jailed Cuban dissident died from a hunger strike. Speaking at a press conference, he practically blamed the prisoner for dying and said he disapproved of that "form of struggle." Just hours later, he posed, beaming, for a photograph with Fidel and Raúl Castro.

Lula also gave Iranian President Mahmoud Ahmadinejad a hero's welcome in Brasília and São Paulo (the latter home to a majority of Brazil's significant Jewish community) just a few months after Ahmadinejad stole his country's 2009 election and the Iranian government violently suppressed the resulting public demonstrations. Within a few months of that visit, Lula traveled to Tehran. To Venezuelan President Hugo Chávez's increasingly heavy hand, Lula has also turned a blind eye. He never questions the jailing of political opponents; crackdowns on the press, trade unions, and students; or tampering with the electoral system in Venezuela. Brazilian corporations, especially construction companies, have huge investments there, and Lula has used his friendship with Chávez and the Castro brothers to placate the left wing of his party, which is uncomfortable with his orthodox economic policies. He systematically cloaks his pragmatic—some would say cynical—approach in the robes of nonintervention, self-determination, and Third World solidarity.

Recently, Brazil seems to have changed its tune somewhat, moving slightly away from its traditional stance of nonintervention after a coup in Honduras last year. When Honduran President Manuel Zelaya was ousted from office in June 2009, Lula suddenly became a stalwart defender of Honduras' democracy. Together with allies of Zelaya, such as Raúl Castro, Chávez, and the presidents of Bolivia, Ecuador, and Nicaragua,

Lula convinced other members of the OAS, including Mexico and the United States, to suspend Honduras from the organization. Lula subsequently granted Zelaya asylum in the Brazilian embassy in Tegucigalpa, allowing him to mobilize his followers and organize against the coup's instigators from there. But since Porfirio Lobo Sosa was chosen to be Honduras' new president in free and fair elections late last year and several Latin American countries and the United States have recognized his government, Brazil's enduring support for Zelaya has increasingly come to seem intransigent and quixotic. One wonders whether Lula's position expresses the reflexive solidarity of a state that once suffered military coups itself, signals a new willingness to stand up for democratic principles, or is yet another concession to Chávez and his friends in an effort to quiet the restless and troublesome left wing of Lula's party by defending its disciple in Tegucigalpa. But this much seems clear: Brazil's first attempt to take a stance on an internal political conflict in another Latin American country did not turn out too well, and Brazil does not yet feel comfortable with leaving behind its traditional policy of nonintervention in the name of the collective defense of human rights and democracy.

It's the Bomb!

These States' ambivalence on so-called soft issues, such as human rights and democracy, tends to go hand in hand with their recalcitrance on "harder" issues, such as nuclear proliferation. With the exception of South Africa, which unilaterally gave up the nuclear weapons it had secretly built under apartheid, Brazil, China, and India have opposed the international nonproliferation regime created by the NPT in 1968. India has not deliberately helped or encouraged other countries with their nuclear ambitions. But it has never ratified the NPT, and the very fact that it went nuclear in 1974 led Pakistan, its neighbor and enemy, to do the same in 1982. Pakistan has since become one of the world's worst proliferators, thanks to the shenanigans of the rogue nuclear scientist A. Q. Khan. India cannot rightly be faulted for the actions of Pakistan, but it can be for not signing the NPT, for not doing more to assist the Nuclear Suppliers Group, and for not sanctioning states that aspire to get the bomb. It has coddled Tehran even as Tehran has seemed increasingly determined to build a nuclear weapon; it has repeatedly rejected imposing sanctions. In opposing the last batch in June of this year, Indian Prime Minister Manmohan Singh stated that Iran had every right to develop a peaceful nuclear industry and that there was scant evidence that any military intent was driving its program. He did not need to say that India is developing an important energy relationship with Iran and is seeking to build gas and oil pipelines from Iran all the way to New Delhi.

China, for its part, has an "execrable" record on proliferation, according to *The Economist* earlier this year—or rather it did until it joined the NPT in 1992 (after that, it at least nominally began to improve). The Chinese government helped Pakistan produce uranium and plutonium in the 1980s and 1990s, and it gave Pakistan the design of one of its own weapons. Beijing has not been especially constructive in trying to hinder North Korea's efforts to acquire nuclear weapons, and it has been downright unhelpful regarding Iran, systematically opposing or undermining sanctions against Tehran and threatening to use its veto on the UN Security Council if the Western powers go too far. Its recent decision to sell two new civilian nuclear power reactors to Pakistan will ratchet up the nuclear rivalry between India and Pakistan and undercut the work of the Nuclear Suppliers Group by making it easier for Islamabad to build more bombs.

Neither China nor India can be counted on to defend the nonproliferation regime. Both states seem too attached to the recent past, especially to the notion that they, huge developing nations once excluded from the atomic club, were able to challenge the nuclear monopoly held by the West and the Soviet Union thanks to the genius, discipline, and perseverance of their scientists. Not that there is anything wrong with being faithful to the past. But perhaps those states that remain faithful to the past best belong there—and not among those that will build a new international order.

Nostalgia is not the problem when it comes to Brazil. Brazil cannot be counted on when it comes to nuclear nonproliferation either, but for reasons having less to do with its past than its future. In the 1960s, it signed the Treaty of Tlatelolco, which banned nuclear weapons from Latin America, and in the 1990s, together with Argentina, it agreed to dismantle its enrichment program. When it finally ratified the NPT, in 1998, Brazil was perceived as a strong supporter of nonproliferation. But this May, eager to cozy up to Iran and wanting to be treated as a world power, it suddenly teamed up with Turkey to propose a deal that would lift sanctions on Iran if Iran took its uranium to Turkey to be enriched. Tehran nominally accepted the arrangement; the rest of the world did not. Lula and Turkish Prime Minister Recep Tayyip Erdogan claimed that the arrangement simply replicated a proposal previously put forth by the P-6 and that Obama supported their effort. Washington nonetheless called for stronger sanctions against Iran. Twelve of the UN Security Council's 15 members, including China and Russia, voted for the sanctions; only Brazil and Turkey opposed them. (Lebanon abstained.) In the end, the episode was widely seen as a clumsy scheme to get Tehran off the hook and a gambit by Lula to get the world to take Brazil more seriously. (Turkey was also deemed to be a spoiler, but at least it has real interests in the Middle East.) What Lula achieved instead was to show that Brazil is still more interested in Third World solidarity than in international leadership. Worse, now some are speculating that Brazil is laying the groundwork to resurrect its own nuclear program.

One might say that in behaving in these ways, the emerging powers of today are acting no differently from the established powers—and that this is the best proof that they have come of age. They are rising powers, and—just like the states that came before them—they act increasingly on the basis of their national interests, and those national interests are increasingly global and well defined. But unlike the existing global players, they are not subject to enough domestic or international safeguards, or checks and balances, or, mainly, pressure from civil society—all forces that could limit their power and help them define their national interests beyond the economic realm and the short term. Their discourse and conduct may seem to be as legitimate as those of the traditional powers, but they are in fact far more self-contradictory. On the one hand, the rising powers still see themselves as members of and spokespeople for the developing world, the Non-Aligned Movement, the world's poor, and so on; on the other hand, they are staking their reputations on having become major economic, military, geopolitical, and even ideological powers, all of which not only distinguishes them from the rest of the Third World but also involves subscribing to certain universal values.

To Be or Not to Be

The stance of these countries on climate change also illustrates this persistent ambivalence about what role they are ready to assume. Brazil, China, and India are among the world's top emitters of carbon dioxide (China and India are among the top five). Last December, at the Copenhagen conference on climate change, they, along with South Africa (and Sudan, which was chairing the UN's Group of 77, or G-77, a coalition of developing nations), put forward a position that they said reflected the interests and views of "the developing nations." Building on a statement they had made at the 2008 G-8 summit, they called for assigning states' responsibilities for fighting climate change according to states' capacities. They believe that reducing emissions is above all the responsibility of the developed countries. They are willing to do their share and reduce their own emissions, they say, but rich countries will have to do more, such as make deeper, legally binding emissions cuts and help the most vulnerable nations pay for the expenses of mitigating and adapting to the effects of global warming. Their case rests on a strong foundation: after all, it was over a century of the rich countries' industrial growth and unrestricted emissions that led to climate change, and the poorer countries are only now beginning to develop strongly. Placing proportional limits on the emissions of all states, the reasoning goes, would amount to stunting the economic growth of developing countries by imposing on them requirements that did not exist when the developed countries were first growing.

Perhaps, but this argument also raises the question of whom these countries are speaking for and what role they envision for themselves. Brazil's emissions are mainly the byproduct of extensive agricultural development, deforestation, and degradation; India's, like China's, come from industrialization, which both countries claim they have a right to pursue despite the pollution it causes. These are not traits common to the vast majority of the world's poor nations. On the eve of the Copenhagen summit, Jairam Ramesh, India's environment minister, described India's position clearly: "The first nonnegotiable is that India will not accept a legally binding emission cut. . . . We will not accept under any circumstances an agreement which stipulates a peaking year for India." He did say that India was prepared to "modulate [its] position in consultation with China, Brazil, and South Africa" and to "subject its mitigation actions to international review." But he added, apparently in all earnestness, that India's acceptance of such a review would depend on how much "international financing and technology" the country got.

Do the emerging powers identify more with the rich polluters whose ranks they want to join or with the poor nations, which are both potential victims of and contributors to climate change? The groups overlap (the rich nations also are victims, and the poor ones also pollute), and Brazil, China, India, and South Africa have much in common with both groups, but they cannot be part of both at once. For now, these states seem to have chosen to side with the poor countries. Partly because of that decision, the Copenhagen summit failed, and the Cancún climate summit scheduled for the end of 2010 will probably fail, too. Marina Silva, a former environment minister under Lula who is running for president against her former boss' chosen candidate, seems to have grasped the contradiction in Brazil's official position more clearly than Lula. She has made the case that Brazil should do more. "It must admit global goals of carbon dioxide emissions reduction," she said a few weeks before the Copenhagen summit last year, "and contribute to convincing other developing countries to do the same."

Some candidates for emerging power status are beginning to understand this, but just barely. Mexico, for example, had originally subscribed to the joint stance of Brazil, China, India, and South Africa on emissions caps in 2008 and 2009, but by the time of the Copenhagen summit, it realized that its $14,000 per capita income (in 2008 purchasing parity prices) placed it closer to the states of the Organization for Economic Cooperation and Development (to which it already belongs) than to those of the G-77 or the Non-Aligned Movement (to which it does not belong) and stopped signing their common documents. Similarly, during the Doha Round of trade negotiations, Mexico grasped that its myriad free-trade agreements and low levels of agricultural exports put it in the camp of the industrialized nations rather than the camp of Brazil, China, India, and South Africa. Those states presented something of a common front on behalf of, as Lula put it, "the most fragile economies," although Brazil was more interested in opening up agricultural markets and China and India were more concerned with protecting small farmers. But these are exceptions, like Turkey's attempt to join the European Union, accepting all of its conditions regarding values and institutions. None of the emerging countries, democratic or otherwise, richer or poorer, more integrated into regional groups or not, has truly undergone its political or ideological aggiornamento.

Pay to Play

The ongoing discussion about whether emerging powers should be admitted to the helm of the world geopolitical order emphasizes the economic dimension of their rise and its geopolitical consequences. Not enough attention has been paid to the fact that although these countries are already economic powerhouses, they remain political and diplomatic lightweights. At best, they are regional powers that pack a minuscule international punch; at worst, they are neophytes whose participation in international institutions may undermine progress toward a stronger international legal order. They might be growing economic actors, but they are not diplomatic ones, and so as they strive to gain greater political status without a road map, they fall back on their default option: the rhetoric and posturing of bygone days, invoking national sovereignty and nonintervention, calling for limited international jurisdiction, and defending the application of different standards to different nations.

Given this, granting emerging economic powers a greater role on the world stage would probably weaken the trend toward a stronger multilateral system and an international legal regime that upholds democracy, human rights, nuclear nonproliferation, and environmental protection. An international order that made more room for the BRICS, for Mexico and South Africa, and for other emerging powers, would be much more representative. But it would not necessarily be an order whose core values are better respected and better defended.

The world needs emerging powers to participate in financial and trade negotiations, and it would benefit immensely from hearing their voices on many regional and international issues, such as the killings in Darfur, instability in the Middle East, repression in Myanmar, or the coup in Honduras. For now, however, these states' core values are too different from the ones espoused, however partially and duplicitously, by the international community's main players and their partners to warrant the emerging powers' inclusion at the helm of the world's top organizations.

These states still lack the balancing mechanisms that have helped curb the hypocrisy of great powers: vibrant and well-organized civil societies. This lack is more obvious in some countries (China, South Africa) than in others (Brazil, India), but there is a fundamental difference between the terms of their inclusion into the inner sanctum and that of those countries that are already there (although this difference obviously applies to Russia also). Before a serious debate takes place within these countries regarding their societies' adherence to the values in question, it might not be such a good idea for them to become full-fledged world actors. Maybe they should deliberate more prudently over whether they really want to pay in order to play, and the existing powers should ponder whether they wish to invite them to play if they will not pay.

Critical Thinking

1. What countries are likely contenders for leadership roles in international institutions?
2. What are the issues that raise questions about these countries' leadership?
3. What positions on these issues are the most troubling?
4. What are the arguments in favor of admitting these emerging countries to leadership positions in international institutions?

Jorge G. Castañeda was Mexico's Foreign Minister in 2000–2003. He teaches at New York University and is a member of the Board of Directors of Human Rights Watch and a Fellow at the New America Foundation.

Unit 5

UNIT

Prepared by: Robert J. Griffiths, *University of North Carolina at Greensboro*

Population, Resources, Environment, and Health

The developing world's population continues to increase at an annual rate that exceeds the world average. The average fertility rate (the number of children a woman will have during her life) for all developing countries is 2.9, while for the least developed countries the figure is 4.9. Although growth has slowed considerably since the 1960s, world population is still growing at the rate of over 70 million per year, with most of this increase taking place in the developing world. Increasing population complicates development efforts, puts added stress on ecosystems, and threatens food security. World population now exceeds seven billion and, if current trends continue, could reach 9 billion or more by 2050. Even if, by some miracle, population growth was immediately reduced to the level found in industrialized countries, the developing world's population would continue to grow for decades.

Almost one-third of the population in the developing world is under the age of 15, with that proportion jumping to 40 percent in the least developed countries. The population momentum created by this age distribution means that it will be some time before the developing world's population growth slows substantially. Some developing countries have achieved progress in reducing fertility rates through family planning programs, but much remains to be done.

Over a billion people live in absolute poverty, as measured by a combination of economic and social indicators. Economic development has not only failed to eliminate poverty but has actually exacerbated it in some ways. Ill-conceived economic development plans have diverted resources from more productive uses and contributed to environmental degradation. Industrialization increases resource consumption and pollution. Morover, as resources are depleted, extraction becomes more difficult and dangerous. If developing countries try to follow Western consumption patterns, sustainable development will be impossible. Furthermore, economic growth without effective environmental policies can lead to the need for more expensive clean-up efforts in the future. As population increases, it becomes more difficult to meet the basic human needs of the citizens of the developing world. Indeed, food scarcity looms as a major problem as the world struggles with a global food crisis, triggered by higher demand, skyrocketing oil prices, and the diversion of agricultural production to biofuels. The world's capacity to increase food production is limited and food shortages are likely to be more common, perhaps triggering conflict. Trade disputes, resource scarcity, and the uncertainties of alternative energy supplies potentially make the world's efforts toward a greener environment a significant security challenge. Growing demand for water is rapidly depleting available supplies. Competition for scarce water resources not only affects agricultural production, but it also threatens to spark conflict. By some estimates, over the next 20 years, a gap of over 40 percent will exist between global demand and reliable water supplies. Greenhouse gas emissions are accelerating climate change and the adverse effects will be felt first by the developing world. For instance, flooding in densely populated coastal areas of Bangladesh is likely to increase as sea levels rise and provides a clear indication of the potential for climate change displacement.

Divisions between the North and the South on environmental issues became evident at the 1992 Rio Conference on Environment and Development. The conference highlighted the fundamental differences between the industrialized world and developing countries over the causes of, and the solutions to, global environmental problems. Developing countries pointed to consumption levels in the North as the main cause of environmental problems and called on the industrialized countries to pay most of the costs of sustainable development designed to conserve the resources used to modernize and develop. These divisions have deepened on the issues of climate and greenhouse gas emissions. The Johannesburg Summit on Sustainable Development, a follow-up to the Rio conference, grappled with many of these issues, achieving some modest success in addressing water and sanitation needs. The Copenhagen Climate Conference aimed at establishing a new limit on greenhouse gases further demonstrated this rift between industrial and developing countries.

Article

The End of Easy Everything

The transition from an easy to a tough resource era will come at a high price.

MICHAEL T. KLARE

According to some experts, many of the world's key energy and mineral supplies are being rapidly depleted and will soon be exhausted. Other experts say that new technology is opening up vast reserves of hitherto inaccessible supplies. Oil, coal, uranium, and natural gas will soon be scarce commodities or will be more plentiful than ever, depending on whom you ask. The same holds true for copper, cobalt, lithium, and other critical minerals.

Those unfamiliar with the distinctive characteristics of the extractive industries can find it difficult to make sense of all this. But in truth, the contending positions on resource availability largely obscure an essential reality: Instead of moving from plenty to scarcity or from plenty to even greater abundance, we are moving from "easy" sources of supply to "tough" ones. This distinction carries immense implications for international politics, the world economy, and the health of the global environment.

Toughest for Last

Extraction of resources, whatever the material, follows a predictable pattern. Whenever a natural resource is first found to possess desirable characteristics (whether as a trade commodity, source of energy, manufacturing input, or luxury product), producers seek out and exploit the most desirable deposits of that material—those easiest to extract, purest, closest to markets, and so on. In time, however, these deposits are systematically depleted, and so producers must seek out and develop less attractive deposits—those harder to extract, of poorer quality, further from markets, and posing hazards of various sorts.

Very often technology is brought to bear to exploit these tougher deposits. Mining and drilling go deeper underground and extend into harsher climate zones. In the case of oil and gas, drilling moves from land to coastal waters, and then from shallow to deeper waters. Technological innovations allow increasingly unappealing sources of supply to be exploited—but they also pose evergrowing risks of accidents, environmental contamination, and political strife.

The Deepwater Horizon disaster that began on April 20, 2010, is a perfect expression of this phenomenon. Until relatively recently, offshore oil and gas drilling had been confined to relatively shallow waters, at depths of less than 1,000 feet. Over the past few decades, however, the major oil firms have developed incredibly sophisticated offshore drilling rigs that can operate in waters over one mile deep. One such rig, called Mars, was deployed in deep Gulf of Mexico waters six months before NASA's celebrated 1996 launch of its Pathfinder probe to the planet Mars. At a total cost of $1 billion, Shell's Mars platform was more than three times as expensive as Pathfinder, and its remote-sensing technologies and engineering systems are arguably more sophisticated.

The use of such costly and advanced technology has allowed BP, Shell, and other well heeled companies to extract ever-increasing volumes of oil from the Gulf's deep waters, helping to compensate for production declines at America's onshore and shallow coastal deposits. But operating in the Gulf's deep waters is far more difficult and hazardous than doing so in shallow waters, and the deep underground pressures encountered by these rigs are proportionally more difficult to manage. Intricate safety devices have been developed to reduce the risk of accident, but, as shown by the fate of the Deepwater Horizon, these cannot always be relied on to prevent catastrophe.

Despite this reality, oil companies will continue to drill in the Gulf's deep waters—and other challenging environments—because they see no other choice. Most of the "easy" oil and gas deposits on land and in shallow coastal waters in the United States and in friendly countries around the world have now been discovered and exploited, leaving only "tough" deposits in deep waters, the Arctic, areas with problematic geological formations, and dangerous or inhospitable countries like Iran, Iraq, and Russia. However daunting a task, the giant firms must find ways to operate in such areas if they intend to survive as major energy providers in the years to come.

And there is no question but that a vast abundance of "tough" oil and natural gas remains to be exploited. Resources in this category, which are often grouped together as "unconventional" fuels, include Canadian tar sands, Venezuelan heavy oil, shale oil and oil shale (two different things), shale gas, ultra-deepwater oil and gas, and Arctic hydrocarbons. The Orinoco Belt of Venezuela, for example, is said by the US Geological Survey (USGS) to contain as many as 1.7 trillion barrels of oil equivalent—easily exceeding the world's 1.3 trillion barrels in "proven" reserves of conventional (liquid) petroleum. The Arctic region, claims the USGS, harbors an estimated 1,700 billion cubic feet of natural gas, or the equivalent of 320 billion barrels of oil.

The Deepwater Horizon disaster may be the first ominous sign of what we can expect as we rely more heavily on unconventional fuels.

Even more astonishing is the amount of kerogen (an immature form of oil) contained in the oil shales of western Colorado and eastern Utah: as many as 2.8 trillion barrels of oil equivalent, or twice the tally of proven conventional reserves. Mature oil and gas deposits encased in hard shale formations, such as the Bakken oil formation of North Dakota, Montana, and Saskatchewan and the Marcellus gas formation of Pennsylvania, New York, and West Virginia are thought to be of a comparable scale.

Peak and Plateau

Such assessments of potential resource availability, coupled with recent advances in extractive technology, have led many energy experts to proclaim a new golden age of fossil fuel production—contradicting those in the field who speak of an imminent peak (and subsequent decline) in the output of oil, natural gas, and coal. Adherents of the "peak oil" theory see a significant contraction in petroleum supplies just around the corner, while the new-energy optimists believe that with sufficient investment, new technologies, and the relaxation of environmental regulations, all of humankind's future energy needs can be met.

Among the most vocal and prominent critics of production pessimism is Daniel Yergin, the author of a classic history of the oil industry, *The Prize: The Epic Quest for Oil, Money, and Power* and a just published study of energy's future, *The Quest: Energy, Security, and the Remaking of the Modern World.* "The peak oil theory," Yergin writes in his new volume, "embodies an 'end of technology/end of opportunity' perspective, that there will be no more significant innovation in oil production, nor significant new resources that can be developed. . . . But there is another, more appropriate way to visualize the course of supply: as a plateau. The world has decades of further production growth before flattening out into a plateau—perhaps some time around midcentury—at which time a more gradual decline will begin."

To buttress this contention, Yergin highlights the promising outlook for deep offshore drilling, shale oil, and Canadian tar sands. He also speaks with great enthusiasm about the "natural gas revolution"—the potential for recovering vast quantities of gas from shale rock through the use of horizontal drilling and hydraulic fracturing ("hydro-fracking," or simply "fracking"). When combined, these techniques allow for the extraction of gas from the shale deposits of the giant Marcellus formation, as well as others in the United States and around the world. "As a result of the shale revolution," he asserts, "North America's natural gas base, now estimated at 3,000 trillion cubic feet, could provide for current levels of consumption for over a hundred years—plus."

Yergin's writings, in turn, have spawned an outpouring of Pollyannaish commentary about the unlimited future for unconventional oil and gas production in the United States and elsewhere. Writing in *The New York Times,* columnist David Brooks has described shale gas as a "wondrous gift" and a "blessing."

That production of unconventional oil and gas is rising, and that these fuels will constitute an increasing share of America's energy supply, are unquestionable—as long as we rely on fossil fuels for the lion's share of our energy supply. But to view such options as blessings, wondrous gifts, or even as easily obtainable resources is misleading. Even putting aside the fact that continued dependence on fossil fuels will lead to increased emissions of greenhouse gases and an acceleration in climate change, the extraction of these materials will involve ever greater cost, danger, and environmental risk as energy firms operate deeper underground, further offshore, further north, and in more problematic rock formations. Indeed, the Deepwater Horizon disaster may be the first ominous sign of what we can expect as we rely more heavily on unconventional fuels.

The Turning Point

Perhaps the first person to grasp the significance of this shift toward tough energy was David O'Reilly, the former chairman and chief executive officer of Chevron. In February 2005, O'Reilly startled participants at an annual oil-industry conference in Houston by declaring that their business was at an epochal turning point. After more than a hundred years during which the global availability of petroleum had always kept pace with rising world demand, he said, "oil is no longer in plentiful supply. The time when we could count on cheap oil and even cheaper natural gas is clearly ending." In an open letter published in many newspapers, O'Reilly then put the matter in even starker terms: "The era of easy oil is over. . . . New discoveries are mainly occurring in places where resources are difficult to extract, physically, economically, and even politically."

Nations will fight for access to new supply sources as easy reserves are depleted.

A closer look at O'Reilly's speech and accompanying advertisements shows that he was less interested in defining a momentous historic transition than in lobbying for more favorable government policies and reduced environmental regulation. Nevertheless, his description of the global situation has been widely embraced as an explanation for prevailing energy trends. *The Wall Street Journal,* for example, recently summed up a story about the rise of unconventional petroleum in Saudi Arabia with the headline "Facing up to End of 'Easy Oil.'"

As the paper explained, "As demand for energy grows and fields of 'easy oil' around the world start to dry up, the Saudis are turning to a much tougher source: the billions of barrels of heavy oil trapped beneath the desert."

The impact of the changeover from "easy oil" to tougher alternatives is partly financial and technical. Extracting light crude in Saudi Arabia once was accomplished for a few dollars per barrel, whereas making a barrel of usable liquid from sulfurous heavy oil requires sophisticated technology and can cost as much as $60 or $70 per barrel. But the pursuit of new petroleum sources to replace the exhausted "easy" deposits also has other costs, such as a growing reliance on oil acquired from countries in conflict or controlled by corrupt dictators.

Nigeria, for example, has become America's fourth-leading supplier of oil—yet Nigerian production is constantly imperiled by sabotage and the kidnapping of oil workers by militants opposed to the inequitable allocation of the country's petroleum revenues. Russia is another large source of oil and gas, yet Prime Minister Vladimir Putin's relentless drive to impose state control over the extraction of natural resources has resulted in the de facto seizure of foreign assets by government-owned firms. Iraq, with the world's second largest petroleum reserves, is theoretically capable of producing three or four times as much as it does now, but any such increase would require a significant increase in domestic security as well as a predictable legal regime—neither of which appears in the offing any time soon.

The Arctic is another promising source of tough oil and gas. According to the USGS, the land above the Arctic Circle, representing about 6 percent of the world's total surface area, contains approximately 30 percent of the world's undiscovered hydrocarbon reserves. As the planet warms and new technologies are perfected, it will become increasingly possible to extract this untapped energy. But operations in the Arctic are exceedingly difficult and hazardous. Winter temperatures can drop to well below minus 40 degrees Fahrenheit, and severe storms are common. Thick ice covers the Arctic Ocean throughout the winter, and drifting ice threatens ships and oil platforms in the summer. Many endangered species inhabit the area, and any oil spill is likely to prove devastating—especially since the oil companies' capacity to conduct cleanup operations in the Arctic (such as those performed in the Gulf of Mexico following the Deepwater Horizon spill) is severely limited.

Of all unconventional sources of oil and gas, none perhaps is more controversial than shale gas, when extracted by the hydro-fracking method. To obtain gas in this manner, a powerful drill is used to reach a gas-bearing shale formation, often thousands of feet underground, and then turned sidewise to penetrate the shale layer in several directions. After concrete is applied to the outer walls of the resulting channels, explosives are set off to penetrate the rock; then millions of gallons of water—usually laced with lubricants and toxic chemicals—are poured into the openings to fracture the stone and release the gas. The "frack" water is then pumped back up and stored on site or sent for disposal elsewhere, after which the gas is sucked out of the ground.

The big problem here is the risk of water contamination. Water extracted from the wells (or "flowback") contains toxic chemicals and radioactive materials released from underground rock and cannot be returned to local streams and rivers; any seepage, either from the well itself (due to cracks in the well bore) or from on-site storage ponds could contaminate local drinking supplies—a major worry in New York and Pennsylvania, where the Marcellus formation overlaps with the watershed for major metropolitan areas, including New York City. Cavities created by the fracturing process could also connect to other underground fissures and allow methane to escape into underground aquifers, with the same risk of water contamination. Dangers like these have led some states and municipalities to place a moratorium on hydro-fracking, or ban its use near major watershed areas.

Advocates of shale gas and hydro-fracking say that the technique can be performed safely and to great benefit—if only regulators and environmentalists will stand aside and let the companies get on it with it. "There have been over a million wells hydraulically fractured in the history of the industry, and there is not one, not one, reported case of a freshwater aquifer having ever been contaminated from hydraulic fracturing," said Rex W. Tillerson, the chief executive of ExxonMobil, in testimony before Congress. But investigation by reporters for *The New York Times* has uncovered numerous examples of contamination, including cases in which flowback that contained unsafe levels of radioactive materials has been dumped into rivers that supply drinking water to major communities.

Coal, too, is becoming increasingly difficult and dangerous to extract. In the American West, many once-prolific coal deposits have been exhausted, forcing miners to dig ever deeper into the earth—increasing the risk of cave-ins and seismic jolts known as "bounces," since less stone is left after the mining process to support the weight of the mountains above. The end of easy coal is also evident in a growing reliance on "mountaintop removal," a technique used to uncover buried coal seams in Appalachia by blasting off the peaks of mountains and dumping the rubble in the valleys below. While considered a practical method for reaching otherwise inaccessible coal deposits, the technique has devastating environmental consequences, such as the destruction of woodland habitats and the contamination of valley streams with toxic chemicals.

Never Had It So Hard

What is true of oil, gas, and coal is also true of many other natural resources necessary for modern industry, including iron, copper, cobalt, and nickel. "With easy nickel fading fast, miners go after the tough stuff," read one characteristic headline in *The Wall Street Journal,* describing ongoing mining difficulties in the South Pacific islands of New Caledonia. At one time, New Caledonia's ore had been so rich—as much as 15 percent nickel—that miners could simply dig it out with pickaxes and haul it away on donkeys.

Those reserves are long gone, however, and the mine's current owner, the Brazilian mining giant Vale, has been left trying to extract the valuable metal from ores that contain less than 2 percent nickel. This requires treating the rough ore with acid under intense heat and pressure, an inherently costly and risky process. Massive acid spills have occurred on several occasions, delaying the opening of Vale's $4 billion nickel refinery in New

Caledonia. Adding to the company's problems, indigenous groups have repeatedly stormed the site, demanding that Vale halt its operations and restore the original forested landscape.

Copper, another critical mineral, likewise is seeing the end of easy supplies. With many existing mines in decline, the major mining firms are searching for new sources of supply in the Arctic and in countries recovering from conflict. Freeport-McMoRan Copper and Gold, for example, has acquired a majority stake in the Tenke Fungurume copper/cobalt mine in the southern Katanga region of the Democratic Republic of the Congo, one of the most war-ravaged countries on the planet. Said to contain ore that is up to 10 times as rich as copper found in older mines elsewhere, Tenke Fungurume was originally developed by other companies, but was abandoned in the 1990s when fighting among various militias and rebel factions made it unsafe to operate in the area. Freeport has now rebuilt much of the damaged infrastructure at the site and hired a small army of private guards to protect the installation and its staff from continuing outbursts of violence. But security conditions remain a concern.

As easy-to-access deposits of all these natural resources disappear, the price of many basic commodities will rise, requiring lifestyle changes from people in wealthy countries—and extreme hardship for the poor, especially when it comes to food prices. The cost of corn, rice, wheat, and other key staples doubled or tripled in 2008, provoking riots around the world and leading to the collapse of Haiti's government; then, after a brief retreat, food prices rose again in 2010 and 2011, reaching record highs and sparking a fresh round of protests.

Analysts have given many reasons for this alarming trend, including soaring global demand, scarcity of cropland, and prolonged drought in many parts of the world (widely attributed to climate change). But according to a World Bank analysis, the catastrophic 2008 spike in food prices, at least, was largely driven by rising energy costs. With oil prices expected to remain high in the years ahead, food will remain costly, producing not just hardship for the poor but also a continuing risk of social instability.

Ferocious Competition

Skyrocketing commodity prices are among the most visible effects of the end of "easy" resources, and they will be felt by virtually everyone on the planet. But the transition away from an easy resource world will not only affect individuals. It will also set the stage for ferocious competition among major corporations and for perilous wrangling among nation-states.

As existing reserves of vital materials are exhausted, the major energy and minerals firms will have to acquire new sources of supply in distant and uninviting areas—an undertaking that will prove increasingly costly and dangerous, exposing many smaller and less nimble companies to a risk of seizure by larger and more powerful firms. It has been reported, for example, that Shell and ExxonMobil both considered an unfriendly takeover of BP following the Deepwater Horizon disaster, when that company's stock fell to record lows. Many mining firms have also been targets of corporate attack as existing deposits of key minerals have been exhausted and industry giants compete for control over the few promising alternative reserves.

Nations, too, will fight among themselves for access to new supply sources as easy reserves are depleted and everyone must rely on the same assortment of tough deposits. This is evident, for example, in the Arctic, where formerly neglected boundary disputes have acquired fresh urgency with the growing appeal of the region's oil, gas, and mineral reserves. Canada and Russia have been particularly assertive in their claims to Arctic territory, saying not only that they will not back down in disputes over the location of contested offshore boundaries but that they will employ force if necessary to protect their Arctic space.

A similar pugnaciousness is evident in the East and South China Seas, where China has claimed ownership over a constellation of undersea oil and gas deposits but faces challenges from neighboring states that also assert ownership over the subsea reserves. In the East China Sea, China is squared off against Japan for control of the Chunxiao natural gas field (called Shirakaba by the Japanese), located in an offshore area claimed by both countries. Periodically, Chinese and Japanese ships and planes deployed in the area have engaged in menacing maneuvers toward one another, though no shots have yet been fired.

The situation in the South China Sea is even more complex and volatile. China and Taiwan claim the entire region, while parts are claimed by Brunei, Malaysia, Vietnam, the Philippines, and Indonesia—and here, shots have been fired on several occasions, when Chinese warships have sought to drive off oil-exploration vessels sanctioned by Vietnam and the Philippines.

The end of easy everything will not result in scarcity, as predicted by some—at least not in the short term. Instead, the use of advanced technologies to extract resources from hitherto inaccessible reserves will result in a continued supply of vital energy and mineral supplies. But the transition from an easy to a tough resource era will come at a high price, both in economic costs and in terms of environmental damage, social upheaval, and political strife. Only by reducing consumption of traditional fuels and metals and accelerating the development of renewable alternatives will it be possible to avert these perils.

Critical Thinking

1. What is the predictable pattern in resources extraction?
2. What is the "shale revolution"?
3. How does Klare assess this so-called revolution?
4. What is meant by the end of easy oil?
5. Compare the prospects of energy resources to mineral resources.
6. Do the authors of Article 1 give the same priority to the changing circumstances of natural resource extraction that Klare gives?

Michael T. Klare, a *Current History* contributing editor, is a professor at Hampshire College and author of the forthcoming *The Race for What's Left* (Metropolitan Books, 2012), from which this article is drawn.

Article

The World's Water Challenge

If oil is the key geopolitical resource of today, water will be as important—if not more so—in the not-so-distant future.

Erik R. Peterson and Rachel A. Posner

Historically, water has meant the difference between life and death, health and sickness, prosperity and poverty, environmental sustainability and degradation, progress and decay, stability and insecurity. Societies with the wherewithal and knowledge to control or "smooth" hydrological cycles have experienced more rapid economic progress, while populations without the capacity to manage water flows—especially in regions subject to pronounced flood-drought cycles—have found themselves confronting tremendous social and economic challenges in development.

Tragically, a substantial part of humanity continues to face acute water challenges. We now stand at a point at which an obscenely large portion of the world's population lacks regular access to fresh drinking water or adequate sanitation. Water-related diseases are a major burden in countries across the world. Water consumption patterns in many regions are no longer sustainable. The damaging environmental consequences of water practices are growing rapidly. And the complex and dynamic linkages between water and other key resources—especially food and energy—are inadequately understood. These factors suggest that even at current levels of global population, resource consumption, and economic activity, we may have already passed the threshold of water sustainability.

An obscenely large portion of the world's population lacks regular access to fresh drinking water or adequate sanitation.

A major report recently issued by the 2030 Water Resources Group (whose members include McKinsey & Company, the World Bank, and a consortium of business partners) estimated that, assuming average economic growth and no efficiency gains, the gap between global water demand and reliable supply could reach 40 percent over the next 20 years. As serious as this world supply-demand gap is, the study notes, the dislocations will be even more concentrated in developing regions that account for one-third of the global population, where the water deficit could rise to 50 percent.

It is thus inconceivable that, at this moment in history, no generally recognized "worth" has been established for water to help in its more efficient allocation. To the contrary, many current uses of water are skewed by historical and other legacy practices that perpetuate massive inefficiencies and unsustainable patterns.

The Missing Links

In addition, in the face of persistent population pressures and the higher consumption implicit in rapid economic development among large populations in the developing world, it is noteworthy that our understanding of resource linkages is so limited. Our failure to predict in the spring of 2008 a spike in food prices, a rise in energy prices, and serious droughts afflicting key regions of the world—all of which occurred simultaneously—reveals how little we know about these complex interrelationships.

Without significant, worldwide changes—including more innovation in and diffusion of water-related technologies; fundamental adjustments in consumption patterns; improvements in efficiencies; higher levels of public investment in water infrastructures; and an integrated approach to governance based on the complex relationships between water and food, water and economic development, and water and the environment—the global challenge of water resources could become even more severe.

Also, although global warming's potential effects on watersheds across the planet are still not precisely understood, there can be little doubt that climate change will in a number of regions generate serious dislocations in water supply. In a June 2008 technical paper, the Intergovernmental Panel on Climate Change (IPCC) concluded that "globally, the negative impacts of climate change on freshwater systems are expected to outweigh the benefits." It noted that "higher water temperatures and changes in extremes, including droughts and floods, are projected to affect water quality and exacerbate many forms of water pollution."

Climate change will in a number of regions generate serious dislocations in water supply.

As a result, we may soon be entering unknown territory when it comes to addressing the challenges of water in all their dimensions, including public health, economic development, gender equity, humanitarian crises, environmental degradation, and global security. The geopolitical consequences alone could be profound.

Daunting Trends

Although water covers almost three-quarters of the earth's surface, only a fraction of it is suitable for human consumption. According to the United Nations, of the water that humans consume, approximately 70 percent is used in agricultural production, 22 percent in industry, and 8 percent in domestic use. This consumption—critical as it is for human health, economic development, political and social stability, and security—is unequal, inefficient, and unsustainable.

Indeed, an estimated 884 million people worldwide do not have access to clean drinking water, and 2.5 billion lack adequate sanitation. A staggering 1.8 million people, 90 percent of them children, lose their lives each year as a result of diarrheal diseases resulting from unsafe drinking water and poor hygiene. More generally, the World Health Organization (WHO) estimates that inadequate water, sanitation, and hygiene are responsible for roughly half the malnutrition in the world.

In addition, we are witnessing irreparable damage to ecosystems across the globe. Aquifers are being drawn down faster than they can naturally be recharged. Some great lakes are mere fractions of what they once were.

And water pollution is affecting millions of people's lives. China typifies this problem. More than 75 percent of its urban river water is unsuitable for drinking or fishing, and 90 percent of its urban groundwater is contaminated. On the global scale, according to a recent UN report on world water development, every day we dump some 2 million tons of industrial waste and chemicals, human waste, and agricultural waste (fertilizers, pesticides, and pesticide residues) into our water supply.

Over the past century, as the world's population rose from 1.7 billion people in 1900 to 6.1 billion in 2000, global fresh water consumption increased six-fold—more than double the rate of population growth over the same period. The latest "medium" projections from the UN's population experts suggest that we are on the way to 8 billion people by the year 2025 and 9.15 billion by the middle of the century.

The contours of our predicament are clear-cut: A finite amount of water is available to a rapidly increasing number of people whose activities require more water than ever before. The UN Commission on Sustainable Development has indicated that we may need to double the amount of freshwater available today to meet demand at the middle of the century—after which time demand for water will increase by 50 percent with each additional generation.

Why is demand for water rising so rapidly? It goes beyond population pressures. According to a recent report from the UN Food and Agriculture Organization, the world will require 70 percent more food production over the next 40 years to meet growing per capita demand. This rising agricultural consumption necessarily translates into higher demand for water. By 2025, according to the water expert Sandra Postel, meeting projected global agricultural demand will require additional irrigation totaling some 2,000 cubic kilometers—roughly the equivalent of the annual flow of 24 Nile Rivers or 110 Colorado Rivers.

Consumption patterns aside, climate change will accelerate and intensify stress on water systems. According to the IPCC, in coming decades the frequency of extreme droughts will double while the average length of droughts will increase six times. This low water flow, combined with higher temperatures, not only will create devastating shortages. It will also increase pollution of fresh water by sediments, nutrients, pesticides, pathogens, and salts. On the other hand, in some regions, wet seasons will be more intense (but shorter). In underdeveloped communities that lack capture and storage capacity, water will run off and will be unavailable when it is needed in dry seasons, thus perpetuating the cycle of poverty.

Climatic and demographic trends indicate that the regions of the world with the highest population growth rates are precisely those that are already the "driest" and that are expected to experience water stress in the future. The Organization for Economic Cooperation and Development has suggested that the number of people in water-stressed countries—where governments encounter serious constraints on their ability to meet household, industrial, and agricultural water demands—could rise to nearly 4 billion by the year 2030.

The Geopolitical Dimension

If oil is the key geopolitical resource of today, water will be as important—if not more so—in the not-so-distant future. A profound mismatch exists between the distribution of the human population and the availability of fresh water. At the water-rich extreme of the spectrum is the Amazon region, which has an estimated 15 percent of global runoff and less than 1 percent of the world's people. South America as a whole has only 6 percent of the world's population but more than a quarter of the world's runoff.

At the other end of the spectrum is Asia. Home to 60 percent of the global population, it has a freshwater endowment estimated at less than 36 percent of the world total. It is hardly surprising that some water-stressed countries in the region have pursued agricultural trade mechanisms to gain access to more water—in the form of food. Recently, this has taken the form of so-called "land grabs," in which governments and state companies have invested in farmland overseas to meet their countries' food security needs. *The Economist* has estimated that, to date, some 50 million acres have been remotely purchased or leased under these arrangements in Africa and Asia.

Although freshwater management has historically represented a means of preventing and mitigating conflict between countries with shared water resources, the growing scarcity of water will likely generate new levels of tension at the local, national, and even international levels. Many countries with limited water availability also depend on shared water, which increases the risk of friction, social tensions, and conflict.

The Euphrates, Jordan, and Nile Rivers are obvious examples of places where frictions already have occurred. But approximately 40 percent of the world's population lives in more than 260 international river basins of major social and economic importance, and 13 of these basins are shared by five or more countries. Interstate tensions have already escalated and could easily intensify as increasing water scarcity raises the stakes.

Within countries as well, governments in water-stressed regions must effectively and transparently mediate the concerns and demands of various constituencies. The interests of urban and rural populations, agriculture and industry, and commercial and domestic sectors often conflict. If allocation issues are handled inappropriately, subnational disputes and unrest linked to water scarcity and poor water quality could arise, as they already have in numerous cases.

Addressing the Challenge

Considering the scope and gravity of these water challenges, responses by governments and nongovernmental organizations have fallen short of what is needed. Despite obvious signs that we overuse water, we continue to perpetuate gross inefficiencies. We continue to skew consumption on the basis of politically charged subsidies or other supports. And we continue to pursue patently unsustainable practices whose costs will grow more onerous over time.

The Colorado River system, for example, is being overdrawn. It supplies water to Las Vegas, Los Angeles, San Diego, and other growing communities in the American Southwest. If demand on this river system is not curtailed, there is a 50 percent chance that Lake Mead will be dry by 2021, according to experts from the Scripps Institution of Oceanography.

Despite constant reminders of future challenges, we continue to be paralyzed by short-term thinking and practices. What is especially striking about water is the extent to which the world's nations are unprepared to manage such a vital resource sustainably. Six key opportunities for solutions stand out.

First, the global community needs to do substantially more to address the lack of safe drinking water and sanitation. Donor countries, by targeting water resources, can simultaneously address issues associated with health, poverty reduction, and environmental stewardship, as well as stability and security concerns. It should be stressed in this regard that rates of return on investment in water development—financial, political, and geopolitical—are all positive. The WHO estimates that the global return on every dollar invested in water and sanitation programs is $4 and $9, respectively.

Consider, for example, how water problems affect the earning power of women. Typically in poor countries, women and girls are kept at home to care for sick family members inflicted with water-related diseases. They also spend hours each day walking to collect water for daily drinking, cooking, and washing. According to the United Nations Children's Fund, water and sanitation issues explain why more than half the girls in sub-Saharan Africa drop out of primary school.

Second, more rigorous analyses of sustainability could help relevant governments and authorities begin to address the conspicuous mismanagement of water resources in regions across the world. This would include reviewing public subsidies—for water-intensive farming, for example—and other supports that tend to increase rather than remove existing inefficiencies.

Priced to Sell

Third, specialists, scholars, practitioners, and policy makers need to make substantial progress in assigning to water a market value against which more sustainable consumption decisions and policies can be made. According to the American Water Works Association, for example, the average price of water in the United States is $1.50 per 1,000 gallons—or less than a single penny per gallon. Yet, when it comes to the personal consumption market, many Americans do not hesitate to pay prices for bottled water that are higher than what they pay at the pump for a gallon of gasoline. What is clear, both inside and outside the United States, is that mechanisms for pricing water on the basis of sustainability have yet to be identified.

Fourth, rapid advances in technology can and should have a discernible effect on both the supply and demand sides of the global water equation. The technology landscape is breathtaking—from desalination, membrane, and water-reuse technologies to a range of cheaper and more efficient point-of-use applications (such as drip irrigation and rainwater harvesting). It remains to be seen, however, whether the acquisition and use of such technologies can be accelerated and dispersed so that they can have an appreciable effect in offsetting aggregate downside trends.

From a public policy perspective, taxation and regulatory policies can create incentives for the development and dissemination of such technologies, and foreign assistance projects can promote their use in developing countries. Also, stronger links with the private sector would help policy makers improve their understanding of technical possibilities, and public-private partnerships can be effective mechanisms for distributing technologies in the field.

Fifth, although our understanding of the relationship between climate change and water will continue to be shaped by new evidence, it is important that we incorporate into our approach to climate change our existing understanding of water management and climate adaptation issues.

Sixth, the complex links among water, agriculture, and energy must be identified with greater precision. An enormous amount of work remains to be done if we are to appreciate these linkages in the global, basin, and local contexts.

In the final analysis, our capacity to address the constellation of challenges that relate to water access, sanitation, ecosystems, infrastructure, adoption of technologies, and the mobilization of resources will mean the difference between rapid economic development and continued poverty, between healthier populations and continued high exposure to water-related diseases, between a more stable world and intensifying geopolitical tensions.

Critical Thinking

1. In what way will the geopolitical patterns of water resources and consumption be different than the geopolitical patterns of oil resources and consumption?
2. Why does "an obscenely large portion of the world's population lack regular access to fresh water and sanitization?"
3. Refer to your map, and map out the "profound mismatch between the distribution of the human population and the availability of fresh water." Make some critical observations regarding that pattern.
4. How might climate change make the world's future water challenge even more challenging?
5. How might the water challenges of the industrialized world be different than the challenges facing "developing" nations?

Erik R. Peterson is senior vice president of the Center for Strategic and International Studies and director of its Global Strategy Institute. **Rachel A. Posner** is assistant director of the CSIS Global Water Futures project.

Article

Bangladesh's Climate Displacement Nightmare

While scientists and the international community endlessly debate and argue, millions of Bangladeshi citizens have already been displaced by climate change—for them the worst-case "nightmare" climate scenario is already real.

SCOTT LECKIE, ZEKE SIMPERINGHAM, AND JORDAN BAKKER

Climate displacement has arrived without mercy in Bangladesh. In Khulna district alone, some 60,000 Bangladeshi citizens have fled what has become permanent coastal flooding in the remote southwest of the country. With no option of returning home, and little access to new land thus far, these climate displaced persons (CDPs) are forced to survive on a 25 kilometre long, 2m high and 3–4 m wide embankment.

This desperate community in Dacope sub-district in Khulna has built rudimentary, makeshift shelters along the length of the levee that was originally designed to protect their now destroyed villages, land and homes. The levee failed, and all they now have are insecure and instable shelters perched precariously atop the embankment, surrounded by unruly water on both sides at high tide and at low tide by thousands of hectares of desolate muddy land that was once fertile paddy and farmland.

Living in this isolated and impoverished corner of Bangladesh, which borders on the famous Sundarban National Park, and completely segregated from political life in Dhaka (and the officials that could assist them in finding new land), the people of the delta see all too little hope or viable options for the future. Ninety-per cent of the CDPs are now without livelihoods, forced to live day by day from aid handouts and are unable to return to lives, land and homes that were completely obliterated by coastal erosion and storm surges. Nor do the displaced in Dacope see any solutions coming from the Government of Bangladesh any time soon, with officials seeming thus far resistant to suggestions that they may need to assist this and other climate-affected communities to relocate to safer areas and provide them with new land.

And as bad as things may be for the delta dwellers, this CDP community is only the tip of the displacement iceberg eating away at Bangladesh's land and populace. Comprehensive surveys carried out in 2010 by over 200 community-based organisations and coordinated by the remarkable efforts of the Association of Climate Refugees, found that a staggering 6.5 million citizens (1.3 million households) of Bangladesh have already been displaced by the effects of climate change.

Uniquely vulnerable to frequent and severe river, rainwater and tidal flooding, Bangladesh today has the sad distinction of being the world's most vulnerable country to climate displacement. While climate scientists, the international community and academics vigorously debate about the potential for climate change to affect future population displacement, the millions of Bangladeshi citizens already displaced by the effects of climate change are no longer simply waiting for solutions to their plight, and have begun to organise for climate justice and their basic human rights. For them the worst-case future climate scenarios have already arrived; for them the future is now.

Earth's Most Climate Vulnerable Communities

Bangladesh is a low lying, largely flat country with two-thirds of the country located less than 5m above sea level. Situated in the delta region of three of the world's largest rivers—with a combined annual discharge second only to that of the Amazon—it is no surprise that Bangladesh suffers from catastrophic floods every year. According to government statistics, 25 percent of Bangladesh is inundated every year and 60 percent of the country suffers from severe flooding every 4–5 years. What makes the situation so dire now is that the flooded land in the delta is seemingly gone for good. In Khulna, the flood will simply not recede.

And yet, this is far from the extent of climate vulnerability in Bangladesh. The country is also hit by a severe tropical cyclone on average once every three years. These storms form in the months before and after the monsoon season and intensify as they move over the warm waters of the Bay of Bengal. They are accompanied by winds of up to 150kph and can result in storm surges of up to several metres. As experienced by the 60,000 people crammed in miserable conditions on the embankments of Khulna, the results for housing, land, property and livelihoods are devastating.

Of the 160 million citizens of Bangladesh, it is the more than 50 million people who live in the most extreme poverty that are and will continue to be most affected by climate change. These are the people who are forced to live in remote, exposed and vulnerable locations—often on river islands and cyclone prone coastal regions—where the land is cheap but the risks are high. Of Bangladesh's 64 districts, 24 are already severely affected by growing numbers of climate displaced persons.

As sure as the effects of climate change are in devastating lives and communities in Bangladesh today, it is also clear that the devastation is only going to increase in the future. The Intergovernmental Panel on Climate Change (IPCC) predicts that floods, tropical cyclones and storm surges will all become more frequent and more severe in the future due to the effects of climate change. The IPCC also forecasts even higher flows in the rivers that flow into Bangladesh from India, Nepal, Bhutan and China—as a direct result of increasing monsoon rainfalls and the melting of the Himalayan glaciers. Sea level rise as a result of global warming will also result in even more severe coastal flooding in Bangladesh as well as saline intrusion into rivers across the entire southern regions of the country.

The Need for Solutions to Climate Displacement

While the full impact of future climate change is notoriously difficult to accurately predict, it is clear that the 6.5 million climate displaced people in Bangladesh in January 2011 will be joined by many millions more in the future. The effects on communities and the devastation of lands and homes will only become more intense. It is clear that the future is not bright for the people of Bangladesh and equally that land-based solutions are required now.

As poor as they may be, under human rights law, these impoverished and marginalised communities are also the people most in need of having their housing, land and property rights respected, protected and fulfilled. Combined efforts to tackle the challenges of climate displacement with a renewed commitment to HLP rights just might hold out the best hope that CDP's will a secured a future worth living. And this is precisely what the joint Bangladesh HLP Initiative of Displacement Solutions and the Association of Climate Refugees intends to do.

Despite the considerable efforts of the Bangladeshi Government to combat and address the effects of climate change—including the adoption of the 2005 Bangladesh National Adaptation Programme of Action and the 2009 Bangladesh Climate Change Strategy and Action Plan—the Government has yet to propose clear or practical land-based solutions for addressing the plight of Bangladesh's current and future climate displaced people.

Though one of the pillars of the Bangladesh Climate Change Action plan is to "ensure that the poorest and most vulnerable in society are protected from climate change," it is clear that the climate displaced communities living on the embankment in Khulna province and indeed the many millions more across Bangladesh, have thus far received all too little protection, safe housing, or access to basic services from the Government.

Enter the Association for Climate Refugees

Some 200 community-based NGOs throughout the country have recently banded together to form the Association of Climate Refugees (ACR) and to actively find solutions for the citizens of Bangladesh who have already been displaced by climate change. ACR's founder and director, Muhammad Abu Musa, has chosen for himself one of the world's more difficult tasks. For this jolly and remarkably optimistic 52 year-old Bangladeshi activist has dedicated his life in recent years towards the gargantuan goal of finding permanent and sustainable residential solutions to the millions of climate displaced people across Bangladesh. If predictions by the IPCC and others are correct, the sprightly Abu Musa will need to find new homes for a further 30 million displaced people in the coming years.

The ACR is focusing on capacity building and empowerment at the local level—directly among the climate affected communities themselves. ACR relies on partner organisations—grassroots activists in 24 of the countries 64 districts, often working out of a single room in the middle of affected communities, to promptly relay first hand information about any developments in climate affected communities.

Abu Musa believes that it is the affected communities themselves who have the best knowledge and resources for self-protection and adaptation. He also strongly believes that having local communities own the problem is the only way for the Government of Bangladesh to listen to their plight—"If we showed up as an NGO describing this problem, the Government door would be immediately closed, it is essential that the local communities take action themselves," he says with conviction.

The ACR plans to continue its work of monitoring climate displacement across Bangladesh and in the near future to implement a system of both emergency and permanent relocation out of climate vulnerable locations together with their international partners, in particular Displacement Solutions. ACR is aware that some CDPs have relocated to the distant Chittagong Hill Tracts (some 600 kms from Khulna), and in January 2011, ACR acquired a small land plot of 1.65 acres in Kamarkhola Union in Khulna district, donated by a local landowner sympathetic to ACR's aims.

The land represents the first such acquisition of land for climate affected communities, and will be transformed into a community land trust aptly named "Community Land Trust for Climate Displacement Solutions in Bangladesh." This symbolic gesture, which will provide land solutions for some twenty families, will surely not resolve climate displacement in the country, but will hopefully inspire other landowners to donate larger pieces of unused land to assist in finding solutions to the dismal displaced population of Bangladesh.

Abu Musa and many others believe that the climate displacement solution for Bangladesh will frequently lie in relocation to safer areas, and not solely on building higher and higher embankment walls. Many of the 60,000 people on the embankment in Khulna province expect that in the next monsoon season the entire embankment will be under water and that they will have to move again. Accessing new and viable land will be the secret to ACR's success.

What Will the Future Hold?

The work of ACR is admirable and essential, but alone it is unlikely to be able to find land-based solutions for the climate-displaced people of Bangladesh. Similar to popular movements in other climate affected countries such as Tulele Peisa in Papua New Guinea, path breaking groups like ACR need to be able to work with much more than their currently meagre, shoestring budget. Funds from the newly established Green Fund under the Cancun Adaptation Framework (meant to reach 100 billion USD in coming years) need to be earmarked for groups such as ACR and Tulele Peisa to enable them to resolve the displacement caused by climate change.

It is essential for these groups and governments to band together to develop and clarify land-based solutions as rapidly as possible, before the already drastic situation becomes exponentially worse as the effects of climate change become more severe and more frequent.

Importantly, it is increasingly clear that the imperative to resolve climate displacement in Bangladesh is not only a matter of human dignity and human rights, but also one of security. The marginalised communities most affected by climate change may also be the most susceptible to influence by extremists. As a country with a large Muslim population, thus far largely spared the fundamentalist-driven ravages now so commonplace in Pakistan and elsewhere, some analysts have noted that the most disenfranchised and affected communities could turn to Islamic militantism—and transform Bangladesh into another breeding ground for violent fundamentalism.

Unless climate displaced persons are treated as the rights-holders that they actually already are, and enabled to access new housing, land and property, this looming security threat may become ever more real.

The international community now has an opportunity to address the immediate and future climate displacement crisis in Bangladesh. The world needs to capture the momentum of recent positive developments at the 2010 United Nations Climate Change Conference held in Cancun, where national, regional and international coordination and cooperation was encouraged in implementing planned relocation of climate displaced communities and where it was stated that human rights should be fully respected in all climate change related actions.

States across the globe should take heed of the climate displacement nightmare that is unfolding in Bangladesh, and at the same time focus on the emerging dream of durable land solutions for all. Land-based solutions to climate displacement can and should be identified now, and excellent community led groups—such as the Association for Climate Refugees—need to be sufficiently well resourced to be able to implement emergency and permanent relocation strategies. The Government of Bangladesh should also be encouraged—through bilateral, regional and international advocacy—to do more to respect the human rights of all people in Bangladesh, including the 6.5 million people already displaced by climate change.

The development of a National Plan to Resolve Climate Displacement, prepared jointly with civil society groups such as ACR, could go a long way to ensure a brighter future for the displaced millions in this country. The situation in Bangladesh is as clear a demonstration to the world as any that contrary to what many people still think, climate displacement is not a problem for the future—for 2020, or 2030 or 2050—it is a problem now, and one that urgently requires solutions.

Critical Thinking

1. What makes Bangladesh particularly vulnerable to the effects of climate change?
2. What are the obstacles to dealing with climate displacement in Bangladesh?
3. How might this problem become a security concern?
4. What steps are needed to address this problem?

Article

Prepared by: Robert J. Griffiths, *University of North Carolina at Greensboro*

Climate Change and Food Security

"The dual forces of population growth and climate change will exacerbate pressures on land use, water access, and food security."

BRUCE A. MCCARL, MARIO A. FERNANDEZ, JASON P. H. JONES, MARIA WLODARZ

Learning Outcomes

After reading this article, you will be able to:

- Recognize the impact of climate change on the variability of crop and livestock yields.
- Describe the policies necessary to address the impact of climate change on agricultural production.

Of the 10 warmest years in recorded history, 9 have appeared in the past 10 years, and all since 1998. Furthermore, 2012, the 9th-warmest year in history, was the 36th year in a row above the twentieth century average. Simultaneously, precipitation patterns are changing, with rainfall generally becoming more concentrated. Not surprisingly, the effects on agriculture from such climate change are proving significant and worldwide, including in the United States. The US National Oceanic and Atmospheric Administration estimated, for instance, that climate change made a 2011 drought in the American Southwest 20 times more likely to occur.

At the same time, the role of agriculture, a sector highly vulnerable to climate change, is changing globally. Not only does farming remain vital for food and fiber supplies; it is also growing in importance as a source of feedstock for energy production. It is frequendy mentioned, too, as a possible source of offsets to the greenhouse gas emissions that contribute to global warming.

Climate trends, in short, raise critical questions for the future of agriculture. What influence is climate change having on agricultural yields? Does it imply that farming might be less able to supply future food needs, especially given the likely demands from a growing population and from populations with growing income? And what might nations do to lessen the disruptive influence of climate change on agriculture?

To help put these questions in perspective, it is worth mentioning a couple of climate changes fundamental characteristics. First, the preponderance of evidence indicates that it is likely to make conditions hotter and overall wetter; but with a more variable set of weather patterns. Second, climate change has not been observed to, nor is it projected to, have geographically uniform effects. In particular, while most every place is expected to be hotter with more variable conditions, some regions are likely to be drier while others will be wetter.

The Culprits

A changing climate certainly alters agricultural productivity. Ultimately, conditions involving extreme heat or extreme cold, as well as extreme wetness or extreme dryness, are unsuitable for raising crops. Crops fare best within narrow temperature and precipitation bands. Fortunately, temperature and precipitation conditions vary geographically. Conditions near the poles are generally too cold, while those near the equator can be too hot. Not all crops need the same ranges: Wheat, for example, fares best under comparatively colder conditions, and cotton or rice under hotter ones, while corn and soybeans need moderate conditions. This means a warmer climate will benefit certain crops and regions but harm others. It will also alter the geographic distribution of crop production, causing current crop ranges to move generally poleward.

Carbon dioxide is a related factor that will also affect agriculture. Considerable scientific evidence indicates that today's climate change is being driven in large part by increasing atmospheric greenhouse gas concentrations. Increases in carbon dioxide, the most abundant of greenhouse gases, stimulates the growth of certain classes of crops (so-called C3 crops such as rice, wheat, barley, oats, soybeans, potatoes, and most fruits), while the growth of others (so-called C4 crops like corn, sugarcane, sorghum, millet, and some grasses) is not greatly stimulated, but does better under drought conditions. Carbon dioxide effects on production are not strictly positive: Weed competition, for instance, also will be stimulated. However, carbon dioxide effects could partially offset yield losses that will occur solely based on temperature and precipitation changes.

And these are far from the only climate change factors with important effects on agriculture. Sea-level rise caused by ice melt and thermal expansion of the ocean could inundate substantial areas of agricultural land, particularly in low-lying producing countries such as Egypt, Bangladesh, India, and

Vietnam. Pest populations are likely to be affected, and significant shifts have already been observed in pest extent and incidence. Observations show that weed and pest damages are greater in warmer areas, portending an expanding region of damage as the climate warms. Decreased frequency of extreme cold spells can also stimulate pest spread, as has been observed in North American forests with the wide spread of the destructive pine bark beetle.

Climatic extreme events—for example, droughts, floods, heatwaves, and extreme cold—are projected to increase, and these can lead to lower, less stable agricultural yields, while also inducing greater incidence of famine and shifts in land use away from cropping. The Intergovernmental Panel on Climate Change (IPCC) recently published a report on extreme events suggesting that droughts may intensify in many parts of the world, including North and South America, Central Europe, and Africa. This in turn could reduce production and cause domestic and international food prices to increase, as was seen during 2012. Countries whose inhabitants already spend a large portion of their income on food will be most severely affected, resulting in increased malnourishment and poverty.

The IPCC report on weather extremes indicates the likelihood of more heat waves, which would stress water availability, crop production, and livestock production. They could as well decrease livestock disease resilience. The IPCC also provides evidence of an increase in the proportion of heavy rainfall events, relative to total rainfall. This would increase soil and fertilizer runoff, in turn causing water pollution and algae blooms.

Climate variation does not arise from a single source. Earth's climate has always exhibited strong natural variability on a seasonal, annual, and multiyear basis. Such variation originates from interactions within and among the atmosphere, ocean, land, sea ice, and glaciers, among other factors. One widely discussed cause of between-year climate variability is the El Niño Southern Oscillation (ENSO). Arising from interactions between the ocean and the atmosphere, ENSO causes shifts in the jet steam with effects on climate over large areas. For example, in Texas the occurrence of the La Niña phase of ENSO has been associated with the driest years in recorded history, including the record drought in 2011.

Many other major ocean-atmosphere interactions have been identified as contributing factors as well, including longer-term phenomena like the so-called North Atlantic Oscillation. Interestingly, some analysts have projected interaction between climatic change forces and the ocean phenomena with, for example, extreme ENSO events becoming more common and stronger. The jury is still out on whether this is likely to happen.

Crop and Livestock Yields

Certainly there is reason for concern given climate change effects and natural variability coupled with agriculture's enormous dependence on climate. And this concern is borne out in current agricultural production trends.

Recent years have witnessed substantial variability in agricultural yields. Consider data from the United States. During the 2011 drought in the Southwest, nearly 40 percent of the cotton crop was abandoned, with yields judged insufficient to merit harvest. Cattle were widely sold off. Irrigators in many areas found that they could not pump enough water to compensate for the extremely dry conditions. The net loss was estimated at $7.4 billion. Then came a 2012 drought in America's Midwest, resulting in a corn crop estimated to be 25 percent smaller than expected, and a near-doubling of corn prices.

Increasing variability in yields is also evident in developing countries. In subsistence areas, dry conditions have led to widespread famine in some instances, while extremely wet and favorable conditions can cause an oversupply in markets not capable of moving the commodities, resulting in a collapse in prices.

Some of climate change's damaging effects on agricultural yields are offset by technological progress. Indeed, increases in yield stimulated by research investment and technology dissemination have been a key feature of agriculture for many years. In some areas of the world, food supply has grown faster than the population—leading to declining real prices and enhancing nations' ability to export more food. This also has allowed farmers to devote increasing amounts of land to bioenergy resources.

However, recent years have seen an overall decline in rates of yield growth. In the United States, corn yield growth until the 1970s exceeded 3 percent per year; now it is below 1.7 percent. Many complex factors have led to this result, including reductions in yield-enhancing investment levels. But certainly climate change has been a factor, and will be one in the future. This portends lower future growth in yields relative to demand growth, and perhaps may restrict agriculture's ability to meet the multiple demands now placed upon it. It also calls for larger levels of investment in productivity-increasing factors like research and technology dissemination.

The agricultural impacts of climate change and climate variation show considerable geographic differences, both within and across regions, due to differing soil characteristics, regional climates, and socioeconomic conditions. For example, according to projections reviewed in IPCC reports, rain-fed agricultural production in sub-Saharan Africa will decline by up to 50 percent by 2020. Maize production in Africa and Latin America is projected to fall by 10 percent to 20 percent by 2050. Yet the maize yield on China's Loess Plateau is projected to increase by around 60 percent during 2070–99. Wheat yields in southern Australia are projected to drop by 13.5 percent to 32 percent by 2050, yet over the same period winter wheat production in southern Sweden will increase by 10 percent to 20 percent.

In areas of Illinois and Indiana, due to an increase in daily maximum temperatures, some analysts project long-season maize yields will decline by 10 percent to 50 percent between 2030 and 2095. However, maize yields in the Great Plains area are projected to increase 25 percent by 2030 and 36 percent by 2095. A warming of 9 degrees to 11 degrees Fahrenheit by 2050 would cause a projected 10 percent decline in livestock yields, on average, in cow and calf and dairy operations in the Appalachian region, the Southeast (including the Mississippi Delta), and the southern plains.

Simultaneously, water is expected to become a growing issue. IPCC projections indicate that water availability within some dry regions at mid-latitudes and in the dry tropics will experience a reduction of 10 percent to 30 percent by 2050. The projections also show that, at higher latitudes and in some wet tropical areas, water supplies will increase by 10 percent to 40 percent over the same period. Also, the portion of river basins under severe water stress is expected to expand, with the ability to withdraw water either stabilizing or declining in 41 percent of global river basins. On the one hand, such impacts are expected to be more prevalent in developing countries than in industrialized ones. On the other hand, warming may well help in regions closer to the poles by limiting cold stress, even as it raises the heat stress in regions closer to the equator.

As already hot regions grow hotter, cows and pigs will not eat as much; the heat suppresses their appetites. This will negatively affect their growth performance. Additionally, evidence suggests that higher average temperatures cause lower birth rates and reduced milk and wool production. A study by the US Department of Agriculture (USDA) estimates that additional stress from heat will cause the beef industry to lose $370 million per year. This, coupled with altered feed availability, could cause large pole-ward shifts in regions of livestock production.

850 million of the earth's inhabitants lack access to a secure food supply.

Forage properties are also at issue. Under hotter conditions in already hot areas, the quality of forage deteriorates and its protein content worsens. Also, grass and hay are projected to grow at a slower pace; thus livestock stocking rates per unit of land area will go down.

Livestock diseases and pests are projected to become more prevalent. For example, higher temperatures have been found to increase the probability of avian influenza outbreaks, raising threats to poultry as well as human populations. In Niger, an invasion of desert locusts in 2005–06 caused massive damage to pasture lands and was followed by an extreme food crisis, with around 4 million people facing chronic famine.

Collectively, the water and agricultural implications of climate change will add to the developmental challenges of ensuring food security and reducing poverty.

Adapt and Mitigate

The 2007 IPCC report identifies two basic forms of actions for addressing the impact of climate change on agriculture. First, society can alter agricultural production processes to accommodate the altered climate. Second, society can act to reduce greenhouse gas emissions in an effort to mitigate (or limit). the extent of future climate change, with farming playing a role in this effort. Climate change likely will affect agriculture negatively where societies do not find ways to adapt.

To prepare for changing climate conditions, policy makers require a clear picture of the risks that their country or region will face in the future. The extent of these risks is generally uncertain. Traditionally we have used historical climate behavior as a starting point for predictions. That is, we typically assumed that any climatic cycles or phenomena that occurred in the past will likely recur (for example, the 100-year flood). This was a reasonable approach in earlier times, but in a future with climate change the repeatability of the past is not likely to hold.

Climate change alters the variability of droughts, heat waves, and floods. Not only will it affect future average crop and livestock yields; it will also make more uncertain the year-to-year variations in production. Thus, it will not be appropriate to assume that, for example, an observed flood or drought of a particular severity that occurred once in the past hundred years will occur with such frequency in the future.

Agriculture can be adapted to climate change by altering the management and location of production. Indeed, adaptation is not a new concept in agriculture. Producers in any region are faced with local conditions in terms of climate, pests, water availability, demand, land suitability, environmental regulation, and market competition. In turn, they choose an appropriate mix of crops, livestock, and management techniques to accommodate those conditions. As we have noted, for instance, areas where rice and cotton are grown are generally hotter than areas where wheat grows. As climate heats up, relocation of negatively affected crops toward the poles is an effective adaptation.

At the same time, selection of animal, crop, and forage species or breeds that are more resistant to heat and drought might help, along with the provision of irrigation and shade for animals. These possibilities will aid agricultures adaptation, but likely will not alleviate difficulties in particularly vulnerable regions. In these regions a lack of resources such as available capital producer education and knowledge, and available information, together with the infeasibility of certain actions, might preclude full adaptation, leaving residual damages from climate change.

In general, adaptations can be private and autonomous or public in nature. Producers often undertake adaptations autonomously. For example warmer conditions historically have caused crop shifts. In the United States, the geographic center of corn and soybean production in 1990 showed a northwestern shift of approximately 120 miles, in comparison with production locations in the early 1900s. More recent data show a further northwestern shift of more than 75 miles since 1990.

Policy Strategies

Public adaptations, on the other hand, encompass actions that are beyond the capabilities of individuals, or are far too costly for individuals to invest in, or once developed are not the kind of practices that an individual can patent and be paid for by other users. Public adaptations range from developing heat-resistant crop and livestock varieties, to disseminating climate-forecasting information to populations that need the knowledge in order to adapt.

A warmer climate will benefit certain crops and regions but harm others.

For one example, the US National Aeronautics and Space Administration, the National Oceanic and Atmospheric Administration, and the US Geological Survey have created a famine early-warning system using satellite information on soil moisture levels and crop health. The system is designed to help farmers adapt to projected unfavorable climate change and to lower the cost of extreme events.

Publicly supported adaptations can also involve the development of institutions such as financial systems that reduce farmers, exposure to risk, or the implementation of a freer trade policy that more readily provides food to areas where climate change reduces production. However, in this regard there is a serious risk of public underinvestment. The World Bank estimates a current need for between $9 billion and $40 billion in annual climate change adaptation funding. The United Nations' Food and Agriculture Organization (FAO) indicates that in 2011, some $244 million was dispersed to all countries in total.

Agricultural damages from climate change impacts are expected to be greatest among countries with the least ability to adapt, primarily poor countries. When such nations face a prolonged drought or multiyear crop failures, their strained food supply could cause a collapse of rural production, large-scale out-migration, social unrest, and famine. The severity of impact is related to the limited human and physical resources available for investments in technological knowledge, human capital, water and food storage, processing, and distribution.

What's at Stake

There is increasing evidence that the welfare of current and future generations will depend heavily not only on atmospheric greenhouse gas concentration levels, but also on the actions taken to stop and reverse greenhouse gas accumulation. In 2012 carbon dioxide levels in the atmosphere were measured to be more than 40 percent higher than pre-industrial levels. Agriculture itself is the source of between 50 percent and 70 percent of methane and nitrous oxide emissions, and atmospheric concentrations of these greenhouse gases also have increased significantly.

Agriculture can play a role in reducing atmospheric greenhouse gases by increasing carbon storage (sequestration), increasing tree planting, easing tillage, converting croplands to grasslands, or otherwise managing to increase soil organic content. Agriculture can also help avoid emissions by reducing fossil fuel use, altering nitrogen fertilization practices, better managing ruminant livestock and manure, and reducing rice methane emissions, among other means. Finally, agriculture can provide substitute products that can be used in place of fossil-fuel-intensive products. For example, biomass-based feedstocks can be substituted for liquid energy or electricity production, and new building materials can replace steel and concrete.

In considering adaptation and mitigation, one must be cognizant of the fact that land use for some environmentally adaptive alternatives can come into competition with land use for the food supply. The recent corn ethanol boom in the United States is an important example: An expansion of ethanol consumption from roughly 6 percent to nearly 40 percent of the US corn crop between 2002 and 2012 has, coupled with other factors, led to increased land use, diverted production, higher food prices, and some degree of increased price instability.

Rising food prices are not the only problem caused by expanded mitigation activity. Increased biomass production and utilization (for example, removal of corn residues from fields) cause increases in pesticide use, ground water depletion, soil erosion, and biodiversity loss. Furthermore, the rise in commodity prices can induce expansions in domestic and international agricultural land use, possibly leading to greater rates of deforestation and losses in associated carbon sequestration.

FAO figures show that the world's agricultural production has more than doubled in the past 50 years, and in developing countries it has more than tripled. The amount of available food has grown steadily, allowing the fulfillment of basic nutritional requirements for an increasing share of a growing global population. In part, advances in farmers management skills, fertilizers and pesticides, and irrigation supply have contributed to increasing crop productivity in formerly famine-prone areas, particularly in Africa.

Still, the USDA estimates that, 850 million of the earth's inhabitants currently lack access to a secure food supply. Oxfam, an international organization for famine relief, recently projected a doubling of prices for the world's staple food products over the next 20 years, with half of the increase attributed to climate change. This would likely result in major food security issues, particularly in areas of Africa, India, and Southeast Asia.

Population growth also contributes to the problem. By 2050 the world is projected to have 3.3 billion more mouths to feed. The challenge is feeding them while also adapting to or mitigating climate change. The dual forces of population growth and climate change will exacerbate pressures on land use, water access, and food security.

It is likely that the impacts of climate change on agriculture will affect everyone. However, the degree of impact will vary depending on how or whether one's society chooses to adapt, and how or whether we act on a national and global basis to limit the extent of future impacts by mitigating atmospheric greenhouse gas concentrations. Both adaptation and mitigation require actions and investments that will compete with each other and with conventional production and consumption. Food security in some regions is certainly at stake.

Critical Thinking

1. How does climate change affect crop and livestock yields?
2. What factors affect the ability to adapt agriculture to changing climate patterns?
3. How are the countries least able to adapt likely to be affected by climate change?

Create Central

www.mhhe.com/createcentral

Internet References

Earth Pledge Foundation
www.earthpledge.org

EnviroLink
http://envirolink.org

Greenpeace
www.greenpeace.org

Linkages on Environmental Issues and Development
www.iisd.ca/linkages

Population Action International
www.populationaction.org

World Health Organization (WHO)
www.who.ch

The Worldwatch Institute
www.worldwatch.org

Bruce A. McCarl, *a professor of agricultural economics at Texas A&M University, has contributed to the work of the Intergovernmental Panel on Climate Change.* Mario A. Fernandez, Jason P. H. Jones, *and* Marta Wlodarz *are graduate students at Texas A&M.*

Article

The New Geopolitics of Food

From the Middle East to Madagascar, high prices are spawning land grabs and ousting dictators. Welcome to the 21st-century food wars.

LESTER R. BROWN

In the United States, when world wheat prices rise by 75 percent, as they have over the last year, it means the difference between a $2 loaf of bread and a loaf costing maybe $2.10. If, however, you live in New Delhi, those sky-rocketing costs really matter: A doubling in the world price of wheat actually means that the wheat you carry home from the market to hand-grind into flour for chapatis costs twice as much. And the same is true with rice. If the world price of rice doubles, so does the price of rice in your neighborhood market in Jakarta. And so does the cost of the bowl of boiled rice on an Indonesian family's dinner table.

Welcome to the new food economics of 2011: Prices are climbing, but the impact is not at all being felt equally. For Americans, who spend less than one-tenth of their income in the supermarket, the soaring food prices we've seen so far this year are an annoyance, not a calamity. But for the planet's poorest 2 billion people, who spend 50 to 70 percent of their income on food, these soaring prices may mean going from two meals a day to one. Those who are barely hanging on to the lower rungs of the global economic ladder risk losing their grip entirely. This can contribute—and it has—to revolutions and upheaval.

Already in 2011, the U.N. Food Price Index has eclipsed its previous all-time global high; as of March it had climbed for eight consecutive months. With this year's harvest predicted to fall short, with governments in the Middle East and Africa teetering as a result of the price spikes, and with anxious markets sustaining one shock after another, food has quickly become the hidden driver of world politics. And crises like these are going to become increasingly common. The new geopolitics of food looks a whole lot more volatile—and a whole lot more contentious—than it used to. Scarcity is the new norm.

Until recently, sudden price surges just didn't matter as much, as they were quickly followed by a return to the relatively low food prices that helped shape the political stability of the late 20th century across much of the globe. But now both the causes and consequences are ominously different.

In many ways, this is a resumption of the 2007–2008 food crisis, which subsided not because the world somehow came together to solve its grain crunch once and for all, but because the Great Recession tempered growth in demand even as favorable weather helped farmers produce the largest grain harvest on record. Historically, price spikes tended to be almost exclusively driven by unusual weather—a monsoon failure in India, a drought in the former Soviet Union, a heat wave in the U.S. Midwest. Such events were always disruptive, but thankfully infrequent. Unfortunately, today's price hikes are driven by trends that are both elevating demand and making it more difficult to increase production: among them, a rapidly expanding population, crop-withering temperature increases, and irrigation wells running dry. Each night, there are 219,000 additional people to feed at the global dinner table.

More alarming still, the world is losing its ability to soften the effect of shortages. In response to previous price surges, the United States, the world's largest grain producer, was effectively able to steer the world away from potential catastrophe. From the mid-20th century until 1995, the United States had either grain surpluses or idle cropland that could be planted to rescue countries in trouble. When the Indian monsoon failed in 1965, for example, President Lyndon Johnson's administration shipped one-fifth of the U.S. wheat crop to India, successfully staving off famine. We can't do that anymore; the safety cushion is gone.

That's why the food crisis of 2011 is for real, and why it may bring with it yet more bread riots cum political revolutions. What if the upheavals that greeted dictators Zine el-Abidine Ben Ali in Tunisia, Hosni Mubarak in Egypt, and Muammar al-Qaddafi in Libya (a country that imports 90 percent of its grain) are not the end of the story, but the beginning of it? Get ready, farmers and foreign ministers alike, for a new era in which world food scarcity increasingly shapes global politics.

The doubling of world grain prices since early 2007 has been driven primarily by two factors: accelerating growth in demand and the increasing difficulty of rapidly expanding production. The result is a world that looks strikingly different from the bountiful global grain economy of the last century. What will the geopolitics of food look like in a new era dominated by scarcity? Even at this early stage, we can see at least the broad outlines of the emerging food economy.

On the demand side, farmers now face clear sources of increasing pressure. The first is population growth. Each year the world's farmers must feed 80 million additional people, nearly all of them in developing countries. The world's population has nearly doubled since 1970 and is headed toward 9 billion by midcentury. Some 3 billion people, meanwhile, are also trying to move up the food chain, consuming more meat, milk, and eggs. As more families in China and elsewhere enter the middle class, they expect to eat better. But as global consumption of grain-intensive livestock products climbs, so does the demand for the extra corn and soybeans needed to feed all that livestock. (Grain consumption per person in the United States, for example, is four times that in India, where little grain is converted into animal protein. For now.)

At the same time, the United States, which once was able to act as a global buffer of sorts against poor harvests elsewhere, is now converting massive quantities of grain into fuel for cars, even as world grain consumption, which is already up to roughly 2.2 billion metric tons per year, is growing at an accelerating rate. A decade ago, the growth in consumption was 20 million tons per year. More recently it has risen by 40 million tons every year. But the rate at which the United States is converting grain into ethanol has grown even faster. In 2010, the United States harvested nearly 400 million tons of grain, of which 126 million tons went to ethanol fuel distilleries (up from 16 million tons in 2000). This massive capacity to convert grain into fuel means that the price of grain is now tied to the price of oil. So if oil goes to $150 per barrel or more, the price of grain will follow it upward as it becomes ever more profitable to convert grain into oil substitutes. And it's not just a U.S. phenomenon: Brazil, which distills ethanol from sugar cane, ranks second in production after the United States, while the European Union's goal of getting 10 percent of its transport energy from renewables, mostly biofuels, by 2020 is also diverting land from food crops.

This is not merely a story about the booming demand for food. Everything from falling water tables to eroding soils and the consequences of global warming means that the world's food supply is unlikely to keep up with our collectively growing appetites. Take climate change: The rule of thumb among crop ecologists is that for every 1 degree Celsius rise in temperature above the growing season optimum, farmers can expect a 10 percent decline in grain yields. This relationship was borne out all too dramatically during the 2010 heat wave in Russia, which reduced the country's grain harvest by nearly 40 percent.

While temperatures are rising, water tables are falling as farmers overpump for irrigation. This artificially inflates food production in the short run, creating a food bubble that bursts when aquifers are depleted and pumping is necessarily reduced to the rate of recharge. In arid Saudi Arabia, irrigation had surprisingly enabled the country to be self-sufficient in wheat for more than 20 years; now, wheat production is collapsing because the non-replenishable aquifer the country uses for irrigation is largely depleted. The Saudis soon will be importing all their grain.

Saudi Arabia is only one of some 18 countries with water-based food bubbles. All together, more than half the world's people live in countries where water tables are falling. The politically troubled Arab Middle East is the first geographic region where grain production has peaked and begun to decline because of water shortages, even as populations continue to grow. Grain production is already going down in Syria and Iraq and may soon decline in Yemen. But the largest food bubbles are in India and China. In India, where farmers have drilled some 20 million irrigation wells, water tables are falling and the wells are starting to go dry. The World Bank reports that 175 million Indians are being fed with grain produced by overpumping. In China, overpumping is concentrated in the North China Plain, which produces half of China's wheat and a third of its corn. An estimated 130 million Chinese are currently fed by overpumping. How will these countries make up for the inevitable shortfalls when the aquifers are depleted?

Even as we are running our wells dry, we are also mismanaging our soils, creating new deserts. Soil erosion as a result of overplowing and land mismanagement is undermining the productivity of one-third of the world's cropland. How severe is it? Look at satellite images showing two huge new dust bowls: one stretching across northern and western China and western Mongolia; the other across central Africa. Wang Tao, a leading Chinese desert scholar, reports that each year some 1,400 square miles of land in northern China turn to desert. In Mongolia and Lesotho, grain harvests have shrunk by half or more over the last few decades. North Korea and Haiti are also suffering from heavy soil losses; both countries face famine if they lose international food aid. Civilization can survive the loss of its oil reserves, but it cannot survive the loss of its soil reserves.

Beyond the changes in the environment that make it ever harder to meet human demand, there's an important intangible factor to consider: Over the last half-century or so, we have come to take agricultural progress for granted. Decade after decade, advancing technology underpinned steady gains in raising land productivity. Indeed, world grain yield per acre has tripled since 1950. But now that era is coming to an end in some of the more agriculturally advanced countries, where farmers are already using all available technologies to raise yields. In effect, the farmers have caught up with the scientists. After climbing for a century, rice yield per acre in Japan has not risen at all for 16 years. In China, yields may level off soon. Just those two countries alone account for one-third of the world's rice harvest. Meanwhile, wheat yields have plateaued in Britain, France, and Germany—Western Europe's three largest wheat producers.

In this era of tightening world food supplies, the ability to grow food is fast becoming a new form of geopolitical leverage, and countries are scrambling to secure their own parochial interests at the expense of the common good.

The first signs of trouble came in 2007, when farmers began having difficulty keeping up with the growth in global demand for grain. Grain and soybean prices started to climb, tripling by mid-2008. In response, many exporting countries tried to control the rise of domestic food prices by restricting exports. Among them were Russia and Argentina, two leading wheat exporters. Vietnam, the No. 2 rice exporter, banned exports entirely for several months in early 2008. So did several other smaller exporters of grain.

With exporting countries restricting exports in 2007 and 2008, importing countries panicked. No longer able to rely on the market to supply the grain they needed, several countries took the novel step of trying to negotiate long-term grain-supply agreements with exporting countries. The Philippines, for instance, negotiated a three-year agreement with Vietnam for 1.5 million tons of rice per year. A delegation of Yemenis traveled to Australia with a similar goal in mind, but had no luck. In a seller's market, exporters were reluctant to make long-term commitments.

Fearing they might not be able to buy needed grain from the market, some of the more affluent countries, led by Saudi Arabia, South Korea, and China, took the unusual step in 2008 of buying or leasing land in other countries on which to grow grain for themselves. Most of these land acquisitions are in Africa, where some governments lease cropland for less than $1 per acre per year. Among the principal destinations were Ethiopia and Sudan, countries where millions of people are being sustained with food from the U.N. World Food Program. That the governments of these two countries are willing to sell land to foreign interests when their own people are hungry is a sad commentary on their leadership.

By the end of 2009, hundreds of land acquisition deals had been negotiated, some of them exceeding a million acres. A 2010 World Bank analysis of these "land grabs" reported that a total of nearly 140 million acres were involved—an area that exceeds the cropland devoted to corn and wheat combined in the United States. Such acquisitions also typically involve water rights, meaning that land grabs potentially affect all downstream countries as well. Any water extracted from the upper Nile River basin to irrigate crops in Ethiopia or Sudan, for instance, will now not reach Egypt, upending the delicate water politics of the Nile by adding new countries with which Egypt must negotiate.

The potential for conflict—and not just over water—is high. Many of the land deals have been made in secret, and in most cases, the land involved was already in use by villagers when it was sold or leased. Often those already farming the land were neither consulted about nor even informed of the new arrangements. And because there typically are no formal land titles in many developing-country villages, the farmers who lost their land have had little backing to bring their cases to court. Reporter John Vidal, writing in Britain's *Observer,* quotes Nyikaw Ochalla from Ethiopia's Gambella region: "The foreign companies are arriving in large numbers, depriving people of land they have used for centuries. There is no consultation with the indigenous population. The deals are done secretly. The only thing the local people see is people coming with lots of tractors to invade their lands."

Local hostility toward such land grabs is the rule, not the exception. In 2007, as food prices were starting to rise, China signed an agreement with the Philippines to lease 2.5 million acres of land slated for food crops that would be shipped home. Once word leaked, the public outcry—much of it from Filipino farmers—forced Manila to suspend the agreement. A similar uproar rocked Madagascar, where a South Korean firm, Daewoo Logistics, had pursued rights to more than 3 million acres of land. Word of the deal helped stoke a political furor that toppled the government and forced cancellation of the agreement. Indeed, few things are more likely to fuel insurgencies than taking land from people. Agricultural equipment is easily sabotaged. If ripe fields of grain are torched, they burn quickly.

Not only are these deals risky, but foreign investors producing food in a country full of hungry people face another political question of how to get the grain out. Will villagers permit trucks laden with grain headed for port cities to proceed when they themselves may be on the verge of starvation? The potential for political instability in countries where villagers have lost their land and their livelihoods is high. Conflicts could easily develop between investor and host countries.

These acquisitions represent a potential investment in agriculture in developing countries of an estimated $50 billion. But it could take many years to realize any substantial production gains. The public infrastructure for modern market-oriented agriculture does not yet exist in most of Africa. In some countries it will take years just to build the roads and ports needed to bring in agricultural inputs such as fertilizer and to export farm products. Beyond that, modern agriculture requires its own infrastructure: machine sheds, grain-drying equipment, silos, fertilizer storage sheds, fuel storage facilities, equipment repair and maintenance services, well-drilling equipment, irrigation pumps, and energy to power the pumps. Overall, development of the land acquired to date appears to be moving very slowly.

So how much will all this expand world food output? We don't know, but the World Bank analysis indicates that only 37 percent of the projects will be devoted to food crops. Most of the land bought up so far will be used to produce biofuels and other industrial crops.

Even if some of these projects do eventually boost land productivity, who will benefit? If virtually all the inputs—the farm equipment, the fertilizer, the pesticides, the seeds—are brought in from abroad and if all the output is shipped out of the country, it will contribute little to the host country's economy. At best, locals may find work as farm laborers, but in highly mechanized operations, the jobs will be few. At worst, impoverished countries like Mozambique and Sudan will be left with less land and water with which to feed their already hungry populations. Thus far the land grabs have contributed more to stirring unrest than to expanding food production.

And this rich country-poor country divide could grow even more pronounced—and soon. This January, a new stage in the scramble among importing countries to secure food began to unfold when South Korea, which imports 70 percent of its grain, announced that it was creating a new public-private entity that will be responsible for acquiring part of this grain. With an initial office in Chicago, the plan is to bypass the large international trading firms by buying grain directly from U.S. farmers. As the Koreans acquire their own grain elevators, they may well sign multiyear delivery contracts with farmers, agreeing to buy specified quantities of wheat, corn, or soybeans at a fixed price.

Other importers will not stand idly by as South Korea tries to tie up a portion of the U.S. grain harvest even before it gets to market. The enterprising Koreans may soon be joined by China, Japan, Saudi Arabia, and other leading importers. Although South Korea's initial focus is the United States, far and away the world's largest grain exporter, it may later consider brokering deals with Canada, Australia, Argentina, and other major exporters. This is happening just as China may be on the verge of entering the U.S. market as a potentially massive importer of grain. With China's 1.4 billion increasingly affluent consumers starting to compete with U.S. consumers for the U.S. grain harvest, cheap food, seen by many as an American birthright, may be coming to an end.

No one knows where this intensifying competition for food supplies will go, but the world seems to be moving away from the international cooperation that evolved over several decades following World War II to an every-country-for-itself philosophy. Food nationalism may help secure food supplies for individual affluent countries, but it does little to enhance world food security. Indeed, the low-income countries that host land grabs or import grain will likely see their food situation deteriorate.

After the carnage of two world wars and the economic missteps that led to the Great Depression, countries joined together in 1945 to create the United Nations, finally realizing that in the modern world we cannot live in isolation, tempting though that might be. The International Monetary Fund was created to help manage the monetary system and promote economic stability and progress. Within the U.N. system, specialized agencies from the World Health Organization to the Food and Agriculture Organization (FAO) play major roles in the world today. All this has fostered international cooperation.

But while the FAO collects and analyzes global agricultural data and provides technical assistance, there is no organized effort to ensure the adequacy of world food supplies. Indeed, most international negotiations on agricultural trade until recently focused on access to markets, with the United States, Canada, Australia, and Argentina persistently pressing Europe and Japan to open their highly protected agricultural markets. But in the first decade of this century, access to supplies has emerged as the overriding issue as the world transitions from an era of food surpluses to a new politics of food scarcity. At the same time, the U.S. food aid program that once worked to fend off famine wherever it threatened has largely been replaced by the U.N. World Food Program (WFP), where the United States is the leading donor. The WFP now has food-assistance operations in some 70 countries and an annual budget of $4 billion. There is little international coordination otherwise. French President Nicolas Sarkozy—the reigning president of the G-20—is proposing to deal with rising food prices by curbing speculation in commodity markets. Useful though this may be, it treats the symptoms of growing food insecurity, not the causes, such as population growth and climate change. The world now needs to focus not only on agricultural policy, but on a structure that integrates it with energy, population, and water policies, each of which directly affects food security.

But that is not happening. Instead, as land and water become scarcer, as the Earth's temperature rises, and as world food security deteriorates, a dangerous geopolitics of food scarcity is emerging. Land grabbing, water grabbing, and buying grain directly from farmers in exporting countries are now integral parts of a global power struggle for food security.

With grain stocks low and climate volatility increasing, the risks are also increasing. We are now so close to the edge that a breakdown in the food system could come at any time. Consider, for example, what would have happened if the 2010 heat wave that was centered in Moscow had instead been centered in Chicago. In round numbers, the 40 percent drop in Russia's hoped-for harvest of roughly 100 million tons cost the world 40 million tons of grain, but a 40 percent drop in the far larger U.S. grain harvest of 400 million tons would have cost 160 million tons. The world's carryover stocks of grain (the amount in the bin when the new harvest begins) would have dropped to just 52 days of consumption. This level would have been not only the lowest on record, but also well below the 62-day carryover that set the stage for the 2007–2008 tripling of world grain prices.

Then what? There would have been chaos in world grain markets. Grain prices would have climbed off the charts. Some grain-exporting countries, trying to hold down domestic food prices, would have restricted or even banned exports, as they did in 2007 and 2008. The TV news would have been dominated not by the hundreds of fires in the Russian countryside, but by footage of food riots in low-income grain-importing countries and reports of governments falling as hunger spread out of control. Oil-exporting countries that import grain would have been trying to barter oil for grain, and low-income grain importers would have lost out. With governments toppling and confidence in the world grain market shattered, the global economy could have started to unravel.

We may not always be so lucky. At issue now is whether the world can go beyond focusing on the symptoms of the deteriorating food situation and instead attack the underlying causes. If we cannot produce higher crop yields with less water and conserve fertile soils, many agricultural areas will cease to be viable. And this goes far beyond farmers. If we cannot move at wartime speed to stabilize the climate, we may not be able to avoid runaway food prices. If we cannot accelerate the shift to smaller families and stabilize the world population sooner rather than later, the ranks of the hungry will almost certainly continue to expand. The time to act is now—before the food crisis of 2011 becomes the new normal.

Critical Thinking

1. Food prices have recently increased substantially and future prices will go higher according to Brown. What explains these trends?
2. What are some of the major changes in the environment that are affecting food production?

Lester R. Brown, president of the Earth Policy Institute, is author of *World on the Edge: How to Prevent Environmental and Economic Collapse.*

Article

Prepared by: Robert J. Griffiths, *University of North Carolina at Greensboro*

A Light in the Forest: Brazil's Fight to Save the Amazon and Climate Change Diplomacy

JEFF TOLLEFSON

Learning Outcomes

After reading this article, you will be able to:

- Trace the trends in the clearing of the rainforest in Brazil.
- Describe the features of the REDD (reducing emissions from deforestation and forest degradation) program.

Across the world, complex social and market forces are driving the conversion of vast swaths of rain forests into pastureland, plantations, and cropland. Rain forests are disappearing in Indonesia and Madagascar and are increasingly threatened in Africa's Congo basin. But the most extreme deforestation has taken place in Brazil. Since 1988, Brazilians have cleared more than 153,000 square miles of Amazonian rain forest, an area larger than Germany. With the resulting increase in arable land, Brazil has helped feed the growing global demand for commodities, such as soybeans and beef.

But the environmental price has been steep. In addition to providing habitats for untold numbers of plant and animal species and discharging around 20 percent of the world's fresh water, the Amazon basin plays a crucial role in regulating the earth's climate, storing huge quantities of carbon dioxide that would otherwise contribute to global warming. Slashing and burning the Amazon rain forest releases the carbon locked up in plants and soils; from a climate perspective, clearing the rain forest is no different from burning fossil fuels, such as oil and gas. Recent estimates suggest that deforestation and associated activities account for 10-15 percent of global carbon dioxide emissions.

But in recent years, good news has emerged from the Amazon. Brazil has dramatically slowed the destruction of its rain forests, reducing the rate of deforestation by 83 percent since 2004, primarily by enforcing land-use regulations, creating new protected areas, and working to maintain the rule of law in the Amazon. At the same time, Brazil has become a test case for a controversial international climate-change prevention strategy known as REDD, short for "reducing emissions from deforestation and forest degradation," which places a monetary value on the carbon stored in forests. Under such a system, developed countries can pay developing countries to protect their own forests, thereby offsetting the developed countries' emissions at home. Brazil's preliminary experience with REDD suggests that, in addition to offering multiple benefits to forest dwellers (human and otherwise), the model can be cheap and fast: Brazil has done more to reduce emissions than any other country in the world in recent years, without breaking the bank.

The REDD model remains a work in progress. In Brazil and other places where elements of REDD have been applied, the funding has yet to reach many of its intended beneficiaries, and institutional reforms have been slow to develop. This has contributed to a rural backlash against the new enforcement measures in the Brazilian Amazon—a backlash that the government is still struggling to contain. But if Brazil can consolidate its early gains, build consensus around a broader vision for development, and follow through with a program to overhaul the economies of its rainforest regions, it could pave the way for a new era of environmental governance across the tropics. For the first time, perhaps, it is possible to contemplate an end to the era of large-scale human deforestation.

Lula Gets Tough

The deforestation crisis in Brazil ramped up in the 1960s, when the country's military rulers, seeking to address the country's poverty crisis, encouraged poor Brazilians to move into the Amazon basin with promises of free land and generous government subsidies. In response, tens of thousands of Brazilians left dry scrublands in the northeast and other poor areas for the lush Amazon basin—a mass internal migration that only increased in size throughout the 1970s and beyond.

But the government did not properly plan for the effect of a population explosion in the Amazon basin. The result was a land rush, during which short-term profiteering from slash-and-burn agriculture prevented anything resembling sustainable development. Environmental and social movements arose in response to the chaotic development, but it was not until the 1980s, when scientists began systematically tracking Amazonian deforestation using satellite imagery, that the true scale of the environmental destruction under way in the Amazon became apparent. The end of military rule in 1985 and Brazil's transition to democracy did nothing to slow the devastation; the ecological damage only worsened as road-building projects and government subsidies for agriculture fueled a real estate boom that wiped out forests and threatened traditional rubber tappers and native peoples. Meanwhile, the total population of the Amazon basin increased from around six million in 1960 to 25 million in 2010 (including some 20 million in Brazil), and agricultural production in the Amazon region ramped up as global commodity markets expanded.

Things began to change in 2003, when Luiz Inácio Lula da Silva, the newly elected Brazilian president, known as Lula, chose Marina Silva as his environment minister. A social and environmental activist turned politician, Silva hailed from the remote Amazonian state of Acre and had worked alongside Chico Mendes, a union leader and environmentalist whose murder in 1988 at the hands of a rancher drew global attention to the issue of the Amazon's preservation. With Lula's blessing, Silva immediately set about doing what no Brazilian government had previously attempted: enforcing Brazil's 1965 Forest Code, which had set forth strong protections for forests and established strict limits on how much land could be cleared. Doing so represented a major shift in domestic policy and was equally striking at the international level: Brazil chose to act at a time when most developing countries were resisting any significant steps to combat global warming absent the industrialized world's own more aggressive actions and provision of financial aid.

After peaking in 2004, when an area of rain forest roughly the size of Massachusetts was mowed down in a single year, Brazil's deforestation rate began to fall. Then, in late 2007, scientists at Brazil's National Institute for Space Research warned that the rate of deforestation had spiked once again. The increase coincided with a sudden rise in global food prices, which created an incentive for landowners in the Amazon to illegally clear more forest for pasture and crops. This suggested that the earlier decline in the rate of deforestation might have been driven by market forces as much as by government intervention, but Lula nevertheless doubled down on enforcement. The government deployed hundreds of Brazilian soldiers in early 2008 to crack down on illegal logging, issuing fines to those who broke the law and in some instances hauling lawbreakers to jail.

The following year, Brazil announced that its rate of deforestation had hit a historic low, and Lula pledged that by 2020 the country would reduce its deforestation to 20 percent of the country's long-term baseline, then defined as the average from 1996 to 2005. His plan to achieve that goal was based on one version of the REDD model, which had vaulted onto the international agenda several years earlier as scientists made advances in quantifying the impact of tropical deforestation on climate change.

Green-Lighting Redd

Politicians and commentators usually describe global warming as a long-term threat, but scientists also worry about transgressing invisible thresholds and thus provoking potentially rapid and irreversible nearterm changes in the way environmental and biological systems function. During the past decade, based in part on the results of intensive climate modeling, some scientists began to grow concerned that the Amazon could represent one of the clearest examples of such tipping points.

Think of the rainforest not as a collection of trees but as a hydrologic system, a massive machine for transporting and recycling water in which trees act as pumps, pulling water out of the ground and then injecting it, through transpiration, into the air. This process ramps up as the sun rises over the Amazon each day; as the forest heats up, evaporation increases, and trees transpire water to stay cool, simultaneously increasing the amount of water they take up through their roots. By constantly replenishing the atmosphere with water vapor, the Amazon helps create its own weather on a grand scale.

Humans interfere with this process whenever they chop down rain forests, and at some point, the system will begin to shut down. And this is not the only threat. Studies suggest that the Amazon could also be susceptible to rising temperatures and shifting rainfall patterns due to global warming. The nightmare scenario is known as "Amazon dieback," wherein the rains decrease and open savannas encroach on an ever-shrinking rain forest. The resulting loss of fresh water could be catastrophic for communities, agriculture, and hydropower systems in the Amazon, and dieback would have drastic effects on biodiversity and the global carbon dioxide cycle. The Amazon stores some 100 billion metric tons of carbon, equivalent to roughly a decade of global emissions. Converting carbon-rich rain forests into open savannas would pump massive quantities of carbon dioxide into the atmosphere, making it even harder for humans to prevent further warming.

Roughly 20 percent of the Amazon has been cleared to date, and there is already evidence that precipitation and river-discharge patterns are changing where the deforestation has been most intense, notably in the southwestern portion of the basin. And some scientists fear that the shifting climate may already be exerting an influence. In the past seven years, the Amazon has suffered two extremely severe droughts; normally, such droughts would be expected to occur perhaps once a century. One of the most comprehensive modeling studies to date, conducted in 2010 under the auspices of the World Bank, suggests that even current levels of deforestation, when combined with the impacts of increasing forest fires and global warming, are making the Amazon susceptible to dieback.

Such projections have heightened the sense of urgency in climate policy circles and helped focus attention on the REDD model. The concept has been around in some form for more than 15 years, but it was first placed on the international agenda in 2005 by the Coalition for Rainforest Nations, a group of

41 developing countries that cooperates with the UN and the World Bank on sustainability issues. At the core of the model is the belief that it is possible to calculate how much carbon is released into the atmosphere when a given chunk of forest is cut down. Fears that this would prove impossible helped keep deforestation off the agenda when climate diplomats signed the Kyoto Protocol in 1997. Scientists are steadily improving their methods for estimating how much carbon is stored in forests, however, and most experts agree that carbon dioxide can be tracked with enough accuracy to calculate baseline figures for every country.

Under various proposed versions of the REDD model, wealthy countries or businesses seeking to offset their own impact on the climate would pay tropical countries to reduce their emissions below their baseline levels. There is no consensus about the best way to design such a system of payments; since REDD was formally adopted as part of the agenda for climate negotiations at the UN Climate Change Conference in Bali, Indonesia, in 2007, dozens of countries and nongovernmental organizations have put forward a range of ideas. Most of these call for the creation of a global market that, like the European carbon-trading system, would allow industrial polluters to purchase carbon offsets generated by rain-forest preservation. Some environmentalists and social activists worry about the validity and longevity of such credits, as well as the prospect of banks and traders entering the conservation business. One fear is that "carbon cowboys," a new class of entrepreneurs specializing in the development of carbon-offset projects, would sweep through forests, trampling the rights of indigenous and poor people by taking control of their lands and walking away with the profits. This concern is valid, as there is always a danger of bad actors. But civil-society groups and governments, including Brazil's, are aware of the problem and are working on safeguards.

Brazilian officials have also expressed worries that the ability to simply purchase unlimited offsets would allow wealthy countries to delay the work that needs to be done to reduce their own emissions. An alternative backed by Brazil's climate negotiators and others would be a state-based funding system, in which money would flow from governments in the developed world to governments in the developing world, which would guarantee emissions reductions in return.

Norwegian Wood

In 2008, Lula, perhaps hoping to preempt an interminable debate over how best to design a global REDD system, announced the establishment of the Amazon Fund, calling on wealthy countries to contribute some $21 billion to directly fund rainforest-preservation measures. The proposal went against the market-based approach being pushed by the Coalition for Rainforest Nations. Based on a more conventional system of government donations, the Amazon Fund would allow Brazil to control the money and manage its forests as it saw fit. To the fund's backers, the resulting reductions in emissions would represent offsets of a sort.

Only one country decided to take up Lula's challenge: Norway, which stepped forward with a commitment of up to $1 billion. Coming well in advance of any formal carbon market and the international treaty that many hoped would be signed at the UN climate summit in Copenhagen in 2009, Norway's pledge was largely an altruistic vote of confidence in Brazil's approach, with donations conditioned on measurable progress. Since 2010, when the funding began, the Brazilian Development Bank, which manages the fund, has undertaken 30 projects, costing nearly $152 million. These projects include direct payments to landowners in return for preserving forests and initiatives to sort out disputes over landownership, educate farmers and ranchers about sustainability, and combat forest fires.

Although environmentalists and scientists have criticized some delays in the program, Brazil's deforestation rate has continued to plunge. Each year from 2009 to 2012, the country registered a new record low for deforestation; in 2012, only 1,798 square miles of forest were cleared. That is 76 percent below the long-term baseline, leaving Brazil just 4 percent shy of its Copenhagen commitment with eight years to go. Recent calculations by Brazilian scientists suggest that the cumulative release of carbon dioxide expected as a result of deforestation in the Brazilian Amazon dropped from more than 1.1 billion metric tons in 2004 to 298 million in 2011—roughly equivalent to the effect of France and the United Kingdom eliminating their combined carbon dioxide emissions for 2011.

REDD remains a distant promise for most landowners and communities, and the precipitous drop in deforestation in Brazil is more a function of broader government policy than the result of any individual project. Still, the Amazon Fund is demonstrating the promise and practicality of the REDD model. Although the actual cost of preventing emissions remains unclear, Brazil is offering donors carbon offsets at a discounted price of $5 per metric ton of carbon dioxide, intentionally underestimating how much biomass its forests contain in order to avoid arguments over the price. Of course, implementing the REDD model could prove significantly more expensive elsewhere. But the price would nonetheless be significantly cheaper than for many other methods of cutting emissions, such as capturing carbon dioxide from a coal-fired power plant and pumping it underground, which could cost upward of $100 per metric ton in the initial stages.

Rousseff and the Ruralistas

Lula was succeeded by his protégé and former chief of staff, Dilma Rousseff, in 2011. Although environmentalists have been critical of her broader development agenda in the Amazon and beyond, Rousseff has upheld Lula's deforestation policies. And she has done so despite intense pressure from the so-called ruralista coalition of landowners and major agricultural interests, which currently exercises tremendous influence in Brasília.

In the spring of 2012, the Brazilian Congress passed a bill that would have eviscerated the country's vaunted Forest Code by scaling back basic protections for land alongside rivers and embankments and offering outright amnesty to companies and landowners who had broken the law. Rousseff fought back, and a prolonged tussle ensued. The final result was a law that is generally more favorable to agricultural interests but that nonetheless retains minimum requirements for forest protection and recovery on private land.

More troubling than the new law itself, perhaps, is the political polarization that accompanied its passage. Brasília now seems divided into rigid environmentalist and agricultural factions. Fierce opposition to Brazil's rainforest-preservation efforts is sure to persist, and many observers fear that landowners, impatient with the slow pace of progress on REDD, will ultimately begin to test the limits of the newly revised Forest Code. As if on cue, last September, Brazilian scientists announced that deforestation was 220 percent higher in August than it had been in August of 2011. But it is too early to tell what this latest outbreak might mean. After all, prior spikes have incurred a government response, and each time the damage has been contained.

It is also worth noting that not only has Brazilian deforestation decreased overall, but the size of the average forest clearing has also decreased over time. The powerful landowners and corporate interests responsible for large-scale deforestation have apparently decided that they can no longer cut down rain forests with impunity. The upshot is that for the first time ever, in 2011, the amount of land cleared in the Brazilian Amazon dropped below the combined amount cleared in the surrounding Amazon countries, which make up 40 percent of the basin. In those countries, the trend is not so encouraging: deforestation in the non-Brazilian Amazon increased from an estimated annual average of 1,938 square miles in the 1990s to 2,782 square miles last year, according to an analysis published by the World Wildlife Fund.

Missing the Forest for the Trees?

There was very little progress on REDD at the most recent UN climate summit, in Doha, Qatar, last November. Negotiators left the door open to a full suite of REDD-style models, from government-to-government financial transfers to a privatized carbon market, but failed to agree on the details. Regardless of which particular models are codified in a hypothetical future treaty on climate change, countries need to focus on making the money flow: Some studies suggest that halving deforestation would cost $20-$25 billion annually by 2020. So far, governments have committed several billion dollars to forest protection through various bilateral and multilateral agreements. Through the UN, the industrialized countries have also made impressive commitments to combating climate change in the developing world, promising to contribute up to $100 billion annually by 2020, a portion of which could fund forest protection.

But it is not at all clear that this money will materialize, due in part to the current weakness of the global economy. And there is a limit to government largess. Advocates of rainforest preservation are now trying to convince governments to commit money from revenue streams that do not depend on annual appropriations, which are more vulnerable to political and economic pressure. But that, too, is an uphill battle. Indeed, forest-preservation advocates cannot rely on governments alone; they will ultimately need to attract private-sector investment.

In the meantime, the fight against deforestation will rely on a patchwork of international partnerships and initiatives. Most significant, perhaps, Norway has transferred the model it developed with Brazil to Indonesia, which now ranks as the largest emitter of carbon dioxide from tropical deforestation. Just as in Brazil, the promise of REDD helped inspire some bold political commitments by Indonesian authorities, who have agreed to reduce their greenhouse gas emissions—most of which come from deforestation—by up to 41 percent by 2020 if international aid materializes. But Indonesia has neither the monitoring technology nor the institutional wherewithal of Brazil, so Norway's $1 billion commitment is aimed at helping the country build up its scientific and institutional capacity. Progress has been slow, but the advantage of a results-based approach, such as REDD, is that these initiatives cost money only if they yield positive results.

Brazil's experience offers some lessons for other tropical countries. The first is that science and technology must be the foundation of any solution. Brazil's progress has been made possible by major investments in scientific and institutional infrastructure to monitor the country's rain forests. Nations seeking to follow suit must invest in tools that will help them not only monitor their forests but also estimate just how much carbon those forests store. Working with scientists at the Carnegie Institution for Science, the governments of Colombia and Peru are deploying advanced systems for tracking deforestation from readily available satellite data. Combined with laser-based aerial technology that can map vast swaths of forest in three dimensions, these systems will be able to more accurately calculate and monitor stored carbon across an entire landscape-a feat that could allow these countries to leapfrog Brazil.

Brazil's Amazon Fund also shows that it is possible to move forward despite lingering scientific uncertainty about how to quantify the carbon stored in forests. Some critics of the REDD model have worried that it could draw attention away from the enforcement of existing forestry laws, ultimately increasing the cost of conservation and rewarding wealthy lawbreakers. But Brazil's experience shows that the two approaches can go hand in hand. Indeed, most of Brazil's progress to date has come from simply enforcing existing rules. The government has also created formal land reserves, outlawing development on nearly half its territory, and environmental groups have played a role by rallying public opinion and partnering with industry groups to improve agricultural practices. Still, enforcement can go only so far with the smaller landholders and subsistence farmers who are responsible for an increasingly large share of the remaining deforestation. Brazil must focus the Amazon Fund and other government initiatives on projects that will create more sustainable forms of agriculture for these small-scale farmers and ranchers.

The government also needs to look ahead. Cities in the Amazon are booming, and larger populations will translate into additional demands for natural resources and food. The Brazilian government has sought to increase agricultural productivity across the basin, recognizing that there is more than enough land available to expand production without clearing more of it. But Brazil should also encourage more forest recovery, which would bolster the Amazon's ability to produce rain and absorb carbon dioxide from the atmosphere. Globally, forests currently absorb roughly a quarter of the world's carbon emissions, thanks to the regrowth of forests cut down long ago in places such as the United States, and they could provide an even larger buffer going forward. Roughly 20 percent of the areas once cleared in the Amazon are already regrowing as so-called secondary forest. Scientists have calculated that if the government can increase that figure to 40 percent, the Brazilian Amazon will transition from a net source of carbon dioxide emissions to a "carbon sink" by 2015, taking in more carbon dioxide than it emits.

Deforestation is just one of many challenges buffeting the Amazon region, and improvements on this front should not obscure the ongoing problems of poverty, violence, and corruption. But at a time when expectations for progress on climate change are falling, Brazil has given the world a glimmer of hope. In many ways, the hard work is just beginning, but the results so far more than justify continuing the experiment.

Critical Thinking

1. What initially drove deforestation in Brazil?
2. How does deforestation contribute to climate change?
3. How does the REDD program work?
4. What are the obstacles to such efforts to reduce deforestation?

Create Central

www.mhhe.com/createcentral

Internet References

Earth Pledge Foundation
www.earthpledge.org

EnviroLink
http://envirolink.org

Greenpeace
www.greenpeace.org

Linkages on Environmental Issues and Development
www.iisd.ca/linkages

Population Action International
www.populationaction.org

World Health Organization (WHO)
www.who.ch

The Worldwatch Institute
www.worldwatch.org

Jeff Tollefson is a U.S. correspondent for Nature, where he covers energy, climate, and environmental issues.

Unit 6

UNIT

Prepared by: Robert J. Griffiths, *University of North Carolina at Greensboro*

Women and Development

There is widespread recognition of the crucial role that women play in the development process. Women are critical to the success of family planning programs, bear much of the responsibility for food production, account for an increasing share of wage labor in developing countries, are acutely aware of the consequences of environmental degradation, and can contribute to the development of a vibrant, civil society and good governance. Despite their important contributions, however, women lag behind men in access to health care, nutrition, education, and legal protection while continuing to face formidable social, economic, and political barriers. Women's lives in the developing world are invariably difficult. Often female children are valued less than male offspring, resulting in higher female infant and child mortality rates. In extreme cases, this undervaluing leads to female infanticide.

Those females who do survive often face lives characterized by poor nutrition and health, multiple pregnancies, hard physical labor, discrimination, and in some cases violence. Women are particularly vulnerable to human rights abuses and the consequences of armed conflict and must be included in transitional justice efforts in post-conflict societies.

Clearly, women are central to any successful population policy. Evidence shows that educated women have fewer and healthier children. This connection between education and population indicates that greater emphasis should be placed on educating women. Female school enrollments are often lower than those of males because of state priorities, insufficient family resources to educate both boys and girls, female socialization, and cultural factors. Education is the largest single contributor to enhancing the status of women and promoting development, but access to education is still limited for many women. Sixty percent of children worldwide not enrolled in schools are girls. Education for women leads to improved health, better wages, and greater influence in decision making, which benefits not only women but the broader society as well. Educated women contribute more to their families, are less likely to subject their daughters to female genital mutilation, and are three times less likely to contract HIV.

Women make up a significant portion of the agricultural workforce. They are heavily involved in food production right from planting to cultivation, harvesting, and marketing. Despite their agricultural contribution, women frequently do not have adequate access to advances in agricultural technology or the benefits of extension and training programs. They are also discriminated against in land ownership. As a result, important opportunities to improve food production are lost when women are not given access to technology, training, and land ownership commensurate with their agricultural role.

The industrialization that has accompanied the globalized production has meant more employment opportunities for women, but often these are low-tech, low-wage jobs. The lower labor costs in the developing world that attract manufacturing facilities are a mixed blessing for women. Increasingly, women are recruited to fill these production jobs because wage differentials allow employers to pay women less. On the other hand, expanding opportunities for women in these positions contribute to family income. The informal sector, where jobs are small scale, more traditional, and labor-intensive, has also attracted more women. In many cases, these jobs are their only employment option due to family responsibilities or discrimination.

Women also play a critical role in the economic expansion of developing countries. Nevertheless, women are likely to be the first to feel the effects of an economic slowdown. The consequences of the structural adjustment programs that many developing countries adopted fell disproportionately on women. When employment opportunities decline because of austerity measures, women lose jobs in the formal sector and face increased competition from males in the informal sector. Cuts in spending on health care and education also affect women, who already receive fewer of these benefits. Because of the gender division of labor, women are often more aware of the consequences of environmental degradation. Depletion of resources such as forests, soil, and water are much more likely to be felt by women, who are responsible for collecting firewood and water and who raise most of the crops. Women are an essential component of successful environmental protection policies, but they are often overlooked in planning environmental sustainability projects.

Enhancing the status of women has been the primary focus of several international conferences. The 1994 International Conference on Population and Development (ICPD) focused attention on women's health and reproductive rights, and the crucial role that these issues play in controlling population. The 1995 Fourth World Conference on Women held in Beijing, China, proclaimed women's rights to be synonymous with human rights. Along with the Convention on the Elimination of All Forms of Discrimination against Women, these developments represent a turning point in women's struggle for equal rights and have prompted efforts to pass legislation at the national level to protect women's rights.

There are indications that women have made progress in some regions of the developing world. The election of Ellen John-Sirleaf as president of Liberia and Africa's first female head of state is the most visible indicator of a trend toward greater political involvement of women in Africa. In the Middle East, women's rights continue to lag behind those of their counterparts in other regions of the world. Women were important actors in the struggle for political reform during the Arab Spring. While this may open further opportunities to increase women's political participation, early indications suggest that the gains Egyptian women made under previous regimes may be at risk in the post-revolution political upheaval. In several other Middle Eastern countries, women continue to face obstacles to political participation and human rights.

There continues to be a wide divergence in the status of women worldwide, but the recognition of the valuable contributions they can make to society is increasing the pressure to enhance their status. Reflecting this recognition, multinational corporations are increasingly seeking to empower women and enhance their status.

Article

The Women's Crusade

The oppression of women worldwide is the human rights cause of our time. And their liberation could help solve many of the world's problems, from poverty to child mortality to terrorism. A 21st-century manifesto.

NICHOLAS D. KRISTOF AND SHERYL WUDUNN

In the 19th century, the paramount moral challenge was slavery. In the 20th century, it was totalitarianism. In this century, it is the brutality inflicted on so many women and girls around the globe: sex trafficking, acid attacks, bride burnings and mass rape.

Yet if the injustices that women in poor countries suffer are of paramount importance, in an economic and geopolitical sense the opportunity they represent is even greater. "Women hold up half the sky," in the words of a Chinese saying, yet that's mostly an aspiration: in a large slice of the world, girls are uneducated and women marginalized, and it's not an accident that those same countries are disproportionately mired in poverty and riven by fundamentalism and chaos. There's a growing recognition among everyone from the World Bank to the U.S. military's Joint Chiefs of Staff to aid organizations like CARE that focusing on women and girls is the most effective way to fight global poverty and extremism. That's why foreign aid is increasingly directed to women. The world is awakening to a powerful truth: Women and girls aren't the problem; they're the solution.

One place to observe this alchemy of gender is in the muddy back alleys of Pakistan. In a slum outside the grand old city of Lahore, a woman named Saima Muhammad used to dissolve into tears every evening. A round-faced woman with thick black hair tucked into a head scarf, Saima had barely a rupee, and her deadbeat husband was unemployed and not particularly employable. He was frustrated and angry, and he coped by beating Saima each afternoon. Their house was falling apart, and Saima had to send her young daughter to live with an aunt, because there wasn't enough food to go around.

"My sister-in-law made fun of me, saying, 'You can't even feed your children,'" recalled Saima when Nick met her two years ago on a trip to Pakistan. "My husband beat me up. My brother-in-law beat me up. I had an awful life." Saima's husband accumulated a debt of more than $3,000, and it seemed that these loans would hang over the family for generations. Then when Saima's second child was born and turned out to be a girl as well, her mother-in-law, a harsh, blunt woman named Sharifa Bibi, raised the stakes.

"She's not going to have a son," Sharifa told Saima's husband, in front of her. "So you should marry again. Take a second wife." Saima was shattered and ran off sobbing. Another wife would leave even less money to feed and educate the children. And Saima herself would be marginalized in the household, cast off like an old sock. For days Saima walked around in a daze, her eyes red; the slightest incident would send her collapsing into hysterical tears.

It was at that point that Saima signed up with the Kashf Foundation, a Pakistani microfinance organization that lends tiny amounts of money to poor women to start businesses. Kashf is typical of microfinance institutions, in that it lends almost exclusively to women, in groups of 25. The women guarantee one another's debts and meet every two weeks to make payments and discuss a social issue, like family planning or schooling for girls. A Pakistani woman is often forbidden to leave the house without her husband's permission, but husbands tolerate these meetings because the women return with cash and investment ideas.

Saima Muhammad, lives near Lahore, Pakistan. She was routinely beaten by her husband until she started a successful embroidery business.

Saima took out a $65 loan and used the money to buy beads and cloth, which she transformed into beautiful embroidery that she then sold to merchants in the markets of Lahore. She used the profit to buy more beads and cloth, and soon she had an embroidery business and was earning a solid income—the only one in her household to do so. Saima took her elder daughter back from the aunt and began paying off her husband's debt.

When merchants requested more embroidery than Saima could produce, she paid neighbors to assist her. Eventually 30 families were working for her, and she put her husband to work as well—"under my direction," she explained with a twinkle in her eye. Saima became the tycoon of the neighborhood, and she was able to pay off her husband's entire debt, keep her daughters in school, renovate the house, connect running water and buy a television.

Goretti Nyabenda Musiga Commune, Burundi

In Burundi, which is one of the poorest counteries in the world, Goretti Nyabenda used to be largely a **prisoner in her hut.** In Keeping with tradition in the region where she lived, she could not leave without the permission of her husband, Bernard. Her interactions with Bernard consisted in good part of being beaten by him. "I was wretched" she remembers. Then Goretti joined an empowerment program run by CARE, taking out a $2 microloan to buy fertilizer. The result was an excellent crop of potatoes worth $7.50—and Goretti began to build a small business as a farmer, goat breeder and banana-beer brewer. When Bernard fell sick with malaria, it was Goretti who was able to pay the bill. Today Goretti is no longer beaten, and she comes and goes freely. Her children, including her second daughter, Ancilla, have been able to afford school with Goretti's earnings.

"Now everyone comes to me to borrow money, the same ones who used to criticize me," Saima said, beaming in satisfaction. "And the children of those who used to criticize me now come to my house to watch TV."

Today, Saima is a bit plump and displays a gold nose ring as well as several other rings and bracelets on each wrist. She exudes self-confidence as she offers a grand tour of her home and work area, ostentatiously showing off the television and the new plumbing. She doesn't even pretend to be subordinate to her husband. He spends his days mostly loafing around, occasionally helping with the work but always having to accept orders from his wife. He has become more impressed with females in general: Saima had a third child, also a girl, but now that's not a problem. "Girls are just as good as boys," he explained.

Saima's new prosperity has transformed the family's educational prospects. She is planning to send all three of her daughters through high school and maybe to college as well. She brings in tutors to improve their schoolwork, and her oldest child, Javaria, is ranked first in her class. We asked Javaria what she wanted to be when she grew up, thinking she might aspire to be a doctor or lawyer. Javaria cocked her head. "I'd like to do embroidery," she said.

As for her husband, Saima said, "We have a good relationship now." She explained, "We don't fight, and he treats me well." And what about finding another wife who might bear him a son? Saima chuckled at the question: "Now nobody says anything about that." Sharifa Bibi, the mother-in-law, looked shocked when we asked whether she wanted her son to take a second wife to bear a son. "No, no," she said. "Saima is bringing so much to this house.... She puts a roof over our heads and food on the table."

Sharifa even allows that Saima is now largely exempt from beatings by her husband. "A woman should know her limits, and if not, then it's her husband's right to beat her," Sharifa said. "But if a woman earns more than her husband, it's difficult for him to discipline her."

What should we make of stories like Saima's? Traditionally, the status of women was seen as a "soft" issue—worthy but marginal. We initially reflected that view ourselves in our work as journalists. We preferred to focus instead on the "serious" international issues, like trade disputes or arms proliferation. Our awakening came in China.

After we married in 1988, we moved to Beijing to be correspondents for *The New York Times.* Seven months later we found ourselves standing on the edge of Tiananmen Square watching troops fire their automatic weapons at prodemocracy protesters. The massacre claimed between 400 and 800 lives and transfixed the world; wrenching images of the killings appeared constantly on the front page and on television screens.

Yet the following year we came across an obscure but meticulous demographic study that outlined a human rights violation that had claimed tens of thousands more lives. This study found that 39,000 baby girls died annually in China because parents didn't give them the same medical care and attention that boys received—and that was just in the first year of life. A result is that as many infant girls died unnecessarily every week in China as protesters died at Tiananmen Square. Those Chinese girls never received a column inch of news coverage, and we began to wonder if our journalistic priorities were skewed.

A similar pattern emerged in other countries. In India, a "bride burning" takes place approximately once every two hours, to punish a woman for an inadequate dowry or to eliminate her so a man can remarry—but these rarely constitute news. When a prominent dissident was arrested in China, we would write a front-page article; when 100,000 girls were kidnapped and trafficked into brothels, we didn't even consider it news.

Amartya Sen, the ebullient Nobel Prize-winning economist, developed a gauge of gender inequality that is a striking reminder of the stakes involved. "More than 100 million women are missing," Sen wrote in a classic essay in 1990 in *The New York Review of Books,* spurring a new field of research. Sen noted that in normal circumstances, women live longer than men, and so there are more females than males in much of the world. Yet in places where girls have a deeply unequal status, they vanish. China has 107 males for every 100 females in its overall population (and an even greater disproportion among newborns), and India has 108. The implication of the sex ratios, Sen later found, is that about 107 million females are missing from the globe today. Follow-up studies have calculated the number slightly differently, deriving alternative figures for "missing women" of between 60 million and 107 million.

The U.N. has estimated that there are 5 thousand honor killings a year, the majority in the Muslim world.

Girls vanish partly because they don't get the same health care and food as boys. In India, for example, girls are less likely to be vaccinated than boys and are taken to the hospital only when they are sicker. A result is that girls in India from

1 to 5 years of age are 50 percent more likely to die than boys their age. In addition, ultrasound machines have allowed a pregnant woman to find out the sex of her fetus—and then get an abortion if it is female.

The global statistics on the abuse of girls are numbing. It appears that more girls and women are now missing from the planet, precisely because they are female, than men were killed on the battlefield in all the wars of the 20th century. The number of victims of this routine "gendercide" far exceeds the number of people who were slaughtered in all the genocides of the 20th century.

For those women who live, mistreatment is sometimes shockingly brutal. If you're reading this article, the phrase "gender discrimination" might conjure thoughts of unequal pay, underfinanced sports teams or unwanted touching from a boss. In the developing world, meanwhile, millions of women and girls are actually enslaved. While a precise number is hard to pin down, the International Labor Organization, a U.N. agency, estimates that at any one time there are 12.3 million people engaged in forced labor of all kinds, including sexual servitude. In Asia alone about one million children working in the sex trade are held in conditions indistinguishable from slavery, according to a U.N. report. Girls and women are locked in brothels and beaten if they resist, fed just enough to be kept alive and often sedated with drugs—to pacify them and often to cultivate addiction. India probably has more modern slaves than any other country.

Another huge burden for women in poor countries is maternal mortality, with one woman dying in childbirth around the world every minute. In the West African country Niger, a woman stands a one-in-seven chance of dying in childbirth at some point in her life. (These statistics are all somewhat dubious, because maternal mortality isn't considered significant enough to require good data collection.) For all of India's shiny new high-rises, a woman there still has a 1-in-70 lifetime chance of dying in childbirth. In contrast, the lifetime risk in the United States is 1 in 4,800; in Ireland, it is 1 in 47,600. The reason for the gap is not that we don't know how to save lives of women in poor countries. It's simply that poor, uneducated women in Africa and Asia have never been a priority either in their own countries or to donor nations.

Abbas Be, a beautiful teenage girl in the Indian city of Hyderabad, has chocolate skin, black hair and gleaming white teeth—and a lovely smile, which made her all the more marketable.

Money was tight in her family, so when she was about 14 she arranged to take a job as a maid in the capital, New Delhi. Instead, she was locked up in a brothel, beaten with a cricket bat, gang-raped and told that she would have to cater to customers. Three days after she arrived, Abbas and all 70 girls in the brothel were made to gather round and watch as the pimps made an example of one teenage girl who had fought customers. The troublesome girl was stripped naked, hogtied, humiliated and mocked, beaten savagely and then stabbed in the stomach until she bled to death in front of Abbas and the others.

Abbas was never paid for her work. Any sign of dissatisfaction led to a beating or worse; two more times, she watched girls murdered by the brothel managers for resisting. Eventually Abbas was freed by police and taken back to Hyderabad. She found a home in a shelter run by Prajwala, an organization that takes in girls rescued from brothels and teaches them new skills. Abbas is acquiring an education and has learned to be a bookbinder; she also counsels other girls about how to avoid being trafficked. As a skilled bookbinder, Abbas is able to earn a decent living, and she is now helping to put her younger sisters through school as well. With an education, they will be far less vulnerable to being trafficked. Abbas has moved from being a slave to being a producer, contributing to India's economic development and helping raise her family.

Perhaps the lesson presented by both Abbas and Saima is the same: In many poor countries, the greatest unexploited resource isn't oil fields or veins of gold; it is the women and girls who aren't educated and never become a major presence in the formal economy. With education and with help starting businesses, impoverished women can earn money and support their countries as well as their families. They represent perhaps the best hope for fighting global poverty.

In East Asia, as we saw in our years of reporting there, women have already benefited from deep social changes. In countries like South Korea and Malaysia, China and Thailand, rural girls who previously contributed negligibly to the economy have gone to school and received educations, giving them the autonomy to move to the city to hold factory jobs. This hugely increased the formal labor force; when the women then delayed childbearing, there was a demographic dividend to the country as well. In the 1990s, by our estimations, some 80 percent of the employees on the assembly lines in coastal China were female, and the proportion across the manufacturing belt of East Asia was at least 70 percent.

The hours were long and the conditions wretched, just as in the sweatshops of the Industrial Revolution in the West. But peasant women were making money, sending it back home and sometimes becoming the breadwinners in their families. They gained new skills that elevated their status. Westerners encounter sweatshops and see exploitation, and indeed, many of these plants are just as bad as critics say. But it's sometimes said in poor countries that the only thing worse than being exploited in a sweatshop is not being exploited in a sweatshop. Low-wage manufacturing jobs disproportionately benefited women in countries like China because these were jobs for which brute physical force was not necessary and women's nimbleness gave them an advantage over men—which was not the case with agricultural labor or construction or other jobs typically available in poor countries. Strange as it may seem, sweatshops in Asia had the effect of empowering women. One hundred years ago, many women in China were still having their feet bound. Today, while discrimination and inequality and harassment persist, the culture has been transformed. In the major cities, we've found that Chinese men often do more domestic chores than American men typically do. And urban parents are often not only happy with an only daughter; they may even prefer one, under the belief that daughters are better than sons at looking after aging parents.

Why do microfinance organizations usually focus their assistance on women? And why does everyone benefit when women enter the work force and bring home regular pay checks? One reason involves the dirty little secret of global poverty: some of the most wretched suffering is caused not just by low incomes but also by unwise spending by the poor—especially by men. Surprisingly frequently, we've come across a mother mourning a child who has just died of malaria for want of a $5 mosquito bed net; the mother says that the family couldn't afford a bed net and she means it, but then we find the father at a nearby bar. He goes three evenings a week to the bar, spending $5 each week.

Our interviews and perusal of the data available suggest that the poorest families in the world spend approximately 10 times as much (20 percent of their incomes on average) on a combination of alcohol, prostitution, candy, sugary drinks and lavish feasts as they do on educating their children (2 percent). If poor families spent only as much on educating their children as they do on beer and prostitutes, there would be a breakthrough in the prospects of poor countries. Girls, since they are the ones kept home from school now, would be the biggest beneficiaries. Moreover, one way to reallocate family expenditures in this way is to put more money in the hands of women. A series of studies has found that when women hold assets or gain incomes, family money is more likely to be spent on nutrition, medicine and housing, and consequently children are healthier.

In Ivory Coast, one research project examined the different crops that men and women grow for their private kitties: men grow coffee, cocoa and pineapple, and women grow plantains, bananas, coconuts and vegetables. Some years the "men's crops" have good harvests and the men are flush with cash, and other years it is the women who prosper. Money is to some extent shared. But even so, the economist Esther Duflo of M.I.T. found that when the men's crops flourish, the household spends more money on alcohol and tobacco. When the women have a good crop, the households spend more money on food. "When women command greater power, child health and nutrition improves," Duflo says.

Such research has concrete implications: for example, donor countries should nudge poor countries to adjust their laws so that when a man dies, his property is passed on to his widow rather than to his brothers. Governments should make it easy for women to hold property and bank accounts—1 percent of the world's landowners are women—and they should make it much easier for microfinance institutions to start banks so that women can save money.

Of course, it's fair to ask: empowering women is well and good, but can one do this effectively? Does foreign aid really work? William Easterly, an economist at New York University, has argued powerfully that shoveling money at poor countries accomplishes little. Some Africans, including Dambisa Moyo, author of "Dead Aid," have said the same thing. The critics note that there has been no correlation between amounts of aid going to countries and their economic growth rates.

Our take is that, frankly, there is something to these criticisms. Helping people is far harder than it looks. Aid experiments often go awry, or small successes turn out to be difficult to replicate or scale up. Yet we've also seen, anecdotally and in the statistics, evidence that some kinds of aid have been enormously effective. The delivery of vaccinations and other kinds of health care has reduced the number of children who die every year before they reach the age of 5 to less than 10 million today from 20 million in 1960.

Abbas Be was held captive in a Delhi brothel. After she was freed, she returned to her home city of Hyderabad, became a bookbinder and now puts her sisters through school.

In general, aid appears to work best when it is focused on health, education and microfinance (although microfinance has been somewhat less successful in Africa than in Asia). And in each case, crucially, aid has often been most effective when aimed at women and girls; when policy wonks do the math, they often find that these investments have a net economic return. Only a small proportion of aid specifically targets women or girls, but increasingly donors are recognizing that that is where they often get the most bang for the buck.

In the early 1990s, the United Nations and the World Bank began to proclaim the potential resource that women and girls represent. "Investment in girls' education may well be the highest-return investment available in the developing world," Larry Summers wrote when he was chief economist of the World Bank. Private aid groups and foundations shifted gears as well. "Women are the key to ending hunger in Africa," declared the Hunger Project. The Center for Global Development issued a major report explaining "why and how to put girls at the center of development." CARE took women and girls as the centerpiece of its anti-poverty efforts. "Gender inequality hurts economic growth," Goldman Sachs concluded in a 2008 research report that emphasized how much developing countries could improve their economic performance by educating girls.

98 percent of people in Egypt say they believe that 'girls have the same right to education as boys.'

Bill Gates recalls once being invited to speak in Saudi Arabia and finding himself facing a segregated audience. Four-fifths of the listeners were men, on the left. The remaining one-fifth were women, all covered in black cloaks and veils, on the right. A partition separated the two groups. Toward the end, in the question-and-answer session, a member of the audience noted that Saudi Arabia aimed to be one of the Top 10 countries in the world in technology by 2010 and asked if that was realistic. "Well, if you're not fully utilizing half the talent in the country," Gates said, "you're not going to get too close to the Top 10." The small group on the right erupted in wild cheering.

Policy makers have gotten the message as well. President Obama has appointed a new White House Council on Women and Girls. Perhaps he was indoctrinated by his mother, who was one of the early adopters of microloans to women when she worked to fight poverty in Indonesia. Secretary of State Hillary Rodham Clinton is a member of the White House Council, and she has also selected a talented activist, Melanne Verveer, to direct a new State Department Office of Global Women's Issues. On Capitol Hill, the Senate Foreign Relations Committee has put Senator Barbara Boxer in charge of a new subcommittee that deals with women's issues.

Yet another reason to educate and empower women is that greater female involvement in society and the economy appears to undermine extremism and terrorism. It has long been known that a risk factor for turbulence and violence is the share of a country's population made up of young people. Now it is emerging that male domination of society is also a risk factor; the reasons aren't fully understood, but it may be that when women are marginalized the nation takes on the testosterone-laden culture of a military camp or a high-school boys' locker room. That's in part why the Joint Chiefs of Staff and international security specialists are puzzling over how to increase girls' education in countries like Afghanistan—and why generals have gotten briefings from Greg Mortenson, who wrote about building girls' schools in his best seller, "Three Cups of Tea." Indeed, some scholars say they believe the reason Muslim countries have been disproportionately afflicted by terrorism is not Islamic teachings about infidels or violence but rather the low levels of female education and participation in the labor force.

So what would an agenda for fighting poverty through helping women look like? You might begin with the education of girls—which doesn't just mean building schools. There are other innovative means at our disposal. A study in Kenya by Michael Kremer, a Harvard economist, examined six different approaches to improving educational performance, from providing free textbooks to child-sponsorship programs. The approach that raised student test scores the most was to offer girls who had scored in the top 15 percent of their class on sixth-grade tests a $19 scholarship for seventh and eighth grade (and the glory of recognition at an assembly). Boys also performed better, apparently because they were pushed by the girls or didn't want to endure the embarrassment of being left behind.

Another Kenyan study found that giving girls a new $6 school uniform every 18 months significantly reduced dropout rates and pregnancy rates. Likewise, there's growing evidence that a cheap way to help keep high-school girls in school is to help them manage menstruation. For fear of embarrassing leaks and stains, girls sometimes stay home during their periods, and the absenteeism puts them behind and eventually leads them to drop out. Aid workers are experimenting with giving African teenage girls sanitary pads, along with access to a toilet where they can change them. The Campaign for Female Education, an organization devoted to getting more girls into school in Africa, helps girls with their periods, and a new group, Sustainable Health Enterprises, is trying to do the same.

Claudine Mukakarisa Kigalf, Rwanda

Claudine Mukakarisa spent much of the genocide in Rwanda **imprisoned in a rape house.** She escaped, and afterward she found that she was the only one left alive in her family—she was pregnant, homeless and 13 years old. Claudine gave birth in a parking lot, and hating the child because its father was a rapist, she initially left him to die. But then she returned to the parking lot, picked up her son and nursed him. She survived by begging and washing laundry; eventually, another child followed—the father was a man who raped her after offering her shelter. Claudine, with her two children, received help from an aid organization called Women for Women International, which paired her with Murvelene Clarke, a bank employee from Brooklyn. Clarke began donating $27 a month, and that money (together with training in making beadwork, which can be sold) helped Claudine educate her children.

And so, if President Obama wanted to adopt a foreign-aid policy that built on insights into the role of women in development, he would do well to start with education. We would suggest a $10 billion effort over five years to educate girls around the world. This initiative would focus on Africa but would also support—and prod—Asian countries like Afghanistan and Pakistan to do better. This plan would also double as population policy, for it would significantly reduce birthrates—and thus help poor countries overcome the demographic obstacles to economic growth.

But President Obama might consider two different proposals as well. We would recommend that the United States sponsor a global drive to eliminate iodine deficiency around the globe, by helping countries iodize salt. About a third of households in the developing world do not get enough iodine, and a result is often an impairment in brain formation in the fetal stages. For reasons that are unclear, this particularly affects female fetuses and typically costs children 10 to 15 I.Q. points. Research by Erica Field of Harvard found that daughters of women given iodine performed markedly better in school. Other research suggests that salt iodization would yield benefits worth nine times the cost.

We would also recommend that the United States announce a 12-year, $1.6 billion program to eradicate obstetric fistula, a childbirth injury that is one of the worst scourges of women in the developing world. An obstetric fistula, which is a hole created inside the body by a difficult childbirth, leaves a woman incontinent, smelly, often crippled and shunned by her village—yet it can be repaired for a few hundred dollars. Dr. Lewis Wall, president of the Worldwide Fistula Fund, and Michael Horowitz, a conservative agitator on humanitarian issues, have drafted the 12-year plan—and it's eminently practical and built on proven methods. Evidence that fistulas can be prevented or repaired comes from impoverished Somaliland,

Do-It-Yourself Foreign AID

People always ask us: How can I help the world's needy? How can I give in a way that will benefit a real person and won't just finance corruption or an aid bureaucracy? There are innumerable answers to those questions, but it's becoming increasingly clear that many of them involve women. From among the examples in our book "Half the Sky," here are a handful:

Choose a woman to lend to on kiva.org. The minimum amount is $25, and you can choose from people all over the world. The money will be used to support a business and will be paid back. Or go to globalgiving .com, find a woman abroad whose cause you identify with and make a small gift. On GlobalGiving, for example, we have supported a program to prevent runaway girls from being trafficked into brothels.

Sponsor a girl abroad through one of the many child-sponsorship organizations. We do so through Plan USA (planusa.org), but there are many other great ones, including Women for Women International (womenforwomen.org).

Become an advocate for change by joining the CARE Action Network at care.org. CARE is now focused on assisting women and girls for the pragmatic reason that that is where it can get the best results. The network helps people speak out and educate policy makers about global poverty.

Find a cause that resonates with you, learn more about it and adopt it. For example, we send checks to support an extraordinary Somali woman, Edna Adan who has invested her savings and her soul in her own maternity hospital in Somaliland (ednahospital.org).

Even school kids can make a difference. Jordana Confino, an eighth grader in Westfield N.J., started an initiative with friends to help girls go to school in poor countries. The effort grew to become Girls Learn International (girlslearn.org), which now pairs American middle schools and high schools with needy classrooms in Africa, Asia and Latin America. An expanded list of organizations that specialize in supporting women in developing countries is at nytimes.com/magazine.

— N.D.K. and S.W.D.

a northern enclave of Somalia, where an extraordinary nurse-midwife named Edna Adan has built her own maternity hospital to save the lives of the women around her. A former first lady of Somalia and World Health Organization official, Adan used her savings to build the hospital, which is supported by a group of admirers in the U.S. who call themselves Friends of Edna Maternity Hospital.

For all the legitimate concerns about how well humanitarian aid is spent, investments in education, iodizing salt and maternal health all have a proven record of success. And the sums are modest: all three components of our plan together amount to about what the U.S. has provided Pakistan since 9/11—a sum that accomplished virtually nothing worthwhile either for Pakistanis or for Americans.

One of the many aid groups that for pragmatic reasons has increasingly focused on women is Heifer International, a charitable organization based in Arkansas that has been around for decades. The organization gives cows, goats and chickens to farmers in poor countries. On assuming the presidency of Heifer in 1992, the activist Jo Luck traveled to Africa, where one day she found herself sitting on the ground with a group of young women in a Zimbabwean village. One of them was Tererai Trent.

Tererai is a long-faced woman with high cheekbones and a medium brown complexion; she has a high forehead and tight cornrows. Like many women around the world, she doesn't know when she was born and has no documentation of her birth. As a child, Tererai didn't get much formal education, partly because she was a girl and was expected to do household chores. She herded cattle and looked after her younger siblings. Her father would say, Let's send our sons to school, because they will be the breadwinners. Tererai's brother, Tinashe, was forced to go to school, where he was an indifferent student. Tererai pleaded to be allowed to attend but wasn't permitted to do so. Tinashe brought his books home each afternoon, and Tererai pored over them and taught herself to read and write. Soon she was doing her brother's homework every evening.

The teacher grew puzzled, for Tinashe was a poor student in class but always handed in exemplary homework. Finally, the teacher noticed that the handwriting was different for homework and for class assignments and whipped Tinashe until he confessed the truth. Then the teacher went to the father, told him that Tererai was a prodigy and begged that she be allowed to attend school. After much argument, the father allowed Tererai to attend school for a couple of terms, but then married her off at about age 11.

Tererai's husband barred her from attending school, resented her literacy and beat her whenever she tried to practice her reading by looking at a scrap of old newspaper. Indeed, he beat her for plenty more as well. She hated her marriage but had no way out. "If you're a woman and you are not educated, what else?" she asks.

Yet when Jo Luck came and talked to Tererai and other young women in her village, Luck kept insisting that things did not have to be this way. She kept saying that they could achieve their goals, repeatedly using the word "achievable." The women caught the repetition and asked the interpreter to explain in detail what "achievable" meant. That gave Luck a chance to push forward. "What are your hopes?" she asked the women, through the interpreter. Tererai and the others were puzzled by the question, because they didn't really have any hopes. But Luck pushed them to think about their dreams, and reluctantly, they began to think about what they wanted.

Tererai timidly voiced hope of getting an education. Luck pounced and told her that she could do it, that she should write down her goals and methodically pursue them. After Luck and her entourage disappeared, Tererai began to study on her own, in hiding from her husband, while raising her five children. Painstakingly, with the help of friends, she wrote down her goals on a piece of paper: "One day I will go to the United States of America," she began, for Goal 1. She added that she would earn a college degree, a master's degree and a Ph.D.—all exquisitely absurd dreams for a married cattle herder in Zimbabwe who had less than one year's formal education. But Tererai took the piece of paper and folded it inside three layers of plastic to protect it, and then placed it in an old can. She buried the can under a rock where she herded cattle.

Then Tererai took correspondence classes and began saving money. Her self-confidence grew as she did brilliantly in her studies, and she became a community organizer for Heifer. She stunned everyone with superb schoolwork, and the Heifer aid workers encouraged her to think that she could study in America. One day in 1998, she received notice that she had been admitted to Oklahoma State University.

Some of the neighbors thought that a woman should focus on educating her children, not herself. "I can't talk about my children's education when I'm not educated myself," Tererai responded. "If I educate myself, then I can educate my children." So she climbed into an airplane and flew to America.

At Oklahoma State, Tererai took every credit she could and worked nights to make money. She earned her undergraduate degree, brought her five children to America and started her master's, then returned to her village. She dug up the tin can under the rock and took out the paper on which she had scribbled her goals. She put check marks beside the goals she had fulfilled and buried the tin can again.

In Arkansas, she took a job working for Heifer—while simultaneously earning a master's degree part time. When she had her M.A., Tererai again returned to her village. After embracing her mother and sister, she dug up her tin can and checked off her next goal. Now she is working on her Ph.D. at Western Michigan University.

Tererai has completed her course work and is completing a dissertation about AIDS programs among the poor in Africa. She will become a productive economic asset for Africa and a significant figure in the battle against AIDS. And when she has her doctorate, Tererai will go back to her village and, after hugging her loved ones, go out to the field and dig up her can again.

Edna Adan A former first lady of Somalia and World Health Organization official, she built her own maternity hospital in the enclave of Somaliland.

There are many metaphors for the role of foreign assistance. For our part, we like to think of aid as a kind of lubricant, a few drops of oil in the crankcase of the developing world, so that gears move freely again on their own. That is what the assistance to Tererai amounted to: a bit of help where and when it counts most, which often means focusing on women like her. And now Tererai is gliding along freely on her own—truly able to hold up half the sky.

Critical Thinking

1. What abuses do women often suffer in developing countries?
2. What impact does empowering women have on their families?
3. How might governments and donor countries help to improve women's lives?
4. Aside from the economic benefits, what other reasons are there to educate and empower women?
5. What steps are needed to more fully involve women in the fight against poverty?

Nicholas D. Kristof is a *New York Times* Op-Ed columnist and **Sheryl WuDunn** is a former *Times* correspondent who works in finance and philanthropy. This essay is adapted from their book *"Half the Sky: Turning Oppression Into Opportunity for Women Worldwide,"* which will be published next month by Alfred A. Knopf. You can learn more about *Half the Sky* at nytimes.com/ontheground.

Article

Gender and Revolution in Egypt

It is an old story that women participate in popular revolutions, only to be told later that their concerns must assume a lower priority than "national" issues. Egyptian women face the added problem that many of their contemporary gains are associated with the authoritarian state.

MERVAT HATEM

During the 18 days of the uprising against Husni Mubarak's autocratic rule, the streets were filled with women from across the Egyptian social spectrum. Young and old, veiled and unveiled, poor and affluent—women came out in force to support the movement for a democratic revolution. Yet the gender politics of post-Mubarak Egypt look startlingly familiar, with women's participation in rebuilding the Egyptian state tightly controlled by the transitional government. No women were appointed to the committee convened by the Supreme Council for the Armed Forces (SCAF) to propose amendments to the constitution in the wake of Mubarak's forced resignation. The various cabinets interim Prime Minister 'Isam Sharaf has convened in the last eight months have included only one female minister, Fayza Abu al-Naga, a holdover from Mubarak's regime.

Neither the Islamic nor the Christian establishment has engaged with the public debate about the role of women in Egyptian civil society. Still on the defensive for their early opposition to the protest movements, both institutions have been cautious about anything controversial. As the government, the SCAF, al-Azhar and the Coptic Church work to maintain the gender order associated with the old regime, activist women are using their numerical predominance and high profile in the media and the universities to push for institutional reform as a key step forward in the struggle for democracy.

"Suzanne's Laws"

Public campaigns to discredit the old regime have targeted the state-sponsored feminism that has defined women's civic and social roles since the formation of the Egyptian republic in 1952. The constitution of 1956 guaranteed women the right to vote and run for public office, in exchange for controlling the content and scope of women's political agendas. State policies and resources explicitly shaped the role that women were to play in the development of society. During the 1950s and 1960s, the state emphasized the productive roles of women outside the home by expanding educational and employment opportunities and encouraging birth control. With the onset of economic crisis in the 1970s and 1980s, the state encouraged women's return to the home through the availability of unpaid maternity leave for women in the state sector and attractive early retirement packages.

The Egyptian state consolidated control over the women's rights agenda in 2000 with the creation (by presidential decree) of the National Council for Women. Led by Mubarak's wife Suzanne and headquartered in the National Democratic Party (NDP) offices in Cairo, the National Council collected data on illiteracy among women, disseminated information about health services and disease prevention, partnered with international and aid organizations to provide training and microcredit for women, facilitated the acquisition of ID cards that granted access to existing resources and recruited women interested in running for local and national office to the ruling NDP. Important legislation regarding personal status was proposed by the NDP through the People's Assembly. These incrementally progressive gender policies sought both to legitimize the Mubarak regime as a supporter of women's rights and to promote the National Council as the official representative of Egyptian women in international fora. As a result, the National Council drew international donor money away from non-governmental organizations, many of which provide women with the social services abandoned by the state, such as birth control, employment training, income-generating activities and professional work. The state has also used the Ministry of Social Affairs—which must approve domestic and international funding for NGOs—to rein in civil society institutions that oppose the state's policies on women, human rights and other issues.

The National Council's close association with Mubarak's regime fueled attacks on state-sponsored changes to the personal status code, which critics termed "Suzanne's laws." This label refers to four specific reforms: the right to a "no-fault" divorce *(khul')*, in which a woman forfeits financial claims on her spouse in exchange for divorce; mothers' right to retain custody of sons until they are 15 years old and daughters until they are married, as well as to make important decisions regarding their children's education; the right of Egyptian women married to foreign nationals to pass Egyptian nationality to their children; and electoral quotas for women.

Discrediting gender laws by ascribing them to the undue influence of the president's wife is, of course, not new. Expansions of the personal status law and a parliamentary quota for women enacted under Anwar al-Sadat in 1979 were similarly ridiculed as "Jehan's laws" before they were repealed by the High Constitutional Court in 1985. Both the personal status law and the electoral quotas were struck down: the former for being passed by a presidential decree when a sitting parliament was in session and the latter for violating Article 7 of the constitution, which grants all Egyptian citizens equality before the law and prohibits discrimination due to race, origin, language or religion. In 2011, positive discrimination in favor of women's rights in the family and political representation continues to be viewed as a sign of unchecked or illegal executive power. Quotas granting 50 percent representation to workers and peasants, however, have been debated frequently since 1961, but remain unchallenged as a corrective for historical political exclusion.

Popular debate about the proper role of a president's wife has surged in 2011 with the publication of Tahiyya Abdel Nasser's memoirs, which were also serialized in the daily newspaper *al-Shurouq.* In *Memories with Him,* Abdel Nasser defines herself as the wife of the president and the mother of their children and evinces the belief that maintaining a limited formal role earned her the respect of many Egyptians.[1] (Indeed, using *Him* in the title seems to relegate Abdel Nasser to the background of her husband Gamal's public life.) In contrast, Jinan al-Sadat and Suzanne Mubarak staked out powerful public roles by claiming to advance policy goals for women and children. Their reliance on executive authority has made these women—as well as the programs and laws they championed—symbols of political corruption and the abuse of power.

Rejecting the "Femocrats"

Since Mubarak's departure, women's groups have vigorously opposed the revival of the National Council, half of whose board members resigned after the mass demonstrations of January 25. In March, a leading coalition of feminist women's organizations, the Alliance of Women's Organizations, sent statements to Sharaf and the SCAF demanding the replacement of the National Council with a democratic, transparent body of representatives from civil society groups rather than party-appointed bureaucrats. A second statement in June asked international donors to stop their support of the National Council until it is restructured. Activist critiques of the National Council gained momentum from sympathetic coverage by official media outlets trying to dissociate themselves from the corruption of the old regime; news reports in May 2011 revealed that the National Council failed to provide proper accounting for some $800 million of international aid.[2]

In response to bad publicity and activist pressure, Sharaf has proposed the creation of a Commission for Women, though its functions and policies remain undefined. Dramatic reform of the National Council will be hampered, however, by government policies that seek further to restrict the independence of NGOs and limit criticism of the military and civilian leadership. Minister of Planning and International Cooperation Abu al-Naga, a career diplomat whom Sharaf reappointed from Mubarak's cabinet, has moved to cut off the flow of international funding for civic organizations not approved by the Egyptian state in the interest of "national sovereignty." This policy continues the Mubarak-era project to limit the activities of civil society groups—and to rely on female spokespersons to do so. Law 153, sponsored by Minister of Insurance and Social Affairs Mervat al-Tallawi in the late 1990s, initiated the "governments micromanagement of all aspects of NGO operations."[3] Her successor, Amina al-Gindi, replaced Law 153 with the even more restrictive Law 84, which allowed the government to unilaterally dissolve NGOs for any violation of its terms.

Both Muslim and Coptic women are treated as community property, rather than individuals with personal problems and personal prerogatives.

While some women's organizations have been supportive of plans for a restructured Commission, others are skeptical of the state's involvement in formulating a women's rights agenda. A June 2011 conference organized by the Alliance of Arab Women, a member of the new coalition of feminist NGOs, along with the Association of Former United Nations Employees and other members, drew 3,000 men and women activists from across Egypt under the banner, "Women Are Partners in the Revolution." The discussion ranged from traditional women's issues like family law to broad questions about the constitution, civil liberties and economic and social justice. Some activists within this coalition, including Muna Zulfiqar (a former member of the National Council) and Iqbal Baraka, who have previously been sympathetic to state feminism, have gone further by proposing an independent union for Egyptian women to determine their own agendas outside of state control. This push to explore new forms of organization indicates that the state's institutional relationship to women—one that has allowed the former to dominate the latter in exchange for some concessions—has been significantly challenged.

Personal Status Laws in Crisis

The religious establishment has responded to the push for new approaches to women's rights and family issues in a limited fashion. While there has been some reshuffling of interests around certain reformed family laws, deep tensions remain about the role of Muslim and Christian institutions in either shaping or adhering to laws about marriage, divorce and the family.

According to critics, the advent of no-fault divorce precipitated a crisis of the Egyptian family. No group has been more vocal, however, than the ranks of unwillingly divorced men. Though no formal studies have traced the social effects of *khul',* critics claim it has accelerated overall rates of divorce, destabilized the family and created a mental health crisis for abandoned husbands, who now face social humiliation and attachment disorders.[4] The anger felt by some of these divorcés has inspired groups such as the "Revolt of the Men of Egypt" and the "Movement to Save the Egyptian Family," both of which have created popular Facebook pages and staged protests at al-Azhar, the Ministry of Justice and the Press Syndicate. Associations of divorced women have also organized and held their own demonstrations in front of the Ministry of Justice. While women's concerns about their vulnerability to divorce and the effects of divorce on their children have been largely ignored, these issues seem to be taken seriously now that they are being raised by men.

Divorce has remained a contentious issue since the late 1990s, and the political opportunity created by Mubarak's departure has revitalized the debate. Yet the partisan character of these discussions has been coupled with the rise of new alliances among secular and religious men and women to defend existing family laws. Some voices at al-Azhar—including the widely respected and conservative Islamic Research Complex—have defended their involvement in and the revisions to family law as necessary to accommodate changing demands on parents. Professor of Islamic law Abdallah al-Naggar has argued that extending the age for maternal custody to 15 is compatible with *shari'a* conventions about children's welfare in light of the fact that fathers are spending more time outside the home. Despite reservations about the social effects of higher divorce rates, Islamic philosopher Amena Nusayr has criticized attacks on family law as misplaced anger at Mubarak's regime. She supports the alliance of men and women activists to defend these reforms.[5] More conservative university figures like Su'ad Salih, however, condemn these laws as threatening the primacy of the father in child rearing and unfairly tipping the scale of justice in favor of women.

The Coptic Church, which represents most of the 8 million Christians in Egypt, holds firm that adultery is the only grounds for divorce. In the minority of cases in which divorce is granted, a cumbersome system exists for securing Church permission to remarry. In May 2010, two Christian men who had received divorces won a legal case challenging the Church in the Supreme Administrative Court for violating their constitutional right to remarry. The court agreed. In response, the Church used the decision to mobilize the community to defend the Church against this state attack on its autonomy, its power and its right to legislate personal behavior for its members. The ensuing publicity, including a formal appeal by Pope Shenouda, forced the state to back off from implementing the decision. Activism around the right to divorce has reappeared since Mubarak's departure in the shape of demonstrations by divorced Christian men in front of the main Cairo cathedral of the Coptic Church. They have demanded reform of the Ecclesiastical Council, a body that sets marriage policy and decides individual cases of divorce and remarriage, and called for the formation of provincial councils to take on these roles.

Two recent high-profile cases of Christian women in troubled marriages have highlighted the increasingly tense relations between the Church's position regarding divorce and the personal needs of its members under conditions of intensified sectarian conflict. Given the Church's restrictive laws governing divorce and remarriage, conversion to Islam has sometimes been used as a desperate and difficult solution. In 2010, the story of Camillia Shehata Zakhir, a teacher in Minya in Upper Egypt, stoked sectarian tension and captured national media attention for weeks. Rumors surrounding Camillia's disappearance from her home following a dispute with her husband, a Coptic priest, led her family to report her missing. State security located Camillia several days later and placed her in the care of her father and brother. Because she refused to return to her marital home, rumors circulated by Christians suggested she was being pressured to convert to Islam, provoking opposite rumors that she had converted to Islam but that she was being coerced by her husband and the church to leave her new faith. These stories provoked public clashes between Muslims and Christians, with each group claiming Camillia as their co-religionist. Camillia finally appeared on TV to declare that she never abandoned her Christian faith and that the whole matter was the result of a marital rift.

In April 2011, 'Abir Tal'at left her Christian husband and daughter in Asyout in Upper Egypt, and entered into an *'urfi* (informal Muslim marriage) with Yasin Thabit. Her subsequent disappearance led Yasin to claim Abir had been kidnapped and locked up against her will in the Mar Mina church in the Cairo neighborhood of Imbaba. Muslim demonstrators attempting to liberate 'Abir set the church alight. 'Abir, who was not in the church, eventually gave herself up to the military police and was charged with inflaming public opinion and disturbing the peace. Almost 200 others were arrested and tried in military courts.

These incidents expose the traditional treatment of both Muslim and Christian women as the collective property of the community, not as individuals who confront personal and legal problems in families hampered by restrictive personal status laws. The hollow displays of sheikhs and priests meeting to kiss and make up fail to address the underlying conflicts over citizenship and personal status. While both al-Azhar and the Coptic Church have consolidated power from their control over personal status laws, their social authority faces growing pressure from men and women who see these institutions as insensitive or indifferent to their interests.

Democracy in Action

Resistance to change in the political and religious spheres contrasts with the successful push by women for democratization in other arenas. Popular support for women activists targeted by the SCAF, and for democratic reforms in the media and in the universities, shows dramatic changes in women's consciousness and public attitudes. Continued protests over stalled reforms and the military's obstruction of democratic process have led to a crackdown on public dissent. Since March, the SCAF has arrested and tried 20,000 people in military courts, most of them young men and women. Military police have attempted to intimidate and delegitimize female protesters in particular. After arresting a large group of women in Tahrir Square on March 9, military police subjected them to so-called virginity tests. After repeated military denials of the use of this practice, a senior general eventually admitted to CNN that conducting the tests was a preemptive measure against potential charges of sexual assault. He claimed none of the women who were subjected to the tests were virgins. In the coded language of the military police, this charge implied the women were prostitutes not entitled to any rights. While the state and satellite media outlets did not report this abuse, outrage over the incident led women's groups and human rights organizations to file a lawsuit against the head of the armed forces and the minister of defense for violating the constitutional rights of women to express their opinions and participate in politics without fear of bodily harm.

Broad public support for women activists has caused the SCAF to back off from several campaigns against media figures. Reem Maged, the well-respected host of a popular talk show "Our Country in Dialect," along with blogger Hossam al-Hamalawy and author Nabil Sharaf al-Din (two recent guests on her show), was summoned to the Military Prosecution Office on May 26 to explain her critical views of the military police and the SCAF. Before the meeting, a large crowd of youth and representatives of human rights organizations showed up to support the three dissenters. Demonstrators carried signs reading, "The SCAF does not represent a red line in any discussion; the people are the only red line" and "Freedom of expression is a basic right." Faced with this public backlash, the military retreated, claiming they only invited Maged and her guests to chat over coffee. When the military detained and charged prominent activist and blogger Asma' Mahfouz with inciting violence against the armed forces, a broad coalition of activist groups rallied around her. Leftist law professor Husam 'Isa represented her in court and the Egyptian Mainstream, an Islamic party she had recently joined, paid for her bail. The military ultimately dropped the charges.

Maged used her brush with the SCAF to host an episode with colleague Yusri Fouda of "The Last Word," discussing freedom of speech, the role played by professional reporters, the use of sources and the need to cover different perspectives so that viewers are able to get a better understanding of important issues and events. Muna al-Shazli, another popular television personality, conducted a forceful interview with 'Abboud al-Zumur of the Gama'a Islamiyya. In what became a media event, al-Shazli asked al-Zumur about his role in supporting the 1981 assassination of Anwar al-Sadat, and grilled him about the *salafi* group's religious interpretations of the relationship between rulers and the ruled, the role that religion should play in society and why Egyptians should view him and the Gama'a as legitimate partners in a new democratic Egypt. For supporters of the Gama'a, al-Shazli's antagonistic questions were made more outrageous by the fact that she was unveiled. For other viewers, her professionalism was a bold statement in the wake of the spectacular failure of state television in reporting and analyzing the initial 18 days of protests. (Telecasters Suha al-Naqqash and Shahira Amin protested this failure in public ways during the revolution, with the former taking an open-ended leave of absence and the latter resigning her post.)

In the universities, women have pushed for institutional democratization, academic freedom and an end to corruption since 2004 through the March 9 movement for university independence. Since February 2011, women academics have expanded their role in this movement. At Cairo University, they took the lead in the campaign to replace the dean of the Faculty of Arts, a position that has been appointed by the state since 1993. Hala Kamal, Randa Abu Bakr, Madiha Duss, 'Abir 'Abd al-Hafiz and Sayyid Bahrawi initiated the discussion of electoral alternatives in general faculty meetings, conducted a survey to test faculty support and drafted provisions for a new, free electoral process. Abu Bakr was elected dean of the Faculty of Arts in June 2011, though her appointment was blocked by the Ministry of Higher Education due to her affiliation with the March 9 movement.[6] When 4,000 university professors went on strike in September 2011 supported by thousands of student demonstrators, the Ministry was forced to organize its own elections, which Abu Bakr boycotted. Twelve of the 17 faculties at Cairo University elected new deans.

Moving Forward

Unlike in Tunisia, where feminist activists have been less eager to dismantle the structures of state-directed gender policies (with the family code as its cornerstone), activist Egyptian women have expressed a clear desire to distance themselves from the institutional and political legacies of state feminism. This decision is partly motivated by their success in the establishment of NGOs that articulate the multiplicity of voices and approaches to women's interests and concerns. Feminist organizations seek to solidify their institutional accomplishments, the result of many struggles against an aggressive authoritarian state, through coalition politics that allow different groups to work together without undermining the diversity of views, expertise, interests and agendas.

While the Sharaf government has attempted to reassert state control over the discussion of women's rights, these independent organizations advocate a more transparent and balanced relationship between the state and society. The flow of foreign aid to support Egypt's transition to democracy, especially aid earmarked for women, has provided incentives for the state's continued involvement in the affairs of these civil society groups. By complicating the funding of independent organizations, the government may hope that international donors will eventually funnel some of the money through the state.

Despite distancing themselves from the negative legacy of state feminism, the advocates of women's rights have mostly defended the modest changes it introduced in divorce, custody and nationality laws as gains made by Egyptian women reflecting the changing needs of society. The visible roles that these women are playing in the call for the reform of important institutions of society suggest the development of a new consciousness in which some segments of the middle classes reject the state's restriction of women's voices to gender questions. While most women activists acknowledge the work that remains to be done to advance women's education, employment and the integration of the rural, Upper Egyptian and Bedouin women into society, many no longer see themselves as dependents of the state in this process.

Notes

1. Tahiyya Gamal Abdel Nasser, *Dhikrayat Ma'ahu* (Cairo: Dar al-Shurouq, 2011).
2. *Sabah al-Khayr,* May 17, 2011.
3. Human Rights Watch, *World Report 2000* (New York, 1999), p. 347.
4. *Al-Ahram,* August 9, 2011; and *al-Ahram,* June 25, 2010.
5. *Al-Misri al-Yaurm,* May 31, 2011.
6. E-mail communication from Hala Kamal, October 15, 2011.

Critical Thinking

1. What accounts for opposition to women's rights progress in Egypt?
2. Why are women skeptical that their interests will be protected in the post-Mubarak era?
3. How have women responded to threats to their freedoms?

Mervat Hatem is professor of political science at Howard University.

Author's Note: I wish to acknowledge the helpful feedback of two professors, Vickie Langohr of the College of Holy Cross and Hala Kamal of Cairo University.

Article

Prepared by: Robert J. Griffiths, *University of North Carolina at Greensboro*

Why Do They Hate Us?

The real war on women is in the Middle East

MONA ELTAHAWY

Learning Outcomes

After reading this article, you will be able to:

- List the range of abuses against women in the Arab world.
- Summarize the argument for why the revolutions in the Arab world might have a limited impact on women's rights.

In "Distant View of a Minaret," the late and much-neglected Egyptian writer Alifa Rifaat begins her short story with a woman so unmoved by sex with her husband that as he focuses solely on his pleasure, she notices a spider web she must sweep off the ceiling and has time to ruminate on her husband's repeated refusal to prolong intercourse until she too climaxes, "as though purposely to deprive her." Just as her husband denies her an orgasm, the call to prayer interrupts his, and the man leaves. After washing up, she loses herself in prayer—so much more satisfying that she can't wait until the next prayer—and looks out onto the street from her balcony. She interrupts her reverie to make coffee dutifully for her husband to drink after his nap. Taking it to their bedroom to pour it in front of him as he prefers, she notices he is dead. She instructs their son to go and get a doctor. "She returned to the living room and poured out the coffee for herself. She was surprised at how calm she was," Rifaat writes.

In a crisp three-and-a-half pages, Rifaat lays out a trifecta of sex, death, and religion, a bulldozer that crushes denial and defensiveness to get at the pulsating heart of misogyny in the Middle East. There is no sugarcoating it. They don't hate us because of our freedoms, as the tired, post-9/11 American cliché had it. We have no freedoms because they hate us, as this Arab woman so powerfully says.

Yes: They hate us. It must be said.

Some may ask why I'm bringing this up now, at a time when the region has risen up, fueled not by the usual hatred of America and Israel but by a common demand for freedom. After all, shouldn't everyone get basic rights first, before women demand special treatment? And what does gender, or for that matter, sex, have to do with the Arab Spring? But I'm not talking about sex hidden away in dark corners and closed bedrooms. An entire political and economic system—one that treats half of humanity like animals—must be destroyed along with the other more obvious tyrannies choking off the region from its future. Until the rage shifts from the oppressors in our presidential palaces to the oppressors on our streets and in our homes, our revolution has not even begun.

So: Yes, women all over the world have problems; yes, the United States has yet to elect a female president; and yes, women continue to be objectified in many "Western" countries (I live in one of them). That's where the conversation usually ends when you try to discuss why Arab societies hate women.

But let's put aside what the United States does or doesn't do to women. Name me an Arab country, and I'll recite a litany of abuses fueled by a toxic mix of culture and religion that few seem willing or able to disentangle lest they blaspheme or offend. When more than 90 percent of ever-married women in Egypt—including my mother and all but one of her six sisters—have had their genitals cut in the name of modesty, then surely we must all blaspheme. When Egyptian women are subjected to humiliating "virginity tests" merely for speaking out, it's no time for silence. When an article in the Egyptian criminal code says that if a woman has been beaten by her husband "with good intentions" no punitive damages can be obtained, then to hell with political correctness. And what, pray tell, are "good intentions"? They are legally deemed to include any beating that is "not severe" or "directed at the face." What all this means is that when it comes to the status of women in the Middle East, it's not better than you think. It's much, much worse. Even after these "revolutions," all is more or less considered well with the world as long as women are covered up, anchored to the home, denied the simple mobility of getting into their own cars, forced to get permission from men to travel, and unable to marry without a male guardian's blessing—or divorce either.

Not a single Arab country ranks in the top 100 in the World Economic Forum's Global Gender Gap Report, putting the region as a whole solidly at the planet's rock bottom. Poor or rich, we all hate our women. Neighbors Saudi Arabia and Yemen, for instance, might be eons apart when it comes to

GDP, but only four places separate them on the index, with the kingdom at 131 and Yemen coming in at 135 out of 135 countries. Morocco, often touted for its "progressive" family law (a 2005 report by Western "experts" called it "an example for Muslim countries aiming to integrate into modern society"), ranks 129; according to Morocco's Ministry of Justice, 41,098 girls under age 18 were married there in 2010.

It's easy to see why the lowest-ranked country is Yemen, where 55 percent of women are illiterate, 79 percent do not participate in the labor force, and just one woman serves in the 301-person parliament. Horrific news reports about 12-year-old girls dying in childbirth do little to stem the tide of child marriage there. Instead, demonstrations in support of child marriage outstrip those against it, fueled by clerical declarations that opponents of state-sanctioned pedophilia are apostates because the Prophet Mohammed, according to them, married his second wife, Aisha, when she was a child.

But at least Yemeni women can drive. It surely hasn't ended their litany of problems, but it symbolizes freedom—and nowhere does such symbolism resonate more than in Saudi Arabia, where child marriage is also practiced and women are perpetually minors regardless of their age or education. Saudi women far outnumber their male counterparts on university campuses but are reduced to watching men far less qualified control every aspect of their lives.

Yes, Saudi Arabia, the country where a gang-rape survivor was sentenced to jail for agreeing to get into a car with an unrelated male and needed a royal pardon; Saudi Arabia, where a woman who broke the ban on driving was sentenced to 10 lashes and again needed a royal pardon; Saudi Arabia, where women still can't vote or run in elections, yet it's considered "progress" that a royal decree promised to enfranchise them for almost completely symbolic local elections in—wait for it—2015. So bad is it for women in Saudi Arabia that those tiny paternalistic pats on their backs are greeted with delight as the monarch behind them, King Abdullah, is hailed as a "reformer"—even by those who ought to know better, such as Newsweek, which in 2010 named the king one of the top 11 most respected world leaders. You want to know how bad it is? The "reformer's" answer to the revolutions popping up across the region was to numb his people with still more government handouts—especially for the Salafi zealots from whom the Saudi royal family inhales legitimacy. King Abdullah is 87. Just wait until you see the next in line, Prince Nayef, a man straight out of the Middle Ages. His misogyny and zealotry make King Abdullah look like Susan B. Anthony.

SO WHY DO THEY HATE US? Sex, or more precisely hymens, explains much.

"Why extremists always focus on women remains a mystery to me," U.S. Secretary of State Hillary Clinton said recently. "But they all seem to. It doesn't matter what country they're in or what religion they claim. They want to control women." (And yet Clinton represents an administration that openly supports many of those misogynistic despots.) Attempts to control by such regimes often stem from the suspicion that without it, a woman is just a few degrees short of sexual insatiability. Observe Yusuf al-Qaradawi, the popular cleric and longtime conservative TV host on Al Jazeera who developed a stunning penchant for the Arab Spring revolutions—once they were under way, that is—undoubtedly understanding that they would eliminate the tyrants who long tormented and oppressed both him and the Muslim Brotherhood movement from which he springs.

I could find you a host of crackpots sounding off on Woman the Insatiable Temptress, but I'm staying mainstream with Qaradawi, who commands a huge audience on and off the satellite channels. Although he says female genital mutilation (which he calls "circumcision," a common euphemism that tries to put the practice on a par with male circumcision) is not "obligatory," you will also find this priceless observation in one of his books: "I personally support this under the current circumstances in the modern world. Anyone who thinks that circumcision is the best way to protect his daughters should do it," he wrote, adding, "The moderate opinion is in favor of practicing circumcision to reduce temptation." So even among "moderates," girls' genitals are cut to ensure their desire is nipped in the bud—pun fully intended. Qaradawi has since issued a fatwa against female genital mutilation, but it comes as no surprise that when Egypt banned the practice in 2008, some Muslim Brotherhood legislators opposed the law. And some still do—including a prominent female parliamentarian, Azza al-Garf.

Yet it's the men who can't control themselves on the streets, where from Morocco to Yemen, sexual harassment is endemic and it's for the men's sake that so many women are encouraged to cover up. Cairo has a women-only subway car to protect us from wandering hands and worse; countless Saudi malls are for families only, barring single men from entry unless they produce a requisite female to accompany them.

We often hear how the Middle East's failing economies have left many men unable to marry, and some even use that to explain rising levels of sexual harassment on the streets. In a 2008 survey by the Egyptian Center for Women's Rights, more than 80 percent of Egyptian women said they'd experienced sexual harassment and more than 60 percent of men admitted to harassing women. Yet we never hear how a later marriage age affects women. Do women have sex drives or not? Apparently, the Arab jury is still out on the basics of human biology.

Enter that call to prayer and the sublimation through religion that Rifaat so brilliantly introduces in her story. Just as regime-appointed clerics lull the poor across the region with promises of justice—and nubile virgins—in the next world rather than a reckoning with the corruption and nepotism of the dictator in this life, so women are silenced by a deadly combination of men who hate them while also claiming to have God firmly on their side.

I turn again to Saudi Arabia, and not just because when I encountered the country at age 15 I was traumatized into feminism—there's no other way to describe it—but because the kingdom is unabashed in its worship of a misogynistic God and never suffers any consequences for it, thanks to its double-whammy advantage of having oil and being home to Islam's two holiest places, Mecca and Medina.

Then—the 1980s and 1990s—as now, clerics on Saudi TV were obsessed with women and their orifices, especially what came out of them. I'll never forget hearing that if a baby boy urinated on you, you could go ahead and pray in the same clothes, yet if a baby girl peed on you, you had to change. What on Earth in the girl's urine made you impure? I wondered.

Hatred of women.

How much does Saudi Arabia hate women? So much so that 15 girls died in a school fire in Mecca in 2002, after "morality police" barred them from fleeing the burning building—and kept firefighters from rescuing them—because the girls were not wearing headscarves and cloaks required in public. And nothing happened. No one was put on trial. Parents were silenced. The only concession to the horror was that girls' education was quietly taken away by then-Crown Prince Abdullah from the Salafi zealots, who have nonetheless managed to retain their vise-like grip on the kingdom's education system writ large.

This, however, is no mere Saudi phenomenon, no hateful curiosity in the rich, isolated desert. The Islamist hatred of women burns brightly across the region—now more than ever.

In Kuwait, where for years Islamists fought women's enfranchisement, they hounded the four women who finally made it into parliament, demanding that the two who didn't cover their hair wear hijabs. When the Kuwaiti parliament was dissolved this past December, an Islamist parliamentarian demanded the new house—devoid of a single female legislator—discuss his proposed "decent attire" law.

In Tunisia, long considered the closest thing to a beacon of tolerance in the region, women took a deep breath last fall after the Islamist Ennahda party won the largest share of votes in the country's Constituent Assembly. Party leaders vowed to respect Tunisia's 1956 Personal Status Code, which declared "the principle of equality between men and women" as citizens and banned polygamy. But female university professors and students have complained since then of assaults and intimidation by Islamists for not wearing hijabs, while many women's rights activists wonder how talk of Islamic law will affect the actual law they will live under in post-revolution Tunisia.

In Libya, the first thing the head of the interim government, Mustafa Abdel Jalil, promised to do was to lift the late Libyan tyrant's restrictions on polygamy. Lest you think of Muammar al-Qaddafi as a feminist of any kind, remember that under his rule girls and women who survived sexual assaults or were suspected of "moral crimes" were dumped into "social rehabilitation centers," effective prisons from which they could not leave unless a man agreed to marry them or their families took them back.

Then there's Egypt, where less than a month after President Hosni Mubarak stepped down, the military junta that replaced him, ostensibly to "protect the revolution," inadvertently reminded us of the two revolutions we women need. After it cleared Tahrir Square of protesters, the military detained dozens of male and female activists. Tyrants oppress, beat, and torture all. We know. But these officers reserved "virginity tests" for female activists: rape disguised as a medical doctor inserting his fingers into their vaginal opening in search of hymens. (The doctor was sued and eventually acquitted in March.)

What hope can there be for women in the new Egyptian parliament, dominated as it is by men stuck in the seventh century? A quarter of those parliamentary seats are now held by Salafis, who believe that mimicking the original ways of the Prophet Mohammed is an appropriate prescription for modern life. Last fall, when fielding female candidates, Egypt's Salafi Nour Party ran a flower in place of each woman's face. Women are not to be seen or heard—even their voices are a temptation—so there they are in the Egyptian parliament, covered from head to toe in black and never uttering a word.

And we're in the middle of a revolution in Egypt! It's a revolution in which women have died, been beaten, shot at, and sexually assaulted fighting alongside men to rid our country of that uppercase Patriarch—Mubarak—yet so many lowercase patriarchs still oppress us. The Muslim Brotherhood, with almost half the total seats in our new revolutionary parliament, does not believe women (or Christians for that matter) can be president. The woman who heads the "women's committee" of the Brotherhood's political party said recently that women should not march or protest because it's more "dignified" to let their husbands and brothers demonstrate for them.

The hatred of women goes deep in Egyptian society. Those of us who have marched and protested have had to navigate a minefield of sexual assaults by both the regime and its lackeys, and, sadly, at times by our fellow revolutionaries. On the November day I was sexually assaulted on Mohamed Mahmoud Street near Tahrir Square, by at least four Egyptian riot police, I was first groped by a man in the square itself. While we are eager to expose assaults by the regime, when we're violated by our fellow civilians we immediately assume they're agents of the regime or thugs because we don't want to taint the revolution.

So What is to be Done?

First we stop pretending. Call out the hate for what it is. Resist cultural relativism and know that even in countries undergoing revolutions and uprisings, women will remain the cheapest bargaining chips. You—the outside world—will be told that it's our "culture" and "religion" to do X, Y, or Z to women. Understand that whoever deemed it as such was never a woman. The Arab uprisings may have been sparked by an Arab man—Mohamed Bouazizi, the Tunisian street vendor who set himself on fire in desperation—but they will be finished by Arab women.

Amina Filali—the 16-year-old Moroccan girl who drank poison after she was forced to marry, and be beaten by, her rapist—is our Bouazizi. Salwa el-Husseini, the first Egyptian woman to speak out against the "virginity tests"; Samira Ibrahim, the first one to sue; and Rasha Abdel Rahman, who testified alongside her—they are our Bouazizis. We must not wait for them to die to become so. Manal al-Sharif, who spent nine days in jail for breaking her country's ban on women driving, is Saudi Arabia's Bouazizi. She is a one-woman revolutionary force who pushes against an ocean of misogyny.

Our political revolutions will not succeed unless they are accompanied by revolutions of thought—social, sexual, and cultural revolutions that topple the Mubaraks in our minds as well as our bedrooms.

"Do you know why they subjected us to virginity tests?" Ibrahim asked me soon after we'd spent hours marching together to mark International Women's Day in Cairo on March 8. "They want to silence us; they want to chase women back home. But we're not going anywhere."

We are more than our headscarves and our hymens. Listen to those of us fighting. Amplify the voices of the region and poke the hatred in its eye. There was a time when being an Islamist was the most vulnerable political position in Egypt and Tunisia. Understand that now it very well might be Woman. As it always has been.

"When an article in the Egyptian criminal code says that if a woman has been beaten by her husband 'with good intentions' no punitive damages can be obtained, then to hell with political correctness.

"When more than 90 percent of ever-married women in Egypt—including my mother and all but one of her six sisters—have their genitals cut in the name of modesty, then surely we must all blaspheme.

"When Egyptian women are subjected to humiliating virginity tests merely for speaking out, it's no time for silence.

"Yes: They hate us. It must be said."

Critical Thinking

1. In what ways are Arab women subject to human rights abuses?
2. What rationale do men provide for the treatment of women in the Arab world?
3. Why is it unlikely that the revolutions in the Arab world will bring changes in attitudes about women's rights?

Create Central

www.mhhe.com/createcentral

Internet References

WIDNET: Women in Development NETwork
www.focusintl.com/widnet.htm

Women Watch/Regional and Country Information
www.un.org/womenwatch

Mona Eltahawy is an Egyptian American columnist. In November 2011, Egyptian police beat her, breaking her left arm and right hand, and sexually assaulted her. She was detained by the Interior Ministry and military intelligence for 12 hours.

Article

Girls in War

Sex Slave, Mother, Domestic Aide, Combatant

RADHIKA COOMARASWAMY

"The attackers tied me up and raped me because I was fighting. About five of them did the same thing to me until one of the commanders who knew my father came and stopped them, but also took me to his house to make me his wife. I just accepted him because of fear and didn't want to say no because he might do the same thing to me too." This is the testimony of a young girl of 14 from Liberia as told to the *Machel Review* in a focus group conducted jointly by the United Nations Children's Fund (UNICEF) and the Office of the Special Representative of the Secretary-General for Children and Armed Conflict (OSRSG/CAAC).

This story shows how vulnerable girls are in armed conflict. Actually, they can be affected by war in five different ways. Firstly, they are often direct victims of violence—killed, maimed or sexually violated as war crimes are committed against them. Secondly, they can be recruited and used as combatants for fighting in the battlefield. Thirdly, as refugees and internally displaced persons (IDPS), they remain in insecure environments, often deprived of basic amenities. Fourthly, they are frequently trafficked and exploited, as perpetrators abuse their vulnerability. Finally, when they become orphans, some of them have to manage child-headed households, eking out a living for themselves and their siblings.

Direct Violence

The number of children who are victims of direct violence, especially killings, has greatly increased in the last few years. Many have lost their lives in the confrontation between terrorism and counter terrorism. We have seen the phenomenon of children being used as suicide bombers and we have seen children as victims of aerial bombardment, a part of what is euphemistically called "collateral damage".

In Afghanistan I met Aisha, a girl whose home had been destroyed during an air raid which killed many of her family members, and whose school had been attacked by insurgents opposing education for girls. But Aisha was determined to go on with her studies so that she could become a school teacher.

Sexual Violence

Girls are often raped or violated in situations of conflict. Raping girls and women is often a military strategy aimed at terrorizing the population and humiliating the community. At other times, the climate of impunity in war zones leads to rape and exploitation by individual soldiers who know they will not be punished. Eva was a young girl I met in the Democratic Republic of the Congo. She and her friend were walking to school when they were waylaid by armed members of the Democratic Liberation Forces of Rwanda. They were taken to the camp, repeatedly raped, compelled to live in a state of forced nudity and assigned to domestic chores for the members of the group. Eva finally escaped and found shelter in Panzi hospital, a refuge for victims of sexual violence, where she found out that she was pregnant. She was 13 years old. When I met her, Panzi hospital was taking care of her child while she was attending school. They were trying to trace her family, even though they knew that girls who are victims of rape are often shunned by their next of kin.

Girl Soldiers

Increasingly, girls are being recruited into fighting forces as child soldiers. Some are abducted and have to play the dual role of sex slave and child combatant. This was particularly true in the wars of Sierra Leone and Liberia. In other cases, girls join the fighting forces for a multitude of reasons because they identify with the ideology, they want to run away from home or they have no other option for survival. Maria was a former girl child soldier whom I met in Colombia. She joined the rebel groups because her brothers had joined before her. Subjected to domestic violence at home, she ran away. She fought with the rebels and was then captured during one of the confrontations. Today she feels very lost. She does not want to go back home and she feels she has neither the education nor the skills to survive alone. When I met her, she was being taken care of by a foster parent. She felt boys were frightened of her because of her past. She also told me that many girls who had left the movement finally end up in sex work as a survival strategy.

Internally Displaced

Eighty percent of the world's refugees and internally displaced are women and children. Displaced children are perhaps one of the most vulnerable categories. In many parts of the world they are separated from their families while fleeing, becoming orphans overnight. And living in camps, they are often recruited into the fighting forces. Displaced children also suffer from high rates of malnutrition and have little access to medical services. Many girls are victims of violence in the camp or when they leave the camp to gather firewood and other necessities. For those who advocate for the rights of displaced children, the first priority should be security. The objective is to ensure that children are safe, protected from sexual violence and recruitment, and that there are child-friendly spaces in the camp. The second priority is education. Recently, UN agencies and non-governmental organizations (NGOS) have partnered to advocate strongly that education is an integral part of emergency response and not a luxury development. This was one of the key messages of the General Assembly debate on Education in Emergencies, in March 2009. It is important to plan for schools and play areas for children as the camp is constructed and provisions are made for families to be settled. It gives children a sense of normalcy and routine when they live in the camps.

Trafficking and Sexual Exploitation

Another concern we have for girl children in situations of armed conflict is that they are often trafficked and sexually exploited. At the international level, commentators have always pointed to "waves" of trafficking: that is, particular groups being trafficked in large numbers at a particular time. These waves often occur in areas of armed conflicts; women flee in large numbers, and being sex workers is their only survival strategy. They become victims of terrible exploitation by ruthless international criminal gangs. So many of these stories have been chronicled and a great deal of effort has been made over the last two decades to tackle the phenomenon. Nevertheless, the ground realities of conflict still lead to the sexual vulnerability of girls and women. Our own peacekeepers have not been immune to these situations. The UN Department of Peacekeeping Operations has made it a priority through their zero tolerance policy and code of conduct and discipline to ensure that this type of activity ceases and that peacekeepers will only be seen as protectors.

In areas of armed conflicts women flee in large numbers, and being sex workers is their only survival strategy. They become victims of terrible exploitation by ruthless international criminal gangs.

Orphans and Child-Headed Households

The terrible toll of war also makes many children into orphans overnight. In many parts of the world, we are seeing child-headed households where children have to fend for themselves as well as for other children. This happens especially to girl children who have to take over the role of parents. Parentless children often live in deplorable conditions such as broken-down buildings with leaky roofs, or no roofs at all. They sleep together under torn plastic sacks and cook with old rusty cans and broken pottery. They are susceptible to all manner of diseases and their situation is terribly vulnerable and heartbreaking. UN agencies are trying ways of giving these children a future without institutionalizing them in centres. It is their aim to keep children in the community and make it the responsibility of the community to take care of its children. Through schemes that find foster homes and foster mothers, they hope to let the children enjoy the benefit of family life.

The terrible toll of war also makes many children into orphans overnight. In many parts of the world, we are seeing child-headed households where children have to fend for themselves and also other children. This happens especially to girl children who have to take over the role of parents.

The International Tribunals and the Fight against Impunity

How has the international community responded to these devastating descriptions of what girl children suffer during war time? Recently things are slowly beginning to change, especially in the fight against impunity. The first breakthrough for children was the establishment of international tribunals which began to hold perpetrators accountable for international crimes. The cases before the tribunals of the Former Yugoslavia and Rwanda that dealt with sexual violence, created a framework of international jurisprudence that will help us in the future. Individual women found justice, and there is always the deterrent effect that cannot be measured in an empirical manner. Recently, the Special Court for Sierra Leone found several commanders of the Revolutionary United Front guilty of 16 charges of war crimes and crimes against humanity including conscription and enlistment of children under 15 into the fighting forces. The setting up of the International Criminal Court was the culmination of this trajectory. Their first case, the Thomas Lubanga case, involved the recruitment and use of children as child soldiers, strengthening the cause for children. Our office submitted an amicus curiae to the court in that case, arguing that girl children should be brought into the ambit of protection. We advocate for the young, abducted girls who play multiple roles in camps, to receive the protection of the law against being recruited, used, as well as forced to participate in the hostilities. We hope to get our day in court to argue this point of view so that the enormous suffering of girl children does not remain invisible.

Involvement of the Security Council

In the area of children in armed conflict, another mechanism that has begun to chip away at impunity is Security Council resolution 1612. The resolution, passed in 2005, created a Working

Group on Children and Armed Conflict. It also established a monitoring and reporting mechanism involving a Task Force at the national level made up of all the UN agencies, assigned to report on the violations. The Task Force is chaired by either the Resident Co-ordinator or the Special Representative and is often co-chaired by UNICEF. Through this mechanism, OSRSG/CAAC receives bimonthly reports on grave violations against children in war zones. The Security Council process is informed by the Annual Report of the Secretary-General to the Council which lists parties that recruit and use child soldiers. Resolution 1612 recommends the prospect of targeted measures against persistent violators of children's rights. The hope in 2009 is to extend these measures, beyond the recruitment and use of child soldiers, to include sexual violence against children, such that those who persistently use sexual violence in war be listed, shamed and face the possibility of sanctions. Having received the full support of the UN system, it is hoped that Member States, especially those in the Security Council, will help our office deliver on this promise.

In a world where there is so much abuse against women and children, one may become cynical about these small steps that the international community has begun to take to fight impunity, but we must not underestimate their effects. Recently, I was in the Central African Republic and met three generations of women in one family who had been raped when Jean-Pierre Bemba's troops attacked the capital, Bangui. They were getting ready to go to The Hague to testify against him. Their elation at the possibility of justice, and their gratitude that these things have come to pass has convinced me that we are on the right path. Grave violations, war crimes and crimes against humanity must be taken seriously, so that the culture of impunity that often hangs over warfare be broken.

Reintegration of Former Child Soldiers

Another area where the international community can help is the field of rehabilitation and reintegration. Reintegrating children affected by war is a major task facing governments, UN agencies and NGO partners working in the field. The Paris Principles give us a framework on how to reintegrate children associated with armed groups, but these principles are also a guide to reintegrating all children. The call for community-based programming that works with the child, while developing the family and the community in an inclusive manner, must be the starting point for child-based programming. And yet, some children need special attention. Research shows that children who were forced to commit terrible crimes and children who were victims of sexual violence need special care and attention. Girl children often have different needs from boys. Treating children as important individuals while, at the same time, developing the community in a holistic manner, is the only sustainable way forward.

Finally we cannot even begin to speak of the psychological toll that war takes on children. When I was in Gaza, I went to a school and entered a classroom of nine year-old girls, who were drawing in an art class. I moved from one to the other, and then I just looked down at one girl's drawing, Ameena's. She had drawn a house and she explained to me that the two figures in the house were her mother and herself. Above the house there was a mangled object which I gather was a helicopter gunship; to the left of the house there was an imposing looking tank and to the right of the house, a soldier. All these were firing at the home. Her sad, dull eyes on her beautiful face told the rest of the story. Meeting the day to day reality of war is a terrible calling for all of my colleagues working in the field. But rebuilding the shattered lives of children is an even more daunting task; to make them smile again, care again and live with purpose is the challenge of the hour.

Critical Thinking

1. In what ways are girls vulnerable in conflict situations?
2. How are internal displacement and vulnerability linked?
3. How has the international community responded to this vulnerability?

Radhika Coomaraswamy is the Special Representative of the UN Secretary-General for Children and Armed Conflict (www.un.org/children/conflict).

Article

Prepared by: Robert J. Griffiths, *University of North Carolina at Greensboro*

Increasing Women's Access to Justice in Post-Conflict Societies

MICHELLE BACHELET

Learning Outcomes

After reading this article, you will be able to:

- Identify the effects of conflict on women and the impact this has on the ability of women to fully participate in peacebuilding and reconstruction.
- Discuss the efforts to incorporate a women's agenda into peacebuilding and transitional justice in post-conflict societies.

For centuries, sexual violence and other atrocities committed against women were considered inevitable during times of war. Today, legal frameworks and institutions are in place to provide justice to women affected by conflict and progress is being made.

In all situations of conflict, women are disproportionately affected by sexual and gender-based violence, forced displacement, the destruction of civilian infrastructure and the range of rights violations. The legacy of this violence endures long after a peace agreement is signed.

In the past three decades, significant gains have been made in building an international justice architecture which includes accountability for sexual and gender-based crimes. The prosecution of these crimes serves as an important signalling of a break with the past, an assertion of the equal rights of women and an international willingness to protect these rights. For the first time in history, these significant advances have made it possible to prosecute sexual and gender-based violence in conflict.

However, much remains to be done. The rule of law still often rules out women. Obstacles that prevent women from accessing legal protection for their rights persist, resulting in discrimination and inequality that hamper their ability to live free of violence and contribute to society as full and equal citizens.

In the wake of fighting and destruction, institutions are only rudimentarily functioning, community networks are weakened, small arms proliferate and violence against women continues. The devastation of conflict exacerbates both the challenges and the impact of discrimination. As a result, women have the least access to justice precisely when they need it most.

The absence of a strong framework of laws to protect women's rights, backed by effective security and justice institutions to enforce these rights, has wide-ranging impacts. The 2011 World Development Report of the World Bank made important findings on the nexus among justice, security and development in conflict-affected States. The report noted that where the rule of law and justice are not secured, insecurity and violence continue and development is hampered. As some have noted, violent conflict, with its deaths, disease, destruction and displacement, is equal to "development in reverse".

Furthermore, this insecurity and violence, facilitated by a lack of justice or legal frameworks, effectively prevent women's participation in rebuilding their nations—in efforts for reconstruction, peacebuilding and development. Without security, women and girls will not engage in field-based farming or market activity, which is crucial for early recovery and family survival. Girls will not enroll in school. Women will not engage in public life. In short, without justice and security, societies impede the ability of half their population and human resources to contribute to development and peace.

One of the most significant measures of enabling women's participation is through the provision of reparations. As the 2007 Nairobi Declaration on Women's and Girls' Right to a Remedy and Reparation notes, "[justice and] reparations must go above and beyond the immediate reasons and consequences of crimes and violations; they must aim to address the political and structural inequalities that negatively shape women's and girls' lives". This is paramount because women are more than victims of conflict; they are leaders of peace, justice and democracy.

The post-conflict momentum presents unique opportunities for transformation. UN Women's report, "Progress of the World's Women: In Pursuit of Justice", found that transitions following conflict present not only important opportunities to address injustices faced by women during times of war, but also a chance to transform underlying inequalities and gender-based discrimination through the new constitutions, legislative reforms and institution-building put in place.

Research shows that restoring basic services, such as education and health care, is vital to women's ability to access justice.

To move this forward, the United Nations advocates prioritizing women's security in rule of law initiatives and creating a protective environment for women. Key to success is the provision of support for women's access to justice and law enforcement institutions, and the application of gender expertise and guidance to the formulation of truth commissions, reparations programmes and other transitional justice mechanisms. Also of critical importance are economic recovery programmes that prioritize women's involvement in employment creation schemes, community development programmes and delivery of front-line services, This commitment is outlined in the 2010 Report of the Secretary-General "Women's Participation in Peacebuilding," and his 2011 report "Rule of Law and Transitional Justice in Conflict and Post-Conflict", which called for an increased focus on addressing the underlying economic and social issues that drive inequality.

Most recently on 24 September 2012, the United Nations General Assembly held a High-level Meeting on the Rule of Law during which Member States adopted a Declaration reaffirming their commitment to the rule of law as a foundation to peace and security, development and respect for human rights. The Declaration recommitted States to "establishing appropriate legal and legislative frameworks to prevent and address all forms of discrimination and violence against women and to secure their empowerment and full access to justice".

Complementing the work of international criminal proceedings, UN Women continues to work towards extending the notion of gender justice to a much-needed focus on the victim. UN Women's approach envisions a comprehensive justice that includes the critical component of reparations, which are a victim's right under international law.

In order to strengthen the United Nations approach to women's access to justice post-conflict, UN Women is currently reviewing all programming and funding undertaken in this area. This landmark effort will contribute to placing the issue of women's access to justice at the centre of efforts made by the United Nations in promoting the rule of law in post-conflict societies.

It is important that all transitional justice measures—courts, truth commissions and reparations programmes—place women's needs at their core and further justice for women. UN Women works to ensure that every United Nations Commission of Inquiry has the investigative expertise on gender crimes needed to secure accountability. Most recently, these efforts have strengthened the likelihood that the International Criminal Court will prosecute these crimes in relation to the conflict in Libya. We have also supported truth commission processes in a range of contexts, for example in Kenya, the Solomon Islands and Sierra Leone, to promote women's access to justice.

"We must improve measures to ensure the protection of victims and witnesses and enhance women's participation so that they can benefit from transitional justice processes and reparations programmes."

In order to protect and share the wealth of experience accumulated within the International Criminal Tribunal for the Former Yugoslavia and Rwanda and the Special Court for Sierra Leone, we support the legacy and documentation of their work. As part of this endeavour, UN Women and the United Nations Development Programme facilitated a New York visit of the leadership of the Sierra Leone Special Court, comprised of women, to brief the Security Council on their work. Their contributions made it evident that these women were not only an important model of women's leadership in post-conflict decision-making but, more importantly, they created foundational international jurisprudence on gender-based crimes, and actively increased women's access to the court through their support for innovative gender-sensitive outreach programmes. These programmes are now replicated by other courts.

UN Women is moving forward by working with governments to support legal and institutional reforms, and training and building capacity of those responsible for delivering justice, including the police, lawyers and judges. We are also working to get more women serving on the front lines of justice.

In Liberia, UN Women supported women in the communities to become crucial players in peacebuilding and conflict resolution. This was done by facilitating the establishment of so-called Peace Huts that are based on traditional justice systems. At first, these Peace Huts focused on a "shedding the weight" process and counselled women who experienced grief and trauma, as well as supported ex-child soldiers after the civil war. Then, Peace Hut women began hearing cases, and these huts became a safe space where village women came together to mediate and resolve community disputes. This is where they gather to discuss matters that affect their daily lives, where the reconciliation and resolution of conflicts takes place and where women demand police action to end violence against women. It is also where rural women openly and safely discuss issues of inequality, take decisions on peace and security, and seek justice.

In Haiti, UN Women supports associations in helping female survivors of gender-based violence receive medical and legal care in rural areas. Broad sensitization campaigns and cooperation with local security committees led to less tolerance of violence against women in the community. These changes send a strong message to potential perpetrators. Men are now more hesitant to beat women because they are aware of the measures and laws in place and do not want to be punished or imprisoned.

In Kenya, we are supporting the Government to establish an association of women police officers to promote their role in law enforcement and security reform. This association will be a platform where policewomen can develop leadership skills, support one another and advance gender-sensitive policies and practices throughout the force.

We must further increase our support for paralegal centres and mobile courts in conflict-affected societies and improve comprehensive training on justice for gender-based crimes for all actors in the justice chain, from prosecutors to judicial investigators and public defenders. We must improve measures to ensure the protection of victims and witnesses and enhance women's participation so that they can benefit from transitional justice processes and reparations programmes.

Harnessing the potential of this moment and sustaining the required political will remains a challenge. It demands not only a greater emphasis on rule of law and justice, but a dedicated focus on justice for women. In peacebuilding settings, the focus of the support of the United Nations should, therefore, include three core elements: to secure justice and accountability for the crimes experienced by women in conflict; to rebuild national justice systems from the ground up, with women's participation, access and gender sensitivity as central components; and to link the judicial response to a broader and transformative notion of justice and equality for all.

Ultimately, the rule of law must empower individuals and further their participation in reconstructing their societies, so that all people have an opportunity to contribute and share in the dividends of peace and justice.

Critical Thinking

1. Why are women vulnerable in post-conflict societies?
2. How does a lack of justice and security affect women's participation in peacebuilding and reconstruction?
3. What steps has the UN taken to address these issues?

Create Central

www.mhhe.com/createcentral

Internet References

WIDNET: Women in Development NETwork
www.focusintl.com/widnet.htm

Women Watch/Regional and Country Information
www.un.org/womenwatch

Michelle Bachelet is Under-Secretary-General and Executive Director of UN Women.

Article

Women in the Shadow of Climate Change

BALGIS OSMAN-ELASHA

Climate change is one of the greatest global challenges of the twenty-first century. Its impacts vary among regions, generations, age, classes, income groups, and gender. Based on the findings of the Intergovernmental Panel on Climate Change (IPCC), it is evident that people who are already most vulnerable and marginalized will also experience the greatest impacts. The poor, primarily in developing countries, are expected to be disproportionately affected and consequently in the greatest need of adaptation strategies in the face of climate variability and change. Both women and men working in natural resource sectors, such as agriculture, are likely to be affected.[1] However, the impact of climate change on gender is not the same. Women are increasingly being seen as more vulnerable than men to the impacts of climate change, mainly because they represent the majority of the world's poor and are proportionally more dependent on threatened natural resources. The difference between men and women can also be seen in their differential roles, responsibilities, decision making, access to land and natural resources, opportunities and needs, which are held by both sexes.[2] Worldwide, women have less access than men to resources such as land, credit, agricultural inputs, decision-making structures, technology, training and extension services that would enhance their capacity to adapt to climate change.[3]

Worldwide, women have less access than men to resources such as land, credit, agricultural inputs, decision-making structures, technology, training and extension services that would enhance their capacity to adapt to climate change.

Why Women Are More Vulnerable

Women's vulnerability to climate change stems from a number of factors—social, economic and cultural.

Seventy percent of the 1.3 billion people living in conditions of poverty are women. In urban areas, 40 percent of the poorest households are headed by women. Women predominate in the world's food production (50–80 percent), but they own less than 10 percent of the land.

Women represent a high percentage of poor communities that are highly dependent on local natural resources for their livelihood, particularly in rural areas where they shoulder the major responsibility for household water supply and energy for cooking and heating, as well as for food security. In the Near East, women contribute up to 50 percent of the agricultural workforce. They are mainly responsible for the more time-consuming and labour-intensive tasks that are carried out manually or with the use of simple tools. In Latin America and the Caribbean, the rural population has been decreasing in recent decades. Women are mainly engaged in subsistence farming, particularly horticulture, poultry and raising small livestock for home consumption.

Women have limited access to and control of environmental goods and services; they have negligible participation in decision-making, and are not involved in the distribution of environment management benefits. Consequently, women are less able to confront climate change.

During extreme weather such as droughts and floods, women tend to work more to secure household livelihoods. This will leave less time for women to access training and education, develop skills or earn income. In Africa, female illiteracy rates were over 55 percent in 2000, compared to 41 percent for men.[4] When coupled with inaccessibility to resources and decision-making processes, limited mobility places women where they are disproportionately affected by climate change.

In many societies, socio-cultural norms and childcare responsibilities prevent women from migrating or seeking refuge in other places or working when a disaster hits. Such a situation is likely to put more burden on women, such as travelling longer to get drinking water and wood for fuel. Women, in many developing countries suffer gender inequalities with respect to human rights, political and economic status, land ownership, housing conditions, exposure to violence, education and health. Climate change will be an added stressor that will aggravate women's

Oxfam International reported disproportional fatalities among men and women during the tsunami that hit Asia at the end of 2004. According to an Oxfam briefing, females accounted for about three quarters of deaths in eight Indonesian villages, and almost 90 percent of deaths in Cuddalore, the second most affected district in India. Of the 140,000 who died from the 1991 cyclone disasters in Bangladesh, 90 percent were women.[6]

Women and girls in many rural societies spend up to three hours per day fetching water and collecting firewood. Droughts, floods, and desertification exacerbated by climate change make women spend more time on these tasks, diminishing their ability to participate in wage-earning activities.[7]

During natural disasters, more women die (compared to men) because they are not adequately warned, cannot swim well, or cannot leave the house alone.

Moreover, lower levels of education reduce the ability of women and girls to access information, including early warning and resources, or to make their voices heard. Cultural values could also contribute to women's vulnerability in some countries. For example, in Bangladesh, women are more calorie-deficient than men (the male members in a family have the "right" to consume the best portions of the food, and the female members have to content themselves with the left-overs) and have more problems during disasters to cope with.

In Sudan, the increase in the migration of men from the drought-hit areas of western Sudan increased the number of female-headed households, and consequently their responsibilities and vulnerabilities during natural disasters.

—Balgis Osman-Elasha

vulnerability. It is widely known that during conflict, women face heightened domestic violence, sexual intimidation, human trafficking and rape.[5]

According to the IPCC in Africa, an increase of 5–8% (160–90 million hectares) of arid and semiarid land is projected by the 2080s under a range of climate change scenarios.

Improving Women's Adaptation to Climate Change

In spite of their vulnerability, women are not only seen as victims of climate change, but they can also be seen as active and effective agents and promoters of adaptation and mitigation. For a long time women have historically developed knowledge and skills related to water harvesting and storage, food preservation and rationing, and natural resource management. In Africa, for example, old women represent wisdom pools with their inherited knowledge and expertise related to early warnings and mitigating the impacts of disasters. This knowledge and experience that has passed from one generation to another will be able to contribute effectively to enhancing local adaptive capacity and sustaining a community's livelihood. For this to be achieved, and in order to improve the adaptive capacity of women worldwide particularly in developing countries, the following recommendations need to be considered:

- Adaptation initiatives should identify and address gender-specific impacts of climate change particularly in areas related to water, food security, agriculture, energy, health, disaster management, and conflict. Important gender issues associated with climate change adaptation, such as inequalities in access to resources, including credit, extension and training services, information and technology should also be taken into consideration.
- Women's priorities and needs must be reflected in the development planning and funding. Women should be part of the decision making at national and local levels regarding allocation of resources for climate change initiatives. It is also important to ensure gender-sensitive investments in programmes for adaptation, mitigation, technology transfer and capacity building.
- Funding organizations and donors should also take into account women-specific circumstances when developing and introducing technologies related to climate change adaptation and to try their best to remove the economic, social and cultural barriers that could constrain women from benefiting and making use of them. Involving women in the development of new technologies can ensure that they are adaptive, appropriate and sustainable. At national levels, efforts should be made to mainstream gender perspective into national policies and strategies, as well as related sustainable development and climate change plans and interventions.

Notes

1. ILO, 2008. Report of the Committee on Employment and Social Policy, Employment and labour market implications of climate change, Fourth Item on the Agenda, Governing Body, 303rd Session (Geneva), p. 2.
2. Osman-Elasha, 2008 "Gender and Climate Change in the Arab Region", Arab Women Organization, p. 44.
3. Aguilar, L., 2008. "Is there a connection between gender and climate change?", International Union for Conservation of Nature (IUCN), Office of the Senior Gender Adviser.
4. Rena, Ravinder and N. Narayana (2007) "Gender Empowerment in Africa: An Analysis of Women Participation in Eritrean Economy", New Delhi: *International Journal of Women, Social Justice and Human Rights,* vol.2. no.2., pp. 221–237 (Serials Publishers).
5. Davis, I. et. al. 2005, "Tsunami, Gender, and Recovery".

6. IUCN 2004 (a), "Climate Change and Disaster Mitigation: Gender Makes the Difference". Intergovernmental Panel on Climate Change, 2001. Climate Change: Impacts, Adaptation and Vulnerability, Contribution of Working Group II to the Third Assessment Report of the IPCC.
7. IUCN 2004 (b), "Energy: Gender Makes the Difference". Gender Action, 2008. Gender Action Link: Climate Change (Washington, D.C.), www.genderaction.org/images/Gender%20Action%20Link%20-%20Climate%20Change.pdf
8. Third Global Congress of Women in Politics and Governance, 2008. Background and Context Paper for the Conference, Manila, Philippines, 19–22 October, www.capwip.org/3rdglobalcongress.htm IUCN 2007, "Gender and Climate Change: Women as Agents of Change"

Critical Thinking

1. Why are women particularly vulnerable to climate change?
2. Why are they less able to deal with the consequences of climate change?
3. How do socio-cultural norms affect women's ability to meet the challenge of climate change?

Balgis Osman-Elasha is Principal Investigator with the Climate Change Unit, Higher Council for Environment and Natural Resources, Sudan; and a lead author of the Intergovernmental Panel on Climate Change's Fourth Assessment Report.

POL 217 American Constitutional Law TR 9:45am - 11:20am ~~[illegible]~~ Chase Sherrett

POL 434 Senior Seminar T: 3-430 Jenks 114 Sherrett

NSM ~~202B~~ 202C Scientific Enterprise MW ~~12-2~~ 2:30-4:30 Kos 214 Seibert
↳ says prerequisite has not been met

HIS 121 D HISTORICAL PERSPECTIVES MWF 1-2 Goss

Need: BCM, NSM, HIS, OT

Article

The Global Glass Ceiling

Why Empowering Women Is Good for Business

Isobel Coleman

Over the last several decades, it has become accepted wisdom that improving the status of women is one of the most critical levers of international development. When women are educated and can earn and control income, a number of good results follow: infant mortality declines, child health and nutrition improve, agricultural productivity rises, population growth slows, economies expand, and cycles of poverty are broken.

But the challenges remain dauntingly large. In the Middle East, South Asia, and sub-Saharan Africa, in particular, large and persistent gender gaps in access to education, health care, technology, and income—plus a lack of basic rights and pervasive violence against women—keep women from being fully productive members of society. Entrenched gender discrimination remains a defining characteristic of life for the majority of the world's bottom two billion people, helping sustain the gulf between the most destitute and everyone else who shares this planet.

Narrowing that gulf demands more than the interest of the foreign aid and human rights communities, which, to date, have carried out the heavy lifting of women's empowerment in developing countries, funding projects such as schools for girls and microfinance for female entrepreneurs. It requires the involvement of the world's largest companies. Not only does the global private sector have vastly more money than governments and nongovernmental organizations, but it can wield significant leverage with its powerful brands and by extending promises of investment and employment. Some companies already promote initiatives focused on women as part of their corporate social-responsibility programs—in other words, to burnish their images as good corporate citizens. But the truly transformative shift—both for global corporations and for women worldwide—will occur when companies understand that empowering women in developing economies affects their bottom lines.

The majority of global population growth in the coming decades will occur in those countries where gender disparities are the greatest and where conservative religious traditions and tribal customs work against women's rights. As multinational corporations search for growth in the developing world, they are beginning to realize that women's disempowerment causes staggering and deeply pernicious losses in productivity, economic activity, and human capital. Just as many corporations have found that adopting environmentally sensitive business practices is not only good public relations but also good business, companies that embrace female empowerment will see their labor forces become more productive, the quality of their global supply chains improve, and their customer bases expand. They will also help drive what could be the greatest cultural shift of the twenty-first century.

Benefits Package

In 2006, General Electric was facing a growing disaster. Its ultrasound technology had spread to India, and Indian human rights groups and gender activists began to accuse the company of being complicit in female feticide. This was a burgeoning public relations nightmare that also threatened GE's profitable Indian ultrasound business.

In India, as in many other countries in South and East Asia, the heavy burden of dowry payments and/or patriarchal traditions make parents prefer male children to female ones. The spread of GE's portable sonogram machines to clinics across rural India brought low-cost fetal sex screening to millions—which meant that parents could now easily abort unwanted girls. Although in 1994 the Indian government passed a law prohibiting sex-selective abortion, the problem persists. In some parts of the country, as many as 140 boys are born for every 100 girls. Comparing the cost of an abortion to a future dowry, abortion clinics lure customers with advertisements warning that it is better to "pay 500 rupees now, save 50,000 rupees later." Because abortion providers have continued to flout the 1994 law, in 2002 the Indian government amended it to make the manufacturers and distributors of sonogram equipment responsible for preventing female feticide.

To protect its ultrasound business and avoid legal damages, GE created a series of training programs, sales-screening procedures, and post-sale auditing processes designed to detect misuse, and it also put warning labels on its equipment. Nonetheless, GE was caught off-guard by the media campaign launched by Indian activists, who accused it of enabling female feticide. Before long, GE realized that if it hoped to continue to dominate the country's ultrasound market, it would have to confront the low status of women in Indian society. It met with activist groups and launched a poster campaign to change attitudes about women's rights. At the same time, it began to fund education for girls and to sponsor a hip, young Indian female tennis star as a progressive role model.

As often happens when the private sector gets involved in the touchy subject of women's rights in the developing world, the case of GE in India was disappointingly reactive. Too often, companies act only after they face a public relations problem, whether being charged with female feticide or with hiring underage girls in sweatshops. Perhaps it is not surprising that multinational companies tend to approach the topic gingerly and belatedly, given the cultural sensitivities regarding women in many emerging markets and the fact that the senior management of local subsidiaries is often overwhelmingly male.

Slowly, however, attitudes are beginning to change. Partly in response to shareholder demands, some companies are becoming increasingly proactive regarding women's empowerment. In addition, investors have put more than $2 trillion into socially responsible investment funds, which weigh both financial returns and societal impact. Although supporting women's rights is not yet a primary concern of most such funds, it is becoming an increasingly high-profile component of the larger social justice agenda that dictates how and where socially responsible investment funds invest. Meanwhile, the rise of female senior managers, board members, and CEOs in Western companies is also raising the profile of women's rights in the global corporate agenda.

Nike is one company that has decided to take a proactive approach to women's empowerment. Having been regularly hit in the 1990s with accusations of relying on sweatshop labor abroad, Nike instituted an elaborate inspection system to root out the worst labor practices among its suppliers. Along the way, it realized that many of its overseas factories were overwhelmingly staffed with female workers, meaning that the problems of oppressed girls and women—including a lack of education and access to health care, child marriage, vulnerability to HIV/AIDS, human trafficking, and domestic violence—were its problems, too. In 2004, the company created the Nike Foundation, which invests in health, education, and leadership programs for adolescent girls in the developing world. So far, it has distributed close to $100 million. Perhaps more important, Nike has deployed its powerful brand and marketing skills in support of young girls. In 2008, it launched *The Girl Effect,* a dramatic, smartly produced video that has since gone viral on the Internet.

In 2008, Goldman Sachs put its own recognizable brand and considerable resources behind female empowerment when it launched a program called 10,000 Women, a five-year, $100 million global initiative to invest in business and management education for female entrepreneurs in developing countries. The initiative helps make up for the lack of business education available to women in the developing world: in all of Africa, for example, there are fewer than 3,000 women enrolled in local MBA courses. Goldman touts the program on the economic grounds that closing employment gender gaps in emerging markets stimulates growth. The company's CEO, Lloyd Blankfein, says that the program is a way of "manufacturing global GNP," which, in the long run, is good for Goldman. Early assessments in the press indicate that graduates of the program have seen increases in the revenues of their businesses and have hired more employees, thus growing local GNP and raising the economic stature of women. The 10,000 Women program is also funding new teachers and curricula to educate future generations of female entrepreneurs in Africa, Asia, Latin America, and the Middle East. Just as governments and international development organizations have realized that empowering women is much more than a human rights issue, leaders in the private sector, such as Goldman Sachs and Nike, are starting to understand that enhancing women's economic power is good business.

Rani the Riveter

A 2009 McKinsey survey of corporations with operations in emerging markets revealed that less than 20 percent of the companies had any initiatives focused on women. Their executives have simply not made the issue a strategic priority. Perhaps they should reconsider. According to the same study, three-quarters of those companies with specific initiatives to empower women in developing countries reported that their investments were already increasing their profits or that they expected them to do so soon. Such investments pay off by improving a company's talent pool and increasing employee productivity and retention. Corporations also benefit as new markets are created and existing ones expand. In the developing world especially, networks of female entrepreneurs are becoming increasingly important sales channels in places where the scarcity of roads and stores makes it difficult to distribute goods and services.

One example of how a corporation can simultaneously expand its business and empower women is Hindustan Unilever, India's largest consumer goods company. It launched its Shakti Entrepreneur Program in 2000 to offer microcredit grants to rural women who become door-to-door distributors of the company's household products. This sales network has now expanded to include nearly 50,000 women selling to more than three million homes across 100,000 Indian villages. Not only do these women benefit from higher self-esteem and greater status within their families, but they invest their incomes in the health, nutrition, and education of their children, thereby helping lift their communities out of poverty. Hindustan Unilever, for its part, was able to open up a previously inaccessible market.

Training women as local distributors of goods and services is important, of course, but so is incorporating women-owned businesses into global supply chains. As giant retailers such as Walmart and Carrefour move aggressively into emerging markets, they are trying to buy more of their products, particularly food, directly from local producers—both to lower prices and to improve quality. With more than $400 billion in annual sales, Walmart is the world's largest retailer, so its purchasing decisions have a cascading effect throughout the global supply chain. Its recent sensitivity to environmental issues, for example, is starting to transform how companies around the world produce goods. This February, it announced a plan to reduce the greenhouse gas emissions produced by its global supply chain by 20 million metric tons within five years; it plans to do this by forcing its suppliers to adjust how they source, manufacture, package, and transport their products.

Similarly, there are signs that Walmart is beginning to understand the importance of women's empowerment in the developing world, where it projects that most of its future growth will take place. Since almost 75 percent of its employees are women, the company has a clear interest in promoting women's economic empowerment in its new markets. Working alongside CARE, a humanitarian organization that combats global poverty, Walmart has launched several pilot programs to teach literacy and workplace skills in the developing world. In Peru, it is helping female farmers meet the company's quality-control standards. In Bangladesh, it is training local women in the garment industry to move up from fabric sorters to seamstresses and cutters. Similarly, it is developing the skills of female cashew farmers in India so that they can progress from low-level pickers to high-end processors. Walmart expects to see increased productivity, higher quality, and greater diversity in its supply chain as a result. "We aren't engaging with Walmart solely for the financial resources they bring to the table," says Helene Gayle, president and CEO of CARE. "We are working together to make change on a global level. Walmart has enormous potential to transform women's lives in the emerging markets in which it operates."

It is ironic, of course, that Walmart is embracing women's empowerment in emerging markets even as it fights the largest class-action sex-discrimination lawsuit in U.S. history. (Walmart is accused of discriminating against women in pay and promotions.) Undoubtedly, its women's empowerment initiatives could have multiple motivations, including diverting negative public attention. But Walmart's efforts will be sustainable only to the extent that the company considers them central to its long-term growth and profitability and not just part of a public relations strategy. The potential for its female employees and suppliers in the developing world is enormous: if Walmart sourced just one percent of its sales from women-owned businesses, it would channel billions of dollars toward women's economic empowerment—far more than what international development agencies could ever muster for such efforts.

Interestingly, one organization that seems to understand the power of using its supply chain to further women's economic empowerment is the U.S. military. In Afghanistan, the United States has made strengthening the role of women in Afghan society a central element of its counterinsurgency strategy. To this end, the U.S. military is experimenting with setting aside some contracts for Afghan women entrepreneurs to supply uniforms for the national police and army. Initial results in the fall of 2009 were disastrous, however: proposals came back with mistakes and with product samples in the wrong color, fabric, and sizes. In response, the U.S. military has held several training courses to educate Afghan businesswomen on how to meet quality standards and navigate the complicated "request for proposal" process. It is too early to tell if any women-owned companies will be able to fill large military orders—the minimum is for $300,000 worth of goods—but according to news reports, the women who have participated in the program say that the experience has been invaluable.

Attitude Adjustment

Companies that are interested in women's empowerment—whether driven by corporate social responsibility or by business strategy—now have more tools and support available to guide their investments than ever before. The World Bank is one example of an institution that is partnering with private-sector firms in this effort. For two decades, economists at the World Bank have been making the case that girls' education and women's economic empowerment are among the best investments that the developed world can make to reduce poverty and stimulate growth in the developing world. As Robert Zoellick, president of the World Bank, frequently says, "Gender equality is smart economics." The World Bank's Gender Action Plan invests in infrastructure in the developing world, in areas such as energy, transportation, agriculture, water, and sanitation, in ways that are specifically focused on promoting women's economic empowerment. But the plan is short on resources, with only $60 million in funding over four years. Not surprisingly, then, the World Bank is looking for other ways to steer funding toward women in the developing world. In April 2008, it launched the Global Private Sector Leaders Forum to engage corporate executives in developing countries. Already, the 23 member companies in the forum and the World Bank itself have committed to spending $3 billion on goods and services from women-owned businesses over the next three years. Initially, much of this procurement will take place in developed economies, where women-owned business are more established and the commitments are easier to track. But these conditions are beginning to change, thanks to organizations such as WEConnect International, which certifies the operations of women-owned businesses in the developing world according to international standards. Although the Global Private Sector Leaders Forum is composed largely of blue-chip companies based in the United States, such as Boeing, Cisco, ExxonMobil, and Goldman Sachs, it also has a sprinkling of prominent companies from emerging-market economies, such as Egypt, India, Peru, and Turkey.

Governments in emerging-market countries are beginning to understand that to be competitive, they will need to respond to the growing demands of the global economy regarding women's empowerment. For example, in 2008, Morocco retracted its reservations about the UN's Convention on the Elimination of All Forms of Discrimination Against Women—the leading international treaty to protect women's rights—partly so that it would become more attractive to foreign companies. Even Saudi Arabia, an oil-rich state that has rejected any international standards on women's rights, is finding it harder to resist the demands of the global economy. In 2009, recognizing that it must upgrade its educational system to produce enough skilled professionals to fuel growth, it opened a new $10 billion university for science and technology—and, for the first time in the country's history, enrolled women alongside men.

The Five-Point Plan

Five principles should guide the efforts of those corporations that are just now beginning to consider women's empowerment as a strategic aspect of their emerging-market operations.

First, success must be defined and measured appropriately. Success cannot be reduced to the types of metrics now familiar in Western corporate suites, such as how many women are in senior management positions. Instead, corporations must track the most basic information about their female employees, suppliers, and customers in emerging markets. For example, do their female employees have access to financial services so that they can actually control their incomes? Do they have identity cards that allow them to be counted as citizens? Do they need a male family member's permission to work? Since obstacles to female empowerment differ across regions, companies should rely on local market studies and workforce surveys to identify the relevant issues for corporate growth in each market.

Second, although donating money to women's empowerment initiatives is a good start, incorporating such objectives into actual business practices is even better. Bringing female farmers into the global supply chain probably has the most potential in this regard. In sub-Saharan Africa and South Asia, for example, although farm labor is more than 70 percent female, women tend to focus on subsistence crops rather than cash crops, a sector that men still dominate. Using women to increase sales also holds great possibility, as the experience of Hindustan Unilever shows. Even sectors that employ a low percentage of women, such as the extractive industries, could target women-owned businesses for support services, such as catering, laundry, office cleaning, and transportation.

Third, companies should concentrate on providing skills and resources to female entrepreneurs and business leaders. For some firms, this could mean expanding their financial services to female clients—not just credit but savings products, too. Or it could take the form of supporting an existing local organization that helps women obtain access to health care, identity cards, or property rights. Leadership training, as well as secondary and university education, is central to developing the next generation of female business leaders and managers.

Fourth, even though companies are understandably wary of being associated with controversy, they cannot deny that they have an interest in the outcome of conflicts taking place over the role of women in many developing countries. Important and growing markets, such as Indonesia, Nigeria, and Pakistan, are home to protracted debates between moderates and extremists. Such thorny subjects as child marriage, domestic violence, and women's access to reproductive health may seem off-limits to corporations. But consider just one example: rapid population growth in Nigeria, already Africa's most populous state, will strain the country's resources and threaten its stability, thus jeopardizing substantial Western investments. Similarly, decades of research have shown that societies with a disproportionately high number of men—as is the case where families prefer male children to female ones—are less stable and more prone to violence, which hinders economic growth.

Fifth, corporations should not try to reinvent methods that have already been perfected by others simply to appear innovative and committed. Instead, they should look to partner with the many excellent nonprofit organizations that have been working on issues of women's empowerment for decades. Organizations such as CARE, Vital Voices, and Women's World Banking are eager to work with the private sector to develop programs that can take advantage of corporations' expertise and assets, including their brands, employees, supplier bases, technology, and funding. Nike and ExxonMobil have formed a number of such partnerships. Likewise, Goldman Sachs is working with more than 70 academic institutions and nongovernmental organizations around the world to develop its 10,000 Women initiative. Walmart, meanwhile, is working with CARE in Bangladesh, where the organization has more than 50 years of on-the-ground experience.

Closing the gender gap and improving women's rights in the Middle East, South Asia, and sub-Saharan Africa may take many generations, but the benefits will be huge—not only for the individual women and their families but also for global markets. As companies seek new sources of revenue in emerging economies, they will find that gender disparities pose an obstacle to doing business. The sooner the private sector works to overcome gender inequality, the better off the world—and companies' own bottom lines—will be.

Critical Thinking

1. How do women's empowerment efforts improve the image and productivity of multinational business?
2. What types of programs have multinationals initiated to enhance women's empowerment?
3. How have international financial institutions supported efforts to empower women?
4. What principles should guide corporate efforts to empower women?

Isobel Coleman is Senior Fellow for U.S. Foreign Policy and Director of the Women and Foreign Policy Program at the Council on Foreign Relations. She is the author of *Paradise Beneath Her Feet: How Women Are Transforming the Middle East.* For an annotated guide to this topic, see "What to Read on Gender and Foreign Policy" at www.foreignaffairs.com/readinglists/gender.